Aerial view of aerodrome and works from the south 1994.
Our Boeing 747/TriStar hangar is in the foreground

Aircraft Design Office portrayal of my career presented to me on my retirement December 1989

THE MARSHALL STORY

A century of wheels and wings

Sir Arthur Marshall

OBE, DL, Hon. DSc. (Cranfield), CRAeS,
Hon. Fellow Jesus College Cambridge

FOREWORD BY SIR PETER MASEFIELD

Patrick Stephens Limited

THE MARSHALL COAT OF ARMS

The bridge symbolizes the roots, the birth place and the bridge of Cambridge.
The busy bees represent the hard work of all those involved with the Company.
The wings represent the relationship with flight and aircraft.
The cock symbolizes the link with Jesus College.
The speedwell flower represents swift action.
The sword symbolizes the appointment as High Sheriff and represents chivalry.
The shovel represents labour.
The motto 'Felix Qui Laborat' translates – 'Happy is he who works'.

To Rosemary

First published in 1994

British Library cataloguing-in-publication data:
A catalogue record for this book is available from the British Library.

ISBN: 1 85260 472 7
Library of Congress 94 77776

Patrick Stephens Limited is an imprint of
Haynes Publishing, Sparkford, Nr. Yeovil, Somerset BA22 7JJ.

Typeset by Character Graphics (Taunton) Ltd
Printed in Great Britain by Butler & Tanner Ltd. of London and Frome

Contents

Foreword

Sir Peter Masefield

HERE AT FIRST-HAND – delightfully and modestly told – is the story of a unique and outstanding contribution to over 80 years of progress and change in British aviation and the automotive scene.

In this engaging book Sir Arthur Marshall takes us step-by-step – with a perceptive insight into the changing industrial and social scene – from the days before the First World War, when the author's father, the sporting David Gregory Marshall, founded a little automobile business in the small university town of Cambridge, to the company's present position of international repute in the modern world of high technology.

What is so attractive about this personal saga is the breadth of view it encompasses and how, through an astute grasp of opportunities, horizons were steadily widened. The personality of Arthur Marshall himself shines through on every page where his forthright reminiscences of years of immersion in a tough industrial world are enhanced and refreshed by his goodwill and energy in a career devoid of uncharitableness or of any snide remarks. Indeed, over the years, few have shown a surer touch towards forward plans and good staff and customer relations, or have attracted, and rejoiced in, a wider circle of friends and colleagues; so well reflected in the record of his day-to-day work and in the range of his university and business contacts.

Bitten by chance in the late 1920s by the aviation bug, from which there is no recovery, Arthur Marshall rapidly earned a reputation for enthusing undergraduates – including me, now a friend for 60 years – with the delights of learning to fly. He did so with that authoritative and kindly approach which has been the hallmark of his whole career.

The Marshall story is a compelling account of a life at the heart of British industry and commerce against a background of a close-knit family in which, in his words, he was blessed by 'the most fortunate event of my life', his marriage to the charming Rosemary Dimsdale. For the next 57 years Rosemary was at his side sharing and helping in every endeavour. And with them, as the years went by, were their two sons, Michael, who now heads the business, and David, their daughter, Judy, six sisters, eleven grandchildren, two great granddaughters and a host of friends across the world.

So, here indeed, is a book to be read and enjoyed – a story of dedication and achievement by a man of extraordinary talent and sensitivity – a modern Bayard 'sans peur et sans reproche'.

PETER MASEFIELD

Preface

I AM FORTUNATE to have lived through this fast moving and exciting era and to have been actively involved in the formative years of the motor and aviation industries. There has never been a dull moment and I have enjoyed every minute. The Marshall story developed from the cumulative effect of unplanned meetings, unforeseen circumstances, recognising and responding to challenges as they occurred, plus hard work, good health and tremendous luck.

I was born in Cambridge in December 1903 and am proud that everything that has been achieved has been within a mile-and-a-half of my birthplace. At the beginning of this century the University was predominant, and during vacations Cambridge reverted to a small market town. During my undergraduate days, and without any plans or ideas of how it might come about, I began to feel I would like to do something to develop commerce and industry, to provide more employment and prosperity in the region. My thoughts were always centred on Cambridge, the last place in the world one would have chosen to establish a major engineering industry. As it turned out, Cambridge is the only place in the world where these events could have taken place and only at this time – it just happened.

The Marshall Company has brought wealth and employment into the Cambridge area and provided the equivalent of a municipal airport for Cambridge at no charge on the rates. It has enhanced the eastern approach to Cambridge with its wide open spaces – partly within the City boundary – which but for the development of the aerodrome and works would have been built over long ago. Our finance has been self-generated with no injection of outside capital. Everything has developed from our first Metallurgique car of 1909 and our first Gipsy Moth aircraft of 1929.

I am proud of my Company's record of service to the country and our involvement in important projects at times of national emergency. Our spontaneous recognition of the need to speed up the training of pilots at the beginning of World War II was vital. Had our proven philosophy and practice of training pilots and young flying instructors been adopted at the outbreak of war, instead of in 1941 and only then after a great deal of pressure, there would have been no shortage of pilots for the Battle of Britain.

Over the years I have come to recognise the importance of good friends and continuity of relationships and, equally important, continuity of business contacts, customers and suppliers. A Minister in recent years during a discussion on the relative merits and pitfalls of accepting the lowest tender regardless of other considerations turned to me and said, 'Marshall, how often do you change your suppliers?' I answered, 'Never, if I can help it – you might as well have asked me how often I change my friends?'

I have always been concerned with the present and the future with no time to look back, but now, with vivid memories going back to 1909, I have been asked by my colleagues and friends to write the history of the Marshall Company against the family background and the atmosphere of the times. I have written my story just as it happened, with no embellishments, and have deliberately minimised technical details of interest only to the experts.

Acknowledgements

I HAVE HAD enthusiastic encouragement, help and advice from friends and colleagues too numerous to mention and I would like to express my sincere gratitude to them all. There are also many who would have been referred to in the text if space had allowed, but I have only mentioned those who come naturally into the flow of the story.

I have had exceptional help from Freda Short, now in her 40th year as my secretary, particularly with her gift for rephrasing, and Lynda Smith, my assistant secretary for many years. It has been a wonderful team for insertions, deletions and corrections, with many hilarious moments.

I have had unique help from Gordon Bruce, who with his own library and wonderful mental archives has supplied, like instant coffee, detailed answers to so many historical questions.

There have been numerous conversations with retired colleagues, many of whom have written to me of their own recollection of events, and I mention in particular Ronnie Bowles, Harold Fairbrother, Roy Gates, Norman Harry, John Huntridge and 'Mac' McMillan.

For allowing me to quote from their speeches and letters and from our conversations I would like to thank Bill Bailey, Dermot Boyle, John Curtiss, Nicholas Dimsdale, Michael Graydon, Allen Greenwood, Johnnie Johnson, John Kellock, Peter Masefield, Doug Page, Dick Reynolds, Thora Saunders and Leslie Scatchard.

I was helped with confirmation of the atmosphere and details of flying training before and during World War II by Herbert Tappin and by Leslie Worsdell. I am grateful to Leslie and to Molly Rose for permission to quote from their Imperial War Museum tapes.

I would like to thank the AAA for information on athletics in the twenties. Michael Bowyer's advice on the selection of photographs was enthusiastically given. Sebastian Cox of the Ministry of Defence Air Historical Branch (RAF) was most patient and helpful in answering my enquiries. The Revd William Girard was a mine of information to fill in historical details about Horseheath. Freddie Henry was generous with his help on the subject of the Austin Motor Company and Lord Austin. I am grateful to Muriel Brittain for help on Jesus College matters, and Elizabeth Gardner-Smith for information about her late husband the Revd Percival Gardner-Smith. Michael Petty of the Cambridgeshire Collection was always ready to respond to any query on local history. Keith Williams read through my account of Tom Bacon's fuel cell work at Cambridge.

I had much general advice and encouragement from my old friends Norman de Bruyne, Hugh and Irene Gordon, Brian Herring, Francis Pemberton, Nat Somers, and Dick Lane who named the book.

Last, and perhaps they should have been first, I would like to thank Michael for his constant enthusiasm and valuable comments on the draft chapters as they were written, and all members of the family, particularly Violet who prepared a log of all my sisters' lives.

I thank these and many others for their help – any errors are mine.

Most of the photographs were taken by Marshall's photographers or commissioned by Marshall. Many were provided by family and friends and I thank them for these. I am pleased to acknowledge other photographers where we have been able to identify them and I apologise for any inadvertent omissions.

I acknowledge gratefully permission to quote from the following books, newspapers, tapes, and articles: The Imperial War Museum for extracts from Leslie Worsdell's and Molly Rose's tapes; The Pitt Club and Prof. Charles Montague Fletcher for extracts and information from *The University Pitt Club* by Sir Walter Morley Fletcher published 1935; Cambridgeshire County Council Libraries for information from *The Cambridge Book of the Silver Jubilee of King George V* and the print of the demolishing of the Jesus Lane wall, both in the Cambridgeshire Collection; Mrs E. Gardner-Smith and Jesus College Cambridge for extracts from the Revd Gardner-Smith's 80th birthday tape; Mr Richard Collier for Sir Keith Park's letter from *The Few – World War II – The Battle of Britain* by Philip Kaplan and Richard Collier published by Cassell 1989; Random House UK Ltd for an extract from *Wing Leader* by Johnnie Johnson published by Chatto & Windus 1956; Reed Business Publishing for extracts from *Flight International*, *Aeroplane* and *Farmers Weekly*; Express Newspapers PLC for photograph and caption published in the *Daily Express* April 1931; Mr R. W. Daynes, Chairman of Horseheath Parish Council, for his speech on 30 July 1989; Times Newspapers Limited for reference to *The Times* article 'RAF Volunteer Reserve' published 12 January 1937; Canon Eric James and Christian Action for references to Canon F. A. Simpson taken from *A Last Eccentric* edited by Canon James published 1991; Sagittarius Bloodstock Associates Ltd for an extract from *The Bloodstock Breeders Review 1942*; Air Transat for an extract from their House Journal 1991; The Hon. Oliver Walston for Lord Walston's address on 3 July 1988; Mr A. A. Boyle for Marshal of the Royal Air Force Sir Dermot Boyle's account of wing walking in May 1929; A. P. Watt Ltd for an extract from *A Rabbit in the Air* by David Garnett published by Chatto & Windus 1932; and Aircraft Owners and Pilots Association for reference to *ABAC Manual of Flying and Ground Training* compiled and edited by Leslie Worsdell, first published in 1964 by the British Light Aviation Centre Ltd.

The quotation from the lyric of *Get Out and Get Under* (Copyright 1913 Mills Music Inc.) is reproduced by kind permission of Redwood Music Ltd UK Administrator and Francis Day & Hunter Ltd, London WC2H OLA.

Information on the beginnings of the RNAS came from *Seaplanes – Felixstowe* by Gordon Kinsey, published in 1948 by Terence Dalton Ltd.

Various photographs and other material are reproduced by courtesy of Cambridge Newspapers Ltd.

List of Abbreviations

AAA	Amateur Athletic Association
A&AEE	Aircraft & Armament Experimental Establishment
ABAC	Association of British Aero Clubs
ADCC	Air Defence Cadet Corps
AEF	Air Experience Flight
AID	Aeronautical Inspection Directorate
AMSO	Air Member for Supply & Organisation
ARO	Aircraft Repair Organisation
ARP	Air Raid Precautions
ATA	Air Transport Auxiliary
ATC	Air Training Corps
BA	British Airways
BAC	British Aircraft Corporation
BAe	British Aerospace
BEA	British European Airways
BOAC	British Overseas Airways Corporation
CA	Controller Aircraft
CAA	Civil Aviation Authority
C of A	Certificate of Airworthiness
CRO	Civil Repair Organisation
CUAC	Cambridge University Athletics Club
CUAS	Cambridge University Air Squadron
DCAS	Deputy Chief of Air Staff
DH	de Havilland
DROPS	Demountable Rack Off-loading/Pick-up System
EFTS	Elementary Flying Training School
E&RFTS	Elementary and Reserve Flying Training School
FVRDE	Fighting Vehicles Research & Development Establishment
HDU	Hose drum unit
HQFTC	Headquarters Flying Training Command
ISO	International Standards of Operation
JPC	Joint Production Committee
LABS	Low Altitude Bombing System
MAP	Ministry of Aircraft Production

MoD	Ministry of Defence
MVEE	Military Vehicle Experimental Establishment
OTC	Officers' Training Corps
QFCF4	Quick Firing Cartridge Factory
RAE	Royal Aircraft Establishment
RARDE	Royal Armament Research & Development Establishment
RFC	Royal Flying Corps
RFS	Reserve Flying School
RNAS	Royal Naval Air Service
SBAC	Society of British Aircraft Constructors
SFIS	Supplementary Flying Instructor School
SMMT	Society of Motor Manufacturers and Traders
TI	Trial installation
WD	War Department

Chapter 1

How it All Began

1873–1914

DAVID GREGORY MARSHALL, my father, was born on Monday 8 September 1873 in Cambridge. The family was poor and he had to make his own way in life, starting work at the age of 14 in Trinity College kitchens. He was very keen on all kinds of sport and was a member of many of the Cambridge University college servant teams. Sport was to play a big part in his life, right up to his death in 1942 whilst riding one of his Arab horses which he had brought back from Egypt.

DGM's all-round sporting interests were summed up by the winner of a *Cambridge Daily News* 'Who Is It?' competition of 1935, who wrote:

> I have seen this back too many times not to recognise the personage in the form of Mr D. G. Marshall, MBE. A typical sportsman through and through, he can still show a large percentage of the modern generation that he can be just as much 'at home' on a pair of skates or in the saddle of a frisky horse.

From an early age my father's main enthusiasm was horse-racing – he was very successful and must have made a lot of money from his betting, clear of all expenses which included taking members of the family to race meetings all over the country and a family dinner party in London on Derby night. He would start betting on the following year's Derby within a few weeks of the current Derby having been run, and would manage to be a winner regardless of which horse won. Usually the horse he wanted to win would finish second or third. He was a very successful, hard working punter – not a gambler – and he thoroughly enjoyed it. He never read a book, but every evening after dinner he would sit down in his armchair concentrating on racing form, with one hand twiddling the hair at the back of his head. He made no notes but kept it all in his head. From 1935 to his death he owned a small string of horses and had a number of winners.

Before and immediately after the First World War he was involved with the University Steeplechases at Cottenham. My father and Jim Runciman, the well-known Cambridge vet and owner of the Cottenham

Steeplechase land, built the stands at Cottenham with the help of donations of items of equipment, including the Runners and Riders board presented by Douglas Crossman, a very well-known county figure.

The seed of my father's initial success and career, and in fact the future of the companies he founded, was sown on the day he started work in Trinity College kitchens in 1887. It is extraordinary how everything snowballed as a result of the interest shown in him by senior members of Trinity College, Local Directors of Barclays Bank, who became Honorary Treasurers and Presidents of the University Pitt Club, and later the Master and some Senior Fellows of Jesus College.

My father was the protégé of Sir Walter Morley Fletcher, an Hon. Fellow of Trinity and President of the University Pitt Club 1900–1914. It all developed within a few hundred yards of Trinity, at the Pitt Club and the garage in Jesus Lane, followed by the aerodrome two miles along the Newmarket Road. Others directly involved were: Edmund Parker, a Founder Member of Barclays Bank, Hon. Treasurer of the Pitt Club 1900–1905 and High Steward of Cambridge; Melluish Clark, a Local Director of Barclays Bank, Hon. Treasurer of the Pitt Club 1905–1920 and President 1921–1930; and Roger Parker (son of Edmund Parker), a Local Director of Barclays Bank and Hon. Treasurer of the Pitt Club 1920–1933. Sir Walter was described by Monty James, Provost of Eton and later Provost of King's, one-time President of the Pitt Club, as the Second Founder of the Club which he re-established with the help of my father during the early part of the century. The name of the original Founder has been lost over the years.

The Pitt was an aristocratic club founded in 1835 to uphold the political principles of William Pitt and assist the local party organisation of the town of Cambridge to return worthy Tory representatives to Parliament and to the Borough Council, all combined with the pleasures of social intercourse at dinner when party fervour might be warmed towards incandescence by the speeches and many successive toasts. The Club held its annual Anniversary Dinner on 28 May, the birthday of William Pitt. All political activity ceased in 1868, and thereafter members were elected without any consideration of political party, and it became purely a social club. Many rowing men were members of the club. The undergraduate members of the Pitt Club during the early part of the century were in the main very wealthy, including some extremely rich Indian princes.

At the beginning of the century the Pitt Club had financial problems. Sir Walter offered my father the Stewardship of the Club and the challenge and responsibility of recovering the Club's financial position. My father entered into this with great enthusiasm, turned it into a university catering establishment and made the Club a lot of money and himself many influential friends. Sir Walter in his *History of the University Pitt Club* wrote of my father:

Mr D. G. Marshall's services to the Club were very remarkable. It was he who instituted a system of catering on a very elaborate scale, and during his Stewardship the Club acquired a large and elaborate kitchen plant which profited very considerably by sales of food and wine. Until he came to office, the dining room accounts showed a regular terminal deficit but, after one term of his management, profits appeared.

Finally, the 'Napoleon of the Pitt', as he came to be called, laid the foundations of his present prosperous garage and aerodrome business by providing private cars which members might hire. One of these with a smart chauffeur was regularly to be seen waiting outside the Club in Jesus Lane.

This nickname 'Napoleon' followed him to his work with the Ministry of Munitions and at Woolwich Arsenal during the 1914 War. Udny Yule, the world famous statistician of St John's, when I was teaching him to fly in his 63rd year in 1930 received a letter from his friend 'Major', an old member of the Pitt Club who had obviously been associated with my father during the war years. 'Major' wrote:

> My dear chap,
>   You *are* a sportsman! I doubt whether I should have the courage to go up even with Napoleon's son (we always used to call Marshall Napoleon in the Health and Munition Workers' days, his knowledge and power of assembling supplies for canteens were really Napoleonic).

The Pitt Club catered for dinners, including the Athenaeum Club dinners which became so rowdy and destructive that they were eventually held in the racquets court at Portugal Place where Billy Beattie, the University Hairdresser, one of the best violin players in the county, provided background music with his quartet. The Club also catered for undergraduates' early morning breakfasts. It was common to see porters walking about with trays on their heads carrying breakfasts to undergraduates' lodgings. The Pitt Club Ball was established in 1905 and the Club also catered for other balls, including the Trinity Ball held in the Guildhall and Corn Exchange before the 1914 War, when the Guildhall and Corn Exchange were connected by a temporary bridge across Corn Exchange Street.

The Pitt Lawn at Grassy Corner, Fen Ditton, was established for the May Races, and a tea marquee was erected. I remember from personal experience the very good teas which were served, including lush ice-cream made at the Pitt from fresh strawberries. The entry track to Grassy Corner was steep, and many of the early cars huffed and puffed to climb back on to the road. Crowds lined Newmarket Road and Maids Causeway to watch and cheer the unusual procession of cars of all makes and sizes returning from the May Races.

Cambridge in the university vacations became a small country town. Some shops closed and many college servants who were only paid during the term sought employment away from Cambridge. My father provided seasonal staff for hotels, including at Scarborough, during the summer months and for the Royal Pavilion at the Royal Agricultural Society's Annual Shows, where there was much competition for the plates used by the King.

In the early hours of the morning of 24 January 1907 a fire broke out which destroyed the Pitt Club dining room, the Steward's rooms and offices. My father was called out in the early morning and got so impatient with his bicycle that he threw it down and ran the last hundred yards. The Town Council had recently bought a new fire engine and this was its baptism. The *Cambridge Chronicle* of 25 January recorded:

> The Council's new investment proved the value of steam pressure in case of emergency. For over two hours a pressure of about 90 lbs to the square inch was maintained, drawn from a fire hydrant in Jesus Lane. When the Fire Brigade arrived they found the cover of the hydrant frozen and were unable to open it. The situation had become serious when it was suddenly relieved by the appearance of Mr Beattie, the University Hairdresser, with a kettle of boiling water. It appeared that it was his invariable, and on this occasion most fortunate, habit to 'pop the kettle on' whenever he got up in the morning even when forcibly awakened at 5.00 a.m.

Sir Walter Morley Fletcher wrote:

> Marshall grappled with the situation with his usual promptness and efficiency. He set the staff to work to clear the water out of the kitchen, which was 2 ft in depth, and breakfasts were dispatched as usual to members who were accustomed to having a substantial breakfast sent to their lodgings from the Pitt kitchen on a hunting morning. The Club was completely re-opened within 24 hours with meals being served in the Club library.

During his time at the Pitt, my father built up a reputation with senior and junior members of the university and Jesus College that he would succeed in anything he undertook, and he was looked upon as being infallible. Apart from his Club work, he helped and advised many Pitt members with their own personal problems. All this provided many valuable contacts as the years went by and many junior members of the University progressively became important figures in industry, the Government and the University itself. There is no doubt that his wide-ranging reputation at the Pitt stood him in good stead throughout his life. I think Barclays Bank must have helped to finance the initial start of the garage business relying entirely on my father's personal integrity and reputation.

My mother, Maude Edmunds Wing, was born in 1879. Her mother, a widow from an early age, was a Trinity College lodging-housekeeper at 14 Park Parade, Cambridge, with four daughters and a son – my mother being the eldest daughter. My father would not get married until he had his own house. In those days, without any National Insurance or social assistance, he always felt that if you had a roof over your head you would survive. He first built 'Maude Villa' in Humberstone Road, which for some reason he did not like, and then built 'Gregory Villa' in De Freville Avenue.

He made sure the foundations were well and truly sound – a friend had recently built a house and had economised on the foundations, and major cracks developed between the back and the front of the house. This question of good foundations was important to him throughout his business life.

My parents were married at St Andrew's Church, Old Chesterton, on 23 September 1902 by the Revd P. R. Arthur of Trinity College. I was born on Friday 4 December 1903 at 75 De Freville Avenue and baptised Arthur Gregory George by the Revd Arthur at St Andrew's Church on 11 January 1904; being named after the Revd Arthur (who was also my godfather), my father and my other godfather George Nobbs, who was the Chief Clerk at Trinity College.

My brother, Ronald Pitt, was born on 20 March 1906, christened by the Revd Arthur on 19 July 1906, and died of meningitis in June 1907. I was the eldest of eight, Ronald being followed by six sisters, who I will be referring to from time to time. I always think of them as 1 to 6. They are: (1) Margery, 1908; (2) Dorothy, 1910; (3) Violet, 1913; (4) Mary, 1916; (5) Molly, 1920; (6) Brenda, 1927.

My mother was an exceptional woman – tall and good looking – full of unflagging energy and a perfectionist. There is no doubt that the Marshall family owe much to her for our upbringing, general health and capacity for long and sustained work. She worked extremely hard to bring up a family of seven children on a comparatively modest income. She made all the girls' clothes and brought us up in a strict and disciplined way.

My mother defended me against my father's wrath for some of my misdeeds by not telling him of them. I created problems as a result of some of my experimentations, such as the occasion when I had a Magic Lantern which operated with an oil lamp. I bought myself some electrical fittings and a length of flex from Allin's in Bridge Street and installed an electric lamp. In wiring up the bulb holder, I thought it was a waste having two wires running to a dead end, and twiddled them together in the bayonet fitting, and of course it fused all the lights. Also, I was not too lucky at playing conkers, which resulted once in a broken kitchen window and on another occasion a broken wrist-watch.

Both my parents had a big influence on the family. My father was very strict and somewhat impatient if one forgot anything or was slow on the uptake. As the years went by he emphasised the importance of not getting married until you were in a position to support a family. I always felt I was brought up too strictly, and more strictly than my friends, but on looking back I would not have had it otherwise.

My first memory is of my mother taking me for a walk with my sister Margery in her pram and returning home down De Freville Avenue. It must have been autumn-time with the leaves on the ground, and I was swinging my right arm and stirring up the leaves as I walked, only to find a dog had got there before me – many tears.

At the age of six I started attending a small private infants' school for six or seven children at 46 Milton Road; and then went to the Perse Preparatory School in Bateman Street. I used to go to Bateman Street by open-top bus from the top of De Freville Avenue, and later by bike, and sometimes I walked the two or so miles via the Fort St George Midsummer Common ferry.

I spent much time in my school holidays at the Pitt Club, and well remember that on one or two occasions I was sent to deliver the cheques for the end of term accounts, and received the odd tip. I particularly remember Sennitt, the fishmonger on Peas Hill, and Nichols, the butcher at the corner of Petty Cury and Guildhall Street, giving me two shillings or a half-crown. Apart from this I had always been warned not to accept money from anybody, but this seemed different. I also remember receiving sixpence from the Revd Arthur, my godfather, which I refused but was told to accept.

In 1906 my father went to Paris for the first time and was amazed at the advanced state of motoring compared with England. He made up his mind that he must somehow get into the motor business. He tried to find somebody to go in with him, initially Ned Lockhart, who was the Chief Clerk at St John's and a member of the Cambridge Banjo Band with my father. The Lockharts lived at Shelford and his father was very well-to-do, but Ned in due course reported that his father held the purse strings and would not agree. The Lockharts were nevertheless great family friends.

Finally, Harry Rayner, the Barclays Bank audit clerk of the Pitt Club accounts, joined my father as a sleeping partner with a quarter share. My father had originally hoped that Harry would take a 50 per cent interest but again his father held the purse strings and would only agree to a quarter share. Within a year Harry Rayner said, 'Greg, I will take that half share after all,' but my father would not agree. He and his wife were great friends of the family and we spent many Christmases and holidays together.

The business started with chauffeur-driven hire cars in a stable in Brunswick Gardens on 1 October 1909. The garage, with some extension to the stable door, was sufficiently large to house the first two cars. The company was known as The Brunswick Motor Car Company, because at that time my father did not want to have his name too closely associated with the enterprise, which he had started with the enthusiastic approval of the Pitt Club Committee. Because of its German association, the name was changed during the war from The Brunswick Motor Car Company to Marshall's Garage and continued as a partnership until 1934 when it was registered as Marshalls (Cambridge) Limited.

Our first two cars were Metallurgiques followed by two Cottin-Desgouttes. The Metallurgique was described as 'the most renowned sporting car of Belgium and beautifully made'. The Cottin-Desgouttes was quoted as 'expensive and beautifully made near Lyons, the centre of manu-facture of many famous marques of French cars'. These cars were for hire to wealthy dons and undergraduates. There was great wealth amongst the university fraternity in those days, with stories such as of Lord Castlerosse who was said on occasions to have lit his cigar with a £5 note. At one time we had as many as 14 millionaire undergraduate customers.

I spent much time at the Brunswick Gardens garage during 1909, and particularly remember one occasion with my mother when she was repairing a cut in the Bedford Cord upholstery of one of the cars with a big curved needle. Another memory is of my father being instructed on how to drive, with the car parked in the small stable garage. Carter, our first driver, was trying to explain the function of the clutch and gears, all with the engine running. My father, impatient and anxious for some action, got the gear in reverse and backed a few inches, buckling the highly-polished brass oil tail-lamp, and all hell was let loose – 'Why did you let me do that?' I remember my father's first venture at driving outside Cambridge. It was a journey to London with my father driving and Harry Rayner and myself as passengers. We stopped every few miles, the first stop at Royston, to check the water level in the radiator. I expect my father was as excited as a flying pupil going on his first solo cross-country.

The hire car business was an immediate success and expanded into King Street in 1910, which date I well remember because I was intrigued with a new type of five-gallon oil drum which was sitting on a shelf. This had a handle which just pushed up and the oil came straight out horizontally into a pint measure. Being an inquisitive little blighter I thought I would see how it worked. I pushed up the handle and of course a whole flood of oil cascaded over my new knickerbocker suit. Fortunately I did not get into trouble because it was the day my second sister Dorothy was born.

We purchased two more cars, one of which was a Cottin-Desgouttes touring car to satisfy the request of Sir Walter Durnford, Hon. Fellow of King's College and President of the Pitt Club 1869–1871. Sir Walter hired this car regularly for long tours during university vacations, including to Scotland in the summer. The touring car was under-powered and Cottins advised: 'No problem – you can fit a bigger engine. Just move the radiator three-and-a-half inches forward, solder three-and-a-half inches onto the bonnet and drop in a bigger engine'. And this is what was done. The Cottin tourer eventually became our family car in the twenties.

The final move was to Jesus Lane as a tenant of Jesus College in the summer of 1912, which year is also well recorded in my memory. During the big Army manoeuvres in September, the Army Airship 'Beta II' had engine trouble over Cambridge soon after dawn and was drifting over a large Army encampment on Midsummer Common. The Captain mega-phoned down handling instructions to the troops and it was manhandled to a clear patch by the River Cam with the intention of carrying out repairs. The 45 hp Clerget engine spluttering overhead had roused the population, who flocked to the common, in many cases with coats thrown over their night attire, crowding around the airship and making it impossible to work. The Captain ordered the removal of sufficient ballast to allow the airship to rise slightly; troops then walked the airship to a position immediately behind our garage in Jesus College grounds where fencing and a stream kept out the crowds. The garage, which was a big converted coaching stable, had windows opening on to Jesus College grounds and I helped carry petrol and oil cans to the airship. The garage workshop was used by the Army technicians to repair the airship's engine.

Prior to the business moving to Jesus Lane its activities had been confined to hire cars, but at Jesus Lane it became a fully-fledged garage offering sales and service. Whilst we had no agencies we were selling some very expensive cars, including Daimler, Panhard and a Rolls-Royce which we sold to Marshall Field, an American millionaire. These were chassis for which we had the bodies built by Windovers of London and Huntingdon, who had built the bodies of our own hire cars. We sold one Bugatti which was said to achieve 60 mph in Jesus Lane. My father's work at the Pitt Club gave him an automatic sales counter, as it were, for car sales and hire cars which became known as the 'Pitt Taxis'.

About 1913 the City Equitable Insurance Company, which had all our garage insurance business, crashed. Apart from the garage loss, my father was concerned that he had recommended all our customers to insure with this company, and he insisted on paying their renewal premiums with the Union Insurance Company. This started my father's friendship with Mr Dunkin, the Manager of Union Insurance's Cambridge office who was eventually promoted to the London head office. As a young boy of nine I knew nothing of all this at the time, of course, and Mr Dunkin told me the story many years later. DGM established a strict discipline throughout life of immediate payment of monthly accounts. This discipline has been adhered to and has been a great benefit in dealing with the company's suppliers, and has resulted in many cases in special prices, discounts and preferential deliveries and preferential consideration of enquiries.

In the summer of 1913 a modern garage was built in Jesus Lane on the site of the old stable garage, with the showroom on the site of the old Crown Inn. Knowing the congestion experienced at most garages, which were in the main converted premises with a single entrance and exit, my father was determined to have the entrance separate from the exit – a drive-through garage. During the building of the new premises, the garage work was temporarily housed in the big stables and coaching-yard behind the lodging-houses in Jesus Lane, now the site of Wesley House Theological College. Whilst we were operating from the stables on this site, I remember the general service work which we undertook on G. P. Hawkins's two-cylinder Napier baker's vans. I was given the job of taking off one of the front axles. The Napier to the best of my knowledge is the only car ever made with a left-hand starting handle swing. Hawkins had a very large bakery with many shops in Cambridge, including the Dorothy Café where they held regular tea dances. They were one of the first companies in Cambridge to use motor vans.

In 1914 we sold our first Austin car to Claude Elliott, a tutor at Jesus. The car was an open two-seater fitted with one of the very first self-starters. It was engaged with a small brass lever, similar to a small gear lever. This was the first Austin car I drove within the garage bounds in Jesus Lane at 11 years old. I remember that on a Sunday I was alone at the garage and had naughtily been driving this car up and down the garage just before Mr Elliott came in. He very suspiciously felt the temperature of the radiator but said nothing – his look was enough!

Just before the War in 1914 I had on another occasion been left in sole charge of the garage on a Sunday afternoon. My only customer was an elderly gentleman on a push-bike who said there was something wrong with his rear wheel. I managed to diagnose that the wheel was loose, which I tightened and all was well – a satisfied customer – and he gave me his loose change of $3^{1}/_{2}d$, about 50p in today's money.

My two friends Eric and Ronald Francis and I spent some Sunday afternoons at the garage in 1914. We had great fun pushing our bikes from one end to the other – a matter of one hundred feet or so. All went well until Eric failed to catch my bike before it hit the wall and buckled the lower tube of the tubular frame. For a few weeks I thought I was going to get away with it. Then the tube divided into two and there was an inquest on how this came about. No more such games in the garage.

On 25 July 1909 Blériot conquered the English Channel in his monoplane, which shook the Government and the Admiralty to the core. Like the motor car, the nation had, apart from a few enthusiasts, ignored the potential of the aeroplane. It was now realised for the first time that the UK could no longer rely on the protection of the English Channel. Even so, it took much private enterprise to persuade the powers that be to get a move on.

Three organisations played an all-important part in the development and co-ordination of British aviation – the Royal Aeronautical Society, the Royal Aero Club and the Air League of the British Empire. The Aeronautical Society was founded in 1866 as the scientific authority on aeronautical matters, the title 'Royal' being conferred on it in 1918; the Aero Club was formed in 1901, gaining its 'Royal' title in 1910; and the Air League of the British Empire was founded in 1909, very much on the lines of its predecessor the Navy League, as a non-party, patriotic organisation to stimulate British interest in aeronautics and demonstrate the vital importance to the British Empire of aerial supremacy upon which its commerce, communications, defence and very existence largely depended.

The Aero Club resulted from Frank Hedges Butler, a big-game hunter, traveller and early motorist, arranging a motor tour from Surrey to Scotland and back for his 20-year-old daughter, Vera – a high adventure then. A petrol leak in Vera Butler's $4^{1}/_{2}$ hp Renault brought that project to an end. Not to be outdone, the enterprising Vera sought out the professional aeronaut Stanley Spencer and arranged with him a first balloon ascent for her father, herself and the leading motorist, The Hon. Charles Stewart Rolls, from Crystal Palace. At a height of 4,000 feet over Kent, and over a tumbler of champagne, Vera launched the idea of an aero club, which was greeted enthusiastically, and out of its balloon beginnings the Aero Club was formed. It became very much the centre of British aeronautics throughout its pioneering days, particularly when it was centred at 119 Piccadilly, where the Royal Aero Club Smoking Room and Bar became the centre of so much aeronautical gathering and discussion for 30 years.

The three organisations met in 1909 to define the nature and scope of the activities of each society in order to avoid the waste of effort and unnecessary friction such as had resulted from the competition between British organisations concerned with advancing the cause of motoring. The meeting agreed a co-ordinated working scheme to induce the Government to take the subject seriously, and a Parliamentary Committee was formed consisting of members of both Houses with the strict understanding that the whole question was entirely outside party politics. It was finally agreed that: the Royal Aeronautical Society would be the paramount scientific authority on aeronautical matters; the Royal Aero Club would be the paramount body in all matters of sport and the development of the art of aeronautics and the issue of pilots' licences; and the Air League would be the paramount body for patriotic movements and for education.

In 1911 the Royal Aero Club informed the Admiralty that one of its members, Francis McClean, would loan two of his aircraft at his own expense to train four Naval Officers to fly, while another Royal Aero Club member, C. B. Cockburn, offered his services as an instructor. As a result Naval aviation was born. This in turn led to the establishment of Felixstowe as a seaplane base, which was to become the training centre for the RAF High Speed Flight preparing for the international Schneider Seaplane Trophy Race, and the formation of the Royal Naval Air Service in 1914.

Winston Churchill was the First Lord of the Admiralty at this time and he took a keen personal interest in the establishment of the seaplane base, to the extent that, much to the concern of the Prime Minister and his Cabinet colleagues, he insisted on getting first-hand experience of the air whenever possible. His initial experiences at Felixstowe were somewhat frustrated, however. On his first flight the aircraft side-slipped into the sea and the shaken First Lord was taken to a hotel for a change of clothes and a hot meal. On the second occasion the seaplane was forced down with an engine failure and was towed into Harwich harbour. On the third occasion, after inspecting the station and watching a fly-past of marine aircraft, he was about to have a flight himself when the seaplane being brought alongside the landing stage capsized and sank – his planned flight therefore having to be abandoned.

In 1911 *The Daily Mail* sponsored a £10,000 Air Race round Great Britain. My father took my friend Douglas Lockhart and myself to Clacton in the Metallurgique for a few days whilst this race was on. We stayed at a hotel on the front, and outside the hotel was a big map of the British Isles with the course marked out, which was flagged up every day indicating the progress of the competitors. The circuit was 1,010 miles, with 13 compulsory stops, starting and finishing at Brooklands. There had been previous long races in Europe but competitors had been allowed to change their machines as often as they pleased. The Round Britain Race was more strenuous and forbade the practice of changing aeroplanes, and some parts of the airframe and engine were sealed to ensure that the contest was a test of the aircraft rather than the pilot.

Of the 30 entrants 21 lined up at the start. The British aircraft consisted of three monoplanes (two Blackburns and a Birdling) and six biplanes (three Bristols, the new Cody, a Howard-Wright and the Grahame-White Baby). Also, four British pilots were flying French Deperdussin and Blériot aircraft. They were up against very strong opposition – there were several French machines in the race, Deperdussins, Blériots, Morane-Borel, Farman, and Nieuport, and an Austrian Etrich. Tens of thousands gathered to see the start at Brooklands, and it was said that half a million gathered at Hendon to see the start of the second leg of the race.

The race was won in a Blériot monoplane by Lieutenant de Vaisseau Conneau ('Beaumont') by one hour and nine minutes from Jules Vedrines in a Morane-Borel, with James Valentine in a Deperdussin finishing third two days later and Cody, in his British-built Cody, coming in fourth three days after the winner. Whilst the race proved that the UK had some pilots who could compete with the best, it showed most conclusively that our aircraft were far behind the continental machines, both in performance and reliability.

William Rhodes-Moorhouse, a graduate of Trinity Hall and a pioneer aviator, first landed on Parker's Piece in the centre of Cambridge in October 1911 to visit his boot-maker, Frank Dalton. On a number of other occasions he landed on Midsummer Common near Jesus College. He kept his aircraft in an old stable at Huntingdon just behind Windovers, our coachbuilders. This was very handy for him as it was close to Huntingdon Common, his home landing ground. My father, through Windovers, arranged for me, at the age of nine, to visit Rhodes-Moorhouse's workshop and aircraft garage. Rhodes-Moorhouse was killed in action and won the first VC awarded to an airman in World War I. His son was killed in the Battle of Britain and won the DSO. He had been stationed at Duxford and was there with Douglas Bader, who often spoke of him. Rhodes-Moorhouse's VC fetched £126,500 at Sotheby's sale on the occasion of the 50th Anniversary of the Battle of Britain in 1990 in aid of the RAF Benevolent Fund.

In July 1914, immediately before the outbreak of war, Gustav Hamel, another frequent flying visitor to Cambridge, gave a flying display and joyrides alongside the Cherryhinton Road, about 400 yards from Hills Road Railway Bridge. Immediately after the flying display he was lost flying back to Germany, with many rumours and newspaper headlines speculating whether he had been lost at sea or was a German spy and had just disappeared?

In 1912 my father purchased a few acres of land on Milton Road opposite the top of Chesterton Hall Crescent, on the corner of Ascham Road and
incorporating Atherton Close. The land was well laid out into a big garden
and fully fenced in, with a long drive from Milton Road – the original gates
are still there. There was a sunken lawn on the right and stone steps leading
up to the site for the proposed house – we used to play bicycle polo on this
lawn. There were two other lawns – one for tennis and the other for a
cricket net. In spite of my father's coaching at the net, I was no good at
cricket. Later I had a reputation at school at Tonbridge as the straightest bat
ever seen, but I never scored any runs. It was a great disappointment to my
father and I was eventually told to run, which I did with reasonable success.
The Milton Road garden included a big summer-house with a cooking stove
and a swing-boat which was made at Cottenham. All the plans for a house
of York stone had been prepared by a Yorkshire architect, but war inter-
vened and the garden later became the County Council's Milton Road
Library and a housing estate.

About this time we had a Carden cycle car – a single-seater with a 4 hp
single cylinder cycle engine at the back. We spent most of our time trying to
start it with a strap and pulley but, when it went, it was good fun to drive. I
seem to have been allowed to drive from a very early age without getting
into trouble. The Tucks who lived in De Freville Avenue had a splendid
new motor bike and side car – I think it was a Matchless – which caused
much excitement, and a small crowd of children used to gather round it in
wonder when it started off on Sunday morning trips. Mr Sibley, the jeweller
in Bridge Street, a very friendly fellow, had a three-wheeled motor cycle
with a double passenger seat between the two front wheels, and the driver
sitting behind. Mr Sibley contracted to go out to big houses to wind their
clocks on a Sunday morning on his motor three-wheeler.

Dr White was our family doctor and lived at 118 Chesterton Road. He
was very kind to me and often took me with him on his rounds in his small,
8 hp Rover. I remember getting into trouble on one occasion. Whilst the
doctor was visiting a patient, I moved the hand ignition lever to advance
without realising the consequence, which was a severe back-fire when
cranking the engine, and the doctor could have suffered a broken hand –
fortunately he was wearing tough gauntlet gloves.

On Christmas Days my father would take me and one or two of my
sisters for a drive in one of the cars whilst my mother cooked the Christmas
dinner. I particularly remember the great excitement on one such occasion
when we topped 60 mph on the slope running down from the Newmarket
July Course towards Cambridge – a mile a minute was quite something in
those days.

For some years before the war my father had a shoot at Thornton's
farm at Quy Water, which gave him much enjoyment – a mixed bag
including snipe and the odd duck – he was a good rifle shot but not much
good with a gun. A frequent companion was Billy Beattie, the University

Hairdresser, who was one of the best shots in Cambridge, perhaps only bettered by Mrs Beattie.

My father had a rifle range in the cellar of the Pitt Club where he held competitions for the Club staff. At the beginning of the 1914 War, when the RNAS armoured cars were in our garage, he adapted it for RNAS revolver practice and I well remember as a boy of 11 being allowed to have a shot – the revolver kicked and the bullet put out all the lights. I also remember being there as a marker when a piece from a ricocheting bullet embedded itself in the lobe of my right ear. I was very lucky – it could have done serious damage. I also remember incurring my father's wrath when I took a pot shot with his .22 rifle from our back bedroom window in De Freville Avenue at a distant neighbour's chimney stack, but fortunately I don't think I succeeded in hitting anything.

Before the 1914 War we spent our summer holidays at Bognor. We used to take the Cottin tourer and there was always great excitement when, still 10 miles from Bognor, we imagined we smelt the sea. We went to every day of the Goodwood Races and on to the Brighton Races the following week. My father's winnings at these two meetings usually more than paid for our holiday. Near our lodgings in Bognor there was a garage where I spent quite a bit of time. I was intrigued with some of the makes of cars, including an Argyll, with its gear lever attached to the steering column, and a Lanchester which, instead of a steering wheel, had a tiller arm coming from the side of the vehicle.

We were at Bognor when war broke out on 4 August 1914. There was initial panic – the price of petrol went up from $1/2\frac{1}{2}d.$ to 10/- a gallon overnight – but within a few weeks things had settled down and there was talk of 'business as usual'.

Chapter 2

World War I
4 August 1914–11 November 1918

THERE IS NO doubt that when war came it was a great shock – we had not been involved in a war on our doorstep since Waterloo. The German invasion of Belgium caused such universal indignation throughout Great Britain that Parliament voted for war by a very large majority of all parties, and thousands of Englishmen volunteered to fight the Germans. So many years had passed since the wars against Napoleon that no-one knew quite what to expect. From the beginning, nearly all English men and women were anxious to do something for their country. But to do what? There was much flag waving and cheering and crowds gathering outside Buckingham Palace.

Our garage, with its new buildings and showrooms completed in 1913, was just getting into its stride. Its business was virtually 100 per cent dependent on senior and junior members of the University and, as many undergraduates who would have come up in October 1914 joined the forces, the garage and hire car work dropped to a trickle overnight. The undergraduate population decreased from over 3,300 in 1913 to 1,600 in October 1914 and down to something of the order of 400 by the end of the war. In those days replacement parts were not so precisely interchangeable as they are today and such things as connecting rod big end bearings had to be replaced with the running in of hot white metal, then turned up on a lathe and hand scraped for final fitting. This meant that garages had machine shop equipment which could be used for the war effort. Early in the war our garage manufactured shell parts, and for a period housed Royal Naval Air Service armoured cars which were part of the anti-invasion patrols protecting the East Coast.

Until the war Great Britain had ignored the development and potential of the armoured car just as it had ignored the development and potential of motor vehicles and aircraft. Prototype armoured cars were being run in the United States, France and Austria-Hungary from the turn of the century. Commander Charles Samson, in charge of the RNAS in Flanders in

September 1914, obtained Admiralty permission to have a local shipyard fix mild steel boiler plate protection to Mercedes, Rolls-Royce and Wolseley cars and these were the UK's first armoured cars. With the support of Churchill, then First Lord of the Admiralty, the Admiralty Air Department developed from this the classic design of an armoured box with a revolving turret mounting a machine gun. The first Rolls-Royce to this design was delivered in December 1914. Armoured cars were also used in Egypt, Jordan and Saudi Arabia, mostly under the RNAS White Ensign. Lawrence of Arabia wrote of his squadron of Rolls-Royce armoured cars: 'A Rolls in the desert was above rubies . . . great was Rolls, and great was Royce. They were worth hundreds of men to us in these deserts.'

Immediately after the outbreak of war, a battalion of the 60th Rifle Brigade was encamped on Midsummer Common, just across the river from De Freville Avenue. Some of them were ex-members of the Pitt Club and came to our home for a bath or a meal. Until the big Fen Drainage Schemes of the twenties, Midsummer Common experienced some flooding every year and I remember the serious flooding during the Rifle Brigade's encampment. The 60th Rifle Brigade suffered heavy losses at Mons during the first few months of the war. A Tommy's pay at that time was one shilling a day, and I thought this was an awful lot of money.

The First Eastern General Military Hospital, projected to be the biggest in the country, had been under consideration for a great many years but no final action had been taken. Within 24 hours of the declaration of war it was opened first at the Leys School and then, after a few weeks, transferred to the cloisters under the Library in Nevile's Court at Trinity College awaiting the building of a hutted hospital on the old King's and Clare playing fields, now the site of the University Library. A convoy of 170 wounded arrived on 31 August. By 10 October the first part of the hutted hospital was available with 500 beds.

The convoys of wounded from the front used to arrive at the old King's Cross line entrance to Cambridge Station at 8 p.m. They included many stretcher cases, and later many suffering from poison gas. The wounded were conveyed to the First Eastern Hospital by ambulances – some privately owned and driven by their owners. I remember a Fiat ambulance owned by one of the Hooleys of Papworth fame – a very smooth running vehicle. These ambulances were garaged with us at Jesus Lane and my father was involved in setting up the operation of the Ambulance Service with volunteer drivers.

The Revd Simpson of Trinity College was in 1914 an Army Chaplain who paid frequent visits to the wounded at the hospital. He was a delightful but eccentric personality who in the years to come played an important part in my life. He was always keen to have the first of any innovation. Early in the war there was a contraption called the Autowheel, which consisted of a two-stroke engine fitted to a bicycle wheel. This was attached alongside the rear wheel of a bicycle with a few inches clearance of the ground. When in use the Autowheel was lowered to make contact with the road, and was started by pedalling. To say the least, they were not very safe or easy to ride. Anyway, the Revd Simpson had one of these and came a purler. With his head bandaged he looked like a wounded soldier. During one of his visits to the wounded at the First Eastern Hospital, he was very upset when some of the small boys who congregated outside the hospital offering cigarettes to wounded soldiers offered him a cigarette.

With the Pitt Club closed and the garage business reduced to a trickle, my father, aged 42 and well over military age, was determined somehow to join the Forces, much to my mother's annoyance. The Quakers had accepted some responsibility for building up catering units for the expeditionary force in France. My father was on good terms with some of the Quaker members of the Pitt Club, including the Cadbury's, and went to France with them for several months in a voluntary capacity with a uniformed officer's ranking. He qualified for the Mons Star and the British War and Victory Medals, and he was presented by the Joint Committee of the British Red Cross Society and the Order of St John of Jerusalem with a parchment entitled 'Recognition of Valuable Service Rendered During the War, 1914–1918'.

With my father away in France, my mother became the focal point for the voluntary ambulance service operated from the Company's garage in Jesus Lane, supported by Mr Macgillivray, the Manager of the Cambridge Electric Supply Company. I remember that the Zeppelin air raid warning was the electric light being dimmed three times and then remaining dim until the raid was over. I also remember going over the Electric Supply Works in Thompson's Lane. Before entering I was instructed to remove my wrist watch as the current generated was DC (direct current) and the watch would become magnetized. After the war, with the establishment of the National Grid, the current generated was AC (alternating current) – no further problems with wrist watches.

With hindsight, I can imagine my mother's anxiety with my father away and a large and expanding family to look after, and with no pension or life insurances or any national or social benefits such as we know them today. It must have been a very worrying time.

Now for the Royal Arsenal, Woolwich. I am sure that my father had never been to Woolwich and knew little or nothing about Woolwich Arsenal, the country's largest ordnance factory manufacturing big guns and ammunition and employing 10,000 at the outbreak of war, increasing to well over 80,000 before the Armistice on 11 November 1918. The concentration in the Woolwich area of the thousands of men, women and boys, who were brought into the neighbourhood to swell the munitions programme, required a big expansion of canteens, hostel accommodation and welfare centres. This expansion was greater and more rapid than anything which could have been envisaged at the outbreak of war, and problems developed.

The YMCA initially undertook the running of the new canteen, hostels and welfare centres, but during 1915 it became apparent that it was going to be a much bigger job than originally anticipated. Lady Henry Grosvenor, a member of the Westminster family, was Chairman of the YMCA Committee which had undertaken this responsibility, and the Committee decided it was essential to find somebody who could take on overall responsibility on their behalf for the YMCA's Woolwich Arsenal activities. Lady Henry Grosvenor's son, George Greaves, remembered 'Napoleon of the Pitt' which resulted in my father, on his return from France, being offered the job. Things were quiet and getting quieter in Cambridge and this challenge was just what the doctor ordered.

The Woolwich appointment meant that my father had to move there, with the occasional weekend as and when possible at Cambridge, and occasional visits by my mother to Woolwich which were not easy with a young and growing family to look after, and very little help. Initially my father lived in one of the new hutments at Plumstead and I remember staying with him there. My main memories are that the hut was very hot and that the bath had a lid on it, and many of the occupants used the baths for storing their coal.

He then found a small house on Shooters Hill, opposite the banker Baron d'Erlanger's estate with its masses of rhododendrons. In 1915 the family spent a short summer holiday at Shooters Hill. The house had a much overgrown field attached and I thought I would clear it up. It turned out to be more difficult than I had anticipated, and then I had a brainwave – why not burn it? And so I got a box of matches and, not being sure what might happen, a bucket full of water, and thought I would try it out. Of course, one match was enough and the field was well and truly alight. The Fire Brigade was called out and I got into serious trouble but fortunately no damage was done, except we had a very black and dusty field around the house.

My father required a bigger house to accommodate a number of senior management staff, and he found one on the Blackheath side of Shooters Hill called Blomfield House. There, with its many acres of garden and paddocks, my father had a suite of rooms and accommodation for 20 to 30 of his senior staff, many of them from his Cambridge Pitt Club catering staff. This included Bill Morley, who had joined him at the Pitt in the early part of the century as a waiter and who became manager of the largest of the new Arsenal canteens, QFCF4 (Quick Firing Cartridge Factory). A description of this canteen at the time reads: 'This splendid canteen situated in the Danger Zone was opened on 11th December 1916 and is one of the best in the country. It was successful in every way from the first day it was opened and has seating accommodation for 2,500 and is open 24 hours a day for all meals, including teas and light refreshments. The prices charged are 8*d.* for dinner, which consists of meat and two vegetables – sweets being charged for at 2*d.* extra.'

Another early employee I particularly remember was Ted Key, who was with my father as a driver at Woolwich. He had started life as a page boy at the Pitt and taught me to ride a bicycle.

My father was faced with the task of establishing an organisation which could cope with rapid expansion. His first office was in the Drill Hall in Beresford Street, originally the London Rifle Brigade Drill Hall, which was used as the central store but very quickly became too small, coupled with the inconvenience of the double tram lines passing the entrance making the unloading of vans difficult and dangerous. I well remember the noisy trams which ran within a few feet of my father's office with their foot-operated clanging bells and powerful Westinghouse brakes which operated by the pads being depressed on to the main tram lines. The office and stores were quickly moved to New Road, Woolwich, which was only a few yards from Beresford Square and 100 or so yards from the Woolwich Arsenal main gate on Beresford Square.

With the central store transferred to New Road, the Drill Hall was chosen to become the first YMCA canteen to be opened because of its central position 200 yards from the famous Woolwich Arsenal main gate in Beresford Square. This bridged the gap until new canteen accommodation would be available within Woolwich Arsenal. After that the Drill Hall became a billiard room with 14 tables, a buffet and a reading room with newspapers and periodicals, open 24 hours a day. It was very popular as a recreation centre for both soldiers and munition workers.

The total dining room accommodation in the Woolwich Ordnance Factory was 28,000, which meant that 56,000 munition workers could be given full meals in the 24 hours, plus accommodation for snacks and hot drinks. My father's morning routine was office work and then a visit to a selected number of canteens, and he would similarly visit some canteens a few evenings a week. On occasions in the holidays I travelled round the Arsenal visiting the canteens with my father, who was always saying 'Remind me of this' and 'Remind me of that,' with all hell let loose if I forgot anything; and so at this early age I started to make notes as we went along, a habit which I have never lost.

I well remember being at QFCF4 one evening when there was a Zeppelin air raid warning. All the girls poured out. We were near the Plumstead Railway Arsenal gate and must have had a dozen girls piled into and onto our Ford car, with some crying for their mothers. All were panicking and anxious to get out of the Arsenal target area which the Zeppelins could easily locate because of its proximity to the Thames.

At Woolwich, for his personal use my father initially had a Model 'T' Ford which did good service. The Model 'T' Ford had two forward gears and a reverse gear. It was very ingenious and simple to drive if you knew how. The driving controls consisted of three foot pedals, a dual purpose handbrake lever and a hand throttle. The right pedal was the brake, the centre pedal was reverse and the left was forward, pushed down for low, the central position neutral and fully extended back for top gear. The handbrake lever pulled back three inches held the left pedal in the central neutral position when the car was stationary. Until the handbrake was moved fully forward the left pedal could only operate in low gear. The gear box provided epicyclic infinitely variable gearing for the forward low and reverse gears, torque controlled, and direct drive for top gear. If you were turning the car round in a confined space, you could have your left foot on the left forward pedal and your right foot on the centre reverse pedal and could move them up and down, backwards and forwards, using the epicyclic gears for braking.

To drive you put the left foot on the left pedal to maintain the central neutral position, released the handbrake and when ready to move forward depressed the left pedal to engage the low forward gear. When sufficient speed had been gained, the left pedal was allowed to come back through the neutral position to the fully extended top gear position. For a person who had not driven a Model 'T' Ford before and had not been carefully instructed, it was natural to take off the handbrake, which released the left forward gear pedal which automatically fully extended into top gear and the engine would stall.

Driving from Cambridge to Woolwich, our normal route was via Bishops Stortford, Epping Forest and the Woolwich Ferry. I had driven pretty well all the cars we had had to date but had never driven the Ford, and at the age of 13 I worried my father to let me drive, which eventually he did. We changed seats and with no instruction I released the handbrake, the top gear was engaged and the engine stalled. The balloon went up – 'You mean you have been sitting there all this way from Cambridge and don't know how to drive it?' No self-starter, and no more driving for me that day.

The Ford car was not easy to start when cold, and it was always parked overnight on a slope just inside the main gate of Blomfield House so it could run down Shooters Hill to start. One morning my father was delayed and, thinking myself clever, I went to start the Ford car by hand, with the intention of bringing it round to the front of the house. I had left the ignition lever fully advanced; the car back-fired and the starting handle broke my wrist.

The Ford was succeeded early in 1918 by a 10 hp two-seater Singer which I used to drive about Woolwich wearing an Eton Collar with only a motor cycle licence. I was lucky not to be stopped, but in those days I would only have been ticked off. I was often sent into Woolwich Arsenal through the main Beresford Square gate to collect petrol, not only for the car but in some three-gallon cans – these were cans in which liquid Chinese eggs had been imported. All our petrol supplies came from the Woolwich Arsenal main fuel storage centre.

The Singer gearbox was incorporated in the differential of the back axle. During my summer holiday at Woolwich in 1918 my father had someone to lunch in his office and had forgotten his small crocodile pocket cigar case. He had left this at Blomfield House and told me to go and fetch it, which I did at great speed in his small Singer car. Coming back I thought I would take a short cut round the back of the Military Academy over a very bumpy road. All went well until after I had passed the Artillery Theatre on my left and was beginning to descend the hill into Woolwich when I suddenly found I had no brakes. There was a lorry coming towards me on the right and a platoon marching towards me on the left. I put the car into reverse and it juddered round in the centre of the road. I then managed to creep back in low gear to my father's office in New Road. The car was jacked up and it was found that the bumpy road had turned the rear shock absorber past centre and this had lengthened the brake cables which resulted in complete brake failure. The shock absorbers were re-positioned and all seemed well until we were returning to Cambridge the next day, when the whole gearbox collapsed in Epping Forest. I was not very popular.

During this time Eric and Ronald Francis and I went for a number of long cycle rides – very much an adventure in those days. I remember cycling to Devil's Dyke near King's Lynn and to Ashwell, the source of the River Cam beyond Royston. We cycled a number of times to Newmarket Heath, which during the war was a Royal Flying Corps aerodrome, where I was known by some of the catering staff provided by my father. This resulted in a good look round the Sopwith Pup and Camel aircraft. Some of the RFC were billeted in the stands, which were also used as messes.

Meanwhile I had continued my schooling at the Perse Preparatory School. I won my first race, the 100 yards, at Fenners, the university cricket and athletics ground. The mistresses gave us a number of trials to assess the handicaps. My father said: 'Oh, don't worry too much about the trials – concentrate on the final race'. I think his horseracing expertise had some influence here. It was thanks to a good handicap that I won the race by a few inches. The first prize was a silver spoon engraved with the Perse School pelican crest. At the end of 1915 I transferred to the Senior Perse School opposite the Catholic church, where those of us who could not swim had a white button on the top of our school caps. In March 1916 I had some further athletic success by winning the lower school quarter-mile and being second in the 100 yards and fourth in the three cross-country races. I was a member of the Perse School Officers Training Corps. Wearing Army uniforms, we felt we were real soldiers when we paraded on Parker's Piece.

Whilst I was at the Senior Perse School Dr Rouse, the Headmaster, gave me six of the best for ragging in Monsieur Chouville's French class. M. Chouville, the second French master at the school, had a very sharp temper. On another occasion I mixed 'le livre' and 'la livre' and M. Chouville said I was to give him a pound of chocolates as punishment. My mother refused to let me have the chocolates until I knew who they were for. I got the question translated into French and was let off.

The senior French master was the flamboyant Monsieur de Glehn, a famous teacher of phonetics, who had changed his family name from 'von Glehn' to 'de Glehn' during the war to make it clear that he was not a German. There are endless stories of both de Glehn and Chouville. M. de Glehn would miss no opportunity to turn an incident to educational advantage. He once appeared before a class with his flies unbuttoned; and a boy had the temerity to tell him of it, in English. Characteristically de Glehn boomed: 'Why didn't you tell me in French?' And then, without a trace of embarrassment, drilled the class: 'Je suis déboutonné; qu'est-ce que je suis?' and made them go through the other persons, 'Tu es . . . ' etc.

My father often said that a good education was the one thing in life which could not be taken away from you, and during 1917 he thought it was time I went to a boarding school. He had for many years an ambition to buy one of three properties around Cambridge – Milton Hall, Howes Close on Huntingdon Road (now the Cambridge Regional College), or Elfleda House on Newmarket Road. Just as he was going to press the button for me to go to a boarding school he heard that Elfleda House might be coming on the market. I remember walking up and down Regent Street with him opposite the Perse while he explained to me that it would be stretching the family's finances to buy the house and for me to go to a boarding school at the same time – what did I think? I was selfish and not very helpful by asking if we could not do both, and in the end this is what we did. It was finally decided that I should go to Hillside, Tonbridge if I could pass the entrance exam, mainly because Tonbridge had some good engineering workshops, and my father knew of H. S. Vere-Hodge, the Housemaster at Hillside, as a good all-round games player in his Trinity days.

Dr W. H. D. Rouse was a tremendous Headmaster and really put the Perse School on the map but, when he heard I was leaving and going to Tonbridge, he was furious and sent for me and said that he had refused to give me the Tonbridge entrance exam at Cambridge. This saved my bacon as I was a slow developer and I am sure I would never have passed. Travel was difficult in the war years and Tonbridge decided to accept me and give me a short test on the first day of term to decide in which form I should start. This of course resulted in starting in the bottom form. I was very backward – as, for example, I wrote out an order application to my Housemaster for a pair of gym shoes, which I spelt 'jim'.

The opportunity to buy Elfleda House materialised, and we moved in during November 1918. This move to Elfleda House turned out to play an important part in the establishment of our Flying School.

As a result of the success of his Woolwich Arsenal work, my father had become involved with a number of Ministry of Munitions canteen and welfare committees. On behalf of these committees he visited factory canteens which were having problems. This would have been of no consequence if the Ministry of Food had not asked him to report and advise on canteen problems at the Austin works, Birmingham. This was his first introduction to the Austin works and the future Lord Austin. My father was most impressed and, having supplied our first Austin to Claude Elliott of Jesus in 1914, he felt something good must come out of this factory after the war. He made up his mind, just as he had decided in Paris to get into the motor business, that he must make a bee-line for an Austin agency as soon as the war was over.

One continuous worry during the war with my father away at Woolwich was the keenness of a number of individuals and companies to acquire some interest in our garage, knowing that we had got to build up our finances to cope with long-term development. Other garages, whose owners were living in Cambridge throughout the war, were acquiring agencies and it is fortunate for us that Austin was not one of them. Coupled with this my father was not mechanically minded, whereas our competitor garages had graduated almost without exception from cycle shops and had some basic mechanical engineering knowledge.

Pressure of work built up for my father and he resigned from his Ministry of Munitions Committee work early in 1918. He was becoming increasingly concerned about his work at Cambridge and finally resigned all his responsibilities at Woolwich after the Armistice was declared in November 1918. With little or no income from the garage during the war, his Woolwich appointment had been of considerable financial importance.

My father was awarded the MBE in the King's Birthday Honours List in 1918 for his work at Woolwich Arsenal and with the Ministry of Munitions.

Chapter 3

Starting All Over Again

November 1918–April 1926

AT THE BEGINNING of autumn 1918 the Germans put out urgent diplomatic feelers which eventually resulted in the Armistice of 11 November that year. From the depths of despair of only a few months before, the fighting had ended almost overnight. There was initial euphoria, with crowds outside Buckingham Palace, singing and dancing in Piccadilly and street parties. The men who survived had had a rough time in the trenches and came back exhausted and feeling very lucky to be alive. Everybody wanted to make up for lost time and enjoy themselves.

Just as my father had recognised the future importance of the development of the motor car after his visit to Paris in 1906, he now realised the future importance of air travel. He thought flying was just around the corner, and he was anxious to get his foot in the door. In 1919 he bought a new Handley-Page 0/400 twin-engined bomber for £5 from the Disposal Board at Fowlmere, near Duxford, and an ex-RAF canvas-covered Bessonneau hangar – named after its French designer. The hangar was dismantled in sections and re-assembled in the paddock at the back of our house by an ex-RAF Pilot Officer – my father thinking that a pilot of the RAF must know how to assemble an Air Force hangar. It gave the family much worry in high winds at night, with canvas flapping and some of it blowing off. Eventually it was sold to the Cement Company on Newmarket Road who added a corrugated iron roof and used it for a great many years.

I travelled backwards and forwards to Fowlmere to dismantle the aircraft in my Easter school holidays of 1919 on an ABC four-speed, horizontally opposed twin-cylinder motor cycle with Dan Morley from the garage workshop on the pillion. This motor bike was a very pleasant, smooth running machine – good performance but lightly built. ABC engines were used in a number of light aircraft in the early twenties, including the de Havilland DH-11.

Our Handley-Page bomber had a pair of undercarriage wheels under each wing and was too wide to tow along the roads. We removed the wings and undercarriages and refitted the undercarriages under the fuselage to tow the aircraft back to Cambridge. Unfortunately we had not considered the height, and the first thing we did on leaving Fowlmere aerodrome was to pull down the telegraph wires.

There were some 20 gallons of petrol left in the aircraft, but petrol at that time was only 1/4d. a gallon. The bomber's centre section fuel tank was used by the garage for their paraffin storage until well into the fifties. Some of the aircraft bits and pieces, including Bowden cables, were used by our garage. Many cars were still not 100 per cent standard, and much of the cabling could be used on cars which had been personally built, some with aero engines. One which was garaged with us, belonging to Sir John Millbank, could only be started by a gang of his friends pushing it down Jesus Lane until it went off with a roar.

When my father purchased Elfleda, the family thought the name rather drab. Discussing this some time after we had bought the aircraft and Bessonneau hangar, on the spur of the moment I suggested 'Aviation Hall' and, much to my surprise, this suggestion was accepted without argument. All this initial family enthusiasm for the air was further encouraged by a growing national interest in aviation.

The Daily Mail 'Round Britain Air Race' of 1911 had highlighted the backward state of the country's aviation interest. As a result, Lord Northcliffe in 1913 had offered a further prize of £10,000 for the first non-stop flight of the Atlantic, which brought much ridicule on himself and *The Daily Mail* but, even so, a number of aircraft were in the course of design and manufacture when the competition was overtaken by the 1914 War. Immediately after the Armistice in 1918 Lord Northcliffe resurrected his offer, and a number of teams started to prepare for the Atlantic Race, but in the end, in June 1919, it became a contest between three.

Fred Raynham and Charles Morgan had the 'Raymor' Martinsyde biplane built with a single Rolls engine. Because of a cross-wind the aircraft crashed on take-off fortunately without injury to the crew.

Tom Sopwith designed an aircraft for Harry Hawker and Mackenzie-Grieve, known as 'The Atlantic Biplane', fitted with one Rolls-Royce engine. This aircraft had engine trouble, resulting from the radiator cooling shutters being wired in reverse, and force landed in the sea alongside a small ship. They had got to within 720 miles of Ireland after 15 hours flying. The ship had no radio and the aircraft crew were reported missing and assumed dead until the ship was able to flag-signal the coastguard at Butt of Lewis some 10 days later to say they were safe. I well remember the drama – the King and Queen had already sent their condolences to Mrs Muriel Hawker. They were welcomed back by a tremendous crowd at King's Cross Station and received by the King and Queen at Buckingham Palace and presented by Lord Northcliffe of *The Daily Mail* with a consolation prize of £5,000.

The third aircraft, a Vickers Vimy converted bomber with two Rolls-Royce engines, was the thirteenth aircraft off the production line and was flown by Captain John Alcock and Lieutenant Arthur Whitten Brown. They took off from St John's Newfoundland. The flight proceeded well for the first 11 hours, until they encountered severe weather conditions with much turbulence and serious icing problems, causing the aircraft to stall and spin. Alcock regained control within 250 feet of the waves and also managed to regain some height, but with altitude icing again became serious and the engines started misfiring, so they decided they must get down into warmer conditions. They came out of the cloud base at 300 feet and continued eastbound at 200 feet. Two small islands appeared and then a coastline which turned out to be Clifden, the chief town of Connemara. They sighted the Marconi wireless station – the base for transatlantic communications. Alongside the Marconi station there appeared to be a green expanse which looked like a firm meadow and they decided to land and continue their journey to Brooklands on the morrow. The green expanse in fact turned out to be the Derrygimla Bog. The Vimy touched down and then came to a sudden stop – its nose dug into soft, spongy earth. Neither Alcock nor Brown was hurt. The flight had been accomplished in 16 hours 12 minutes.

On Friday 20 June 1919 the *Daily Mail* held a luncheon at the Savoy Hotel, when the cheque for £10,000 was presented by Winston Churchill on behalf of Lord Northcliffe who was indisposed.

And so, from take-off from Newfoundland on the late afternoon of Saturday 14 June, Alcock and Brown had had quite a busy week, ending up on the following Saturday with knighthoods from the King at Windsor. The Vimy is now in the London Science Museum at South Kensington.

In 1919 Churchill, on an official visit, addressed the RAF College at Cranwell and spoke of the great future of aviation, and advised that the three things the aircraft industry had got to concentrate on for the future were an alternative propulsion to the propeller, vertical take-off, and an alternative fuel to petrol. Inspired and prophetic advice.

Civilian flying had restarted on 1 April 1919 using 'demobilised' Service aircraft. My father and I had our first flight in July 1919 in a Fairey IIIA seaplane, registration G-EADZ, at ten shillings each from a point opposite Roedean College at Brighton with a flight round the pier and back. The pilot was in the front with the two passengers behind. I remember that we were not strapped in and it was quite easy for me to stand up.

During the immediate post-war years, however, our main concern was to get the garage re-established, remembering that my father still had substantial catering and Pitt Club commitments.

On 19 July 1919 my father was mainly responsible for what the Town Council Catering Committee described as a magnificent dinner on Parker's Piece on the occasion of the Victory Day celebrations, when 1,380 sat down and an additional 1,500 had to be refused. The Town Council was originally worried as to whether this number of meals could be achieved. Mr G. P. Hawkins volunteered that he was sure it could be done, and my father had the responsibility for carrying it out. The Council passed a resolution expressing their deep gratitude to these two gentlemen. This was a voluntary effort by all concerned, including the cooking, loan of catering equipment and seating, all of which was made available by colleges and catering establishments.

The May Week Trinity Ball was normally held in the Guildhall and Corn Exchange with a temporary bridge across Corn Exchange Street, but in 1920 the Corn Exchange was not available. My father persuaded the powers that be to let him put up a marquee on part of Market Square. The marquee was erected after the stall-holders had closed down for the day and all was ready for supper at 11 o'clock with an awning and red carpet over the closed road to connect the Guildhall and Market Square. All was dismantled and cleared ready for the stall-holders first thing the next day.

This Trinity Ball terminated my father's 33 years of catering, and in June 1920 he finished work at the University Pitt Club having satisfied himself that he had become established in the motor industry before finally giving up his original catering profession. The Club then discontinued its outside catering activities.

The garage was extended into the Jesus College grounds with the building of a second bay, and took in the cobbler's shop in Jesus Lane between the garage and Little Trinity for a showroom. Little Trinity is a Grade 1 listed building built in the middle of the eighteenth century, and great care was taken not to clash with its architecture. Jesus Lane in those days was a very narrow lane, half its present width and with a footpath on one side only. The massive old Sidney Sussex College wall, thought to have been built in the fifteenth century and associated with the Friars' House which preceded the College, was pulled down in 1922. The road was then widened and a new wall set a good deal further back into the College grounds.

Some wartime garage employees had pre-war jobs to return to, and new staff had to be found and trained to cover car sales, garaging, servicing and repairs, plus the chauffeur-driven hire car business and a new venture into small buses for conveying college teams to away matches.

The newly appointed Workshop Manager was not satisfactory and was replaced by his deputy, Dan Morley, who was an important member of the team until he set up his own successful garage business. Dan was succeeded in 1937 by Cyril Porter, known as 'Titch' because of his size, and still in his twenties – it was a gamble that paid off. He had started with the Company as an apprentice in 1923 and then drove hire cars and buses when required, including England, Scotland and Wales coach tours with which the Company became involved in the late twenties. His engineering expertise proved very valuable on many occasions when buses had mechanical problems. Titch retired from the Company in 1974 as Technical Director with 51 years service, having worked his way from the bottom to the top. He was very popular with both customers and staff.

Gilly Fromant was another wonderful old friend and loyal employee. He joined the Company as our second driver at Brunswick Gardens. He spent much time in the Middle East in the 1914 War and rejoined the Company after demobilisation in 1919. Fromant had always been very good with a paintbrush and, with the development of the garage workshop, found himself in charge of a small but all-important paintshop, but still ready to turn his hand to anything mechanical, washing cars, and driving cars and buses as required. The one problem with Gilly Fromant was that he was a perfectionist and did not like 'touching up'. If, for example, a wing required a local touch-up, Fromant, unless he had been very carefully instructed and persuaded to do otherwise, would strip and repaint an Austin Seven at a cost of 25/- instead of just a few shillings for touching up. Fromant's high repainting standards brought much other work to our garage, including the Lord Lieutenant Mr Adeane's Rolls-Royce which came to us regularly every three or four years for service and repaint.

Bill Morley (no relation of Dan) and Ted Key, of Pitt Club and Woolwich days, became important members of the garage team, with Bill Morley as the Garage Manager and Ted Key the senior driver of the hire cars and buses and doing whatever else was required of him – general garage work, washing cars and workshop repairs. Bill Morley was with us until he retired. He had the dignity of a duke and was an old family friend. When given a job to do, Bill would see it through. Ted Key left us in the thirties to start his own successful garage.

Another very important early appointment was Edward J. Parr who, after war service in the Army, joined the Company at the beginning of 1920 as a clerk, and was the only clerical staff until Miss Symonds (later Mrs Mitchell) became his assistant in 1932. Eddie, as he was known, kept the books and filled in customers' new car order forms. He did most of his book-keeping standing at a high sloping desk backing up to a very wide window. He was also a fill-in when necessary for anything that was required, serving in the stores, serving petrol and helping in the garage generally. I do not remember Eddie Parr ever having a day off with illness – the amount of illness in those days amongst the staff generally was much less than encountered today. During my school holidays I kept the books when Eddie was on holiday, but there was not much going through during the university vacations. Staff in those days had only one week's holiday a year, plus Bank Holidays if they were lucky. Prince Albert and Prince Henry were undergraduates at Trinity in 1919 and Prince Albert had a motor bike which he kept in our garage. Eddie Parr often told the story of the Prince coming in to pay an account for 19/6d. with a £1 note. Eddie had to go upstairs to get the 6d. change and was surprised that the Prince was quite happy to wait for his 6d.

Being willing and able to turn one's hand to anything one was capable of was all-important – I say willing, but in those days it was normal practice to do whatever was required regardless of the day or night of the week. Our garage had a reputation for good service and customer courtesy. As our alma mater, our Jesus Lane garage in particular maintains this reputation for good service and customer courtesy resulting from detailed and fundamental training and long continuity of staff employment. The garage was open seven days a week, 24 hours a day. The main activity during the night was washing cars and letting in late-comers. The charge for a wash and polish for the average car was five shillings (in current money, say £9) and this included the cleaning and polishing of the brass radiators, door handles and lamps. When a customer came in to enquire about a new or second-hand car, this was looked after by whoever happened to be handy, including Eddie Parr. We did not have a full-time salesman until 1930.

We had two apprenticeship schemes. The first was a three-year apprenticeship with a premium of £25 (nearly £1,000 in today's money) which carried a wage of four shillings a week for the first year and six and eight shillings a week for the second and third years respectively. The second scheme was a four-year apprenticeship carrying a wage of 2/6d., 5/-, 7/6d. and 10/- a week, but with no premium. The pay was for all hours worked. The apprentices were carefully selected and were excellent material. The workshop was run by the manager with an assistant and eight or nine apprentices. A mechanic's or driver's weekly wage in those days was £2.17s.6d. for all hours worked regardless of the days of the week. The normal hours of work were from 8 a.m. to 6 p.m. Monday to Friday and 8 a.m. to 1 p.m. on Saturdays, a 50-hour week, plus weekend work as required.

New cars were in short supply in 1919, and with buyers endeavouring to get preferential delivery a black market developed. There was, however, a supply of ex-military vehicles at large War Department disposal sales. I remember going to a number of these sales with my father at the Elephant and Castle, London where they were held for a time almost daily.

At one sale we bought two Army Crossley Landaulette staff cars with twin tyres fitted to the rear wheels. We had to convert these to single-tyred wheels because they picked up and retained stones between the double tyres which resulted in punctures – there were many more large stones to be picked up on the roads of those days. We also bought a Renault and a Delaunay Belleville, both very heavily built cars. The Delaunay Belleville was considered by many in 1914 to be the best car in the world, with many royal customers. We built a 12-seater bus body on the Renault and a 14-seater bus body on the Delaunay Belleville for conveying college teams to away matches. The Renault and the Delaunay Belleville buses would never have met today's road regulations – no four-wheel brakes – and one cannot possibly imagine building a bus body on any current car chassis.

We also bought an ex-WD Army Daimler 20-seater bus which we used for college away matches and for taking the University Trial Eight crews to Ely for training in the October term. Large pneumatic tyres were just being introduced, and we replaced the solid tyred front wheels with pneumatics. This was one of the first vehicles in the country to be so converted and was quite a novelty. A photograph in *The Daily Mirror* of this vehicle taking the

Trial Eight crews to Ely gave more prominence to the pneumatic tyres than to the crews.

These buses gave yeoman service until they were replaced progressively from 1925 by two Italian Lancia and two French Laffly coaches with armchair seats, map tables and under-floor side-loading lockers for suitcases. The bodies were built to our specification by Hall Lewis, who were (with the possible exception of Metropolitan Cammell Weyman) the biggest bus builders in the country.

Buying these ex-WD vehicles under the hammer was a big gamble and you had to chance your luck after a very superficial and hurried inspection. There was no general description of the vehicle, track record or mileage guarantee, and sales under the hammer were quick-moving. Many short-lived second-hand dealers were attracted into the business of speculating; buying these vehicles for resale to the trade or to individual customers. The majority of these speculators were honourable men, but there were some lesser brethren who botched up cars to give them a showroom sales appeal regardless of the 'innards'. Car transmissions and back axles, with their crown wheel and bevel pinions, were not as silent in those days as they are today, and I remember that some cars were known to have had sawdust introduced into the transmission lubrication to help deaden noisy whines.

Whilst we had supplied numerous very expensive motor cars, we had never held an agency and most of our pre-war millionaires had disappeared. We had to start from scratch to develop a quite different type of business. Having recognised the Austin Motor Company's potential on his visit to the Austin works during the war, my father succeeded in obtaining the agency under Mann Egerton of Norwich in 1919, and at the Motor Show in 1920 Marshall was appointed the Austin distributor for Cambridgeshire. Our Austin agency was all important to us and became the corner-stone of our business.

Austins had made a major contribution to the war effort, for which Herbert Austin was knighted in 1917. During the war Austin's expanded to over 20,000 employees and production was enormous, including a wide range of major military equipment, and manufacture of various makes of aircraft and aero-engines. The Austin flying field was built by German prisoners of war on the rising ground to the south of the works where the current vehicle assembly shop and Leonard Lord's new office block, which became known as 'The Kremlin', were built in the early fifties. The flying ground had a one mile vehicle test track and a railway track round the perimeter.

Sir Herbert had big ambitions to get established in the commercial aircraft industry and had reached an advanced stage of manufacturing Austin's own design aircraft and aero-engines, including a single-seater private owner aircraft, the Austin Whippet, which was basically designed round an Anzani engine. Three were built and one was flying for many years between the wars. Had a suitable engine been available for a two-seater, it might have brought forward the private flying era by several years. The post-war slump and the collapse of the aircraft industry ended Sir Herbert's aviation ambitions. Until recent years I had not realised that Sir Herbert had burnt his fingers so badly with his civil aircraft venture. I remember asking him more than once, 'What about making an Austin aeroplane, Sir Herbert?', and he would usually answer that he had no relations in the undertaking business.

Transferring from war to peace production was a formidable task. Sir Herbert considered many possibilities, including the manufacture of domestic and industrial electric lighting sets, but they all came to nothing. This left him relying on his new 20 hp car to occupy the enormous Longbridge works. The Austin Twenty was planned to sell for £485 but, by the time production began, it had shot up to £685 and it was too big a car for volume production. The company ran into financial problems and a receiver was appointed in 1920, but debts were all finally paid as Austin became progressively re-established with the introduction of a very successful and comprehensive range of models. The Austin Twenty continued in production for the next 20 years. I particularly remember one Austin Twenty two-door sports saloon with a top speed of 80 mph which we supplied to a wealthy Indian undergraduate at Corpus Christi.

In the early twenties there were about 20 distributors and Sir Herbert held an annual Distributors' Meeting in August in anticipation of the forthcoming Olympia Motor Show in October. During my school and university holidays my father succeeded in taking me to all the Distributors' Meetings from 1920 and, after I left college in 1926, to all the annual Austin Motor Show Dinners at the Connaught Rooms, Holborn, and later at Grosvenor House. I now realise I must have been resented by a few, but it was certainly a good apprenticeship for me. Chris Buckley, later the Sales Manager and a long-standing friend in years to come, told me he thought I was a precocious young man in those days. I was surprised as I have always considered myself shy and retiring.

The Austin Twelve was announced at Sir Herbert's Distributors' Meeting in 1920. Sir Herbert suggested a price of, I think, about £340. George Heath, the Birmingham distributor, immediately chimed in with '£240', and the price announced at the Motor Show was, I think, something just under £300. The price of cars reduced between the wars. At the 1922 Meeting, I remember Billy Rootes asking Sir Herbert when the Austin Twelve was going to have front wheel brakes. Sir Herbert replied: 'We don't fit anything unless it is 100 per cent proven, and the best car in the world has not got front wheel brakes'. But sure enough a year later we had front wheel brakes. The Austin Twelve established a reputation for being one of the hardest wearing machines of all time, advertised by the slogan 'You buy a car but you invest in an Austin'. All the inter-war Austin cars were famous for their durability and reliability.

Knowing Sir Herbert's habit of abruptly and automatically turning down suggestions and then, having slept on them, quietly adopting some, I have always wondered whether my father was responsible for the Austin Seven or whether he was just a further encouragement to Sir Herbert for what he had already planned to do. During early 1920 Sir Herbert gave my father a lift from the Queens' Hotel, Birmingham to the Longbridge works. In the course of the journey my father asked Sir Herbert when he was going to make a small motor car, not a cycle car but a real car, to replace all the undergraduate motor bikes and sidecars we had in our garage. Sir Herbert very firmly replied: 'Never – not for you or anybody else, Mr Marshall.' The Austin Seven was announced to the distributors at their meeting in August 1921.

In more recent years I have learnt that Sir Herbert had considerable difficulty in persuading his Board, which included strong bank representation, to agree to the production of the Austin Seven. Whilst the arguments continued Sir Herbert designed the Austin Seven with the help of Stanley Edge, whom he had taken into his home to live and work on the Austin Seven drawings. Sir Herbert personally held all the patent rights. It was the first real car designed as a miniature motor car as compared with the many primitive and improvised cycle cars of that time. It would carry a family of four and was very durable and cheap to run. The Austin Seven was announced as 'The car for the millions' and became the most popular small car in the world. It was the greatest of all baby cars and very important to our fortunes in the twenties.

Whilst still a schoolboy I took delivery of our first Austin Seven in August 1921. The first few were produced with an engine capacity of under 700 cc, which carried a £7 road tax, and hence the name 'Austin Seven'. There are few inclines between Longbridge and Birmingham but I found that on the slightest incline the car was very sluggish and I had to change down to lower gears. This problem was quickly recognised and, after the first 30 or so cars, the Austin Seven cylinders were bored out to provide an engine capacity of just under 800 cc which carried an £8 road tax, but the car continued to be known as the 'Austin Seven'.

When Sir Herbert announced the Austin Seven, my father said he hoped there would be a sports model which would be popular with young members of the University. Sir Herbert said, 'My hands are full. You had better have a chassis and see what you can do.' And so we had the first chassis out of the works and got Carbodies of Coventry to design and build an aluminium two-seater with a sporting pointed tail. Some years later Bill Lyons told me that he had seen our Austin Seven sports car being built by Carbodies and it had given him the idea of what he wanted for his first Swallow sidecar. This was the beginning of SS Cars, now Jaguar. I was given the job during my school holidays of taking our sports car to the Austin works and showing it to Sir Herbert, who grunted and criticised a number of points. Two years later Austins produced an Austin Seven sports two-seater with a pointed tail very similar to our own car.

The Austin Seven was made under licence in America, France, Germany and Japan. In my humble opinion I consider Sir Herbert must have been one of the foremost British design engineers of the century. His cars were a salesman's delight because you could really believe in what you were selling, and the Austin reputation was high throughout the motoring world.

During the twenties we also became agents for Talbot, Belsize and Fiat. The Talbot, manufactured in North Kensington, was a high-performance car for those days and established the slogan 'The Invincible Talbot' as a result of doing well in a number of international competitions, including coming second in the Brooklands One Thousand Mile Race, and third and fourth in Le Mans, and giving a good account of itself in Alpine and other trials. Belsize of Manchester's initial post-war car had a 15 hp engine and was a good motor car. In 1922 Belsize produced a light car known as the Belsize Bradshaw with a 'V' twin oil-cooled engine. Generally speaking it gave good performance but was difficult to start and not too reliable. With their expanding sales and range of models, Austins in the late twenties introduced a 100 per cent loyalty bonus for those distributors who became 100 per cent Austin, and we gave up our other agencies.

In 1919 we resumed our family summer holidays, and the Goodwood and Brighton race meetings continued to be the focal point. My Aunt Madge, housekeeper to the De La Rue family, had moved with them during the war from Six Mile Bottom to Brighton, and my maternal grandmother and her other daughters moved to Hove. And so in 1919 we travelled to Brighton in the Cottin-Desgouttes tourer, which was heavily laden with a family of six and all our baggage. It was the first journey out of Cambridge for the Cottin-Desgouttes since the war. With the car having been jacked up for the duration of the war the metal studded tyres had perished, and they burst and had to be replaced between Cambridge and Baldock. Metal studded tyres were in common use before and during the war; they were designed to give a good grip on the many indifferent road surfaces of those days, and the studs stood proud like flat-headed tin tacks.

In the mid-twenties my father's friend Ned Lockhart persuaded him to rent the bungalow next to theirs on the front at Heacham, near Hunstanton, and this we did for a number of years. The Lockharts were a family of three girls and a boy, the girls all about my sisters' ages.

At Heacham, with the tide out, there was a very big expanse of sand which encouraged us to build a six-seater family sand-yacht which we sailed for a number of years – it was great fun. We used the large undercarriage wheels and axles from our Fowlmere Handley-Page bomber. The Heacham sand was very firm but very wet. It was a big sand-yacht and required a good strong breeze to keep it moving and, with much spray coming up from the sand when travelling at 40 mph, it could be an exhilarating but wet and cold experience. Much good exercise derived from pushing, particularly on days when the wind strength was marginal. Our most exciting runs when the wind was in the right direction were along the 30-degree dry sand embankment, when we achieved speeds of over 45 mph.

We had some narrow squeaks. The first was after the initial assembly of the yacht behind the bungalows at Heacham with many people about. With my father on the tiller, I pulled up the sail for the first time – my father and I knew absolutely nothing about sailing – and the yacht immediately took off along the back of the Heacham bungalows towards Hunstanton and rapidly gained speed. Fortunately, because of the rough ground, the tiller was jogged out of my father's hand and the yacht turned 180 degrees into wind and stopped immediately and before any catastrophic damage was done. And so we had learnt our first lesson. The second serious incident was when my sister Dorothy fell overboard and one of the rear wheels went over her, but fortunately all was well.

With this sand-yachting one could be wet and exhausted but still with a huge smile on one's face, which said it all. It was exciting and good fun. Sitting so close to the ground with the feel of the sea and the spray gave the impression of travelling much faster than you were. The sand-yacht had no brakes – the only means of slowing down was with the adjustment of the sail, which was not easy, or virtually instant stopping by slewing round into wind.

During these happy years when I was at Tonbridge and Jesus I was fortunate to be involved during holidays and vacations in all that was going on in our garage business at Cambridge – salad days.

Chapter 4

Tonbridge
January 1918–April 1922

I STARTED AT Hillside, Tonbridge, on 16 January 1918. There were six Novis (new boys) in our House that term. We started with three in a small study and later two in a study, with the Head of the House having a study to himself. Henry Bateman, Ralph Ferry and I shared a study and the three of us became friends for life. After Ralph left, Henry and I continued to share until we left school in 1922 and went on together to Jesus College, Cambridge in October of that year. Henry was a good scholar and a great help with my homework. Ralph was also a good scholar and a very good all-round games player, particularly cricket, rugger and fives.

Vere Hodge ('Vera'), a bachelor, was for me the best Housemaster ever – a good games player, particularly cricket, fives and racquets, who regularly played with the boys and in teams against the School Cricket XI. He used to have a few boys to breakfast in his own dining room on Sunday mornings – there were 48 boys in the House, which meant four or five boys each Sunday. We looked forward to this. Apart from anything else, Vera always gave us a very good breakfast. He was later Deputy Headmaster or, as they call it at Tonbridge, Second Master. Hillside had a grass tennis court, lawns and flower beds, and a big sloping lawn with some large trees in the middle where we used to lie on Sunday afternoons in the summer and discuss world problems. There was a very good view from the back of the house across the valley. Vera was a keen gardener with a big vegetable garden. When he retired he started a successful market garden with his Hillside gardener. Vera and I remained very good friends until his death in 1970.

At Tonbridge there were School and House praepostors. The Head of the House was usually a School praepostor and he had four or five House praepostors to help him run the House, which they ruled with a rod of iron. There was general fagging, and fags were allocated to individual praes to keep their studies tidy and clean Officers' Training Corps uniform buttons and boots. A call of 'Kid' by one of the praes brought all the fags rushing up the stairs, the last one being chosen to do whatever chore was required such as making a 'brew'. If a fag was slow in responding to the fag call, he might be ticked off or punished in some way, such as being made to run up and down the stairs six times. The Head of the House could beat a boy.

Lionel Hedges, Head of House and Head of School, was described by Vera as the perfect schoolboy. He was a good scholar and quite exceptional at everything – a good all-round games player (captain of cricket, rugger and racquets), and a good actor and speaker. As a result he got away with blue murder on occasions. One evening when Lionel was the praepostor in charge of prep he was quietly demonstrating, to the delight of all present, how he could stand on his head on a table. Lionel was fully stretched vertically upside-down in the centre of the top table when Vera put his head round the door to see what was going on. He looked with horror, quickly shut the door and went away. Lionel got a cricket Blue at Oxford and became a schoolmaster, but unfortunately died at an early age.

Our pocket money was sixpence a week for juniors and a shilling a week for seniors, doled out by Vera round the breakfast table on Friday mornings and put down on the table against each boy rather like receiving at a Communion service. Hillside dress discipline was strict. First two terms – all coat buttons to be done up and no hands in pockets. Third term – one coat button undone. Fourth term – two coat buttons undone and one hand in pocket. Fifth term – three buttons undone and both hands in pockets and allowed to wear socks with 'clocks', coloured embossed lines at the side.

The Tonbridge School was founded in 1553 by Sir Andrew Judde, a local landowner and prosperous city merchant who was six times Master of the Worshipful Company of Skinners. On his death, by his Will the Skinners Company became responsible for the general administration and welfare of the School which was well endowed. On 'Skinners' Day' the Master and many members of the Skinners Company visited the school. The programme was an early rise and visit to the Rose and Crown Hotel before breakfast to greet the Master and then proceed en masse to the school swimming baths on the Shipbourne Road. During the procession there was always the possibility of an unpopular boy or praepostor being thrown into one of the horse drinking troughs on the way to the baths. It was otherwise a day's holiday, with a chapel service in the morning and games and a school cricket match in the afternoon. We used to enjoy watching the school cricket matches on 'The Head' – often referred to as the most beautiful cricket ground in the country – lying under the trees with a few 'Ginger Nut' biscuits.

We were in dormitories for the first term or so and then had individual cubicles. I was in the largest dormitory of six and there was quite a lot of ragging. One incident of which, in retrospect, I am not proud was in my second term. We were ragging after lights out when Vera came in. I did not have time to get into bed and dropped down on my knees at the side of my bed saying my prayers. Vera was very suspicious of this and I got a stinking report which finished: 'This boy does not seem to understand that school rules are not made to be broken.' My father was livid and said that if I had another report like that he would take me away from the school.

But, alas, I got into worse trouble in my third term, the October term of 1918. During the war, with the shortage of masters, we had two or three mistresses, one of whom was a French mistress whom we ragged. She eventually reported me to Vera, who sent for me and said he was going to give me six of the best. 'Oh dear,' I thought, 'What shall I do now?' I knew Vera always wrote to the parents after giving a beating. I could not just ask not to be beaten, and so I took the beating and then explained to Vera that I was very worried because of my last term's bad report and my father's threat to take me away from school if I got another such report. Vera did not write to my parents but gave me a very good report at the end of the term which finished: 'This boy is a very pleasant boy to deal with.'

Another of my wrong-doings was my drawing homework. I was not very good at drawing but, with the swapping which goes on at school, I came across a very good book of ten drawings which I took out of the book and offered up progressively for my homework. Drawing marks were not used for form places. These drawings were always well received by the drawing master, who gave them 10 out of 10, and, with a bit of trimming, they could be recycled.

I don't recollect many other incidents in life of which in retrospect I am ashamed. These first terms at Tonbridge for me must have been very important character-forming years. I learned my lessons and they stuck. This justified my father's concern that I needed the discipline of a boarding school.

During the war there was severe food rationing and a most popular commodity at the 'Grubber' was hot baked potatoes. Fuel was in short supply and we had a large footbath, which we sat round to wash our legs and feet after football, and a weekly bath. Three had to use the same bath water; the juniors went to bed first, and so the water was pretty dirty and cool for the seniors some 20 minutes or so later.

There was much rejoicing on 11 November 1918 for the Armistice. It was a school holiday and we all thronged through the town to the castle grounds in the middle of town. Lionel Hedges, who I think had had a drink or two, much to the delight of everybody got up on a mound and addressed the crowd at large.

Later in November I had 'flu and after a few days went back to school, but I felt like death and it turned out to be jaundice. I was sent to my Grandmother Wing, now living at Hove, to recuperate. Whilst there I had fun with gas-inflated balloons – this was before the days of balloons being sold at fairs and fêtes filled with helium gas and ready to fly. The gas main pressure was not sufficient to inflate the balloons, so I got a 'Y' tube joint, as used on cars for their acetylene gas headlights, with a rubber tube from the gas generator connected to the single end of the 'Y' joint and with the other two ends of the 'Y' joint connected to tubes leading one to each headlight. I used to insert the single end of the 'Y' joint into the balloon and one of the double ends into the gas main and I would blow down the second one at a slightly higher pressure than the gas main pressure to allow the balloon to inflate sufficiently to make it rise. Then I would arrive on Brighton front with three or four gas-inflated balloons and let them go one at a time. This was quite a novelty in those days and attracted a small crowd.

Although backward, I succeeded in moving up a form each term and, being a few months over the average age of each form, managed to collect a number of form prizes. At Tonbridge one could select the prizes and I selected a beautifully bound biography of Nelson and another of Napoleon, which I chose because my father had a particular interest in both Napoleon and Nelson. My father's interest in Napoleon must have resulted from his nickname 'Napoleon of the Pitt'.

I was a member of Tonbridge School Officers' Training Corps, of which Vera was the Commanding Officer, but I was never very good at this. I never quite understood what was going on on field days, with much firing off of blanks in railway carriages. I was one of the OTC Cadets lining The Mall on the occasion of the Victory Parade after the First World War on 19 July 1919. It was a very hot day and we were standing on parade for two or three hours, and many cadets collapsed in the heat.

Ralph Ferry had been brought up by his aunt, who owned or managed the Royal Hotel, Droitwich – Ralph's father was in the Indian Army. I went to stay with Ralph there and we had much fun, with Ralph trying to introduce me to the game of golf. Ralph in turn often stayed with us when sometimes we had good fun hunting my father round the grounds at night. He had a hunting horn and there were many bushes and woods, and the horn was blown here and blown there with the odd blast, and we followed it round until he was eventually caught. Ralph was a very keen naturalist and we spent many Sunday afternoons at school searching for beetles. He left his very good collection of beetles and butterflies to the Mill Green Museum at Welwyn Garden City. On leaving school Ralph was sent to South America to learn Spanish. When he came back he got the idea into his head that he would like to start a small fleet of fried fish vans. He thought he ought to learn the trade from scratch and started off with one van which, perhaps fortunately, on the first night caught fire and was destroyed, and that was the end of the mobile fried fish venture. Next he became Secretary of the Big Tree Burgundy Company. Our garage did good business with Ralph as we changed their fleet of travellers' cars each year for a number of years. Ralph was always good fun, with many roars of laughter. He was engaged to my sister Violet for a short time and they remained very good friends throughout life. He died in 1983 at the age of 80.

H. C. A. Gaunt (always called Tom), a year senior to me, was a good all-round games player and in most school teams. Tom became Head of House and was a good classical scholar and pianist. He won a scholarship to King's

College, Cambridge, where he was a tennis and hockey Blue and often came to play tennis at Aviation Hall. He was appointed Headmaster at Malvern at the early age of 34. On his retirement from Malvern, he took Holy Orders and became Assistant Master and Chaplain of Winchester College. The last time I saw Tom was when Henry Bateman and I attended Vera's Memorial Service in the College chapel in November 1970. Tom gave a most excellent address spoken from the heart. He reminded us of Vera's classic remark after prayers one evening at a time when bicycles were being borrowed or pinched – 'This promiscuous borrowing of bicycles must cease.'

I had been told, and my Housemaster had been told, by my father that I had athletics potential based on comparatively minor successes at the Perse. But having been told to run, run I did. I didn't take any part in the school five-mile cross-country race known as 'The Crass' but I did win a two-mile winter race when the ground was frozen and there were no games.

At the school sports in March 1919 I had my first real athletics success. I won the Under-16 Half-mile in a good time for my age, I was second in the Open Quarter-mile and participated in the Junior and Open House Relay races. All this whetted my appetite for things to come. My House and Games masters were particularly optimistic and encouraging.

In 1920, at 16, I won the Open Quarter-mile in the good time of $54\,^4/_5$ seconds on a grass track within one-fifth of a second of the school record, and I also unexpectedly won the 100 Yards. I did not know I had won the 100 Yards until some minutes after the race – I had assumed that Knox of Park House would win and that he had won. The 100 yards Cup was always presented by the Ladies of Tonbridge and I had to thank the Ladies – very shy and nervous. I was second in the Half-mile Open and ran in the Mile, and in the Hillside team which won the Open Relay. I was third in the Quarter-mile in the Public School Championships at Stamford Bridge, which was won in $54\,^2/_5$ seconds on a cinder track. The press report read: 'A. G. G. Marshall (Tonbridge) who had won his heat in a poor time but in an easy, convincing stride was well up third.'

I have been known by my initials, AGG, throughout life. This was started by R. L. Aston, the Housemaster of Park House, an OT, an Oxford Blue and rugger international, who in class one day called me 'A Gee-Gee', associating this with my running, and the nickname stuck.

In the 1921 school sports I won the Quarter-mile but not in quite such a good time as the previous year. I also won the Half-mile and was second in the Mile, with Hillside second in the House Relay.

At about this time the question of what I was going to do when I left school was raised in earnest. Mr Dunkin, Manager of the Cambridge branch of the Union Insurance Company and a close friend of my father's, advised that, as the son of a Cambridge tradesman, I could not possibly go up to Cambridge and I should go to Oxford. My father did not like this at all and argued that, if I was ashamed of my family and could not stand up for myself and have some family pride and make my own way in life, it would be best that I did not go to any university. The chasm between Town and Gown and between the professions and tradesmen was much more marked in those early post-war years than today. As far as both my father and I were concerned, going to university simply meant going up to Cambridge, and there was never any interest in going anywhere else. As it happened, it was fortunate that I got into Cambridge. Being a Jesus Cambridge man has been a tremendous benefit to me all my life.

With the possibility of some university athletics success ahead, Vera and my father, to say nothing of myself, were very keen and anxious that I should succeed in going to Jesus. For the first time the question was asked, 'Are we sure that he will pass the entrance exam?' and the answer was, 'No, we are not sure.' Fortunately there were three or four other boys in the same predicament and a class was formed for us to study and prepare for the Cambridge 'Little-Go' entrance examination to be held in Cambridge in July 1921. The Latin part of the entrance exam included a set book, which for that year was *Livy XXI*. I failed in Latin but took it again in December and passed. There was a sigh of relief all round and a happy Christmas followed. It was decided that I should leave school after the school sports at the end of the Lent Term 1922 and that I should then work in our garage until going up to Cambridge in October. My school reports indicated the tremendous suspense and excitement as to whether I was going to triumph over the Cambridge University entrance exam. For me, this and my running were at that time my whole life – nothing else mattered. Everything depended on getting to Cambridge and doing well in athletics. I certainly had to work hard, including before breakfast, and I suppose educationally I was about two years behind the real brains. A late developer – I think I still am – but I live and learn.

In the 1922 sports I won the Quarter-mile, the Half-mile and the Mile, with Alex Sadler of Hillside second, I was second in the 100 yards and won the Victor Ludorum. Hillside won the Open House Relay and the House-Points Cup. And so at the end of my last day at school I received on behalf of Hillside all these Challenge Cups. Having won the Quarter-mile for three years, I had won the Challenge Cup outright and my father had a replica made – quite a field day and a wonderful ending to my school days.

Chapter 5

Jesus College, Friends and Personalities

October 1922–April 1926

I WORKED AT our garage during the summer months of 1922. I crashed my $2^3/_4$ hp, two-stroke Levis motorcycle when a dog ran out on the Newmarket Road near East Road Corner when I was on my way home to lunch. There was a bit of blood about and I was taken into Mason's, the chemist, who very kindly bandaged me up, and I proceeded home. The motor cycle was taken from me and I have not been on a motor cycle since. My father thought it was the end of my athletics career and I was not popular, but all was well. Before the accident my father had often travelled to and from the garage on the pillion of the motor cycle, and we often walked, which took us 20 minutes.

My father's friend, Mr Dunkin, again played a part in my education, and this time had more success. He told my father that he could not possibly let me go to a university without having been abroad. This resulted in my father and I going on what we called 'The DGM/AGGM Continental Tour' in August 1922. This was not to my mother's liking because we planned to fly from Croydon to Le Bourget, Paris, as the first leg of the tour. The aircraft was a Handley-Page W8, registration G-EAPJ, a derivative of our Fowlmere bomber with an open cockpit and wicker seats. We flew at a few hundred feet as a result of low cloud and rain. One of our pilots came back into the cabin from time to time wiping the rain off his goggles and reporting on the poor weather conditions.

We stayed in Paris for the first two nights and the rest of the tour was by train and boat. On the third day we travelled to Cologne with a stop for a few hours in Brussels. The next night we travelled by first-class sleepers from Cologne to Berlin costing $10^1/_2d$. each. The German mark was going up by thousands to the pound overnight. We had two days in Berlin and then on to Frankfurt. From Frankfurt we went by train right across France, by sleeper, to Madrid. At Madrid we saw a bullfight and went to Escorial, a few miles from Madrid, to see the tombs of the Kings of Spain. On the way the engine driver stopped once or twice and had a chat with some of his friends. We were told that engine drivers often did this and made their own times for local journeys. If a driver happened to live along the track, it was the custom to stop and have a chat with his wife. From Madrid we proceeded to Barcelona, and Barcelona to Marseilles, and then back via Paris and Calais – all in 14 days.

In the late summer of 1922 I was sent to collect a new Belsize Bradshaw car from Manchester. It would have been my first night away from home on my own, but I managed to get back the same night and I well remember how pleased and relieved my mother was to see me back. It was the first time a car had been collected from Manchester within the day but there was some rumbling from the drivers who complained that, if they had got back within the day, they would have been ticked off for driving too fast. This was in the days of running in cars at not more than 30 mph for the first 500 miles.

At Jesus, first and second year men lived in College and moved into lodgings in their third year. Just before term I was told there were no rooms in College and that I should live at home until accommodation was available – calamity! Fortunately, two days before term started rooms became available on the second floor of K Pump Court, so all was well.

All my lectures and practical engineering work were at the Engineering School at Scroope House, Trumpington Road. My Director of Studies was Mr Womersley, and I had some coaching in Hydraulics from Mr Ball in my second year – both were very good friends.

Edwin Abbott, a great classical scholar, was the Senior Tutor in 1922 and was known to us as 'Bott', and William Welsh was my tutor. I had a very happy relationship with them both throughout my college life. William Welsh had been Senior Wrangler in 1882. He was a very good golfer and died after a round of golf at Brancaster on the eighteenth green in September 1925. He was a good customer at the garage and owned a Talbot car. Mrs Welsh, also a good golfer, was one of the famous Lowe sporting family. We used to see Mrs Welsh at the Old Rectory, Brancaster, which the family rented for the summer holidays for two or three years in the thirties. The big family activity there was croquet on a very sporting lawn – very fierce competition, a game starting at 9 o'clock and, if lucky, finishing by lunch-time.

Known to us all as 'G-S', the Revd Percival Gardner-Smith, our Dean, had joined the College as an undergraduate in 1906, arriving for the first time in a horse-drawn cab. Reminiscing at his 80th birthday celebration dinner in 1968, G-S said:

> The College reputation in 1906 was not good and, when I told my Form Master that my father was sending me to Jesus, he pulled a rather long face and said, 'I don't think you will be happy there. I was up at Cambridge in 1890 and I remember the common saying that you never saw a sober man come out of Jesus.' The College in 1906 had an annual intake of 40 or so undergraduates a year and there were 12 Fellows. By 1906 things had

improved, but drunkenness is a very serious matter and there was a great deal of senseless and brutal rowdyism and the College was rather like an ill-disciplined public school. Some of the rowdyism did not amount to much, but some things were regrettable. But amidst all this there were many good Jesus men in those days, including all those who served with distinction in the First World War.

After graduating from Jesus, G-S became a Curate, and in the First World War was Chaplain of 149 Squadron of the RAF in France. He was appointed Dean in 1922, the same year as my entry into Jesus, and was Dean for 34 years. G-S continued:

> After the First World War Cambridge filled up rapidly with those returned from fighting. It was a very difficult period – two quite different generations but they had been simultaneously installed. There were the men who had been through the war and there were schoolboys, and the Authorities, the University and College really did not know what to do with them. The ordinary traditional discipline of a College seemed ridiculous when it was applied to men who had undergone unimaginable experiences for the last four years. You could not tell a Brigadier or an Air Commodore that he must be in by ten o'clock or pay a fine of tuppence. The result was that discipline rather broke down and the early twenties were no less rowdy a period, or rather more so, than the period at the beginning of this century. The Proctors in the early twenties had a very lively time.

G-S and the first Mrs Gardner-Smith were very kind to all us undergraduates, including happy Sunday afternoon tea at their home on Chesterton Road. G-S was a very good friend and christened my two sons, Michael and David, in the College Chapel. He had a very severe and forbidding expression and tone of speech, but behind it all he was very kind-hearted and had a great sense of dry humour. Mrs Gardner-Smith died at 75 after an extremely happy marriage and a year later he married her niece, Elizabeth Leeke. Having discussed marriage G-S characteristically summed up the proposal, 'It all boils down to this, whether you would rather be a widow than a spinster.' They were married and had an exceptionally happy marriage of over 23 years.

Towards the end of his life G-S laughingly said he hoped that he and Alan Pars might not die at about the same time, which might result in a joint memorial service. As it happened Alan Pars died on 28 January 1985 and Gardner-Smith on 29 May 1985, so all was well. Alan Pars, a University Mathematics lecturer and a life-long family friend, had entered the College as an undergraduate in 1915, was elected Fellow in 1923 and was very much a College man for 70 years. He was a great follower of sport and an enthusiastic supporter of athletics at Fenner's. I particularly remember his excitement when Jesus beat Trinity in the final of the Inter-College Competition in March 1924. On his death, aged 89, Alan was a very great benefactor to the College.

Until the Government amended the University Statutes in 1886 Dons were not allowed to marry. It was said that the Master of Jesus then called all the Dons together and said, 'It won't make any difference, will it?' They were all married within a matter of weeks except Tommy Watt and one other. As an undergraduate I found Tommy Watt still an enthusiastic supporter of all College sports. I remember my first meeting with him. He was talking to Alan Pars in Pump Court and Alan called me over and introduced me. Tommy Watt looked me up and down and said, 'He looks a healthy specimen.' I had received that morning an invitation from Harold Abrahams at short notice to join a small athletics team he was taking to Paris and we discussed whether I should accept as I was not in training at the time. Tommy Watt did not play any major part in the academic life but he was a tremendous asset to the College. He did not go out of his way to be popular with undergraduates – in fact he was very outspoken about everything, including if a pass had been missed at rugger or a failure at cricket. His room was open every evening to undergraduates to drop in for discussion and have tea and biscuits. He was a perfect link between the High Table and the rest of the College.

My particular friends at Jesus were Henry Bateman of Tonbridge days and Frank Morrell, both medical students and permanent family friends. Henry Bateman and Frank Morrell both served in the Navy as doctors during World War II, and it so happened that they met up together in the middle of the Indian Ocean. Henry's father was a Fellow of Jesus at the beginning of the century and died young when Henry was only a year or so old. Henry was very quiet and unassuming but a very good actor, and he was remembered by all and collected friends wherever he went – friends who at a party would make a point of picking him out. He became a very popular and well-loved family doctor.

Eric Gandar Dower was another Jesus College personality I was to see much of in the future. He was a wealthy Armenian who was up at Jesus when war broke out and returned to complete his education after the war. In the pre-war years he had dabbled in theatricals and, when he planned to come up to Jesus wanting to make sure that only students of whom he approved should be in the same lodging-house, he bought a lodging-house in Park Street and got a theatrical manageress trained and licensed by the University as a lodging-housekeeper.

Eric gave tea parties from time to time, and on one occasion he was regretting that Cambridge was not as he knew it before the war; and as an illustration said, 'Look at Marshall and the garage which has blossomed forth from the old stables.' Eric did not realise that I was a Marshall of Marshall's Garage. Years later, when he was anxious to become Chairman of the Aerodrome Owners' Association, he took the trouble to come to Cambridge to gain my support. My colleague, Dick Lane, met him at the station and said Gandar Dower was very agitated, walking up and down between the railway trucks just outside the station. Eric told Dick he thought I was opposing him because of his remarks about the garage at that tea party some 20 years earlier.

Douglas Lowe of Pembroke became a family friend – a world famous athlete and also a soccer Blue. We stayed with one another's families and he and his wife stayed with me a few years before his death, when Douglas and I went to an athletics reunion dinner at St Catharine's College.

Cyril Harrison, the Trinity 100 yards Blue, was an enthusiastic piano player and also became a family friend. I, in turn, tinkered on the banjo with Cyril at the piano. My interest in the banjo was following in my father's footsteps, who in his early days was a member of the Cambridge Banjo Band; but he played rather more serious music with his fingers on a five-string banjo, whereas I played jazz with a plectrum. Cyril and I formed a band in the October term 1924 when I moved from my College rooms into lodgings at 56 Jesus Lane, which fortunately had a piano. We practised in my rooms two or three times a week and I just do not know how the other occupants of the house and adjoining houses put up with this, but we never had a complaint. At one time we peaked to a total of nine. Our best drummer was of a professional standard, G. E. G. Goddard, a Jesus College rowing Blue, who turned out for us on special occasions such as our Guildhall 'Pop' Concert. Donald Stralem, a wealthy American at Trinity and a tennis Blue, was our best player and leader of the band.

During the October term of 1924 Cyril Harrison received an enquiry for a university band from a schoolmaster at Malvern, who organised a 'Chatelet Club' which took over three small hotels in the small village of Gsteig by Gstaad each Christmas. A band of four was required for two weeks immediately after Christmas, with the Club paying all travelling and half hotel expenses. We thought this was a splendid idea. Cyril Harrison, the second best of our two piano players, and I, the worst member of the band, but both of us founder members, said 'Well, we are going.' Arthur Doggett, a hockey Blue and our second best drummer, and Donald Stralem made up the four. We were to provide dance music on alternate nights at each of the three small hotels. And so we were engaged to travel out to Switzerland on Boxing Day. I had 20 or so tunes to learn by heart as I could not read music, and I practised these more or less continuously on the train journey.

Donald Stralem was spending his Christmas in the South of France and planned to meet us at Gsteig on the night of our arrival, but he did not turn up and the band was in absolute chaos. We were entirely dependent on Donald Stralem with his tenor banjo. We got increasingly worried the second day with no Donald Stralem and no message from him, and then suddenly at six o'clock in the evening he turned up and all was well. I marvelled at how they put up with us but they must have thought it was not too bad because they invited us to return the following year, but that was not possible.

As a result of this visit we called ourselves 'The Chatelet Four', regardless of the number actually playing at the time. We played at a number of charity shows and a pop concert at the Cambridge Guildhall. In those days these concerts were held regularly on Saturday evenings, with an entrance charge of sixpence. The press report read:

> Well played dance music is invariably welcome at these concerts. This in fact no doubt accounted in some measure for the welcome which The Chatelet Jazz Four received. As a matter of fact they were not four but seven – but nobody minded that. They played well and gave numerous popular pieces and the audience soon became infected with the rhythm of the music and beat time with their feet. The 'Four' contributions included 'A New Kind of Man', 'It Had To Be You', 'California', 'Somebody Loves Me' – they were obviously great favourites.

Donald Stralem became a close family friend and used to come and play tennis at Aviation Hall on Sundays. He gave my father one of the new (at the time) American racquets with metal strings. My future wife and I stayed with him in America, and Donald and his daughter came to see us during Donald's only visit to Cambridge after the war when he was representing a few Americans, including Jimmy Van Allen, who were making a contribution towards repairing the bomb-damaged wall of the University tennis ground, which adjoined the Fenner's cricket ground and running track. Van Allen was a tennis Blue and captain of the University team in Donald's time and in recent years invented the tie-break. I remember one year I was watching an Oxford and Cambridge tennis match at Cambridge when Donald came up and said they were short of an umpire and, before I knew where I was and with no experience, I found myself umpiring a singles match. No problems – the players seemed to umpire themselves quite happily. All I had to do was keep the score.

One other old friend I should introduce here is Dr Salisbury Woods. 'Rex', as we called him, had been actively associated with Cambridge University athletics since before the war. He became my doctor in 1922 and was the doctor who looked after most of the University athletes. He was a member of the 1924 Olympic team. During the twenties he became our family doctor.

When I speak of family friends for life, I mean friends not only of the immediate family but of my sisters and their families. My sisters played a big part in establishing these friendships. Had I gone to Oxford there would have been little opportunity for my friends to become family friends, as happened as a result of my home at Cambridge being just down the road.

Chapter 6

University Athletics and Olympic Games
1922–1926

THE UNIVERSITY ATHLETICS Ground was at Fenners, which during the summer was the University Cricket Ground with a perimeter cinder running track. The athletes had the use of the track during the two winter terms and after cricket in the summer. The track was three laps to the mile running clockwise, as compared with standard tracks of four laps to the mile running anti-clockwise.

Alec Nelson was the University Athletics Coach. Alec had been a professional runner in his day and he was a good all-round coach and particularly good with field events. He was full of motivation and instilled individual confidence. My father spoke to him about my running and Alec suggested that I should do a little training in the summer, and he would give me a try-out against the clock. This was while I was working in the garage prior to going to Jesus in October. I did some training and Alec timed me over a quarter-mile at Fenners one evening after the cricket had finished. The time was encouraging and it was thought I might have some potential, which resulted in Alec taking an interest in me.

I trained for the 1922 Freshmen's Sports which were held early in the October term and won the Quarter-mile, beating Ernest Fryer the Public Schools Champion, and also the Half-mile. This was thought to be a good omen, with the Cambridge press reporting:

> It was a great day for local runners and in that a local paper is bound to take due pride. A. G. G. Marshall was the only man to win two events, and the value of these wins can be best understood when it is realised that in the Half-mile he recorded a faster time than did D. G. A. Lowe last year.
> (D. G. A. Lowe was my friend Douglas of Pembroke.)

I went on to win the Quarter-mile in the Freshmen v Seniors Sports, took part in the Inter-College Relays and was selected to run for Cambridge in the Oxford and Cambridge One Mile Relay at Oxford, in which we were beaten.

Jesus had an exceptional intake of athletes in the early twenties: Ernest Fryer, the Public Schools Quarter-mile Champion; Jack Rudd, a South African high hurdler, brother of the famous Oxford and international quarter-miler; R. A. L. Everett, a hurdler; L. G. D. Croft, a half-miler; M. R. Sinclair, who was very versatile and, depending on the opposition, would perform for us to good effect in almost anything, particularly the 100 yards, high and long jump and pole-vaulting; and Jack Longland of Everest fame, a pole-jumper.

The Inter-College Athletics Competition was the first main athletic activity of the Lent term of 1923, followed by the University Sports and, for those successful, the Oxford and Cambridge match. There were two divisions in the Inter-College Athletics. Jesus was in the Second Division and, as a result of our abnormal athletic input, we finished head of the Second Division and were promoted to the First.

I went on to win the Quarter-mile in the Cambridge University Sports in March and was awarded my full Blue by the President, Harold Abrahams. A great thrill and great family excitement. My father immediately put on a champagne and oyster supper for the Rayners and the family. In those days it was a great thing for a local tradesman's son to become a Cambridge Blue and there was much exhilaration. I was a bit of a wet blanket at the party as I refused the oysters on the grounds that I was still in training for the Oxford and Cambridge Sports a few weeks later.

I knew I had little chance against W. E. Stevenson, the Oxford Rhodes Scholar and American amateur champion who had beaten 49 seconds. Rhodes Scholarships were established by Cecil Rhodes through his Will in 1902 to provide for the maintenance at Oxford of graduates of other universities from the British Empire and the USA. He defined many aspects of character and education to be considered in awarding the Scholarships which included sporting prowess. In sporting events Oxford has benefited enormously from the participation of Rhodes Scholars in matches against Cambridge, particularly in athletics. Had I gone to Oxford and been up against two Rhodes Scholars, both overseas national champions, I might have scraped a Half-Blue but I certainly would never have got a full Blue.

Stan Nelson, the son of our coach, was at Fitzwilliam Hall, and had run second to me in the Quarter-mile and it was anticipated that he would be my second string. To my surprise, Harold Abrahams, who had never run a Quarter-mile in his life, was selected as my second string and I assumed that Harold thought he might be able to help me win. I never considered Harold as a possible winner and he certainly undertook no special training for this event prior to the Oxford and Cambridge match. The 100 yards and Long Jump, which Harold was expected to win, were programmed before the 440 yards.

The Oxford and Cambridge Sports were held at Queen's Club, London. We went there to get familiar with the track and to do some training on the Saturday before the match, and then travelled direct from Liverpool Street to Hunstanton, with much playing of Vingt-et-un and a little mild gambling. We stayed at the small Le Strange Arms, Old Hunstanton, right on the sea and a few hundred yards from a most excellent golf course – a championship course in all respects except for the lack of hotel accommodation in the area. This was a wonderful week. We did some training on a local school's playing field and played some golf. One or two members of the team who thought they wanted more experience of Queen's Club made another journey to London during the week. The team, with its fun and games with Cyril Harrison at the piano and my banjo, really took over the hotel and I felt sorry for the few other residents, who seemed to take everything in good part. On the Friday the team travelled to London and had a limber up at Queen's Club and stayed at a hotel near Kensington Gardens.

At breakfast on the Saturday morning, the day of the match, Harold asked me to go for a walk with him in the park – we walked to the Peter Pan statue. In the course of our walk, Harold posed the question, 'Do you think you have any chance of winning the Quarter-mile against the American, Stevenson?' I said I didn't think I had a dog's chance. Harold said if we could plan and achieve a very slow race, he might have enough speed left in him to pip Stevenson at the post. He suggested that he should, as the second string pacemaker, set off at a fast pace with me making no attempt to keep up with him. He would then continue at a slower pace until the finishing straight when he would run wide to let me through, but I should not make any attempt to increase the speed or put any pressure on Stevenson. Stevenson would be watching me as the first string and with all his experience would believe he could beat me on the run-in regardless of the speed of the race. Stevenson would never have considered Harold as a possible winner. Harold said Stevenson would think that he, Harold, was dropping out of the race and, if I made no attempt to increase the speed, Harold might be able to keep up with us and have speed left for the final run-in. Harold asked if I would, as first string, sacrifice any chance I had of winning the race, no matter how remote. I readily agreed to his suggestion and this is what we did, and Harold won, with Stevenson second and me third. The press reported:

> Abrahams in the Quarter did his pace-making to perfection. Drawn on the outside, he cut across and took the lead for the first 100 yards, slowed down and kept the race at a slow pace until he went wide to allow Marshall to come through. Stevenson no doubt thought Abrahams was out of the race, and so did many other people, but Abrahams was within striking distance of Stevenson and Marshall on entering the straight until the final run in when he succeeded in beating Stevenson. Abrahams must be the best all-round athlete Cambridge has ever had. Marshall ran a most promising race to finish within a yard of the American amateur champion and Rhodes Scholar.

The race itself had been won by Harold on good tactics and I was pleased to have played a part in the win – a good team effort. The win was important for Cambridge because in those days only event wins counted towards team scoring. After the race it occurred to me that Harold might also have had in mind the fact that if he won, and his plan was to try to win for Cambridge, he would break S. O. Ashington's record of seven medals against Oxford in 1914, a record which it had been thought could never be broken.

It was not until 1970 that I discovered why Stan Nelson had not been my second string. Harold told me that the committee would not accept the son of our professional trainer as a member of the team – an extreme example of the snobbery which existed in those days, not only between University and Town but also between sporting amateurs and professionals. I remarked that it had been good for me to be able to say that Harold Abrahams was once my second string. Harold added that at the time he had no thought of the possibility of breaking Ashington's record.

In the early summer of 1923 Harold was invited at short notice, and at a time when we were not in training, to take a team of four or five to run in what was called 'Le Meeting PréOlympique de Stade Pershing' in Paris. I ran in the 400 metres and qualified for the final, in which I was fifth. As a small team we were not too successful, with Abrahams coming second in the 200 metres. Harold was anxious to get as much international experience as possible in his plan to achieve his life ambition of winning the 100 metres in the 1924 Olympics in Paris.

In July 1923 the Oxford and Cambridge match against Yale and Harvard took place at the new Wembley Stadium. The American team came to Cambridge for part of their training and were given a luncheon in Caius College with a tot of some strong college audit ale, which they treated as ordinary ale and asked for more, but found their legs were not too steady when they got to Fenners for a training session in the afternoon. My parents entertained the teams at an evening garden party which included some live entertainment. The Americans, when invited, asked whether it was 'live' as they had already had much hospitality in America based on radio programmes at a time when radio was just beginning to find its feet.

In October 1923 Jesus beat Trinity in the final of the First Division of the Inter-College Competition. We planned for our best athletes to run in as many events as possible, and planned who should aim to win or be in the first two or three places in each event in order to conserve energies for events to follow. I ran in the Quarter, the Half and the Mile.

In the Cambridge 1924 University Sports, I again won the Quarter, with Stan Nelson second. I was selected first string for the Oxford and Cambridge Match and this time Stan was my second string and was awarded his Half Blue. We were running against the Canadian champion and Rhodes Scholar D. M. Johnson and were once again up against Stevenson, who since the Oxford and Cambridge Match of last year had won the 1923 AAA Quarter-mile Championship and was now running as Johnson's second string. Johnson was first, with myself second and Stevenson third. The press recorded, 'Marshall had his revenge on Stevenson and ran him into third place.'

The Cambridge University Athletics Club had an invitation from Pennsylvania to take a team of seven to the Pennsylvanian Games in 1924 at a personal cost of £28 – everything else was found. The party consisted of: Ronnie Orchard, Ralph Starr, Douglas Lowe and myself to run in the 4 x 440 yards One-mile Relay; W. S. 'Whiskers' Bristowe – a hurdler – President of the CUAC; Pip Powell, a long jumper; and David Burghley, the 440 yard hurdler; plus Eric Liddell, the Scot from Edinburgh University, the 1923 AAA 100 yards Champion, who had been personally invited and travelled with us.

We stayed at the very comfortable Pennsylvanian Cricket Club, which was also a golf course. Even in those days players were queuing up at the first tee from very early in the morning. We were entertained lavishly, both by the University and at large country houses. I remember that at one country house there was a 12 to 14 ft. long tree trunk burning in a large hearth in the hall, and uniformed footmen everywhere. We had a very happy luncheon at Wanamaker's Stores. I am afraid none of us, including Eric Liddell, managed to win an event at the Pennsylvania Games.

We travelled back in a small ship of the American United Line called 'The Republic' which was a liner which had been taken over from Germany as part of the war reparations. It was making its first trip with a scratch crew of several nationalities. When we set sail, the captain did not know how long the crossing would take – anything from nine to 14 days. It was a very enjoyable trip, finally achieved in 10 days, but we ran out of various stores as the days progressed, starting with bananas on the fifth day. Eric Liddell entered into the fun and games on the boat, including the Fancy Dress Dance. Whilst he was very strict about religion, he was not a prude and I do not remember ever having talked to him abut religion. Eric and I became friendly with two American sisters, Freddie and Edith, who were travelling to 'do Europe', including the UK. They said they were going to be in Paris for the Olympic Games, and we said if we were there at the same time we hoped we could meet.

The return journey having taken so long, there were not sufficient days left to complete the Summer term. This necessitated staying up an extra term, and so it was decided I would stay up for three years and two terms to finish in March 1926 and have a chance of running in the 1925 and 1926 Oxford and Cambridge matches.

Having got back from America, with all the sea breezes, I was very fit and full of beans and continued my training feeling I was running better than I had ever run before. I then struck a bad patch during the early summer which was not improved by my initiation ceremony for the Jesus College sportsmen's Rhadegund Society. This was a strenuous exercise in those days and included dinner, followed by three goblets of port which is roughly a bottle-and-a-half, and a cold bath with soot and other ingredients mixed in. I understand the initiation ceremony has been somewhat toned down since my time.

We now come to the period building up to the Olympic Games. The AAA Championships were brought forward from July to June to avoid clashing with the Olympics in July. As part of our training for the AAA Championships, Douglas Lowe, Henry Stallard (the famous Caius College university and international half-mile and mile runner), Tubby Davis, Cyril Harrison and I went to Hunstanton for a few days training immediately before the Championships. The results of these Championships were planned to be the basis for the selection of the Olympic team. I record the results of the relevant events of the 1923 and 1924 AAA Championships which provide a good background to the Harold Abrahams/Eric Liddell saga so well depicted in the film *Chariots of Fire*:

1923

100 yards	220 yards	440 yards
1 E. H. Liddell	1 E. H. Liddell	1 W. E. Stevenson
in $9^7/_{10}$ sec. (A new AAA record)	in $21^3/_5$ sec.	in $49^3/_5$ sec.
2 W. P. Nichol	2 T. Matthewman	2 G. M. Butler
3 T. Matthewman	3 W. P. Nichol	3 J. J. Gillis

Abrahams did not run in the 1923 Championships.

1924

100 yards	220 yards	440 yards
1 H. M. Abrahams	1 H. P. Kinsman	1 E. H. Liddell
in $9^9/_{10}$ sec.	in $21^7/_{10}$ sec.	in $49^3/_5$ sec.
2 W. P. Nichol	2 E. H. Liddell	2 D. M. Johnson
3 L. C. Royle	3 A. E. Porritt	3 W. E. Stevenson

Harold had set his whole life on winning the Olympic 100 Metres – it had become an obsession with him. Liddell's achievement in winning the 1923 AAA 100 yards in the record time of $9^7/_{10}$ seconds was a devastating blow to Abrahams and shook him to the core. To date Abrahams had been a consistent 10 seconds 100 yards winner but had only slightly broken 10 seconds on one or two occasions. He knew in the Olympics he would be up against overseas competition, particularly from the Americans, but this new and very serious opposition out of the blue and on his doorstep had come at a time when Harold had established his 100 yards supremacy in the UK. To achieve level pegging with Eric Liddell's new record time, Harold had to improve his performance by two or three yards with the help of his trainer Sam Mussambini. It must have been a tremendous relief to Harold when it became known early in 1924 that Eric had decided to concentrate on the 400 metres and, because of his religious principles, would not compete in the Olympic 100 metres as the first heats were always run on Sunday.

Eric had in turn become completely dedicated to winning an Olympic Medal within the restrictions of his religion. He was a famous Scottish international rugger player, and gave up his rugger to enable him to concentrate on his Olympic ambitions, which became very deep-rooted, and his work suffered. Winning an Olympic Gold Medal became a priority, second only to his religion, and the ambition to win this event became part of his religion.

I had failed to get into the finals of the Quarter-mile AAA Championships in June 1924, the official trials for the selection of the

Olympic team. In my semi-final heat I ran fourth behind Liddell, Johnson and Stevenson. This heat was won in the same time as the final in which Liddell, Johnson and Stevenson were again first, second and third. (They all a few weeks later won Olympic medals, two of which broke world records.) The press report on the AAA Championships read: 'A. G. G. Marshall was unfortunate to get drawn in a hot heat in the second round of the Quarter and was always badly placed. Despite that he gave his best display for, according to the official report, he was only 2 yards 1 foot outside $49^3/_5$th seconds, which is moving.' I knew my possible selection must be on a knife-edge and I, too, was on edge anxiously awaiting the announcement of the team. The team was announced on the evening of the day I had been to the Wembley Exhibition with my parents and our friends, the Rayners – I was not very good company that day. I was included as a reserve for the 1600 metres relay. I was very lucky indeed to be a member of the team and to be with them throughout the Games in Paris.

The team travelled to Paris four days before the Olympics started and had a big send-off at Victoria Station. We stayed in a hotel in the Place de la République and were taken daily to the stadium for training sessions. At the opening ceremony the British team was lined up under the stands and presented to the Prince of Wales who attended the Games throughout.

The Games were a great excitement. For most of us our main objective was to be selected for the Olympic team and to give a good account of ourselves, and for a few the bigger ambition of winning a medal. An uncanny, almost reverent, silence descended on the whole arena at the start of main events, with tremendous cheering, clapping and shouting during the event and the playing of the national anthem of the winner. The silence at the start of the 100 metres and 400 metres was quite electric.

Of the six finalists in the 100 metres, our main opposition was from four Americans, all with world reputations, and particularly from Scholz. The six runners got off to an excellent start and were all together at 25 metres, but at half way Abrahams was clear of Scholz and held his lead to the tape, winning by 2 feet from Scholz and equalling the Olympic record for the third time in less than two days. Porritt of New Zealand, the Oxford Blue, beat Bowman, the American, on the tape for third place. Abrahams' dedication to the event had been well publicised. The magnitude of the task he had set himself of winning against the proven performances of the Americans was well known. He had won through with sheer guts and determination to bring this particular honour to Great Britain. As a result and with the tensions suddenly released the acclamation was quite exceptional – it was unbelievable.

In spite of all that has been said about Abrahams' 100 metres, the 400 metres in some way provided the greatest thrill of the meeting with the world record being broken three times in two days. The final six were Liddell, Guy Butler, D. M. Johnson, the Canadian champion and Oxford Rhodes Scholar, Imbach of Switzerland and two Americans. It was considered that Butler or Liddell had a good chance of winning, but nobody thought Liddell capable of the amazing performance he achieved in the final. As far as the crowd were concerned they were well informed about Liddell's dedication to his religion and his refusal to run in the first round of the 100 metres on the Sunday; they also knew of his determination to win this event. The occasion was enlivened by the support given to Liddell by the pipes and drums of the Cameron Highlanders.

The silence and pent-up excitement at the start of the race could be felt. Liddell and Butler went ahead at the start. Liddell had started all out and maintained his pace throughout, finishing in what at the time was described as 'a most lion-hearted manner' winning by three yards from Fitch, an American, with Butler third and my old friend of Oxford and Cambridge days, Johnson the Canadian, fourth. Liddell established a new world record in the final. This was probably the greatest achievement of the VIIIth Olympiad, and superlatives were showered on Liddell by the press of the entire world. Liddell was short and not a pretty runner but just pounded along virtually at the same pace all the way, with a finish as if he was making a final dash for a try in a rugger match with an opponent bearing down on him and about to tackle from behind. It was also a wonderful achievement by Butler who was for a second time in an Olympic 400 metres final.

The 800 metres final was sensational. It was well known that Henry Stallard had injured his foot and there had been considerable doubt about his being able to run. In Lowe and Stallard we knew we had two outstanding runners at this distance, and remembering that Stallard had beaten Lowe in the Half Mile AAA Championships a few weeks previously. Stallard, to everyone's surprise, shot straight to the front and set a very fast pace, which was contrary to his usual tactics. Henry was still well ahead at the half way mark and running strongly with five of the runners following in a bunch. With 200 metres to go, the gap between them began to diminish with Lowe and Martin of Switzerland slowly clearing themselves from the rest and closing in on Stallard. At 100 metres both Lowe and Martin sprinted past Stallard, with Lowe lasting and winning by a yard with Martin second, Ensk of America third and Stallard fourth. It was a magnificent race, the time being within half a second of the world record. Douglas Lowe received a great ovation and there was tremendous applause for Henry Stallard – always popular with the crowd – who had shown a great display of pluck in spite of his injured foot. He was a likely winner up to entering the final straight, and on crossing the line he collapsed having run himself completely out. Henry Stallard and Douglas Lowe were also third and fourth respectively in the 1500 metres. Douglas Lowe went on to win the 800 metres again in the 1928 Olympics.

The 1600 metres Relay, for which I was a reserve, was won in a new world-record time by the United States with my old friend Stevenson the Oxford Rhodes Scholar running the last leg. Sweden was second, England third and Canada, which included Johnson the Oxford Rhodes Scholar, fourth.

A summary of Great Britain's results in these five classic events of the Games is: three 1sts – 100 metres, 400 metres, 800 metres; four 3rds – 200 metres, 400 metres, 1500 metres, 1600 metres Relay; two 4ths – 800 metres, 1500 metres; and one 6th – 200 metres. All very satisfactory for Great Britain. After the events had taken place there was no particular fuss made of the winners – just 'Well done, Harold' or 'Jolly good show, Eric.'

After Eric had won the 400 metres Gold Medal, Eric and I made contact with Freddie and Edith, the American girls, and took them to a Tango Tea Dance in the Champs Elysées. Freddie and Edith stayed with my family for a few days at Gorleston during the family holiday in August. Douglas Lowe and Tubby Davis also had a few days with us at Gorleston and we had some very good games of golf on the Gorleston links – the four-some being made up of my father, Doug Lowe, Tubby Davis and myself. Tubby Davis was not in the Olympic team but had stayed with us in Paris throughout the Games.

Eric Liddell had been born in China, where his father was a missionary, and he returned to China as a missionary on completion of his education. He died in 1945 in a Japanese internment camp at Wei-Fang in China. In 1991 a headstone and garden of remembrance were created at the Wei-Fang Second Middle School and a foundation was set up to provide an annual exchange of youngsters, especially aspiring athletes, between Britain, Hong Kong and China. The headstone is red granite from the Isle of Mull. Eric Liddell's sister, Mrs Somerville, provided the inscription from the book of Isaiah: 'They shall mount up with wings as eagles, they shall run and not be weary.'

Harold Abrahams became a successful barrister and a famous BBC broadcaster. For 40 years he presented athletics with a warmth and sense of proportion that made it one of the most popular sports on radio. His athletics career had been brought to an untimely end in May 1925 at Stamford Bridge when he was trying to achieve his ambition to jump over 25 feet. He missed his footing at take-off and crashed with full force on his right leg. Harold said he heard a noise rather like 'Smee tearing cloth in Peter Pan'. Peter Pan was obviously a favourite of Harold, inasmuch as it was to the Peter Pan statue that he walked me on that morning of the Oxford and Cambridge athletics match in 1923.

Very foolishly, at the very beginning of my third year at Cambridge in the October term 1924, before going into full training for the College and Oxford and Cambridge Relays I played a game of rugger thinking it would be a change from athletics. I had only been on the field for a few minutes when I was tackled and I went one way and my left leg went the other with a crowd of players on top. There was a crack and something went in my left ankle. I was completely out of running for two terms and missed the Oxford and Cambridge Sports in 1925. I never fully recovered from this injury as far as short distance running was concerned. My ankle felt dead and never had the lively spring of the past. I did, however, manage to be a member of the winning Achilles One Mile Relay team in the AAA Championships of 1925, with Guy Butler running the last leg.

Concurrently with all this athletics activity my work had progressed at the Engineering Labs but I well remember the awful few minutes I suffered when I thought I had failed my final exams in June 1925. I had not planned to go to the Jesus May Week Ball but my friend Everett, our hurdler, had his family up for the Ball and asked me to join them. This was the night before the exam results were to be posted at 10 a.m. at the Senate House. Having attended the Ball throughout the night, including the photograph at dawn, I went to the Senate House to see the results and was alarmed to find my name was not there. Walking back and wondering how I was going to break the news to my father, I met a friend in Rose Crescent who had taken the same exam and he said, 'Thank goodness I have passed', and asked how I had got on. I said I had failed and he said, 'That's impossible – you couldn't possibly have failed,' and so we went back together and had another look. I had previously only looked in the Third Class passes and found I had got a First in the Ordinary Engineering Degree, and so perhaps I was beginning to grow up academically, but I had had to put in as much hard work and effort as I had done in the days of the 'Little-Go' victory at Tonbridge.

I decided to have a go at cross-country running hoping this might help strengthen my damaged ankle, and I succeeded in getting into the Cambridge Hare and Hounds team. Cambridge won the match against Oxford in December 1925 – the press reporting:

> A. G. G. Marshall's success as a distance runner has been the outstanding feature of the term and he did well considering his experience was limited to three weeks of cross-country. It was particularly good for a Quarter-mile champion and he it was who won the relay against Oxford. Marshall managed to get within the scoring five. He has, however, established what must be a record for a Quarter-mile Blue to get in the cross-country team.

The Cambridgeshire Amateur Athletic Association was established at a meeting held at our Jesus Lane garage on 12 August 1925. There were 21 at the meeting, and Dr Rex Woods was elected Chairman. We held our first County Championships on Jesus Green, on the site of the existing swimming baths, on Saturday 29 May 1926. The officials and athletes roped off a track and provided some seating accommodation with some empty beer crates, and charged sixpence for the programmes – there was no gate money as the sports were being held on open common land. I won the Quarter-mile, and in 1927 won the Quarter and the 100 yards and established a Quarter-mile county record on a grass track which stood to within two years of the Championships being changed from yards to metres in 1969.

These in fact were my last races, but I kept up some form of training and keeping fit by running a few miles whenever possible, whether it be every week or so or every few months, right up to and including the war years, when I used to run round the aerodrome or along the road towards the Gog Magog Hills, a few miles south of Cambridge.

Much has changed in the athletics world since the twenties and thirties. Competition has become intense and performances have improved dramatically. When talking to Harold Abrahams some 15 years ago I said, 'I wonder what would have happened to us guys against all the performances of today, and how do you think you would have come off?' Harold replied, 'I don't know but I am sure I would not have been 10 yards behind the winner.' Harold has been quoted as upholding the *mutatis mutandis* school of thought that outstanding athletes of the past would have reached the same relative level in the competitive field no matter when they were engaged in it. Another dramatic change is the make-up of the Olympic team. In the early twenties and thirties, 30 per cent of the team came from past and present members of Oxford and Cambridge – and now?

My university days were happy and exciting and the fact that I did not do as well as might have been anticipated in the athletics world did not overshadow my day-to-day life at the time. In any case it was fortunate for me that my athletics career did not progress further as it could have distracted me from my work. Any delay in getting established in the Company business would have upset the extraordinary sequence of events that occurred in 1929 which affected my life in a major way and could never have happened at any other time or in any other place.

Chapter 7

'Felix Qui Laborat'

April 1926–December 1928

I JOINED THE family garage business in April 1926 at a salary of £500 a year on six months trial. I lived at home until my marriage and made no financial contribution to my keep. It never occurred to me and nothing was ever said. I worked from the outset during the university terms about sixty hours and seven days a week and I think I was very generously treated. Over the years I had never thought about what I was going to do – I just assumed I was going into the business. My father, convinced that engineering was the thing of the future, had chosen this as my university subject. I knew my father was anxious I should get started. My mother, on the other hand, with the slack university vacation periods in mind, often asked, 'What on earth are you both going to be doing? Is there enough for the two of you?'

Within a few days of starting at the garage, I was very pleased and excited to achieve my first new car sale at 8.45 in the morning. Mrs Heatland, an elderly lady and a Don's wife, came into the garage and said she wanted to buy a small car. I sold her a new Austin Seven – a clear deal without any part exchange. Mrs Heatland was a good customer for many years and changed her car regularly.

A few days later, on Monday 3 May, the 1926 National General Strike began, and there were volunteers for all necessary services. My father was against my volunteering – he was anxious for me to get my nose down to some hard work – but the garage became so quiet that after two days he agreed to my volunteering for the railways. The training was a day cleaning engines, one or two days stoking and you then became a driver. And so I joined the railways on the Wednesday, did my engine cleaning and became second stoker on a 40-truck goods train to Liverpool Street loaded with vegetables. Our first stoker was Burns, a Trinity chap, and our driver was a retired driver from the Indian Railways. We set off from Cambridge, and our driver spent all his time saying, 'Stoke her up,' and this we did – it was a full-time job. All went well until we rounded the left-hand bend under the road bridge as the line runs into Bishops Stortford station and, lo and behold, there was a passenger train sitting in the station on our line.

Brakes on goods trains consisted of a brake on the engine and a manually operated brake in the guard's van at the back of the train. There were no brakes on the individual trucks and so the braking effect was minimal. In spite of the driver pushing the steam control lever into reverse, we continued at a good rate of knots and went slap into the back of the passenger train. The impact threw the rear carriages of the train on top of the engine which in turn knocked down a length of platform roofing onto the adjoining branch line. One man was killed and a few were injured. Fortunately the rear carriages of the passenger train were goods carriages loaded with milk and eggs. The engine was blowing off steam and we all hopped out as fast as we could, but we two stokers were sent back to draw the fire, not realising that most of the steam was escaping from the safety valve which was depressed by the goods carriages sitting on top of the engine.

Our guard, who travelled in the rear guard's van, was a regular railway worker who was not on strike because he was due for retirement within a few weeks and was worried that, if he went on strike, he might lose his pension. We saw nothing of him for some time and when he suddenly appeared he had the biggest bump I had ever seen on his forehead. Having come to after the crash, all he thought about was walking down the line and putting out red lamps to warn on-coming traffic.

An enquiry was held at Bishops Stortford station, at which we were informed that volunteer passenger train drivers had been instructed not to exceed 15 mph and goods trains were not to exceed 12 mph. With all our stoking, we had averaged 45 mph from Cambridge to Bishops Stortford and had caught up with the passenger train which had left Cambridge three quarters of an hour before us. It was reported from the stations through which we had passed that we had been blowing off steam all the way. At the enquiry it was confirmed that the normal signals were not working because of the strike. Improvised strike signals should have been operating at the stations we passed through, but it was established that, for some reason, there was no such signal operating at Stansted station. There was much press publicity and a headline read: 'Stortford Rail Crash Enquiry. No Signals At Stansted – No Blame To Those On Duty.'

The Strike finished on the 12th and, back at the garage, I soon found the university terms overwhelmingly busy and the vacations depressingly slack. To avoid taking on temporary unskilled staff during the terms it was necessary to have a very versatile and dedicated team prepared to work very hard indeed in term time. It was a case of getting a quart out of a pint pot in every section of the business. In other words, it was very much like the travelling theatrical company sending a telegram to a small town saying, 'Arriving three o'clock and want a rehearsal on arrival. Please ensure stage manager, scene shifters, electricians and other staff are all available,' to which they got the reply: 'He will be there.'

I was responsible for the stores, including stock control, serving customers and issuing spares to our workshops. I had a daily session with Eddie Parr to enter all the charges for the previous day's work. I read out the details of the charges and Eddie would enter them in the large day book. Eddie Parr did most of the typing. I also typed and was responsible for ordering vehicles from Austin. I liked to spend as much time as possible about the garage and meeting customers, and minimum time in the office. This workload continued until my eldest sister Margery, having completed her schooling at Bishops Stortford High School and a secretarial course, became secretary to my father and myself in 1928.

I have often been asked if there was any difficulty for me – young and just down from the University – in assuming authority over members of the staff. The answer is no – we had all grown up and worked together and they knew I was willing to turn my hand to anything I was capable of doing. I was accepted as one of the team. Bill Morley in later days, when talking to my son Michael about the past, said they thought my father was fortunate to have a son joining him at that time.

There were no vehicle transporters in those days and all new cars were individually collected from the Austin Works. This meant that we had a car, or cars, being collected most days of the week, including Saturdays. We could send an order for spares on a near daily basis. The driver would either bring the spares back the same day or on his next visit to Austins a day or so later. This minimised the quantity of stock we needed to carry and saved carriage charges.

Our one objective was to sell as many new Austin cars as possible. This was important because the more new cars we sold the higher our percentage rebate. It was also necessary to satisfy Austins that our percentage of Austin penetration in our region was as good as or better than the national average. This was most important with the continuous sniping by competitors trying to get some share of our Austin distribution which was the most sought after agency. I always remember the week when for the first time we sold over 20 new cars to individual customers. Secondhand cars were a secondary consideration, sold retail as the opportunity occurred, but most were sold to the trade. We did very little advertising and relied on personal recommendations based on doing everything we could to give a good, courteous service. Our letters used to finish 'Your obedient servant,' and, if we were quoting for something, 'Thanking you in anticipation, Your obedient servant,' or 'I have the honour to be your obedient servant.' I know we had the reputation of being more expensive but better and more courteous than most of our competitors. Our new car sales efforts were lively and energetic but friendly. Anybody who came into the garage with a car, even for a shilling's-worth of parking for the afternoon, was a potential coconut. Many a stranger, having garaged his car, went away with a new car on the same day. One such customer was Reginald Dixon of Blackpool Tower organ radio fame. He used to visit Cambridge every few years and, having got to know him, we usually managed to sell him a new car during these visits.

Commercial travellers' cars, previously non-existent, were building up during the twenties and we went out of our way to attract this business by giving quick and reliable service, including decarbonizing which in those days was a routine requirement every 3,500 to 5,000 miles. When a commercial traveller came to park his car for the day, we would ask, 'Any service work, sir, including a decarbonize?' and he would say, 'You can't decarbonize in a day.' We would say, 'Yes we can – we only want three hours or so.' Having satisfied him once, he would then say 'The same again' the next time he was in Cambridge. This was work which we were attracting into our territory and often led to new car sales outside our territory which we would otherwise not have achieved. Such contacts with sales representatives of national companies often resulted in the garage obtaining new car fleet business.

Routine service work and decarbonizing were undertaken by apprentices who were as keen as mustard to take on increasing responsibility and were up to a high standard of capability within the first year of their apprenticeship. The apprentices, with their nimble fingers, were particularly good at decarbonising Austin Seven engines and refitting the small valve retaining cotters.

During my first year of work with the garage I became more and more conscious of the financial drain of the university vacations. I knew my father was well aware of the situation but it had never been costed – I think we had just accepted the high peaks and low troughs as the way of business in Cambridge. We had been born to it. I experimented with one or two ideas which might provide some manufacture during vacations. One such experiment in 1926 was a method of operating pneumatic windscreen wipers. During the early twenties various types of hand-operated windscreen wipers were available – up to then one of the methods of improving vision under rain conditions was by rubbing a cut potato over the screen which made the water run off more quickly. It was not until about 1925 that vacuum-operated wipers were introduced. The operating suction was provided by tapping into the induction pipe between the carburettor and the cylinder intake. This resulted in the windscreen wiper operating very quickly when travelling slowly and very slowly when travelling quickly. I fitted a nine-inch venturi extension to the exhaust pipe of an Austin Twelve, with a small tube in the centre with the open end pointing to the rear. This had the desired effect of the wiper operating quickly at speed and more slowly as the speed decreased. I did not pursue this as I realised that arguments would arise about the possibility of creating back pressure in the engine, particularly in small cars.

The first opportunity to reduce our financial losses during the slack university vacations resulted from our Lancia and Laffly coaches. The bodywork of these was well in advance of its time, and it came to the notice of a newly formed company, Continental Motorways Limited, who had a sales centre in Haymarket, just off Piccadilly Circus. Continental Motorways was formed to pioneer coach tours, with the slogan 'See Europe from an Armchair'. We became responsible for the supply of their transport for short tours of five to seven days covering England and Wales, and longer tours of up to 10 days embracing Scotland. The tours were in the main during the university summer vacation and provided employment for the drivers and some bus maintenance for the workshops.

A second big worry overshadowing everything was the increasing number of undergraduates' serious motor accidents. There was one fatal accident with a Lancia owned by a Magdalene undergraduate which occurred on the downhill approach road from London running into Baldock. This received particular press publicity at a time when there had been a spate of accidents in a short space of time. As a result first-year students were for the first time banned from having cars and, within a year or so, the regulations were further tightened making it difficult for second- or third-year undergraduates to have a car, except for special cases such as team captains. An important source of income had been the garaging of 80 or so undergraduates' cars, at charges from three to six guineas per term depending on the size of the vehicle. Fortunately the run-down of the under-graduate trade coincided with cars coming into more general use with the Austin Seven, 'The Car for the Millions', playing a leading part. As a result of the increasing popularity of motoring generally and the popularity of Austin cars in particular, our garage during the late twenties and early thir-ties became less dependent on University business.

The garage remained an unlimited liability partnership with my father having three-quarters interest and Harry Rayner one quarter, until Harry Rayner died in 1928. Harry had succeeded his elder brother as Manager of Barclays Bank, Bene't Street, during the twenties. When he became seri-ously ill I had the job of negotiating with his brother George for the purchase of Harry's interest in the Company. Harry Rayner's quarter share was finally bought for £5,000 in 1927. From then I had a one-third interest in the profits but no interest in the capital. This continued until Marshalls (Cambridge) Limited was established in 1934, with my father having two-thirds of the shares and me one-third. My father and I did not have any divi-dends or directors' fees but drew money as and when it was available on a two-thirds:one-third basis. Separate companies were progressively estab-lished in the years ahead on the same basis until my father died. As a family we lived well and within our means, but there was no reserve or build-up of capital for the future. The garage company's capital was virtually stagnant between 1924 and 1936. When I joined the Company my father insisted on me taking out a £3,000 life insurance policy at a cost of £56 a year – quite a large sum in those days.

In 1927 my sixth and youngest sister Brenda was born, 24 years younger than myself, 19 years younger than my eldest sister Margery and seven years younger than my fifth sister Molly. My mother was 48 – the oldest birth that Rex Woods had experienced. My mother, with her large family, kept open house for all our friends even on holiday at Heacham. It is still a mystery how the whole family crowded into the Heacham bungalow, plus one or two family friends and some domestic help. My mother was still making all the girls' clothes other than school uniforms. There is no doubt that as a family we have inherited much of my mother's stamina and enthusiasm for planned hard work.

At Aviation Hall there was usually some sports activity on Sunday afternoons – in the winter mixed hockey for whoever turned up by about 2.30, and in the summer some tennis or croquet – a very serious game. In the winter, if there was any skating about, it used to be ice hockey either at Grantchester or Swavesey. In those days we seemed to have more winters with some ice than we have had in recent years. My father was the prime mover in all this games activity and was a ferocious mixed hockey player. He was always ready for a game of any kind, with often a call of, 'Come on, let's get the cards out,' and somebody groaning, 'Must we?' – card games of all kinds including Vingt-et-un and Scrap Patience, Shove Ha'penny, and riding out with the training gallops on Newmarket Heath; and, when in Egypt, family races on donkeys, camels and Arab horses. My mother took part in most of the games but not the mixed hockey or the riding.

One of the Sunday hockey enthusiasts was Dorothy Hawkins. We had known one another for many years and played together in a number of tennis tournaments. Dorothy was a good all-round games player. We were engaged for a few months at the end of 1926 and the beginning of 1927 but Dorothy and I soon realised, with my work building up, that we were too young to get married. I should have taken my father's original unsolicited advice to get fully established in one's life's work before considering undertaking the serious responsibility of marriage. Towards the end of our engagement Dorothy and I were on our way back from Cromer in May 1927 and happened to be passing Mousehold Aerodrome, Norwich, which was Boulton & Paul Aircraft Company's aerodrome and the home of the Norfolk & Norwich Aero Club. We stopped to see what was going on. It was as a result of this that I decided to learn to fly.

During the early twenties the Government had realised the importance of making the nation air-minded and of creating an interest in aviation and private flying. Thanks to the inspired efforts of the Royal Aero Club and the enthusiastic support of Major-General Sefton Brancker, the Director of Civil Aviation at the Air Ministry, the Flying Club Scheme was announced in 1926. General Brancker was a dynamic personality, and a breath of fresh air when it came to getting anything done which he considered of importance to the nation. The Flying Club Scheme made available a de Havilland Cirrus Moth to each of the first 10 established Aero Clubs, of which Norfolk & Norwich, which began flying in 1927, was one. In addition a subsidy of £50 per new licence, £10 per renewal and a grant per flying hour all to a limit of £2,000 was paid per club per year. The Scheme was planned to be announced in 1925 but was delayed until 1926 when the right type of aircraft, the de Havilland Cirrus Moth, which had won the King's Cup air race, became available.

I had my first lesson at Norwich with Instructor Lines in their de Havilland Cirrus Moth on 29 June 1927. I continued with further dual instruction to a total of $6\frac{1}{2}$ hours by the end of August and was then unable to spare any more time for flying until the following year. I had not let my parents know that I was having flying lessons as I thought my mother would have done her best to have stopped it and, knowing how anxious my father was for me to concentrate on the business, I was not sure of his reaction. One or other of my sisters on occasions accompanied me on my journeys to Norwich and was sworn to secrecy – we always agreed what we were going to say we had been up to. Flying was considered to be the risky sport of a fast set in the 'Roaring Twenties', and there were many crashes, often resulting from pilots with little experience shooting up their girlfriends and stunting at low altitudes. But before recommencing my flying instruction I thought I had better come clean and, to my surprise, there was no problem. I think my parents may have been pleased that I was considering their feelings; I don't know, but all was well. When my mother eventually had her first flight with me from Cambridge to Hunstanton, she volunteered that she felt safer with me in an aircraft than in a motor car. But little did she know that the landing, taxiing and take-off between the bunkers of the miniature Le Strange Arms golf course at Old Hunstanton had been most hazardous.

When the Norfolk & Norwich Aero Club decided to purchase further aircraft, the committee thought a variety of aircraft would attract members, and the Club purchased a Cirrus-engined Avro Avian and an ex-RAF Avro aircraft with an eight-cylinder Renault engine. They had not considered that, in the event of unserviceabilities, they would not be able to cannibalize parts from a mixed bag of aircraft to keep one or more aircraft in the air. Financially it limited the spares which could be carried for any one aircraft. It often happened that two or three aircraft became unserviceable at the same time with no spares available, and I had many fruitless journeys.

I recommenced my flying lessons on 3 July 1928 and, after a further 45 minutes dual instruction, I was sent solo by Instructor Young. By 13 July I had completed my Pilot's 'A' Licence test which in those days included a flight of five figures of eight over the aerodrome at an altitude of not more than 400 feet – a barometric recorded flight. I obtained my Private Pilot's Licence, and after seven hours solo I flew from Norwich to land by our bungalow at Heacham for lunch having agreed with the instructor that I would not be charged for the time on the ground at Heacham. I had had no compass or cross-country instruction or experience and relied on finding my way by following the roads. A few days later I picked up my father at Heacham and flew him to Cambridge. It was late August and I noted many straw fires burning which provided a good indication of wind direction in the event of a forced landing. In those days one was always looking out for possible emergency landing grounds during the progress of a cross-country flight. I landed on Stourbridge Common and my father found his way to Aviation Hall, half a mile away. I then flew back to Norwich making two or three practice landings on the way including one on Newmarket Golf Course.

By this time my appetite had been whetted – I wanted a machine of my own and it was a matter of making a choice between the Cirrus Moth on which I had all my flying experience to date or the new unproved Gipsy Moth. The Gipsy engine was de Havilland's first engine. Laurence Hope of London Air Taxis, who had their hutted office at the entrance to de Havilland's Stag Lane Aerodrome, had won the 1928 King's Cup air race in a Gipsy Moth G-EBYZ. The Cirrus engine was quoted at 60 hp and the Gipsy at 100 hp. The Gipsy was said to have an increased cruising speed of an extra 10–15 mph. It was hard to get any reliable advice as to whether my aircraft should have a Cirrus or a Gipsy engine. I went to see the Cirrus people in their semi-basement office in Kingsway. I had not realised until then that the four-cylinder Cirrus engine was made up of surplus parts from wartime 8-cylinder Renault engines, including the cylinders, pistons and connecting rods.

By now my father's original enthusiasm for aviation was completely revived and he approved the idea of me buying a new Gipsy Moth aircraft for £740 plus £35 for Handley-Page automatic wing slots which automatically opened at slow speeds to provide extra air flow over the top of the mainplanes which increased the lift and reduced the risk of spinning off a stall, which had been the cause of so many accidents in the twenties. Without any thought of being anything more than a private owner as a hobby, I ordered my machine in the de Havilland wooden hut head office at Stag Lane on Tuesday morning 11 December 1928, on the morning of the Oxford and Cambridge rugger match which I attended with my parents in the afternoon. The Stag Lane hut became a museum piece at de Havilland's, later British Aerospace's Hatfield aerodrome.

Having ordered the machine for delivery by March, my next problem was where to keep it. The ideal location was 45 acres of the Whitehill Farm which adjoined the Aviation Hall paddock. This would provide a landing ground with runs of 400 yards in all directions with a good approach from the north and a particularly good clear take-off flight path into the prevailing south-westerly wind with no obstruction, thanks to the southern boundary of the proposed landing ground being only separated by a stream from the clear expanse of Coldhams Common. We knew that the owner farmer who lived in the small farmhouse was having a difficult time, and started discussions for the possible purchase of his farm. Finally it was left to me to go to see him before breakfast one morning and make him an offer on behalf of my father two-thirds and myself one-third of £2,250, about £35 an acre, with early vacant possession, which he accepted. Whitehill Farm was a few hundred yards nearer Cambridge than the current aerodrome and the entry was from a lane known as Cut-Throat Lane on the east side of the Abbey Football Ground.

By December 1928 I had worked in the garage for just over two-and-a-half years. I had learnt much of the garage business as a result of my vacation work, my visits to Austins and attending distributors' meetings. What did Cambridge and the future hold? I knew the problems many of my ex-college friends had experienced in finding jobs, many of which had limited potential, and that I was lucky to have a job with a possible future. I had come to know the importance of being courteous and satisfying customers, whether the Master of a college, an undergraduate or a chimney-sweep, and the importance of a modest approach. I thought my brain power was limited and that the only chance I had of holding a worthwhile job was by hard work. I realised I had to rely on my own efforts and work hard and long hours and never put off until tomorrow what could be achieved today, plan to start each day with a clear desk and keep fit. I found that I could best learn a subject by practical application and could only perform a task to my own satisfaction if I became involved in the greatest detail. My approach was not quite as single-minded and intense as Abrahams' and Liddell's for their Olympic medals, but I had something of Abrahams' single-mindedness in my ambitions for my family and the Company, coupled with a deep rooted desire to increase the prosperity of Cambridge and the region, if only to provide a bigger outlet for the sale of our Austin cars. I had no clue as to how this might be achieved.

Apart from the University Press, there was little or no industry at Cambridge until a few years before the First World War, when the Cambridge Instrument Company, Pye's and Chivers were getting established. Pye employed a big percentage of unskilled labour, and Chivers much seasonal labour for fruit picking and jam making. I had come to realise that any industrial development should be such that it did not clash with the University environment and certainly not be anything like the Morris Motors development at Oxford which had seriously affected the character of the University city. I felt any new industry should generate jobs for family breadwinners and employ a wide cross-section of trades and professions on work which offered prospects for advancement for those who were prepared to work for it. I recognised that, whilst Cambridge as a non-industrial area did not experience the full benefit of boom periods, neither did it suffer the full blast of depressions. With all this in mind, I was conscious that, with its small population, non-industrial atmosphere, lack of trades and labour, it was one of the last places in the world that anyone would consider for a major industrial development. Cambridge, apart from the all-important University, was a small country town in the centre of a very large natural green belt.

Our Austin Distributor's Agreement was a valuable asset but from my personal contacts with other distributors, most of whom had larger territories, many including industrial areas, I knew that in our sparsely populated area there was no possibility of a rapid expansion of the garage business. Even so I understood that, with the progressive national expansion of the motor industry and with Austins continuing to produce good, saleable motor cars, it should for the foreseeable future provide a good and comfortable livelihood. This was the outlook in December 1928.

Chapter 8

Annus Mirabilis

1929

AT THE BEGINNING of January 1929 we hoped the garage would have a satisfactory year – nothing spectacular, but perhaps some slight improvement.

I, in turn, in January 1929 was looking forward to some fun and games with my new aeroplane, due for delivery by March, and hoped I would not find it too expensive to operate. I thought I should have some refresher flying, so on 12 January I set out for Norwich to find that Captain J. L. Houston was now the Flying Instructor. I was beginning to realise I had been given too much freedom, and I asked to be given a thorough check-out. I was fortunate to have Captain Houston as my instructor at this stage. He was a very experienced instructor and was to be one of the seven members of the Guild of Air Pilots' panel of examiners for passing out instructors when the Air Ministry in 1932 approved the Guild's proposed standard for official licensing of flying instructors. Until 1932 a pilot holding a commercial licence could give flying instruction for 'hire and reward'.

During the first two months of the year a hangar 60 ft wide by 70 ft deep was erected by Boulton & Paul of Norwich in our paddock within a hundred yards of our back door. The hangar had a clear door opening to the airfield to the south of 60 ft and a 12 ft wide vehicle door at the north end. A wide gap was cut in the hedge between our home paddock and the new landing ground of Whitehill Farm, and a petrol pump was installed nearby. The landing ground had to be levelled and sown with grass, and many trees had to be cut down and, in some cases, their roots removed. There was also need of further cutting down of trees and hedges to bring two small fields into the landing area. A small area in the south-east corner was sown with sainfoin and could be used for landings immediately.

My father undertook the preparation of the landing area with the help of some casual labour. He had a good eye for levels and it was just his handwriting. For the levelling we bought an earth scoop which, when full, was towed to a low area where a rope was pulled allowing the scoop to roll over and release its load. It was towed by our, by now old, Cottin-Desgouttes touring car which was also used to tow the grass cutter. We had much trouble with the cutter bearings running hot, as it was a horse-drawn cutter and not up to the higher speed of cutting behind a motor car. Much oil and grease was used and many bearings replaced. My father did much of the driving for the levelling and grass-cutting himself. Getting fed up with the number of trees he was having to deal with, he decided only to remove those in the line of the main flight paths. The largest of the trees was a big oak standing a hundred yards in from the south-east corner of the landing area.

At this opportune time early in February, Sir Sefton Brancker flew in without warning to see what was going on. He was a breath of fresh air and a tremendous enthusiast ready to do anything he could to help the development of civil aviation – just the man to give my father some encouragement and at just the right time. Sir Sefton was particularly impressed that the aerodrome was within the town boundary and less than two miles from the centre of the University and town. Most flying club aerodromes were several miles from towns and located on minor roads which were difficult to find.

During Sir Sefton's visit my father opened his heart about the work involved in preparing the landing area and particularly the problem of the big oak tree. Sir Sefton put on his monocle, looked around and said, 'Mr Marshall, don't worry too much about that tree – if anybody can't land here they ought not to be flying. And as for that tree, it is a fine specimen and a very good place for pilots to have tea in the shade on a Sunday afternoon.' However, not many weeks passed before we decided the tree must come down.

Early in February a tall clergyman walked into the garage showroom and introduced himself as the Revd Simpson of Trinity College. He said he was considering buying an aircraft. I asked one or two questions and Mr Simpson suggested I should dine with him in Trinity and talk about it. During the course of dinner he turned to me and said, 'I want you to get me an aeroplane like yours.' There was no order form or contract, just a verbal go-ahead. His Gipsy Moth G-AAEN was delivered at the end of March.

The Revd Canon F. A. Simpson, Fellow of Trinity since 1911, Chaplain to the Forces for three years during the war and Dean of Trinity 1919–1923, was a famous preacher and historian. He preached few sermons, but those he preached attracted a full congregation in chapel, church or cathedral. Stories of Simpson's sayings and doings are legion. If Mr Simpson took a friend to the Arts Theatre, he would buy three tickets as he did not like to sit next to anybody he did not know and he also liked somewhere to put his coat. Mr Simpson's entries in the Trinity College Combination Room Suggestion Book include: 'Cannot the half set of false teeth which has been lying about the cloakroom for a couple of months now be removed? If the owner does not want them, still less do we.'

As a Senior Fellow and having been Dean, Mr Simpson kept a watchful and not always welcome eye on successive chaplains. When in the fashion of the sixties chaplains in their prayers would solicit sympathy for the oppressed in a long list of international trouble-spots, Simpson audibly groaned his disapproval of the 'chaplains' Cook's tours', as he described them.

The purchase of G-AAEN had resulted from 'Simbo', as we came to know him, meeting Flying Officer Dick Waghorn at Wellington College where Simpson had gone to preach a sermon. Waghorn was at Wellington to expound the merits of an RAF career. In conversation, Waghorn suggested to Simpson that he ought to have an aeroplane. Simpson exclaimed, 'Me? What on earth would I do with an aeroplane? I can't even drive a car!' Waghorn promptly replied, 'Don't worry about that, sir – I will fly it for you.'

The arrangement with Waghorn was that he would keep the aircraft at the RAF Central Flying School, Wittering. Waghorn would have the use of the machine one weekend, and the next weekend would fly to Cambridge and take Simbo for a flight, either to a friend's house for tea or to land in a field some few miles from Cambridge for a walk amongst the buttercups and daisies, and fly back to Cambridge with Simbo feeling pretty good. This had not been going for many weeks before Waghorn found that every weekend was a bit of a tie and asked Mr Simpson if he would mind if one or two of his RAF friends shared the task. Simpson readily agreed and this introduced Flying Officer Dermot Boyle (later a Marshal of the Royal Air Force) and Flying Officer Maurice Wiblin. All this Simbo thoroughly enjoyed, and the RAF contingent equally enjoyed the use of the aircraft, which they took abroad on at least one occasion.

The sale of this aircraft coinciding with collecting my own aircraft from Stag Lane helped establish a happy and long association with de Havillands. This became a case of the poacher turned gamekeeper – de Havilland's the seller to Marshall's the customer in the twenties and thirties, becoming an all-important customer of Marshall's in the late forties and to this day as British Aerospace.

The order for Simpson's Gipsy Moth was an important landmark. For our Company and for me personally this fortuitous meeting with Simpson at this particular time was to have great consequences. It provided my first meeting with my life-long friend, Dr Norman de Bruyne, a Fellow and Junior Bursar of Trinity and a future FRS. Norman had a flight one Sunday afternoon during the summer in Simbo's aircraft and was to become our first pupil when we began flying training in October.

Simbo gave flights to many senior members of the University, which led to introductions in a matter of weeks and months which would otherwise have taken years to achieve, including (to mention but a few) A. S. F. Gow, Tutor for many years; the Revd John Burnaby, Regius Professor of Divinity and Dean of Trinity 1943–58; R. M. Rattenbury, University Registrary; Sir Edward Collingwood (descendant of Admiral Collingwood),

Lecturer and Steward; Udny Yule, the famous statistician; and Victor Rothschild as an undergraduate. Simbo with his aeroplane was virtually a sales beacon in the heart of Trinity. Some learnt to fly with us and many flew with us from time to time. They flew for pleasure or to view areas of archaeological interest and large country houses, including Wimpole Hall, or to see the Cambridge Water Pumping Station on the Fulbourn Road. The Simpson association also gave us an introduction to a number of up and coming RAF personnel, which has been invaluable over the years.

At this point in my story I thought it would be interesting to take stock of my flying experience at the time of taking delivery of my aircraft, and so for the first time in over 60 years I opened my Log Book and was horrified and embarrassed to read of some of my early irresponsible escapades. All very foolish – and I was lucky to get away with it – but, as it happened, it proved a good education which instilled in me a permanent conviction that others must not be let loose in this way.

After only seven-and-a-half hours dual and seven hours solo flying over a period of 12 months, I was allowed to land beside the beach at Heacham, on Stourbridge Common, Cambridge and any other fields I selected from the air for practice landings, and all without any cross-country, compass or map reading instruction or experience. This was not entirely my fault, but I certainly took full advantage of opportunities available and without question or consideration of the risks involved, not only to myself and the aircraft, but to passengers and third parties. I was never questioned or pulled up by my instructors.

My total flying time when I took delivery of my aircraft was 41 hours 10 minutes, made up of 9 hours 50 minutes dual and 31 hours 20 minutes solo. I was otherwise self-taught – eventually to become a self-taught licensed flying instructor, having used some of my sisters as guinea-pig pupils. The great day for collecting my new aircraft arrived on 28 February 1929. I travelled by train to Liverpool Street and then by underground to Burnt Oak, 10 minutes walk from Stag Lane Aerodrome. By air it was possible to get to the middle of London from Cambridge in just over an hour if you were lucky with the trains at Burnt Oak.

At Stag Lane all was ready and I took delivery of my spanking new aircraft G-AAEH, with its side panels painted in Cambridge blue for which I had let de Havilland's have a cutting from my athletics Blue scarf to match the colour – the blue was outlined with a black line and the top of the fuselage and mainplanes were all aluminium. I did one circuit and landing at Stag Lane and then proceeded to Cambridge. It was in fact my first flight away from my *ab initio* area of Norwich, Heacham and Cambridge. I liked to know by continuous map location exactly where I was, and I picked my way across to Hatfield – the Hatfield bypass had not yet been built. I then followed the road to Stevenage, Baldock, Royston and Cambridge and got back in time for lunch, landing on the small sainfoin strip at the south-east corner of the aerodrome, since the main landing area was still being prepared for the sowing of grass.

I used to put in some flying practice before breakfast to avoid encroaching on my time at the garage. I had a narrow escape on one of the first of those early morning flights when, to save time, I very foolishly decided to start my take-off run in the home paddock and fly through the gap in the hedge instead of taxiing. My wheels just left the ground before reaching the gap. A light breeze blowing diagonally from the left drifted the aircraft to the right and I only just missed hitting the hedge. This could have been the end of everything – a lesson well learnt and, once again, what luck!

On 13 March I had my first experience of flying above the clouds with a completely overcast sky, and I was very excited. I dug out my father and suggested he should come with me and see this wonderful sight, but I was not so lucky this second time in finding my way through the clouds and, after two or three attempts and with a cloud base of only a few hundred feet, I gave it up and was pleased to get down in one piece. My father had not noticed anything untoward and just said, 'Never mind, we must try again another day.' All very dangerous – all I recorded in my Log Book was 'Above clouds'.

The above incident was only a few days before setting out with my father on Saturday 17 March on our epic flight to Hooton Park, near Liverpool, to see my second sister Dorothy at her physical training college. The weather was poor with low cloud and, within 16 miles of Cambridge in the Huntingdon area, the cloud base became impossible and we returned to Cambridge, planning to try again the next day. This was my first cross-country flight over completely strange ground navigating by a combination of road, rail and compass under really non-flyable weather conditions – absolutely crackers.

The next day we set out again. The weather, still bad, was at Cambridge a little better than the previous day but deteriorated to very low cloud, some mist and drizzle from Nottingham onwards. We had been flying about 45 minutes from Cambridge when the revs dropped from 1900 to just under 1000, which did not provide sufficient power to maintain flight. Fortunately I located a large field in the Nottingham area and landed. I ran up the engine against the telescopic chocks; all seemed to be well. I decided I had better carry out a check flight and, if OK, land to pick up my father and continue the flight.

A big gap in the hedge ran into another good-sized field, the breeze was light and I could take off directly into wind towards the gap. I remembered my experience of a few days before when I started my take-off at Cambridge in the home paddock through the gap in the hedge nearly coming to grief. On this test flight the wind was directly ahead through the gap but, as I gained speed, just before take-off the revs again dropped and I had to abandon take-off. I asked the farmer, who had joined my father by now, if I could use his telephone. In those days people were all very friendly, interested and helpful when landing in their fields on such occasions. I rang de Havilland's at about lunch-time and fortunately Hubert Broad, de Havilland's Test Pilot, answered. I explained what had happened and he said, 'You have got an air lock. Disconnect the petrol pipe at the carburettor, let the fuel flow and then reconnect the pipe whilst the fuel is flowing.' This I did and off we went.

The weather continued to deteriorate and I got progressively very worried about our fuel supply and the possibility of over-flying Hooton Park aerodrome. I finally decided I must, as a matter of urgency, land and enquire my whereabouts and physically check the fuel position which was getting very low. I located what I thought was a possible landing space in a field with some trees. By now it was very misty and visibility was down to a few hundred yards. I landed, and fortunately there was a man in the field. I asked, 'Where is Hooton aerodrome?' and he said, 'Over the hedge', and so my father walked through a gap in the hedge and I took off and landed on the aerodrome. The next day I filled up with fuel and the tank took its maximum capacity of 19 gallons!! Another bit of unbelievable luck – luck in the aerodrome being there (I did not find it) and luck with the fuel (a few minutes more flying and we would have run out). Even now it makes me shudder, and of course I was irresponsible to have taken off again without a detailed check-up of the fuel position, even if it was only to fly the aircraft over the hedge. Another lesson well and truly and indelibly learnt for the future. There is no doubt that first-hand experience is the best way of learning – always provided your luck holds.

The next day the weather was not good but better than the previous two days. All went well until about 45 minutes from Hooton Park when, at about the same flying time as we had experienced the problem on the previous day, the revs dropped and I had to land. This time the field was very small – too small to attempt a take-off with my father on board. I went through the same procedure as before of disconnecting the fuel pipe and letting the fuel flow. By this time a motorist had pulled up on a minor road. I explained to him that I was going to take off and try to find a larger field to land in and pick up my father. The motorist very kindly volunteered to take my father and all the baggage we had off-loaded, hoping to see me land in another field and bring my father and our baggage along. It was a hundred to one chance against me locating a suitable field within sight of the motorist or within walking distance for my father, but luck was again with us and I fortunately located a field, landed, picked up my father and returned to Cambridge. If I had not found a suitable field nearby, my father would have been left high and dry in a country area 70 miles or so from Cambridge and with all the baggage.

I discussed the fuel flow problem with de Havilland the next day and flew the aircraft to Stag Lane, where they inserted a piece of rubber tubing to increase the length of the vent pipe on top of the fuel tank by three-quarters of an inch, and no further air lock troubles were ever experienced.

The tank is located in the centre of the upper wing and the fuel tank air vent was not sufficiently long to avoid the area of high suction associated with the air flow over the tank. The people at de Havilland were very matter of fact about this, as I think I must have been, because there were no words of major complaint, and there was no complaint from my father, who took it all as a matter of course and part of the flyer's way of life – our luck had prevailed.

On Monday 25 March we had finished lunch and were getting ready to go back to the garage when we heard an aeroplane landing. This proved to be our first meeting with Sir Alan Cobham. He was a national hero, having carried out survey flights all over the world to plot the Empire Air Routes – it is said that he did more than any man to plot, prove and organise air routes, resulting in services of mail to India in 1929 and the Cape in 1931.

On this occasion Sir Alan with his mechanic, in a Cirrus Moth, was surveying for various municipalities to identify sites for possible landing grounds or municipal aerodromes, including for Huntingdon. He had landed because he had a knock in his engine which he thought was either a loose propeller or a big end bearing, but first he asked if there was any chance of getting something to eat? I took them into our house, and my parents were delighted to meet them. As a big family we always had a very large and wonderful sirloin of beef on a Sunday, cooked slightly underdone and red, and very good when cold. My mother produced the cold beef and some pickled shallots, which Sir Alan ate with gusto. I can see him now with a shallot in each hand throwing them into his mouth.

We talked and, having had Murray Pickthorn (famous for his war-time flying) land a week before and now Sir Alan's landing, the conversation led round to the possibility of others being allowed to land. Sir Alan was enthusiastic about this and we discussed the best method of publicising our aerodrome as being open for others. This started a life-long family friendship between my parents and Sir Alan and Lady Cobham which has extended to this day via our two sons, both Michaels, and their wives. Before Sir Alan left we had committed ourselves to a grand opening of our landing ground on Sunday 9 June 1929 during the traditional university 'May Week' celebrations at the end of the academic year – but would our grass have grown sufficiently by then? The work of levelling and seeding had to be speeded up – the race was on – but in the meantime many other things were to happen.

On 9 April I made a flight to Teignmouth and Land's End with my friend Frank Morrell of Jesus days, landing near Land's End in a field I selected from the air. We bought ten gallons of Shell petrol in two-gallon cans from a nearby garage and filled up using a funnel fitted with a chamois leather filter which I always carried. On our return journey all went well until there was a violent and frightening noise from the engine and a hurried landing had to be made. I had little choice, but managed to get down in a very small field with a 20 foot gap in the hedge at the far end, with a Devonshire sunken road on the far side of the hedge. I had not finished the landing run when I got to the hedge and the left wing caught in it. The aircraft swung round and the right wing dropped into the road dyke. There we were with one wing in the air and the other wing in the dyke. With the help of some passers-by we righted the machine and pushed it back into the field. Fortunately there was not too much damage but it would have been impossible to take off from the field even if repairs, including the engine problem, could have been undertaken on site. At the time of the engine failure Frank had been quietly reading poetry in the front cockpit.

The nearby aerodrome at Teignmouth was operated by Mr Parkhouse, who also had a garage. The garage picked us up at our hotel at five o'clock the next morning to proceed to the aircraft and put it on rail to de Havilland's at Stag Lane. We dismantled it and loaded the wings onto a farm cart pulled by a horse. We towed the aircraft with a new Morris Oxford saloon car, putting the tail skid on the luggage grid. I stood on one side of the grid and the mechanic on the other and we slowly proceeded, keeping pace with the horse, to the nearest railway station. Years later we got to know Mr Parkhouse's son John well, when he was for many years a director of British Aerospace. He is a flying enthusiast and personally rebuilt a Gipsy Moth which he kept in immaculate condition.

When my aircraft got back to Stag Lane, at first they found nothing wrong. They then started it up and immediately realised there was a major problem. Insufficient clearance had been left between the valve cap and the valve retaining cotters, with the result that the cap had vibrated against the cotters until the serrations of the retaining cotters had been sufficiently eroded to allow a valve of No. 3 cylinder to drop into the cylinder. As a result all Gipsy engines were checked or modified to ensure that the valve cap/valve cotter gap provided sufficient clearance.

Up to that time I had only insured my aircraft third party. If I had had full comprehensive insurance, I would have been liable for the first £80 of damage. Fortunately, de Havilland's realised they had some major responsibility and, having estimated the cost of repairs at about £100, apart from the engine which was under guarantee, decided not to make any charge. This was all at a critical time when we were planning for the opening of our aerodrome on 9 June and I did not get my aeroplane back from Stag Lane until 2 May.

I maintained my aircraft myself for the first nine months, which was very valuable experience. Fortunately the three serious forced landings I had experienced in 25 days had nothing to do with my maintenance. It is quite extraordinary that nobody, including any member of the family, ever raised the question of how long I would be allowed to go on flying at this rate of forced landings. To be fair to the Gipsy engine, it must be remembered that the two forced landings which occurred on the journeys to and from Hooton Park, Liverpool, were not engine failures but a matter of fuel starvation. The de Havilland Gipsy engine, after a few teething problems, revolutionised the safety of flying, required little maintenance and offered long periods between complete engine overhauls.

I was beginning to realise that I had been very lucky, and I wrote on one of my then blue pocket note cards 'Never get over-confident, and remember that better pilots than you have crashed.' I still have this card which I have carried to this day. I know this card must have been written about May 1929, because after then my blue cards became pink in order to use up the surplus pink tickets from the opening of the aerodrome on May Week Sunday.

Having committed ourselves to 9 June for the official opening of the aerodrome, the gamble with the weather was on. Would the many areas which had been filled in and sown be useable, or would it be a quagmire? May was a particularly wet month. Two or three weeks before the opening a Gipsy Moth circled overhead and landed in pouring rain. The pilot got out and asked, 'Where is the aerodrome?' This was Ivor McClure, the Manager of the AA Aviation Department which in those days provided advice and information for overseas flights, and hired out continental route maps which were suitably marked up, as for example for a flight to the south of France with warnings about bumpy weather conditions in the Rhône Valley. The wet weather had provided a reasonable growth of grass, except in certain areas where there had been a lot of levelling. The weather became dry at the end of May but there was the worry that, if there was an overnight downpour, we could have a problem in deep filled areas. There were also bald earth areas where the grass had not grown, which could be seen from the air. We did not want any more enquiries such as Mr McClure's 'Where is the aerodrome?', so we got some whitewash, put some green dye in it and sprayed the bald patches the day before the opening. This was quite effective, and fortunately the weather remained dry.

Two weeks before the opening the Bishop of Ely, the Rt Revd Lord Leonard Thomson, led a campaign against the event taking place on a Sunday, and this received much publicity. We had had ten thousand tickets printed on pink card for what was called 'The Grand Opening'. We had a crowd of several thousand, but the Bishop's campaign resulted in many senior members of the University not attending, and I was left with a quantity of pink tickets on my hands, which I used for notes until they ran out. I then ordered more pink cards, and I have been identified with these pink cards and have continued to use them to this day.

The opening was a great success. We provided a small refreshment tent for those arriving by air and a separate tea tent for the spectators. We had the bandstand which my father had used on the Pitt Club Lawn for the May Races before the First World War. The bandstand was surrounded by flower beds, and the Cambridgeshire Regimental Band provided the music. Harold Abrahams was our commentator. After the completion of the flying programme, I gave Harold a flight round Cambridge.

The pageant and programme were well reported in the *Aeroplane* magazine which was dominated in those days by the famous C. G. Grey:

The May Week Air Pageant celebrating the opening of Marshall's Aerodrome, Cambridge, was held on the afternoon of Sunday June 9th in very fair weather. Mr D. G. Marshall, MBE, who owns a large and well appointed garage and motor business in Cambridge, has for many years been a keen advocate of aviation.

It was a very gay occasion. The flower beds separating the principal enclosure from the aerodrome, the brilliant uniforms of a full military band and the assorted colour schemes of the forty-odd aircraft assembled made a view rather unusual in flying meetings. The effect was quite cheering and was a pleasant background to the programme of flying.

Sir Alan Cobham was billed to be present and give flights in his Giant Moth or DH-61 but, although present himself, the 61 unfortunately could not be brought along and Sir Alan carried on in a less ambitious manner with a Coupé Moth lent to him by the de Havilland company.

Mr Broad and YK set the programme going with one of his neat displays of aerobatics, which included a new manoeuvre consisting of half an outside loop and half an inward one. The resulting 'S' looks remarkably pretty from the ground. YK, in which Mr Broad performs, is the original Gipsy Moth and has the original Gipsy engine.

After Mr Broad came a parachute descent by Mr Tranum. He and his Russell parachute first of all made a straight drop from a Klemm Salmson piloted by Mr Alliot, and later in the afternoon made a six second delay drop from about two thousand feet. Between these two demonstrations he sandwiched a wing walking exhibition which caused quite a sensation. The sight of Mr Tranum lying horizontally across the undercarriage of a Moth without either a parachute or a care in the world caused many a stout heart to misfire.

Bombing a small car with flour bags and a similar event called aerial golf provided much amusement. Balloon bursting was responsible for more than one thrill. Single balloons only were used and, after they had ascended to about fifty feet, they invariably descended again, with the result that competitors diving on them appeared to be in greater danger of destroying themselves than the balloons.

Two races were held, the first of which ended in a dead heat between the five competing Gipsy Moths and constituted either a rare proof of standardisation of performance or else a very blatant piece of sportive swindling by the pilots, who will therefore remain anonymous. The second race, a relay, was quite serious and ended with Mr Atcherley on the DH Demonstration Moth winning for his team by about half a fuselage length.

Some superb formation flying by Messrs Waghorn, Wiblin and Boyle on three Gipsy Moths aroused everyone's enthusiasm. Flying between the ground and one hundred feet or so, they passed and repassed the enclosure each time in a different manner and ending their display with a fleur-de-lis break-off. [Prince of Wales Feathers]

About seven or eight thousand spectators were present and undoubtedly went away with a good impression. The meeting was a model of organisation and one of the most pleasant and entertaining affairs so far held this season.

When the machines were all lined up for the tea interval, one was better able to appreciate their numbers and variety, which included DH Moths in all their various guises some twenty-strong, two Westland Widgeons, five Avro

Avians, a Cirrus Spartan, a Westland Wood Pigeon, an SE5A, a DH-53, a Klemm and the Avro Baby.

On the day, the aircraft which John Tranum usually used for his wing walking became unserviceable and I asked Dermot Boyle if he would take up John Tranum in my aeroplane. Dermot was a bit worried about his responsibilities, including insurance, but finally agreed and often tells the story:

> Having got a vague idea of what was expected of me and what John Tranum was going to do, I took off, and no sooner was I off the ground than Tranum was getting out of the front cockpit onto the right wing, all without a parachute. He walked to the wing strut and then returned to the cockpit and repeated the exercise on the left wing. Tranum, when returning from the left wing, put his rubber-soled shoe onto the exhaust pipe resulting in a strong smell of burning rubber. He then proceeded to get out on the right wing and disappeared under the wing and onto the undercarriage. My instructions were to circle the aerodrome at not more than two or three hundred feet. This I did, but after a few circuits I became anxious with no sight of Tranum, but went on circling and hoped he was still with me. I was reassured when I noticed the good British public were all still looking up, so presumably Tranum was still with me. Eventually Tranum reappeared and got back into the front cockpit and all was well.

During the first few months of 1929 some competition had developed between ourselves and Conington, near St Ives, an off-shoot of the Suffolk Aero Club at Ipswich, in which King & Harper, the biggest of the Cambridge garages, were becoming interested. The *Aeroplane* magazine reported:

> Apparently the feeling between the Cambridge Aero Club at Conington and the Marshall Aerodrome is not of the best. One may be wrong, but one gathers that the Conington people regard themselves as true blue amateurs and are inclined to look on the Marshall's people as commercial – with somewhat of the Town and Gown spirit. Although Mr Arthur Marshall was himself a member of the University and won his Blue for athletics, he was born and bred in business in Cambridge and is now the Moth agent for that area, besides being in the motor trade – hence the feeling, apparently. One hopes that more friendly feeling may arise and that, though there may be that competition which is so good for trade, it will be of a thoroughly sporting nature.

Although it was a worry at the time, the Conington airfield was remote from Cambridge on a by-road and did not last long.

One good turn the Conington set-up did for us was to get David Garnett, the well-known author, interested in the air. The Conington flying field was just a few fields away from his house, and he and his wife walked across to see the flying one Sunday afternoon, which resulted in a joy-ride and an interest in learning to fly. He later became my pupil and then, with

Hamish Hamilton the publisher, a joint owner of a small German Klemm monoplane.

In July I flew Oswald Chivers to Tangmere, where his wife Marjorie was convalescing after an illness. This resulted in E. W. Wood, Chivers's Motor Department Manager, becoming interested in learning to fly. Chivers the jam manufacturers, the only big car fleet user in the area, were becoming increasingly important garage customers and there was much competition for their business.

One day in July my father phoned me at the garage at midday and asked if I could get him to Newbury Races for the three o'clock race – it was very important. The weather was bad, low cloud and some drizzle, and the nearest field I could identify as being possible for a landing was two or three miles from the course. We landed and hoped that there might be a passing motorist, but the nearest road was a by-road with little or no traffic. So we climbed on board and I made another attempt to find somewhere nearer the course. By now it was past two o'clock and time was getting short for the three o'clock race and for my father to place some complicated bets. I could not find anywhere nearer and told my father I was going to land on the course. He yelled back that under no circumstances must I do that. It was our only chance and I pulled out the interconnecting speaking tube so that I could concentrate, and landed in a starting area on the course. The horses were coming up for the start of the 2.30 race. My father was livid. The jockeys came riding up and I asked, 'Which way is London?' and they all pointed their racing whips towards London. I suggested to my father that he should make his way to the stands and this he started to do. He had not gone far when some officials drove up in a car and picked him up and said that, now we knew where we were, we must take off immediately after the 2.30 race had started, which we did. The horses he had come to back came in first, second and third and no bet. My name was mud. It was the only time I got in the doghouse with my father resulting from any of our flying escapades.

Our Continental Motorways bus tours suffered breakdowns from time to time. I particularly remember two in July 1929 when I helped by flying parts to the vehicles which were in trouble. The first time was when Ted Key, with one of the Laffly coaches and a full load of passengers, was stranded on the Dover Road with valve trouble, a problem we had experienced before. I flew down and landed in a nearby field with the parts which Key was quickly able to fit. The second occasion was when Titch Porter, by then the Deputy Workshop Foreman, was driving one of the Lancias and broke down at Woodstock, Oxfordshire with back-axle trouble. Titch requested a ballbearing, an axle shaft and a sledge-hammer. I easily spotted the coach and landed in a nearby field with the replacement parts within two hours of receiving the call. This Lancia back axle shaft trouble was another problem we had previously experienced. Titch worked through the night with a tarpaulin shelter over the rear wheel-arch to keep off the rain and got the party on the move again by nine o'clock the next morning.

My sister Dorothy had a Dutch doctor friend, August Deutman, who came to stay with us. He had spent the best part of two days travelling from Rotterdam to Cambridge and I suggested that he and I should fly back to Rotterdam for the night. August could not believe that the journey which had taken him of the order of 36 hours had been achieved in two hours or so. This was on 9 August 1929 and was my first crossing of the Channel as a pilot.

The family holiday at Heacham extended into September this year. The Schneider Trophy Race was on Saturday 9 September, and my father and I planned an early morning flight to Hamble near Southampton. We ran into low cloud and mist at Farnham and landed in a field to wait for the weather to improve. Up came a car, with the lady of the house and her butler wanting to know what we were doing. We explained the position. She was not very pleased and instructed us to take off as soon as possible – no offer of breakfast. This is the only time I can remember not having been well received on these occasions. We got to Hamble and saw the race from a liner anchored in the Solent. Flying Officer Waghorn, Simpson's pilot, won the race for Great Britain at a speed of 328.63 mph in a 'Supermarine S6' seaplane with a Rolls-Royce 'R' engine.

The 'Supermarine S6' was the forerunner of the Spitfire. Rolls-Royce's experience with their Schneider Trophy engine played a big part in the development of the Merlin engine which played an all important part in the Battle of Britain. It is interesting to note that up to and including the 1927 race the Napier Lion engine had been predominant, and it was thought that nothing would ever beat it. For the 1929 race more power was required. The Napier Lion was giving about 800 hp which it was thought could be boosted up by a few hundred for the duration of the race. The Rolls-Royce Buzzard engine was giving 925 hp and Rolls managed to boost it to 1850 as the 'R' engine for the duration of the race. Great Britain, having won the Schneider Trophy in 1927 and again in 1929 and having no challenger in the 1931 race, retained the very large trophy, weighing several hundred-weight and standing three or four feet high, which became the property of the Royal Aero Club and was never competed for again. The trophy had been presented by Monsieur Schneider in 1912 for an international air race for seaplanes. It was mainly competed for between the US, Italy and Great Britain.

After the race my father and I flew back to Heacham. It was during this stay at Heacham that I gave my father a flight to seven thousand feet on 10 September, and for the first time was able to let him see something of the world above the clouds.

On Saturday 28 September, Tubby Davis and I set out in G-AAEH for Switzerland and Germany. On Monday 30 September we landed to refuel at Frankfurt at about 11 o'clock in the morning. There was great excitement. Herr Opel was all dressed up and helmeted ready to attempt the first rocket-propelled glider flight, with the glider sitting on a light rail. He climbed on board and the rockets were lit, but the glider had not achieved flying speed

at the end of the rail and tipped on to its nose. Opel was OK and we left
Frau Opel sipping a glass of brandy and recovering from the fright she had
when she thought her husband was going up in smoke. Opel and his rocket
glider achieved flight later that day, the first time that an aircraft had taken
off and sustained flight under reaction power. The rocket glider is in the
Science Museum in Munich. Few people realise that Germany achieved
rocket flight so soon after World War I, at a time when German military
flying was very restricted.

As a result of the successful opening of our aerodrome we began to
receive enquiries for flying training. I discussed this with Clem Pike, the
Assistant Chief Instructor of the de Havilland Flying Training School at
Stag Lane. I was concerned about the costs involved and what we would be
letting ourselves in for at this early stage and without any Aero Club
government subsidy – a full-time licensed flying instructor and a licensed
engineer, etc. Clem said he had two flying instructors, P. P. Grey and F.
Wilkinson, both ex-RAF five-year Short Service Commission officers at de
Havilland's Flying School, who were leaving at the end of the summer to
take a one-year forestry course at Cambridge before going to Nigeria. Both
agreed to help us to get started. Clem Pike was an important and influential
contact at this time and became a life-long friend. He was a Founder
Member of the Guild of Air Pilots and Air Navigators, a Court member
when the Court held their first meeting on 7 October 1929.

Grey was very keen and it was to him that we were indebted for
making it possible for us to start our Flying School in October of 1929. He
instructed three afternoons a week and on Sundays, with occasional help
from Wilkinson – the plan being that Grey would carry on into the Lent
term, by which time it was hoped that I would have obtained my commercial licence and be able to undertake the flying training.

Having decided to open our aerodrome for flying training, we required
more hangar accommodation. We planned to keep the original hangar in the
home paddock private and away from the general business of the aerodrome,
which was now called Cambridge (Fen Ditton) on its Air Ministry licence.
We erected on the aerodrome a hangar 45 feet wide by 40 feet deep, which
would accommodate one Moth in full flying trim with its wings extended,
and two pairs of lock-ups which would house Moths with folded wings.

We engaged an 'A' and 'C' Licensed Ground Engineer, a Mr Honour,
who lived in the small farmhouse on the aerodrome. Remembering my
many fruitless journeys to Norwich only to find all the aircraft unserviceable, usually because the Norwich Club had no two aircraft alike and no
interchangeability of parts, we decided that for our Flying School we must
standardise on one make of aircraft and engine. It is fortunate that we
decided to standardise on the Gipsy Moth. We bought a second-hand Gipsy
Moth G-EBYZ for £375 from London Air Taxis Limited, which had a small
hutted office just inside the entrance to de Havilland's works at Stag Lane.
The Air Taxi company was owned by Laurence Hope and his friend Birkett

Where it all started, in Brunswick Gardens. Originally a stable, this became the first garage premises in 1909. It was converted from a single to a double doorway to take two cars. The old double doors remain in place in this photograph.

A Metallurgique – our first car with first driver Mr A. Carter at the wheel in King Street 1911. (*Cambridge Daily News*).

One of our Cottin-Desgouttes in King Street in 1911.

My mother with, from left to right, Margery, Violet, Dorothy and me in the garden at Milton Road in 1914.

Above Army airship Beta II in Jesus College grounds in September 1912. (*Cambridgeshire Libraries*)

Left My father in France in 1915.

Below QFCF4 Canteen, Woolwich Arsenal, accommodating 1,500 during the First World War.

A Fairey IIIA seaplane identical to that in which my father and I had our first flight at Brighton in July 1919. (*R.T. Jackson*)

Renault and Crossley hire cars in Jesus Lane garage 1919, before the second bay extension, with Bill Morley (left) and Dan Morley.

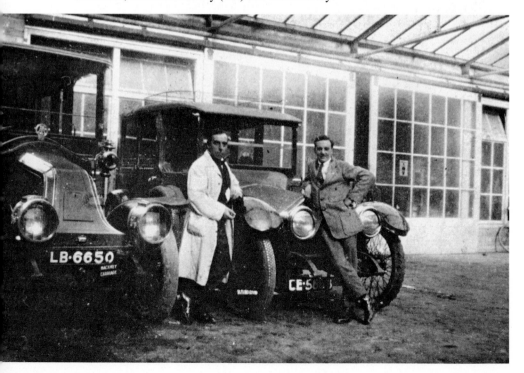

Above An artist's impression of Jesus Lane and the reconstruction of Sidney Sussex College wall, 1922. (*Cambridgeshire Libraries*)

Below Marshall's 1923 Austin 7.

Right The sand-yacht on which we had so much holiday fun – Heacham 1928.

Above left At Hillside, Tonbridge, on a sunny Sunday afternoon between 1918 and 1922.

Above right AGGM winning the Half-mile at Tonbridge in March 1922.

Below The Handley-Page W8 G-EAPJ 'Duchess of York', operated by Handley-Page Transport Ltd, in which my father and I flew from Croydon to Le Bourget, Paris in August 1922. The W8 was a derivative of the 0/400 twin-engined bomber purchased by my father in 1919 for £5. (*R.T. Jackson*)

The finish of the Oxford v Cambridge Quarter-mile in 1923. First Abrahams, second Stevenson, third Marshall.

The finish of the Oxford v Cambridge Quarter-mile in 1924. First Johnson, second Marshall, third Stevenson.

Hunstanton pre-Olympics 1924. Left to right: Henry Stallard, Douglas Lowe, AGGM and Tubby Davis.

Achilles Club members of Olympic team, Paris 1924. From back to front rows:
A. G. de L. Willis, A. G. G. Marshall, R. J. Dickinson, J. H. P. Campbell, L. F. Roberts, W. G. Tatham
W. R. Seagrove, E. A. Montague, G. R. Renwick, L. F. Partridge, Lord Burghley, M. C. Nokes
A. E. Porritt, H.M. Abrahams, P. J. Baker, D. G. A. Lowe, G. M. Butler, H. B. Stallard
R. S. Starr, E.A. Hunter, C.E. Davies
Absent – Sir Park Goff, C. E. W. Mackintosh, B. G. D. Rudd, W. E. Stevenson, R. S. Woods

Above General Strike 1926. Left to right: Burns, Marshall and an ex-Indian Railways driver.

Below Norfolk & Norwich Cirrus Moth G-EBZW, Heacham 1928.

Bottom Marshalls and Lockharts at Heacham in 1929, with Tubby Davis third left back row and Henry Bateman extreme right back row.

Above left My father, Sir Alan Cobham and myself at the opening of our first aerodrome in 1929.

Above right My father on his horse 'Judy' alongside the aerodrome petrol pump in 1930.

Below My first aircraft, Gipsy Moth G–AAEH, which I took delivery of in 1929. In the background is Whitehill, the family home, and on the left our first hangar.

Air race in progress between Dermot Boyle, Dick Waghorn and Maurice Wiblin at the aerodrome opening during 'May Week' in 1929. (*Bystander*)

Fen Ditton aerodrome 1930.

Above My Gipsy Moth and Norman de Bruyne's at Heacham in 1930. Ned Lockhart and my father are in the foreground.

Left Margery at Hanworth before King's Cup Air Race in 1930.

Below One of the cars we took across the stream at Heacham.

Above left Rosemary Dimsdale, 1929.

Above right Mrs Marcus Dimsdale (Rosemary's mother).

Right Marcus Dimsdale (Rosemary's father).

Rosemary and me at Stag Lane immediately after our wedding on 22 April 1931. (*Daily Express*)

Norman de Bruyne's Snark G-ADDL in 1934.

My father entering Monospar G-ADMC on his way to the races in 1936. Peter May is on the far right.

The Austin Twenty converted to a fire engine and crash tender by the Jesus Lane garage for the new aerodrome.

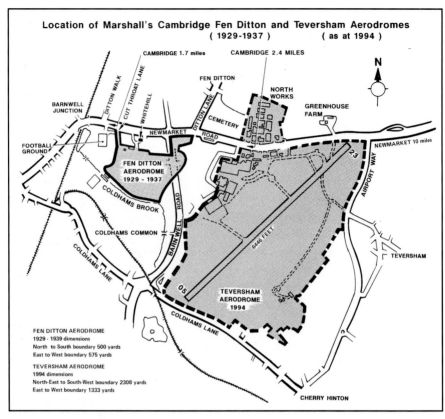

Map locating the original Cambridge (Fen Ditton) and current Cambridge (Teversham) aerodromes.

Airport Hotel, Control Building and No. 1 Hangar from the air in 1938. The Control Building is being considered for Grade II protection by the Department of National Heritage.

– well-known pilots and famous for flying through almost any weather, low cloud and fog conditions to deliver films of special occasions within hours. G-EBYZ was the first production DH60G Gipsy-engined Moth which made its debut by winning the 1928 King's Cup Race piloted by Hubert Broad, the de Havilland Test Pilot. I collected the aircraft from Stag Lane on 4 October. My aircraft G-AAEH during this time was available as a back-up when required for flying training. We purchased a further second-hand Moth, this time an all metal Gipsy Moth, early in 1930.

I consider the Moth is still the best training machine – if you can fly a Moth really well, you can fly anything. It responds naturally. The inspired designer was Sir Geoffrey de Havilland who always carried out the first flight of any machine he had designed. The Moth, which revolutionised private flying in the late twenties, was designed for the amateur, the weekend flyer, and for instruction. Simplicity and safety were paramount. Sir Geoffrey felt that, apart from its designated number, it should have a name, and many ideas were put forward before Sir Geoffrey's enthusiasm for natural history led to the name 'Moth'. It had the right sound, was easy to remember and led to a series of Moths, all named after British insects – Cirrus Moth, Gipsy Moth, Puss Moth, Tiger Moth, Fox Moth, Hornet Moth, Hawk Moth and Leopard Moth. An amateur entomologist defined the Gipsy Moth as being 'usually found in hedges and ditches'. A more reliable ento-mological book states that 'the Gipsy Moth has been extinct in England since about 1850'.

From the day I decided to learn to fly I was only interested in flying to provide the quickest way of getting from A to B regardless of weather conditions. A pilot should be well practised in all basic principles of controlling an aircraft, such as avoiding getting into a stall and how to recover from a spin, but not aerobatics. In the late twenties many of the well-publicised crashes resulted from aerobatics often carried out at low altitudes. Aerobatics is an essential ingredient of military and professional exhibition flying, but should not be connected in any way with commercial and private aviation, just as motor racing has no connection with private motoring. I practised what I preached to the extent that I had never looped or rolled an aircraft until the outbreak of World War II.

With the opening of our Flying Training School we had to prepare our rules and regulations and get them approved by the University for under-graduate flying. The first few undergraduates in October 1929 got their parents' and tutors' permission to learn to fly with us prior to the University Edicts being officially up-dated to recognise the position. There was nothing until then in the University Edicts which said they could or could not fly. All this was at a time when the University regulations regarding the use of motor cars by undergraduates were becoming progressively restric-tive. From our undergraduate motoring experience we knew that, whatever University regulations were in force for undergraduate flying, one serious crash and everything would go back to zero.

With memories of my own recent lack of discipline and control whilst I was learning to fly (I had been given virtually the freedom of the air), I realised that, if we were going to have a chance of survival, we must maintain a very strict discipline which must be rigidly and consistently enforced without any ifs and buts. This was very important, knowing that we would in the main be dealing with high spirited undergraduates. The regulations we wrote in 1929 are virtually the same as our current regulations. Having begun flying training in 1929, we have been fully responsible for all flying training at our Cambridge aerodrome to date, including throughout the war years. It must be one of the few places in the world which has such a continuous and uninterrupted record of flying training.

I think that largely because many senior members of the University became interested and had had some experience of flying with me or in Mr Simpson's aircraft, there were many who were for us rather than against us, including Mr A. S. F. Gow, a Tutor of Trinity. Mr Gow helped to get the University Edicts amended to provide for undergraduates being allowed to learn to fly, and went through his draft proposal with me in his Trinity rooms on Christmas Day 1929. This was approved by the Senate early in 1930.

Our first three pupils were Norman de Bruyne, Junior Bursar of Trinity and the inventor of Aerolite and Redux synthetic glues, Bill Humble, who became Hawker Siddeley's famous Chief Test Pilot during the war, and H. G. Barrington, who became a test pilot at de Havilland's, Hatfield, and then became the Percival Aircraft Company's Chief Test Pilot at Luton. Barrington was killed while test flying during the war. Until we became fully approved at the beginning of 1930, we were not allowed to send pupils on their first solo from our small Cambridge aerodrome. The first two to get their licences were Norman de Bruyne and Bill Humble and, when they were ready for their first solos towards the end of November, we flew to Mousehold, Norwich, with Grey and Norman de Bruyne in one machine and Humble and myself in the second. De Bruyne and Humble having completed their first solos at Norwich, we flew back to Cambridge. Humble and I took off shortly after Grey and de Bruyne and found it was getting dusk sooner than I anticipated and I felt that time was running against us. Humble was in the pilot's cockpit with all the instruments, including the compass. As the ground was looking black I assumed we were on the Ely side of Cambridge over fenland and told Humble to turn 90 degrees to the left. Fortunately Cambridge turned up within a few minutes. Bill Humble and I had not met since his Cambridge days until a chance meeting on the Hunstanton golf course in 1948. One of the first things he asked me was if I remembered when it was getting dark on our return from Norwich after his first solo and I told him to turn left – did I really know where we were? I said I hadn't a clue. It was something he had had in his mind all those years. Bill in recent years wrote, 'Indelibly imprinted is Norman de Bruyne over-shooting one day and brushing through the fence between the aerodrome and the paddock towards your house with your father watching the scene dressed in his stiff white collar and cravat looking very like a member of the cast of *The Forsyte Saga*'.

As soon as we had decided to open a flying school we had to consider what we were going to do about the name of our house, Aviation Hall. It was obvious that the name would attract all business enquiries. At about the same time my father received a letter from his school master friend, Harry Hodges, jokingly addressed to him at 'Motorman's Lodge, Newmarket Road, Cambridge' which did not amuse him. And so overnight we adopted the name of the farm we had bought for the landing field – Whitehill.

On Wednesday 11 December Norman de Bruyne and I flew in G-AAEH on a flight to Berlin and Dresden for five days, returning via Leipzig, Hanover and Dortmund. Whilst Norman and I were away, my father was asked by the Cambridge Town Football Club if there was any possibility of F. A. Ridgeon, the Club's Inside Left, travelling by air to Sussex for the FA Amateur Cup Tie with Southwick. My father made contact with de Havilland and obtained a pilot, who travelled to Cambridge and flew Ridgeon to Sussex in the Company's aircraft. The press reported: 'This is, as far as we have heard, the first time an amateur footballer has travelled to a match by air and the Town Club were very grateful to Mr Marshall for his generous action.' Cambridge won 2–0.

The garage had some benefit from our aviation activities. Whilst the garage provided potential flying pupils, we also obtained some new car sales from our flying contacts, and much time was saved by being able to fly and land in Austin's works. On looking back I am surprised I was never ticked off or banned from landing within the works during those inter-war years.

1929 had been an incredible year. From the purchase of my aeroplane and preparing a landing ground for it, we had progressed to an aerodrome open to the public and successfully launched a flying training school with Mr Grey responsible for the instructing – a responsibility he would relinquish in March, leaving the May term free to prepare for his examinations. The future of the flying training then depended on me qualifying for my commercial flying licence in time to take over all flying training responsibility, knowing that we could not possibly afford to employ a full-time flying instructor at this stage.

Chapter 9

A Critical Year

1930

MY FIRST CONCERN in 1930 was to qualify for my commercial pilot's licence which, as explained, was essential if our flying training was to continue beyond 30 March when Grey would no longer be available.

The 'B' Licence examination started at Northolt with a general flying test and a short cross-country flight with an RAF examiner in an RAF aircraft, followed by a short cross-country flight in my own aircraft. Having cleared these on 9 and 10 January, on 20 January I cleared my solo night-flying test from Croydon in the Company's aircraft G-EBYZ which was fitted with elementary night flying equipment – a red light on the left wing tip and green on the right, a white light on the tail and a small light on the instrument panel. The night flight test procedure was a few circuits and landings with a night flying instructor at Croydon and, if OK, to fly solo to and land at Penshurst, a very large field used as an aerodrome in both wars and maintained on a care and maintenance basis between the wars. The Penshurst caretaker put out goose-neck paraffin flares. The pupil took off from Croydon and landed at Penshurst, got his chit signed, and either stayed the night or flew back to Croydon, which is what I did. Grey gave me my night circuits and landings, plus a leisurely night flight round Croydon, and off I went solo to Penshurst and back. Grey had had five years in the RAF and a period as an instructor at de Havilland's RAFVR School at Stag Lane, but over dinner that night he told me he had never done any night-flying and wanted to see what it was like!

On 5 and 6 February I completed my two outstanding cross-country tests. The first test began with a specific minimum altitude flight from Croydon to Lympne with a recording barograph on board. It was a rough, blustery day with a low cloud base of overlapping cumulus clouds going up to an indefinite altitude. I climbed to my required minimum altitude but soon lost contact with the ground. Just as I was getting anxious and wondering if I should descend with the hope of identifying my position and getting into Lympne within the required time, a gap in the clouds appeared and there, in clear white letters spread across the aerodrome, was 'LYMPNE'. The next leg was to Bristol, where I was ticked off by Cyril Uwins, the Chief Flying Instructor of the Bristol Company's RAFVR Flying School, later a great friend but on this, our first meeting, furious as I had taxied up on the wrong side of a pegged off area of grass which had just been re-seeded. My second solo cross-country test was from Croydon and included a landing at Stag Lane.

My commercial licence was issued on Wednesday 5th March, and on the same day I gave my first 40 minutes flying instruction for 'hire and reward'. Apart from the help I had from Clem Pike on two or three Sundays during the summer term of 1930, I carried out all the flying instruction after Grey ceased operations in March. The university terms were the busiest times for both the garage and flying training. My days were planned on a seven day week from 8.30 a.m. to 7 p.m. in the winter and later in the summer, with my weekday flying activity in the afternoons in the winter and in the evenings in the summer. Saturday was our busiest day at the garage and I was there all day. In term-time there was always a big congestion of cars to be dealt with early every Sunday morning. Cars which had come in late were left at all angles. A general tidy up was necessary to make sure that those cars required early could get away without too much delay. After this, from 9.30 a.m. I was flying all day on Sundays.

At the beginning of the year Udny Yule, the St John's statistician, began flying instruction. He was over 60 and looked somewhat older. In the air he was very good indeed, but the approach and landing speed of the Moth was just too fast for him. I suggested that if he had a German Klemm with a 50 hp Salmson radial engine, which had an approach and landing speed about 12 mph slower than the Moth, he would have a good chance of getting his pilot's licence and would have a few years enjoyable flying. We got him a very good one for £325 and sent him off solo without any problems, and he was soon giving his friends flights. He thoroughly enjoyed the aircraft for a few years.

During the war years, when Udny Yule was confined to his room towards the end of his life, I used to go and see him from time to time. On one occasion he pulled out his private pilot's licence and said, 'Hearing all these bombers overhead at night, going off on their bombing raids, I often show this licence to my friends.' It read 'Udny Yule, licensed to fly all types of aircraft day and night.'

Looking back now I realise how history repeated itself. Just as my father had sold his car hire and cars to members of the Pitt Club in his Pitt days, and this was the key to immediate success, so I in turn sold flying training and flights to garage customers: undergraduates, Dons, and elderly ladies were all potential flyers. My flying philosophy for air taxi work was that, if a customer wanted to go anywhere by air, even if I had never been there before, I would always assume that I could find somewhere to land. As it happened I do not think I ever failed, and now I think I was not just lucky but extremely lucky. We were progressively allowed to land on many racecourses.

To save time at the aerodrome we made the garage the focal point for joining the Flying School, and equipping new pupils with carefully fitted helmets, earphones and goggles. The fitting of the helmet with the earphones positively positioned over each ear was all important to prevent a rush of air into the helmet making it difficult to hear the instructor through the intercommunications speaking tube. A correctly fitted helmet saved many hours of instruction and much frustration. We did not want the trouble of handling cash at the aerodrome (in those days there was no worry about it being pinched) and we sold numbered tickets at Jesus Lane for half-hour flying lessons. The charge for dual and solo flying was 30 shillings an hour. I assumed that the average person who could drive a motor car reasonably well could learn to fly an aircraft and I do not remember any failures.

It was important for the pupil to be sitting at the right height to see forward over the side of the cockpit without straining, which sometimes required one or two extra cushions. This made all the difference to final approach and landing and reduced the instruction time to first solo. After the first lesson, I made the pupil responsible for having the right cushions ready to get into the aircraft without any delay between lessons. Time was always short and the booked flying instruction time included time for pupils to get in and out of the aircraft. The engine was kept running between lessons, with the instructor remaining in the aircraft. The ground engineer would book the time for the next lesson.

I soon found that pupils learning to fly from a small aerodrome such as ours had big advantages. They took no longer to go solo or obtain their licences than those learning on larger aerodromes. They had learnt in this environment from their first lesson and it all came quite naturally to them, with the result that they could land on any aerodrome without difficulty. Learning to fly on a small aerodrome gave pupils greater confidence to face emergency landings.

I remember one casual visitor who asked if he could have an aeroplane and said he had done 70 hours flying. I said yes but he would have to have a dual circuit and landing first, explaining that this was necessary, apart from anything else, to cover our insurances. He was rather put out but he finally agreed. We were very strict about this. In the end he had two hours dual before he could land on our small aerodrome.

The Cambridge University Air Squadron was formed on 1 October 1925 with Town Headquarters in a hut at the University Engineering Laboratories, Scroope House, and started flying at RAF Duxford in February 1926 with two Avro 504K and one Bristol Fighter. Undergraduate Squadron members were not allowed to fly solo at any time. This restriction was amended in 1930 to allow undergraduates to undertake their first solo at the Squadron Summer Camp. Some members came to us, often with their Duxford instructor, to achieve their first solo during the term and get a flying start for the anticipated first solo at the Squadron Summer Camp.

Later the regulations were further relaxed allowing Squadron members to undertake their first solo during the university term at Duxford.

I had no ambitions to take part in air racing but thought that, as part of my flying education, if the opportunity occurred I would like to have at least one experience of a race. The King's Cup, which in those days was a flight round part of England, seemed ideal as compared with short closed circuit races. It was an eight or nine hour race at full throttle and at low altitude. Flying at full throttle was not very good for the engine but it so happened that the engine of our Gipsy Moth G-EBYZ was due for a complete overhaul by the end of the summer. I was not worried under the circumstances about flogging our engine round the course and decided to have a go and take my sister Margery as my passenger.

G-EBYZ, the 1928 winner, was a standard machine except for the faired-in top and bottom fittings of the inter-wing struts and, for the air race, the removal of the exhaust pipe and silencer and the fitting of exhaust stubs. One also played about with propellers to try to find a propeller which gave an extra mile or so per hour. I used to stop-watch time the aircraft with different propellers fitted over a measured mile along the very straight railway line north of the aerodrome between Waterbeach and Ely.

The handicappers, who were becoming very skilled, inspected all aircraft the day before the race. The race started and finished at Hanworth Park, a few miles south of Airworks' Heston Aerodrome, the main private owners' flying centre for London.

I decided on a trial flight round the King's Cup course starting from Hanworth Park with intermediate turning points and landings at Bristol, Manchester and Hull. On Saturday 29 June I set out and stayed the night at Manchester, planning to complete the course on Sunday. On Sunday morning I could not start the engine because the impulse magneto failed. The aircraft had two magnetos, one fitted with an impulse unit having a flick-spring mechanism which, when turning over the engine by hand, delayed the turning of the magneto and held back the spark until the spring flicked and provided a strong spark, as it would do if the engine was running. No replacement impulse unit was available at Manchester, so I persuaded an onlooker with a Morris Cowley car to let me connect one of the ignition leads from his car to one of the aircraft sparking plugs and, with the car engine running, pulled over the propeller and, after a few pulls, I was lucky and the engine started. I kept the engine running and flew back to Cambridge. It was only the impulse unit of the magneto which had failed and so, with the engine started, I was flying on two magnetos. The impulse magneto was changed at Cambridge on the Sunday morning and I flew back to Manchester and completed the course that day, arriving back at Cambridge after eight-and-a-quarter hours flying. The idea of starting an aircraft engine from a motor car when the impulse magneto failed was instantaneous. I have never heard of anybody else trying this, except Leslie Worsdell, of whom more later. Leslie had an impulse magneto failure, having flown Lord Milford to

Llanstephan in Wales in our Puss Moth, and carried out the same exercise with success.

There was nothing particularly eventful about the race itself except that, although the aircraft were started at intervals based on handicap times, they progressively closed up until they were very much bunched together. At Hull it was quite frightening, with all fighting to get refuelled, and aircraft taxiing out with wings almost overlapping. If you found you had got to the take-off point, you took off regardless of whether you were being signalled off or not. There were 101 entrants and, of these, 88 started at Hanworth and 60 finished – the biggest field for the King's Cup Race to date. We were 35th with a speed of 101.1 mph. Winifred Brown in an Avro Avian Cirrus III was the winner at an average speed of 102.7 mph.

It is only in recent years that I have learnt that Margery suffered agony in the front cockpit from fumes coming from the exhaust stubs. I well remember suffering similarly from exhaust fumes when giving instruction from the front cockpit whenever there was a slight leak from a cracked exhaust manifold, which was a common problem. The fumes were strongest with the engine throttled back during the approach. Half an hour's flying instruction with three or four circuits would include three or four approaches. This discomfort was eliminated with the introduction of the Gipsy III inverted engine with the exhaust at the bottom.

During the year the Company bought a further second-hand Gipsy Moth for training purposes as we gradually got more pupils going solo, and this enabled solo flying and dual instruction to proceed concurrently.

The twenties and thirties was a depressed period for the UK which was still recovering from the war. America had not suffered from the big over-seas war debts that the UK had incurred and was making a more rapid recovery until the devastating Wall Street collapse in October 1929. Except for a few individual cases, this did not affect the UK in the same alarming way but it slowed down the nation's recovery. The biggest ripples from the Wall Street Crash reached this country during 1930.

Our most direct experience was that the six or so private owners we had accumulated in less than 12 months decreased to three by the end of 1930. We had earlier in the year built a new workshop hangar 60 feet wide by 40 feet deep which was now no longer required. Mr Wheeler, a wealthy undergraduate, had ordered a Gipsy II Moth and an expensive Invicta motor car for delivery on his return from America at the end of the summer. In July he sent us a cable from America stating that things were much worse than he had expected, as far as his own American finances were concerned, and cancelling both his Moth aircraft and Invicta car.

As many of their passengers were Americans, Continental Motorways were seriously affected by the Wall Street Crash, and during the year ran into financial problems. They finally went bust owing us £1,500 – a considerable sum in those days. It was no use having any recriminations and I remember my father and I giving Mr Lyons, the Continental Motorways Managing

Director, lunch at the Trocadero in Shaftesbury Avenue. With the termination of the Continental Motorways coach tours and the garage space taken by the coaches now being required for general garage use, we ceased coach operations.

I had met Rosemary Dimsdale a few times as a garage customer. Rosemary finished her education at Somerville, Oxford, in June 1930. At Oxford she had had an Austin Seven, and she and her mother thought they would now like something a bit bigger. I tried to sell them an Austin Ten or Twelve but Rosemary had set her heart on a new Wolseley Hornet, a very lively 12 hp, six-cylinder car which had just come on the market. I did all I could to dissuade her but she would not be put off. Saint's in Regent Street near the Catholic Church were the Wolseley agents and I took Rosemary to pick up Saint's demonstration car for a trial run. Rosemary finally had her way, and a Wolseley was ordered. As a result of these meetings and the Wolseley trial run, I started to think more about Rosemary and made up my mind that she was someone it was really worth getting to know. She had a lovely sense of humour, was tall and slim with classical features, quietly elegant, and always looked the part whatever the occasion. But Rosemary was a shy person and so was I. Then I had a brilliant idea and suggested to Rosemary and her mother that they should have a flight. This invitation was accepted and they had their flight on Sunday afternoon, 14 July, which they enjoyed.

I then suggested that Rosemary should learn to fly. I was a little worried about this suggestion as I knew Mrs Dimsdale, a widow, was not too flush with money and Rosemary had just started to earn her living writing fly leaves for new books at Jonathan Cape, the publishers in London. She had a small flat at 4A Duke Street, Marylebone. Rosemary enjoyed her trial lesson and finally decided to go ahead, returning to Cambridge most weekends for a lesson. I was not very pleased when she missed the odd weekend. During the summer I took Rosemary to a Norwich Aero Club 'At Home', where Alan Cobham was helping with joy-riding, and I went in for the balloon bursting competition. Later Norman de Bruyne, with my sister Margery as passenger, and I in a second machine, with Rosemary as passenger, flew to a luncheon given by Lindsay Everard MP in his hangar at his private aerodrome at Radlett, Leicester, in honour of Amy Johnson, who had just returned from her famous flight to Australia in a Moth in 15 days. Lindsay Everard was a great aviation enthusiast and kept his own private twin-engined, six-seater de Havilland Dragon and had his own personal pilot.

The Heacham holiday again extended into September and Norman de Bruyne joined us for two nights, flying down in his Moth. In those days we had quite a menagerie around the bungalow – a pony tethered out, the sand-yacht, an aeroplane, and on this occasion two aeroplanes, plus an old car which with great excitement we just managed, with much pushing and pulling, to get through a stream at low tide. We kept the car for transport to and from the small footbridge half a mile from the bungalow.

On 8 September my father and I were flying from Heacham to the Austin Works, when in the Rugby area we had a sudden engine failure. We landed in a field under some high tension cables. I found a bolt holding No. 3 cylinder valve rocker bracket had broken. I got a bolt which would fit from the local blacksmith and, having fitted it, I ran up the engine against the telescopic chocks and we took off under the high tension cables and completed the journey to Austins. My father was quite unconcerned, except to ask from time to time whilst I was fitting the bolt, 'How much longer are we going to be?' I think my father must have thought that flying was just like those early motoring days so well depicted by that music hall song of the early part of the century:

> A dozen times they'd start to hug and kiss
> And then the darn old engine it would miss.
> And he'd have to get under,
> Get out and get under,
> And fix up his automobile.

By September I felt it was time to stir things up and I told Rosemary I had a meeting in London on 11 September (log book record) and asked her if she would like to fly with me to London via Stag Lane and Burnt Oak tube station, have lunch and fly back? This was accepted. Rosemary and I well remembered walking from Stag Lane to Burnt Oak station and me suggesting that, if she enjoyed the day, we might do it again some time – 'All like having a game of squash, you know.' Of course I had no business engagement, but we split up and arranged to meet at one o'clock at the Trocadero, Shaftesbury Avenue. Rosemary had fillet of plaice and tartare sauce with chipped potatoes, which I soon came to learn was one of her favourite dishes.

Rosemary got her pilot's licence and did sufficient flying each year to keep it valid up to the outbreak of war. Her last solo flight was in one of our new Moth Minor monoplane aircraft which we collected from Hatfield in July 1939.

Civil aviation suffered an irredeemable blow with the death of Sir Sefton Brancker when the R101 airship crashed into high ground at Beauvais in bad weather and low cloud on 5 October 1930. The airship crash had a fundamental effect upon the future of civil aviation, in which it hitherto seemed probable that airships would play an important part in providing the best means of operating long distance commercial routes. As a result of this disaster the R100 was scrapped the following year and the development of airships in the United Kingdom abandoned indefinitely.

In May, Norman de Bruyne had bought a new Gipsy Moth G-AAWN and within weeks decided to design and build his own aircraft. He rented our new workshop hangar, now empty as a result of the Wall Street Crash. His aircraft took four years to build and turned out to be a remarkable machine.

A Mr Armitage completed his flying training and ordered one of the new de Havilland Puss Moths, a high wing, three-seater cabin monoplane with a Gipsy III engine of 120 hp, with a cruising speed of 102 mph and two 17½ gallon fuel tanks. One could get three hours flying out of one wing tank before changing over to the other, giving a range in still air, and without any reserve, of 600 miles. The price, fully equipped, was £1,275. I came to a financial arrangement with him to use his aircraft whilst it was at Cambridge.

During the October term I taught a Mr Salem, an undergraduate at Magdalene College, to fly. He was said to be a wealthy Egyptian whose family was in cotton in a big way. During the term he developed an ambition to be the first Egyptian to fly from England to Egypt and, as he became quite serious about this, we decided he had better have some special training for such a flight.

As part of this training, we flew from Cambridge on 12 December to Amsterdam, and on the next day to Ostend and Brussels and the following day to Paris, and then returned to Brussels. On Monday 15 December, flying from Brussels back to Cambridge, the weather was very bad with low cloud and we crossed the Channel at not more than 50 feet, but could not get into Lympne and landed on a playing field at a girls' school in Folkestone. We were pleased to be down, and anxious to ring Lympne because we had landed without Customs clearance. The headmistress, not concerned about our worries, insisted that I should first give a lecture on flying to the mistresses and girls standing round the aeroplane. The field was too small for take-off with two-up plus baggage, so the next morning I flew to Lympne, and Salem and the baggage went by taxi. We agreed to work out a plan for his flight to Cairo in the Easter vacation.

My sister Violet was at St Croix School near Lausanne in Switzerland, including for Christmas, and so on Saturday 27 December my father and I set off for Switzerland in Mr Armitage's Puss Moth, G-ABEM, but ran into very bad weather after refuelling at Paris. Having made two or three attempts to get through the weather, we returned to Paris, left the machine at Le Bourget and my father and I proceeded by train. Tubby Davis had planned to join us there and arrived at Violet's school the previous day, but was not allowed to take Violet out until her father arrived.

A lucky year with everything still run on a shoe-string but with the feeling that flying had an unlimited horizon, and we had survived so far. We had no anticipation of the eventful year which lay ahead.

Chapter 10

An Eventful Year
1931

MY FATHER AND I returned from our visit to Violet in Switzerland on 5 January and my mother died on 10 January, aged 52.

This was a colossal loss to all of us, and there was a gradual appreciation as the days went by of the big, and now sole, responsibility my father had for the upbringing of six very good-looking girls between four and 23 years of age – from Brenda, the baby, to Margery, the eldest – progressive stages of education, working careers, boyfriends and future possible marriages. One big asset was that my mother and father between them had established a sound foundation – a well-disciplined and close-knit family. Of course my sisters were very much involved with domestic responsibilities. From this sad and devastating moment my father quite deliberately treated the welfare and upbringing of the girls as his first priority and did all he could to ensure that there was never a dull moment. Rex Woods, our family doctor, was a tower of strength.

This is an opportune time to state what my six sisters were doing. Margery was my most excellent secretary, was responsible for the Flying School books and also acted as telephone operator. She was a great help and a very good friend in times of stress. Dorothy had completed her physical training course at Liverpool and was Games Mistress at Tormead Girls' School, Guildford. Violet completed her education in Switzerland and took over responsibility for running Whitehill at the age of 18. She also took part-time coaching for secretarial work to be a stand-in for Margery. Mary was at Paston House in Bateman Street. My father thought she ought to go to a boarding school, either Violet's school in Switzerland or the Convent of the Sacred Heart at Brighton. Mary chose the latter. Molly continued at Paston House for a time and then went as a boarder to Slepe Hall, St Ives. Brenda, aged four, was looked after by a governess, Miss Collins.

As a result of our experience with Mr Armitage's Puss Moth, we ordered a similar aircraft for air taxi work, which I collected from Stag Lane on 21 March 1931 – G-ABIZ. The Puss Moth had been a revelation – an overnight transfer from the open cockpit of a training aircraft to a three-seater heated cabin with comparative silence, a good cruising speed and, for those days, a very long range. The next day I flew the Puss Moth to Lausanne to collect Violet on completion of her education.

The flight of Salem, the Egyptian, to Cairo was planned for the Easter vacation. I insisted that before he left for Egypt he paid all that he owed and the total cost of the hire of the aircraft to Cairo and back. He had always paid to date, and I was foolish enough to accept a cheque at seven o'clock in the morning on the day of his departure – the cheque bounced! After a week we got a letter from Paris saying there might be a problem with the cheque but, if we re-presented it, he was sure it would be all right.

Salem was in fact the first Egyptian to fly to Egypt from England. He was fêted as a hero, with a big press coverage, and received many presents including gold wrist watches. Having taken 10 days to fly out to Cairo, there was not time for him to fly back to England for the beginning of the university summer term and so he came back by boat and train and shipped the aircraft to Marseilles, and we collected it.

The Egyptian Ambassador gave a dinner in his honour at the University Arms, where I had to say a few words in spite of the fact that we had still received no money. Subsequently I met the Ambassador in London but he could do nothing to help. A very big depression had developed in Egypt and the cotton trade was very badly hit.

On Tuesday 14 April I flew to RAF Bircham Newton in Norfolk, a few miles from Ringstead Mill, where Mrs Dimsdale and her family were staying, and that evening I told Mrs Dimsdale I would like to talk about Rosemary. Mrs Dimsdale replied that she wished I would. I said we were considering getting engaged but had no plans for getting married immediately. We talked about the possible future and, as I always do, I talked in the context of planning for the worst and hoping for the best. I told her that I realised this would be a big change for Rosemary – a complete overnight change to the cold world of trade and commerce from the close academic society and environment in which she had been brought up and had lived. On Wednesday 15 April Rosemary and I decided to get engaged.

The next day Rosemary took me back to Bircham Newton for my flight back to Cambridge. The weather was bad, with low cloud and mist coming in from the sea. The mist increased and visibility decreased almost as I taxied. Having taken off, I wished I had not, but could not get back into Bircham Newton and finally got on top of the cloud and all was clear at Cambridge. Rosemary returned to Cambridge on Friday 17 April and we bought the engagement ring.

On the Saturday I wore some plus fours, which Rosemary took an instant dislike to – so much so that she broke off the engagement there and then – just like that. (Today, when I see plus fours on the TV I am immediately reminded of P. G. Wodehouse's Bertie Wooster – so perhaps Rosemary had a point.)

On the Sunday we argued.

On Monday I met Rosemary and said all this was taking up too much time and was interfering with my work and we must get it finally settled one way or the other that day. Rosemary went into solitary meditation for an hour in Comberton Wood, and the result of all this was a decision that there should be no more messing about and we should get married immediately. Wilfrid, Rosemary's brother, and his wife Helen having paved the way by getting married at Marylebone Register Office the year before, we got a licence on Monday afternoon to be married at Marylebone Town Hall on Wednesday afternoon at three o'clock.

On Tuesday I got cold feet and said I thought we ought to delay things. Rosemary was not having any. Rosemary's Welsh obstinate streak came into full play. She said no, we had made up our minds and, come what may, we were jolly well going through with it – and that was that. Rosemary's mother – her father had died in 1919 – and my father had not a clue of what had been going on since our engagement. That evening Rosemary told her mother who, to say the least, was not very pleased. With my father away racing at Newbury, I told my sisters what was happening. They were all very worried and insisted, quite rightly, that I must make sure my father knew all about this before the wedding.

And so at 8.15 a.m. on our wedding day, Wednesday 22 April, I telephoned my father with the girls in the morning room listening with bated breath to hear what happened. My father was horrified but finally accepted the position that we were getting married at three o'clock, and we arranged that Rosemary and I would meet him off his train from London at 6.30 p.m. after the wedding. After the 'phone call to my father I went to the garage for an hour and then did an air taxi trip to Nottingham. In the meantime Rosemary had not been idle. She suddenly realised she had not done anything about a trousseau, so she shot into Cambridge on a shopping spree and bought three things – a new sponge, a toothbrush and a pair of pyjamas.

At one o'clock I collected Rosemary from her mother's flat in Huntingdon Road. We flew in the Puss Moth to de Havilland's aerodrome at Stag Lane, almost in the centre of London. We had a Daimler car waiting for us and drove straight to Marylebone Town Hall where we were married. Our witnesses included Norman de Bruyne, who was best man, and my old friend Frank Morrell. After the ceremony we all bundled out of Marylebone Town Hall – we had made no plans but thought a cup of tea might be a good idea – so we all got into the Daimler and motored round London trying to find somewhere for a cup of tea, and finished up at the Piccadilly.

We flew back to Cambridge and first went to Rosemary's mother's flat to make our peace with her. I corrected the proof of an article I had written for a University paper, which Rosemary re-typed, and we then went to the station to meet my father and made our peace with him and took him home to Whitehill.

Then we thought we had better find somewhere for the night, and we finished up at the Rutland Arms, Newmarket.

The intention was to go back to work the next day but we were told we must have a day or two's holiday, and so we flew to Heston for lunch. Rosemary had her fried fish and tartare sauce and we then flew on to Teignmouth for the night – a champagne dinner, followed by our first Ginger Rogers film.

On Friday 24 April we flew back to Cambridge and back to work, and on the Sunday I did an hour in the garage and then three-and-a-half hours flying instruction. A pilot's log book is a very good diary – certainly one of the first things you must do if you ever commit a crime is to destroy your log book.

When we got back to Cambridge we had nowhere to go and stayed for a few nights at the Blue Boar, Trinity Street. Norman de Bruyne came to the rescue as Junior Bursar of Trinity – he made a set of his undergraduate Trinity lodgings at 56 Chesterton Road available to us. My father thought the undergraduate rooms were not suitably furnished for a young married couple and sent in some furniture, including a very large double bed and the largest double wardrobe you can possibly imagine. Our lodging house-keepers were Mr and Mrs Thurston, known as 'Daddy' and 'Sweetheart'.

The following is the *Cambridge Daily News* report of the wedding:

ROMANCE OF THE AIR
HONEYMOON FLIGHT OF CAMBRIDGE BLUE AND HIS BRIDE

A thrill of romance marked the departure from Marshall's aerodrome to-day of a gleaming silver Puss Moth monoplane, bearing its bridegroom pilot and his bride on the first stage of their honeymoon.

Mr and Mrs Marshall, despite the spectacular nature of their departure from home to-day, manage to do most things quietly. Their take-off from the flying ground was unwitnessed except by the ground engineer and two *Cambridge Daily News* representatives. It was past 12.30 when they appeared from the bridegroom's father's house, near the aerodrome, each carrying a suitcase. The last thing one would have imagined was that this newly-married pair were about to begin a flight, eventually to an unknown destination. Her fair hair fluttering in the breeze, the bride was wearing a green coat, suitable for motoring, and light shoes and stockings. Her husband had a mackintosh over a sports coat and flannel trousers, and he threw a soft hat into the back of his handsome little Moth.

'Is your destination a secret,' asked our reporting representative, 'or may the *Cambridge Daily News* know something of your plans?' Mr Marshall smiled as his wife shyly entered the monoplane. 'I would tell you with plea-sure,' he said, 'but we don't know where we're going – and that's the truth. Anyhow, we propose to have lunch first.' 'That's just like him,' interjected the ground engineer, preparing to start the engine.

Mr Marshall, without more ado, took his seat at the controls, the propeller whirred, and the graceful machine glided forward. In the next few seconds it was rising steeply into the wind, while rain fell from a heavy cloud.

The bridal couple, however, were quite cosy in the saloon cockpit. The ground engineer observed the position of the monoplane a minute or two later. 'That's Stag Lane all right,' he remarked laconically. 'If we're not quick they'll be having lunch in London before we get ours. He can do 120 miles an hour.'

Of all my lucky breaks in life, Rosemary was the luckiest. My father had often advised that it was important to marry somebody better than yourself. I do not know exactly what he meant by 'better', but whatever it was I soon found out that as a matter of luck I must have exceeded his specification. Rosemary was somebody to work for, which for me has always been an important incentive in life. My two basic incentives have been my family and Cambridge. The fact that my wife and I were born in Cambridge has always been of considerable importance to me – I do like roots, and long-term roots.

Later in life I have come to realise that I have never valued anything unless I had to work hard for it. Opportunities were served up on a plate but, having recognised an opportunity, whatever was achieved was only achieved by very hard work. It was good for both of us that Rosemary married me with no financial backing, to the extent that when we were married her Uncle Dick (Sir Laurence Philipps) cut off the £120 a year allowance which had made all the difference to her life at Oxford and since.

Marriage to Rosemary was the most wonderful thing to happen throughout my life. All that has been achieved over the years has only been possible as a result of her dedicated support. Rosemary always remembered the advice of her Aunt Ethel, wife of Uncle Dick, who told her that, in making their way in life, she had always put her husband first in all things and went with him anywhere at any time. Aunt Ethel was the daughter of a clergyman and a descendant of John Hanning Speke, who discovered the source of the Nile at Lake Victoria in 1862.

As far as our parents were concerned, it is hard to define their respective attitudes. I would say that my father, now a widower, and Mrs Dimsdale, a widow for some years, were not one hundred per cent for or against our marriage. My father I think was worried that my attitude to work and days of work might change. Mrs Dimsdale would have preferred to have seen Rosemary marry a budding Don or a Lord rather than the son of a self-made Cambridge tradesman.

Mrs Dimsdale suggested that my father should make a marriage settlement on Rosemary, and this really infuriated him. Mrs Dimsdale then enlisted the help of her brother Dick to persuade my father. Rosemary and I had dinner with Sir Laurence at his home at Dalham, and after dinner we had a very friendly and frank talk. I explained that I owed everything to my parents and that we had not got any money, and even if we had, I would not think of supporting any such suggestion as the proposed marriage settlement. This meeting resulted in a life-long friendship.

The initial family relationship with Mrs Dimsdale was further aggravated by the *Daily Express* photograph of Rosemary and me getting into the

Puss Moth at Stag Lane after the wedding, with Rosemary referred to as 'Miss Dinsdale'. Mrs Dimsdale thought my father had engineered this, but I am quite sure this was not so. Anyway, Mrs Dimsdale retaliated with all guns firing with the following announcement in *The Times*:

INTERESTING WEDDING
MARSHALL-DIMSDALE
The marriage of Arthur Gregory George Marshall, only son of Mr D. G. Marshall, Whitehill, Fen Ditton and Rosemary Wynford Dimsdale, second (twin) daughter of the late Marcus Dimsdale and Mrs Marcus Dimsdale, NIAB, Cambridge, and granddaughter of the Sixth Baron Dimsdale, took place very quietly in London on Wednesday. Mr Arthur Marshall is the well-known Cambridge Running Blue and Director of the Cambridge Flying School, and Miss Rosemary Dimsdale is the niece of Viscount St David's, General Sir Ivor Philipps KCB, Lord Kylsant and Sir Laurence Philipps, Bart.

When I got married I had no idea that Rosemary was a member of such illustrious families. Rosemary's mother was a daughter of the Reverend Canon Sir James Erasmus Philipps, Bt. He was not well off – his sons went to Felstead School and made their own individual ways in life.

I knew nothing of my future mother-in-law other than meeting her, Rosemary and her son Wilfrid as garage customers from time to time. I was soon to learn that she had achieved much in life. Jessie Stewart, her life-long friend, wrote of her:

She took a First Class Honours Degree in History at Somerville, Oxford in 1895 and was the first woman to hold a Research Fellowship at Cambridge and an early Fellow of Newnham College. The students called her 'The Phoenix', she was indeed a *rara avis* among Newnham dons – brilliant, gay, dominant, rather arrogant. She moved in the most intellectual university circles and her friends included the W. N. Whiteheads, Bertrand Russells, Frederick Myers and Jebbs.

In the First World War Mrs Dimsdale became an Assistant Director of Milk Supplies at the Ministry of Health. For many years she was a member of the Cambridgeshire County Council and served on a number of local committees. Her greatest achievement was her work for Papworth Tuberculosis Hospital, of which she was a co-founder.

A formidable mother-in-law but, once the dust had settled, a good friend throughout life who would do anything for us and our family.

Rosemary's father, Marcus Dimsdale, the son of Robert the Sixth Baron Dimsdale, was a fine Classics scholar and Fellow of King's, held in great affection by his many friends. He had an extraordinary knowledge and love of country life and with his friends explored Cambridgeshire on horseback. During World War I he was for a time a Classics Master at Winchester. A distant cousin, the Right Honourable Sir Joseph Dimsdale, Bt., KCVO, MP, Lord Mayor of London 1901–2, claimed that the family was able to trace its roots back to William the Conqueror. The more recent history of the Dimsdale family stems from the barony granted to Dr Thomas Dimsdale, Rosemary's great-grandfather seven generations back, by the Czarina of Russia following his hazardous trip to Russia in 1768 at the invitation of Catherine the Great to inoculate her and her son, Grand Duke Paul, against smallpox. The Russians had a team of horses standing by for his escape if the inoculation went wrong, but all was well.

Rosemary could not have had a more intensely academic life. Her godfather was Dr Monty James, Headmaster and Provost of Eton and Provost of King's 1905–1918. She knew nobody outside the University. Our marriage pitched her into a commercial tradesmen's environment, which she quickly adjusted to, but it was for her a traumatic change.

In June – the university term over and having missed our honeymoon in April – we took the Puss Moth to Switzerland, staying the first night at Ostend and flying on to Zurich and Chur the next day, where we landed on a Swiss Air Force relief landing ground which I had landed on in my Gipsy Moth in September 1929; but there was a difference. In September 1929 the grass had all been cut, but in June 1931 the grass was growing. We went by train from Chur to Pontresina, but became increasingly worried about having left the aircraft picketed out in an isolated area with nobody about and the grass getting longer every day. We were anxious about the effect of the long grass on our take-off and spent much of our time ringing the Commandant. Rosemary had to do most of the talking as, having an Honours Degree at Oxford in Italian, she was the better linguist. We kept asking the Commandant when he was going to cut the grass but could get no clear reply. We went round in circles until it finally emerged that he had no responsibility for cutting the grass as the area was let in small plots to individual peasants who cut the grass at their own personal convenience.

We finally decided to cut short the holiday by two days and went to Chur to pick up the aeroplane. All was well with the aircraft, which was still picketed out and not a soul in sight. The grass was getting long and beginning to seed but I thought we would just about make it. We took off and, immediately after take-off, there was a smell of burning and the carpet round the cabin hot air intake was smouldering, and sparks were blowing into the cabin. I landed as quickly as possible and found that grass seed had entered the cabin heating air intake fitted under the exhaust pipe to provide air to a manifold surrounding the exhaust silencer which heated the air for direct entry into the cabin. We had taken off with the hot air intake partially open as we anticipated flying between six to eight thousand feet and would require some cabin heating. Having made sure that the intake was one hundred per cent closed, we tried again and all was well. This experience resulted in Puss Moth cabin heating air intakes being relocated on top of the exhaust pipe with a filter fitted. Rosemary, who up to then had seen no fear in flying whatsoever, never again felt quite the same, although she flew with me over the years through thick and thin in all weathers without question. It is one of those things which I often quote – until you have personally experienced wind, fire and water out of control, it is hard to imagine how frightening and final they can be.

Whilst in Pontresina, Rosemary had not felt too well and we thought it was perhaps the altitude. Having left Pontresina, we stayed for a couple of nights at Interlaken but she still did not feel too good, and when we got home it was confirmed that she was pregnant. In July we moved to the annexe of Professor Cornford's house at Conduit Head, Madingley Road. This was a great success and, with our first child expected early in the new year, made all the difference to Rosemary's life.

In November Rosemary and I flew for the first time to stay with Uncle Dick and Aunt Ethel at their beautiful home at Llanstephan near Brecon, and landed in one of their fields not far from the house. The comment in my log book is 'Terrible weather conditions'. They were to do much flying with us in the future, often to Llanstephan.

Flying training with some air taxi work continued to make steady progress. By now I had come to realise that flying training and aircraft maintenance was not something which could be treated as a hobby. One had to be completely and deeply involved to have any chance of success. Flying instructors in general were averaging about 250 hours instruction a year and I, part-time but including Sundays, was knocking up 500 hours a year and knew from personal experience that it would be no hardship for full-time instructors to fly considerably more than this.

In 1928 the basic seed had been sown when I ordered my aircraft. As a result of all that developed from the chance meeting in 1929 with the Reverend Simpson and through him the Trinity College contacts, we had achieved within three years what otherwise would have been a long and very expensive slog. Everything developed so quickly and naturally that there was never time to appreciate or consider where the cumulative effect of these happenings might lead if the luck held.

Chapter 11

A Good Apprenticeship
1932–1937

THE FIRST EXCITEMENT in 1932 was Michael being born at 3.30 p.m. on Wednesday 27 January at the Brunswick Nursing Home, a few yards from where our garage was established.

Rosemary rang me at the garage at 11.30 a.m. and said she was not feeling well and would I come home. I spoke to Rex Woods who said he thought she was all right, and the baby was not due for at least another three weeks, so I went back to the garage. I returned home for lunch to find Rosemary still worried, and again I spoke to Rex, who decided that as a precautionary measure she should go into the Brunswick Nursing Home. I had flying instruction booked for the afternoon, so I dropped Rosemary off at the Nursing Home and proceeded to the aerodrome. When I landed at four o'clock, Honour, the Ground Engineer, came out and told me I had a son. At the Nursing Home I found Rosemary in good form and very pleased. I saw Michael for the first time and was horrified at the Easter egg shape of his head, but was assured this was fairly common for first babies and that all would settle down in a few days.

My father and my sisters were all delighted, as were the Dimsdales, but one slight problem rippled the waters for a short time. All my sisters thought they had some claim on Michael, which Rosemary resented. This is something my sisters understood when they married and had their own families, and they often laughed about it over the years – but at the time Rosemary wanted Michael to herself and resented the demands for pushing him out in his pram, and being expected to take him to Whitehill every Sunday for lunch whilst I was giving flying instruction.

Michael was christened in Jesus College Chapel by the Dean, the Revd Gardner-Smith. Norman de Bruyne was Michael's godfather, and after the christening we had tea in my old friend Alan Pars' rooms.

Some years previously I had purchased St Margaret's, 95 Milton Road, pressurised by my father on his principle that you should never consider getting married until you had 'a roof over your head'. In 1932 the tenancy expired and Rosemary and I moved in. We were very lucky with domestic help. It was difficult to obtain good living-in help, and Mrs Dimsdale went with Rosemary to Collins's Employment Agency. Just as they were getting in their car to drive away disappointed, Mrs Dimsdale saw somebody about to go into the agency and rushed up and said, 'Excuse me, are you looking for a job?' This resulted in engaging Dorothy Deer who was with us for over 30 years, including throughout the war years when she worked part-time in our Works Canteen.

In July 1932 Rosemary and I for the first time flew to the south of France for a two week holiday. Lady Philipps, Rosemary's Aunt Ethel, had offered Rosemary the use of a house in the grounds of their villa 'La Primavera' at St Jean, Cap Ferrat. The villa is situated on its own private peninsula with an old world garden; a unique and beautiful site. We had all our meals at a café overlooking St Jean Harbour run by a very pleasant Belgian family. At breakfast we ordered what we wanted for lunch and dinner, all at a charge of 10/6d. for the day. When they gave us the bill they had not included the drinks and insisted that the 10/6d. charge was inclusive of drinks. Unfortunately after two years they went bust.

These happy, sunny holidays in the south of France became an annual pilgrimage from 1932 to 1938. For these flights, depending on the weather and time of day, we refuelled at Le Bourget, Dijon or Lyons. The journeys were very routine, but I do remember that in 1933 on the return journey we landed at Le Bourget with a low cloud base, and it was reported that the weather in England was bad but said to be improving. I met the captain of an Imperial Airways Hannibal airliner, which cruised a little faster than the Puss Moth. The captain said he was planning to fly at 4,000 feet between two cloud layers and I said I would try to follow him. We had not gone far before the cloud layers merged and we lost 'Hannibal'. I was getting worried by the time we should be approaching the coast and was wondering what the cloud base might be, when suddenly there was an opening in the clouds and Le Touquet aerodrome appeared immediately below. We spiralled down and then crossed the Channel at a low level to land at Lympne for Customs.

In the early thirties I taught David Garnett (to whom I have already referred), the well-known author, and his friend Hamish Hamilton, the publisher, to fly. Hamish Hamilton was an ex-Caius man who had stroked the 1928 Olympic crew. Garnett wrote a popular book, entitled *A Rabbit in the Air*, about his experiences learning to fly. He had suffered discouragement by flying club instructors and had been told he would never be a pilot. In his book he wrote, 'I became depressed, and finally abandoned flying, convinced that I was hopeless.' He was eventually tempted to look in to see what we were doing and, after two visits, a chat with engineer Honour and a meeting with me, decided to have another go at learning to fly. He wrote, 'I had really made up my mind to do so the moment that I had met Marshall.' Later David Garnett and Hamish Hamilton clubbed together and bought a

German Klemm, similar to Udny Yule's, which they enjoyed for a few years.

Most pupils were sent solo after eight or nine hours instruction. Some took a little longer but, no matter how good a pupil was, I would not let them go solo until they had made all the common mistakes of under-shooting, over-shooting, levelling off too high and bumpy landings, recog-nised them early and safely corrected them. All these mistakes would be made sooner or later and it was essential that pupils learnt how to correct them before going solo. I sent only one pupil solo with less than eight hours instruction. Two brothers, undergraduates at Downing, had each been left £12,500. The younger one learnt to fly and bought an aeroplane, and his elder brother did much flying with him. In due course the elder brother decided to learn and, as a result of experience gained flying with his brother, he was a perfect pupil and never made a mistake. I foolishly sent him solo with only four-and-a-half hours dual and he made a very good landing. The next day he came for some more flying and, as a matter of normal practice after a first solo, I told him he must have a dual circuit and landing before going solo again. He was surprised, but then started to make the routine mistakes and needed another two hours or so dual instruction before he was allowed to go solo again.

I impressed on pupils going on their first solo that there was no hurry – they had plenty of petrol and plenty of time – and not to land until they were quite happy and comfortable about the approach. One pupil a Dr Loots, a dour Scotsman who had taken a little longer than usual to go solo, went round more than six times before he finally made a perfect landing. We had all begun to get a bit worried and after he had taxied in, he realised we looked a little concerned and said, 'But you told me not to land until I was quite sure. I just did what you told me.' He turned out to be a very good pilot.

Special actions were necessary to encourage some pupils to complete their training. One extreme example was a pupil who was very good in the air – particularly good cross-country, general handling, side-slipping and landing – but had not sufficient confidence to go solo. The instructor occu-pies the front seat of the Moth and the control column is removable and taken out for passenger flying. Unknown to this particular pupil I took a spare stick and, recognising that it was an 'on' day for the pupil, I said, 'Now, you are going solo but I am coming with you. I am passing out my stick, so it's all yours.' When the pupil said, 'No, don't do that,' I said, 'You are perfectly all right and I am quite happy – off you go.' I could feel the pupil's feet shaking on the rudder bar for the first take-off, but a good circuit and landing was made. After a further circuit the pupil went solo and never knew about the spare stick. He was a good pilot and later took part in an air race.

I taught Sabah El Said, the son of the Prime Minister of Iraq, an under-graduate reading Aeronautical Engineering at Corpus, to fly in 1932.

Having completed his first solo, he asked if he could take his friend from London for a flight the next day. He was told that he had to do much more flying and get his licence before he could carry a passenger. The next day he was given a dual check circuit and sent on a solo flight. He was taxiing across the aerodrome when a figure ran out from the far hedge and got in the front cockpit. I was livid – a passenger carried against instructions and after less than half-an-hour solo flying and no pilot's licence. Having said that, El Said and his friend, whom we knew as 'Hussein', were a delightful pair and full of the joys of life, but they wanted much disciplining.

At this time Great Britain was giving up its mandate in Iraq and, with the RAF about to pull out, Iraq was planning to establish its own air force. I asked El Said what aeroplanes they were going to have and he wrote to his father, who replied that they were considering Wapitis – the only aircraft they knew anything about as the RAF had Wapitis in Iraq. I asked if we could supply them, and Sabah's father replied, 'There is no reason why Marshalls should not be on the tender list.'

I contacted Westland Aircraft at Yeovil, the manufacturers, who seemed a bit casual at first. I suggested that young El Said and I should fly down to the Yeovil Works, and Sir Ernest Petter put out the red carpet, gave us lunch and showed us round. Westlands then appreciated that we might have some influence and offered us a discount if new Wapitis were purchased, but by the time the enquiry came through about nine months later Westlands had pulled up the Wapiti jigs and were producing its successor the Wallace. Iraq said if they could not have the Wapiti, the one aircraft they knew, they would consider other makes. Iraq's air force was eventually started with a few Gipsy Moths, most of which were fitted with bomb racks.

I thought no more about Sabah El Said and his friend 'Hussein' until King Hussein of Jordan visited us at Cambridge in 1986. I told the King of the incident and remarked that Sabah's friend's name was also 'Hussein'. The King replied, 'I know all about it – it was my father.' It then became clear that Sabah El Said's friend 'Hussein' was in fact Talal bin Abdullah who became King of Jordan in 1951. The Iraqi Prime Minister General Nuri Es Said and his son Sabah El Said were assassinated in Baghdad with King Feisal II in 1958. King Hussein told us that Sabah El Said's son had been a pilot of the Jordanian Airline until two years previously when he was killed in a car accident.

On 22 June 1932 we had our first Royal visitor when the Prince of Wales, wearing a straw hat, landed at Cambridge in his Puss Moth, G-ABNN, which was painted in the colours of the Brigade of Guards and piloted by Wing Commander 'Mouse' Fielden. The aircraft was left on the aerodrome with one or two other aircraft – no police or security precautions. Today there would be a strong police presence both for the Prince and his aircraft. The Prince drove first to Peterhouse to meet his old wartime associate, Field Marshal Sir William Birdwood, who had commanded the

Anzacs (Australia and New Zealand Army Corps) at Gallipoli in 1915 and was now Master of Peterhouse. After lunch in the Master's Lodge, the Prince proceeded to the Leys School and found all the boys in their own straw hats, blazers and white flannel trousers. Having opened the squash court and additional playing field, the Prince requested that the summer holiday should be extended by three days – a very popular visit.

In the late twenties, Sir Alan Cobham was keen to make the youth of Britain air-minded, and gave flights to thousands of school children. By the early thirties this had become a large patriotic enterprise known as 'Cobham's Flying Circus' – lots of flights including in an autogyro, para-chuting and wing walking – really exciting occasions with the atmosphere of the fun of the fair. We had three visits of Sir Alan's 'Flying Circus' to Cambridge.

Sir Alan did not start his air-to-air refuelling development until the early thirties. At that time he was considering refuelling in the air after take-off in the context of making a contribution to air safety by decreasing the dangers during take-off of passenger aircraft laden with fuel operating with the less reliable engines of the period. In-flight refuelling was in later years to make a vital contribution to military aviation.

Whitney Straight, already in 1933 a national racing driver, was an undergraduate at Trinity and had a Gipsy III Moth which he kept at our aerodrome. Peter Masefield was at Jesus and he recalls:

> I look back with especial pleasure upon my own first flight into Brooklands on April 17th, 1933; flying from Cambridge with Whitney Straight in a DH60 Gipsy III Moth G-ABYV.
>
> One of the endearing features of the aerodrome at Brooklands had always been that the long breakwater, or jetty, in the prominent Queen Mary Reservoir, just north of the Chertsey bend in the River Thames pointed – and still points – directly towards Brooklands, five miles away. To relatively inex-perienced aviators and navigators, such as Whitney and I were at that time, it was a navigational blessing which could not be mistaken.
>
> So, on that April day, we flew down over Shepperton Lock and Weybridge Station (easily identified by the name 'WEYBRIDGE' in white chalk on the north west side of the railway beside a triangle of railway lines). By that time the Byfleet banking stood out prominently ahead.
>
> I remember that on that showery morning the blustery wind was from the south west. So, according to the local regulations, a right-hand circuit was in force. So round we went, over St. George's Hill to the east of the Vickers works, turning just south of the Byfleet banking and back alongside the railway to turn in again from over Weybridge Station to receive an Aldis-light 'green' from the white control tower on the Aero Club House in front of the Hawker and Vickers flight sheds. We came down over the members' banking to land across the River Wey, cautiously towards the extensive sewage farm – inviting a soft but noisome landing should we overshoot.
>
> While I set about filling up with fuel, Whitney rushed off to inspect his beautiful black Maserati, entered that afternoon for a handicap race around the

Mountain Course. After it, Whitney was in high spirits because he had set up a new Mountain Course lap record at something over 78 mph though he did not win the race on handicap. Later that afternoon he did, however, win a second Mountain handicap at a somewhat slower speed from scratch position.

I was equally pleased having had the opportunity to inspect, first of all, Malcolm Campbell's shining Bluebird world's speed record car (which had clocked 272.1 mph in February at Daytona Beach, powered with the Schneider Trophy Rolls-Royce 'R' engine of a phenomenal 36.7 litres).

What had also made my day was having been able to inspect Hawker's latest and most elegant spatted high speed Fury biplane (K3586) which, I see from my notes, was shortly to make its first flight and, with it, to have been able to have a few words with Hawker's Chief Test Pilot, George Bulman, and with the great Sydney Camm, its phlegmatic designer. Both George Bulman and Sydney Camm were later to become valued friends.

At the end of that memorable day, with just time to get back to Marshall's aerodrome at Fen Ditton before dark, we took off in the Gipsy Moth to fly on a compass course, with a spanking tail-wind, overhead Heston, Hendon, close to DH's at Hatfield and over Duxford Aerodrome to land, pleased with ourselves, only 42 minutes later.

Then, because in our 'in statu pupillari' neither of us was allowed to have a motor-car at Cambridge, we both mounted our bicycles and pedalled at modest speed the couple of miles back to our respective colleges.

Whitney Straight later became a famous Battle of Britain pilot. He was shot down over France and reported missing and then reported killed. His obituary appeared in *The Times* and some months later he reappeared, having made his way back through Spain.

We were at a big financial disadvantage when competing with subsidised aero clubs formed in the mid-twenties, so we formed the Cambridge Aero Club in terms which we hoped might be acceptable to the Air Ministry. We managed to persuade them to extend the subsidy to our Cambridge Aero Club in 1934. The subsidy by now was reduced to £25 for each new Pilot's 'A' Licence achieved and £10 for each Pilot's 'A' Licence renewal, all to a maximum of £1,500 per annum per club.

The workload was building up at both the garage and the aerodrome. The immediate urgency was the problem of finding a flying instructor to work with me and carry on the established traditions – not only a good flying instructor and a good disciplinarian but one who would be approachable and popular with all our flying customers – pupils and passengers, senior and junior members of the university and others – and ready to work all the hours necessary. It was important that he should understand that his own future and the future of the Company were dependent on his efforts.

We tried out three flying instructors in 1933, all of whom failed for various reasons, including not being punctual for appointments. It was also difficult to get them to realise that money mattered – they were very shy about asking a passenger to pay for a local flight or an air taxi journey. The fourth recruit, Goodyear, joined us towards the end of 1933. He was the best to date and was with us for nearly two years. He was a good instructor and fitted in well with the pupils, but he was not a salesman who would expand and consolidate our activities. In May 1934 Goodyear was ill with boils on the bottom. This was at the end of the university term, including May Week, always a busy period when we were trying to get pupils to complete their Pilots 'A' Licences before going down at the end of the University year, to avoid the risk of losing the £25 subsidy. Whilst Goodyear was ill we engaged Peter May, an A1 instructor who had just retired from the RAF with a very good record. May was committed to a 12-month engagement in China, starting in September, to instruct the Chinese Air Force. He had been a member of the RAF Hendon Display Team, one of the main attractions of which was an acrobatic display with Eric Greenwood, later Chief Test Pilot of Armstrongs, as the instructor flying in one aeroplane trying to guide his apparently wayward and crazy pupil, Peter May, in another to follow his manoeuvres and make a landing, resulting in thrills of near air collisions and near crashes.

We made a point of flying when weather conditions were bad – low cloud and poor visibility – but still flyable for training with only one aircraft in the air. With the introduction of a full-time instructor, whenever I was available we extended this practice to make it safe for two pupils under instruction to be flying at the same time. The take-off, circuit and landing procedure for two instruction aircraft operating in poor visibility was for the second aircraft to take off as soon as the instructor saw the first machine coming in to land. Most clubs would not have undertaken flying, even with one machine, under these conditions but we found it very good training for our pupils and it added considerably to their confidence.

On 6 June 1934 our second son David was born. He was christened by the Revd Gardner-Smith in Jesus College Chapel. Udny Yule of Klemm fame was his godfather and we again had tea in Alan Pars' rooms. There was no doubt that Rosemary was thoroughly enjoying the children at this time.

In October 1934 Rosemary and I went to see the early morning start of the Mildenhall to Australia Air Race, and went on to have breakfast with Rosemary's uncle, Sir Laurence Philipps, at Dalham. Sir Laurence had supported the development of aviation since the first transatlantic flight by Alcock and Brown, when he had added £1,000 to their prize money, and he had a continuing financial interest in de Havillands. On this day he had Reggie Brie, the internationally known autogyro pilot, at Dalham giving demonstration flights in a Cierva autogyro. Sir Laurence was one of the founder members of the Air Registration Board, which was established in 1937. He represented the general public, and continued as a member of the ARB for several years until after the war. He owned the Sir Laurence Philipps Insurance Company and after we got to know one another he extended his insurance company's interest to aviation, and all our aviation insurances were placed with them until after the war years. His son Jim

Philipps was responsible for the insurance company, and during the thirties he and I used to have an annual meeting with Peter Reiss, a famous under-writer. We discussed the details of the wording and conditions of our policy, including the small print. Our meetings resulted in changes in insurance policy wording, some of which is still used in general aviation policies to this day.

The winners of the England to Australia Air Race in 1934 were Scott and Campbell Black, in one of three Comets designed and built in record time by de Havillands for the race. The Comet had an interesting, little known, French designed two pitch position air screw which was pumped with a bicycle pump to the fine pitch position for take-off. As the aircraft gained speed and pressure built up on the nose of the hub of the propeller, it released the pressure controlling the pitch of the air screw which enabled it to move into coarse pitch for cruise. It was not possible to get back into fine pitch until it was pumped up again after landing. The winning Comet was financed by Grosvenor House Hotel. The DC-2, the forerunner of the famous DC-3 Dakota, performed well in the race, flying with a full load of passengers who were served meals throughout the race. The Comet won both the speed and handicap sections of the race, and the DC-2 was second in both.

On Sunday 16 December 1934 Norman de Bruyne's aeroplane, the Snark G-ADDL, made its first flight. He had entered into the design and building in great detail, attending de Havilland's most excellent technical school and modestly learning aircraft engineering in all its basic aspects. He was entirely responsible for the design and carried out much of the actual construction himself, and for this he obtained his Ground Engineer's Licence and Aircraft Welder's Certificate. Norman named his aeroplane the Snark from Lewis Carroll's *Hunting of the Snark*, which Carroll defined as 'a peculiar creature that won't be caught in a commonplace way'. It was a remarkable low wing, four-seater cabin monoplane fitted with a Gipsy Major engine and had a wide speed range, from stalling at just under 40 mph to a top speed of over 120 mph, and a cruising speed of 110 mph. Norman carried out the first flight himself. The first flight of any new aircraft required the pilot to wear a parachute. Norman's aircraft had not been designed for a parachute and he was sitting in a very high, uncomfort-able position with no head room. The first flight went well.

The machine was of unorthodox construction and Norman had much difficulty in persuading the powers that be that his light construction was as strong as, if not stronger than, the orthodox construction of the day. The Air Ministry finally purchased a second fuselage for testing to destruction, and this passed with flying colours. Dr Harold Roxbee-Cox (later Lord Kings Norton) became involved. At the time of the Norman de Bruyne contacts he was external lecturer to postgraduate students of aircraft structures at Imperial College. He made an analysis of the division of load between the spars in a stress skin wing which Norman used in the final designing of his wings. A full Certificate of Airworthiness was issued to the Snark and the RAE stressing methods were amended.

Lord Kings Norton says that, when Norman attended a small meeting to discuss his unorthodox construction, they were expecting an elderly professor and were surprised to see a man in his twenties. Norman had been in advance of his years even at school at Lancing when, at the age of 16, he wrote a book called *The Electrolytic Rectifier* which was published by Pitman and considered at the time to be the best work on this subject. Many references were made in the press to its excellence and it was taken to be the work of a senior science master at Lancing who, much to his embarrassment, received many letters of congratulation.

During the construction of the Snark, Norman realised the shortcomings of casein glue, the strength of which was seriously affected by humidity, temperature and weather conditions. This generated his interest in adhesives and led to his establishing Aero Research Limited at Duxford (now CIBA-Geigy) where he invented synthetic glues, including Aerolite and Redux, and honeycomb all-metal structures. de Havilland was one of the first aircraft companies to appreciate the importance of Norman's adhesive inventions, which included the adhesion of wood to wood, metal to metal, wood to metal and the adhesion of other materials. Norman became de Havilland's consultant responsible to Mr C. C. Walker, the Director and Chief Engineer, for the introduction of these glues into the future design of de Havilland aircraft. One could see much of Norman's aircraft wood construction principles reflected in the design of the famous Mosquito and its successor, the Hornet.

During the construction of the Snark, Rosemary and I saw much of Norman. We used to discuss what was aerodynamically the most efficient basic design, and generally agreed that this might be a middle wing machine. The big problem in designing a mid-wing aircraft, as compared with high or low wing, was that it necessitated the main spar passing through the centre of the cabin. When Norman started his company he went ahead with the design and building of a small single-seater mid-wing aircraft fitted with a two-cylinder engine (one of the earliest nosewheel aeroplanes), which he called the Ladybird, to carry out experiments with his new synthetic glues. The main spar of the Ladybird passed through the cockpit, the rear side providing the instrument panel.

All this had resulted from Norman de Bruyne's flight one Sunday morning in 1929 in the Revd Simpson's Gipsy Moth. Norman writes of that flight:

> I had been in an aeroplane in 1921, in a Fokker from Amsterdam (Schiphol) to Croydon which was the London Airport. This Moth flight was quite different. It was obviously a private owner's machine; it gave one a feeling of instant exhilaration and opened a new world in the sky waiting to be explored. When I came down people were behaving as though nothing had happened; did they not realise that mankind now had wings? I suppose it was the nearest I shall ever get to a religious conversion.

I began to take an interest in aircraft construction and the more I learnt the more convinced I became that there was room for original work in a branch of aeronautics which seemed to have got in a rut. It is difficult to recall how conservative British aircraft design was in that period. Thick wings were thought to have a large drag. Cantilever wings were thought to be too heavy or too risky. Anything but a biplane was regarded as un-English and not really practical.

Norman flew the Snark for a year or so, including a flight to Berlin with his brother and sister-in-law. In 1936 the Air Ministry purchased the Snark to enable Professor Sir Melvill Jones of the Cambridge University Aeronautical Engineering Department to carry out research on the aerodynamic behaviour of thick winged monoplanes with tufts of wool on the top surface of the wing. The Snark was later sold to Peter Masefield, who towed it to his mother's home near Croydon. By the time he got it home there was not much left of the tyres. The Snark was finally destroyed in a bombing raid on Croydon Aerodrome on 15 August 1940.

In spite of the coming and going of our first few instructors, a high standard of flying training had been established in our first few years of operation. Whilst I continued to give some flying instruction up to 1939, by 1935 it had become a matter of great urgency to find someone to take over the full responsibilities of Chief Flying Instructor on a permanent basis and team up with me to carry on the good work.

Peter May, during the short time he was with us during the summer of 1934 when Goodyear was ill, had been a breath of fresh air enthusiastically fitting in with my own ideas of flying training, getting in as many flying hours as possible and maintaining strict discipline. He had been very popular with the pupils, including the more lively undergraduates whom he had kept under control. I cabled Peter in China suggesting he should come to us on completion of his Chinese commitment. Peter joined us in August 1935, having been given the rank of Colonel in the Chinese Air Force. In addition to flying instruction he had also been involved in helping them with their gliding. He was enterprising, enthusiastic and good company. It was important that Peter should prove to be all that we were looking for – and he did.

In 1935 we realised that the Cambridge Aero Club was going to exceed the £1,500 subsidy limit, so we formed the University Aero Club Limited in April 1936, which was accepted by the Air Ministry for subsidy. Both clubs were sponsored by Marshall's Flying School Limited. In 1936 we trained about 75 new pilots and 40 licence renewals. We did not get more renewals because the undergraduates we trained finished their university careers and were lost to Cambridge.

Soon after Peter May arrived, the Duke of Grafton, a former pupil, asked us to give joy-rides at a fête being held at his home, Euston Hall. Peter and I took two Moths and gave joy-rides until late in the evening, with Rosemary selling the tickets. At that time, to economise on aerodrome maintenance, we had bought some sheep to graze on the aerodrome, and these sheep had not been penned as anticipated for our return from the fête in semi-darkness. We both landed virtually with sheep all around us, by luck without hitting one. The sheep were not a success. There is a stream between the old Fen Ditton aerodrome and Coldhams Common; the sheep were always falling in the brook and much time was spent by the family, particularly it would seem on Sunday afternoons, pulling them out.

The Cambridge University Gliding Club was formed in February 1935. Many of the founder members had been pupils of our Flying School and we gave them all the help and encouragement possible, including free use of the aerodrome, and in due course accommodation in a blister hangar. We gave a number of £10 flying training scholarships to selected experienced members of the Gliding Club. This was an exercise to establish if those with gliding experience would obtain their powered aircraft pilot's licence in fewer hours than pilots trained *ab initio* on powered aircraft. In practice it did effect some saving.

With Peter May installed, and remembering the experience of our first few instructors, I asked myself, apart from luck (and we had had this in abundance), what had been the main reasons for our success? First we had to sell our flying – thanks to the garage we had access to possible flying customers and I seem to have conveyed quite naturally some of my own confidence in aviation to potential pupils and passengers. I had always assumed that there was nothing special about flying – you learnt to ride a bicycle; you learnt to drive a motor car, and so, if you wanted to, you could learn to fly an aeroplane – all quite natural for the average person to be able to do.

I then considered the differences between my own upbringing as a flying instructor and the records of the four instructors who had assisted me in 1933/34. The simple answer was that I had graduated straight from being a pupil to being a flying instructor in a short space of time. I remembered my own problems, experiences and escapades, my enthusiasm to learn more and keenness to build up my flying hours. I was virtually on equal terms with my pupils: we were in it together, and I did not mind the hours I worked – all very exciting. The instructors who had passed through our hands were all good pilots, but they were going back to elementary flying instruction after several years of flying experience. The initial excitement was no longer there.

I concluded that, if other young men were given the same opportunities I had had and, having learnt to fly, went straight on to train to be flying instructors, they could do what I had done. As a result I considered we should train our own flying instructors for the future. Peter May was in full and enthusiastic agreement. The *Cambridge Daily News* at this time published a weekly item written by 'Meteor', who described the flying activities at the Cambridge Aerodrome and any items of general and local aviation interest. In December 1935 he wrote an article describing our proposed Apprenticeship Scheme to train young men with no previous flying experience to become commercial pilots and flying instructors.

A number of young men responded. One of them, Leslie Worsdell, already had 60 hours flying experience with the de Havilland operated RAF Flying Training School at Hatfield. After a test flight with me he was offered an apprenticeship which carried a £100 premium. Leslie Worsdell began his apprenticeship in February 1936 at the age of 19. He was an immediate success and quickly became a qualified flying instructor. This proved the practicality of our revolutionary idea for training first-class flying instructors at a young age. Leslie was the first of many in a scheme which was to be of great national importance.

At the end of 1935 we were approached by the Civil Aviation Service Corps, young working men from London, mostly cockneys, who had a keen interest in aviation, some of whom wanted to learn to fly. Peter May thought they looked good material – good scouts – and we agreed to give them special terms. They clubbed together on a co-operative basis and came to Cambridge at weekends to help generally and wait and fill in gaps in the flying training programme. The Corps was exceptionally well run and they were a pleasant and helpful crowd of young men. Many of them later had good service careers in the RAF as pilots, navigators, Link training instructors and air traffic controllers, and one of them became a flying instructor at Cambridge.

In 1935/6 we started to take on a number of aircraft engineering apprentices, including Peter Else, Humphries and Butcher. Butcher, whom I well remember, was small and was sent to do a job in the tapering confined space of the rear fuselage of David Garnett's Klemm. The aircraft was in my original hangar away from the main workshops. Butcher was missing after lunch and was finally found wedged inside the fuselage of the Klemm patiently waiting to be rescued. All three joined the RAFVR, became pilots and were called up at the outbreak of war. Humphries was killed in the Battle of Britain. Butcher had five tours of Bomber Command operations from Scampton with 49 Squadron, but returning from an early raid over Germany his badly damaged Hampden finally gave up over Holland. He and his crew managed to bale out safely but were rounded up and spent the next four and a half years as guests of the Luftwaffe.

Peter Else was shot down in flames in the Battle of Britain. His Spitfire was hit by cannon fire from a German fighter at 25,000 feet over the Channel. The instrument panel disappeared in a sea of burning petrol and Peter was terribly burnt. The cockpit hood jammed but, with super-human effort, he managed to force it open as the blazing aeroplane plummeted seaward. Somehow Peter managed to get out, as another burst of machine gun fire blew off his left arm. After months of medical treatment and plastic surgery for his burns, he rejoined us and eventually became Chief Engineer of the Light Aircraft Division with responsibility for the maintenance of the Cambridge University Air Squadron aircraft and the Air Training Corps Air Experience Flight Chipmunks. He retired in 1987 after 52 years service, having received an AOC's commendation in 1982 for his services to the RAF.

My father was the enthusiast for the purchase in 1935 of a Monospar, a five-seater low-wing monoplane with a cruising speed of 120 mph. I was not so keen, but he had set his heart on having a two-engine machine, thinking that if you had two engines you had some chance of staying in the air if one engine failed – but this was wishful thinking. We never had any forced landings with the Monospar, although its Pobjoy engines had a very short life between complete overhauls and required much detailed daily maintenance, but when they were running well they were very smooth and a joy to fly. We did much Army co-operation flying with this aircraft, flying over scheduled courses and often up and down the east coast to provide air gunners with sighting experience.

One serious incident with the Monospar was in July 1937. In those days we used to take one or two aircraft to Duxford on 'Empire Air Day' for joy-riding in aid of the RAF Benevolent Fund. On this occasion the first machine had already taken off for Duxford and I was to follow with the Monospar. I started both engines and ran them up, and all seemed well. I took off in an easterly direction, fortunately towards our new aerodrome in the course of construction just over the hedge. Just as I attained flying speed, both engines' revs dropped. I managed to land on the new aerodrome and, in doing so, chewed up some of the grass which my father had recently sown, and I was not very popular. We got some chocks and ran up the engines and they gave full power. There was sufficient room to attain flying speed and pull up within the boundary of the new aerodrome, but the engines again failed as soon as the aircraft attained flying speed.

We got the aircraft back to the old Fen Ditton aerodrome and tried without success to identify the trouble, including checking fuel flows. Then somebody said, 'I suppose the petrol taps are turned on?' and they were not! The petrol taps were about an inch-and-a-half long and located in an inaccessible position between the two front seats. The taps were so stiff and small that they really required a pair of pliers to operate them, so there was a strict instruction always to leave the taps in the 'On' position. We had never realised that we could get full power on the ground with the petrol turned off. The next question was who had turned the taps off? As part of my pre-flight check, I should have checked that they were on. Then somebody remembered that two days before a chap had turned up who wanted to take his licence on a Monospar and had his technical exam the coming week. He had asked if he could have a look over the Monospar, and was given permission to do so. We managed to contact him and he said he had found the taps in the 'On' position and turned them off. The younger brother of Duncan Davis of Brooklands Aviation was killed in a crash resulting from the same problem when taking off at Lympne in a Monospar not long afterwards. It was with a sigh of relief that we sold the Monospar in 1937, destined as we understood for the Spanish Civil War where Monospars were used as air ambulances, transporters and improvised bombers.

With Peter May's enthusiasm, flying training really took off, and additional instructors were engaged. We also took on Dick Stormont Hayes as a flying training 'salesman'. He was responsible for recruiting pupils and chasing up pupils to complete their licences and renewals in order that we could claim the subsidy before they went down. He also sent a weekly report to 'Meteor' of the *Cambridge Daily News* on local flying affairs.

At this time Ronnie Bowles joined us to take over book-keeping, accounts and general administration responsibilities in preparation for the Company's expansion. He was to be a great asset during the war and early post-war years as Personnel Manager.

During this time we began to realise that our flying training expertise could be of national importance with the growing fear of war and the need to train more RAF pilots. A period of good all-round aeronautical apprenticeship had been served. We were poised ready to take advantage of any opportunity which might lie ahead.

Chapter 12

A Close Run Thing

1933–21 October 1937

THE LEAGUE OF Nations disarmament conference in Geneva collapsed in 1933 when Germany withdrew from the conference and from the League itself, following Hitler and the Nazi party coming into full power with the general elections in Germany earlier that year. From that time on, Hitler was emerging as a threat to peace and Britain became increasingly worried about Germany's real intentions. My father and I had always felt that the problems with Germany were not yet over. The pulse was quickening, with rumours of plans for the expansion of the Air Force and its reserves.

I was well acquainted with the flying training schools operated on behalf of the RAF by the main aircraft manufacturers since the early twenties, particularly No. 1 E&RFTS (Elementary and Reserve Flying Training School) run by de Havilland at Stag Lane – later transferred to Hatfield. Having now become involved in flying training, we assumed that any RAF expansion would include an increase in the number of such schools.

In December 1933 a conference was held at the Mansion House to which municipalities were invited. The Prince of Wales was present, and Lord Londonderry, Minister of Air, stressed the need to encourage and help aviation in all its branches, including the teaching of flying and the provision of city and town aerodromes, if we did not want to be left behind other countries. Most aerodromes were some distance from centres of population and it was emphasised that future aerodromes should be built as near as possible to the towns they were to serve.

During 1933 we had realised that our Fen Ditton aerodrome, originally intended only for my own use, was too small for any worthwhile development. We had no premonition of the anxiety and sleepless nights the negotiations for a larger aerodrome would cause or that, as will be seen, it would become a race against time. Our first consideration was the possibility of incorporating 73 acres of land owned by the County Council on the eastern boundary of the aerodrome. We purchased the land in March 1934 unaware that the Borough Council was planning a ring road through part of this land.

Marshall's requested that the route be altered and urgent discussions took place. The Borough Council consulted Alan Cobham who reported favourably on our site. They then consulted the Ministry of Transport who agreed to the altered position of the road and to make a grant towards the cost. However, the Borough Council finally decided to adhere to its plans for the ring road and suggested that Marshall's Aerodrome should be moved to one of several sites around the town.

Meanwhile we had been keeping in touch with the Air Ministry and RAF Flying Training Headquarters at Hendon, which resulted in a visit in May by Group Captain R. Leckie in a Tiger Moth. His immediate reaction was that our Fen Ditton aerodrome was not big enough for an RAF Elementary Flying Training School. We talked about the possible extension of the aerodrome to include the 73 acres just purchased from the County Council, and the Group Captain thought it might then be marginally possible for elementary flying training but not for the larger machines which the RAF might introduce into the next stage of flying training at these schools. With the speed at which aviation matters were developing, we realised that, if we were going to have any chance of any work resulting from the RAF expansion, time was running out. We now required a much larger aerodrome than anything we had considered to date and, if possible, one which could be extended in the future.

We surveyed the area for potential sites, keeping in mind the emphasis on aerodromes being near to the populations they were to serve. The one which best met this criterion was on Newmarket Road and became known as the Teversham Corner site, a major portion of which was owned by the Church. The Borough Council had already earmarked a site on the Milton Road as a possible aerodrome for Cambridge, but it would take some time to acquire the land, obtain vacant possession and develop. With time running against us, we entered into negotiations with the Church for the Teversham Corner site with a view to obtaining an option for submission to the Borough Council for planning consent. The Rector of Teversham was very co-operative in getting a quick decision from the Church to agree to sell the land. He was very proud of his village and I think he foresaw that, if the Teversham Corner land was not used for an aerodrome, it would soon be built over and it would be difficult to identify where Cambridge ended and Teversham began. He looked upon the establishment of an aerodrome as the provision of a lung between the town and the village.

During this time we were having urgent discussions with Borough Council officials. When I say 'we', this was our Counsel Gerald Howard, our solicitor Joe Taylor of Newmarket (a future Chairman of the County Council) and myself. My father decided to remain in the background. In the midst of these talks my father suddenly announced that he had purchased the Teversham Corner site. There is little doubt that in the long run our position was strengthened by the ownership of the land. I was pleased, but it was a bold move and Joe Taylor and I were initially worried that it might put a spanner in the works – it certainly ruffled the Council's feathers.

When we purchased the site its planning designation was 'undetermined'. The Borough Council met on 1 August 1935 and turned down our application for planning permission. Our position was desperate. The Council planned to acquire our Fen Ditton aerodrome under a Compulsory Purchase Order, had refused planning permission for our proposed aerodrome at Teversham Corner, and had rescheduled that site from 'undetermined' to 'housing'.

The Press at this time were stressing the importance to the nation of aviation, the teaching of flying and the provision of aerodromes, and many Borough Councillors were unhappy about the situation. It was being freely said that Marshall's, the pioneers of aviation in the area, were not being given fair consideration and that the Borough Council was deliberately obstructing their business plans. At this stage the unusual action was taken of calling a special Council meeting in the vacation on 15 August. At this meeting, as a result of strong, forthright and determined representations by Councillor John Burnaby, the councillor representing the University, well supported by Alderman Archie Taylor (Proprietor of the *Cambridge Daily News*) and other councillors, the Council agreed that the whole matter would be further debated in open discussion by the Council in October and without prejudice to Marshall's position.

Discussions with Council officials now included the suggestion that the Council should develop the Milton Road site as an aerodrome with Marshall's as tenants with a seven-year lease. Whilst we had made the following points on several occasions, we now took great trouble to re-emphasise that:

> The purchase and development of the Milton Road site as an aerodrome would cost much more than the Council realised and would be a substantial charge on the rates. Cambridge was a sparsely populated area which could not afford the ownership and operation of a municipal aerodrome.
>
> If Marshall developed its own aerodrome, it would be on a commercial basis. A flying school required an aerodrome and from this general aeronautical engineering activities could develop. As a by-product of our commercial aviation activities we hoped to provide Cambridge with the equivalent of a municipal aerodrome without any charge on the rates. We would in turn expect the Council at all times to give full backing to the Company's enterprise knowing the financial benefits this would provide by rates, increased employment and the general expansion of the area.
>
> We did not agree that the Milton Road site was as good or as accessible as the Teversham Corner site – it was more off the beaten track. Further, we felt that the Milton Road site could never be seriously and finally considered for a municipal aerodrome as it would be opposite the sewage farm, which one would hesitate to describe as a fragrant proposition.
>
> We made it clear that the Company would not consider being a tenant; we explained we would not have enough freedom for quick action to meet any opportunity which might arise requiring immediate additional accommodation and an overnight decision.

The Council had gained the impression that a municipal aerodrome would be a good investment, but now began to realise that buying and developing their own aerodrome would cost more than they had anticipated. They tried to gain time for consideration. On the other hand we were short of time and knew that, if we did not get established at the beginning of the anticipated RAF expansion programme, we would never have another such opportunity.

The Borough Council finally agreed at the end of January 1936 that Marshall should go ahead with the development of the Teversham Corner site on the understanding that during 1937 we would occupy the new aerodrome and vacate the old aerodrome which the Council would acquire by Compulsory Purchase Order.

My father took on the responsibility for the considerable work which had to be carried out as a matter of great urgency in levelling and seeding the land – it was essential that the grass of the main landing area should be sown by March/April 1936 if it was going to be suitable for flying during 1937. His experience of preparing the Fen Ditton Aerodrome stood him in good stead. Our garage adapted four old Austin Twelve chassis to pull graders for levelling the site.

The buildings and aerodrome entrances and general layout had to be planned. We decided the entrances should be as near as possible to Cambridge on the Newmarket Road with the hangars and main buildings in the north-west area of the aerodrome with no risk of obstructing prevailing wind flightways. We gave much consideration to the architecture of the two initial buildings. For the Control Building I had helpful advice from my friend Tommy Tomlinson of the University Architectural School. For the hangar I got ideas from new buildings recently erected in America. At that time most hangars were being built to look like big sheds, without introducing any architectural features. We were a bit stumped for inspiration for an attractive architectural approach from Newmarket Road. Rosemary and I motored round many areas to get ideas, particularly along the London Great West Road where a number of commercial premises had recently been built. As a result we decided on the present approach and layout of the Control Building and our first hangar with the low brick wall on the road frontage, all often quoted as a classic example of aerodrome architecture of the late thirties. In 1938 it so happened that there was a local general planning enquiry. The inspector visited the aerodrome and took trouble to say that all concerned were very pleased with the buildings we had erected and, if we continued to offer such buildings for planning permission in the future, we should have no problems.

The Control Building accommodation and layout was designed to provide all the facilities for an RAF Volunteer Reserve flying training centre, including a parachute room (parachutes have to be hung from a height of 20 feet for 24 hours and repacked at specified periods). This was in anticipation of Marshall obtaining an RAF flying training contract to provide trained pilots for the war which now seemed inevitable. The hangar was built by Boulton & Paul of Norwich who had built our original small hangar in 1929.

We were now committed to the early purchase of 13 plots of land around the main Church land to complete the initial development of the Teversham Corner site. In addition we had to consider the provision of catering facilities for flying pupils including, hopefully RAF Volunteer Reservists. To say the least, this additional capital expenditure would have been difficult. My father and I had in 1935 given personal undertakings to the bank for borrowing up to £30,000, which was not very popular with Rosemary as it meant we had pledged all our worldly possessions. Whilst my father's obligation was cancelled at his death in 1942, my obligations were not cleared until 1947.

So we entered into negotiations with Tollemache, the brewers who had recently built what was considered to be a very good modern public house on Milton Road, but we wanted the equivalent of a small hotel. Subject to Marshall obtaining the alcohol licence, Tollemache agreed to build the 'Airport Hotel' with a number of bedrooms, a residents' lounge and a separate dining room reserved for aerodrome visitors, including members of a possible RAFVR Flying Training School – all at a cost to Tollemache of about £20,000 plus the cost of the site. Our licence application was heard at the Bottisham Court and the licence was granted on 1 April 1937. Sir Alan Cobham gave evidence on behalf of the aviation travelling public.

During 1936 the Air Ministry issued an invitation to a number of companies to locate sites and submit proposals for the operation of RAF Volunteer Reserve flying training centres west of a line from Newcastle to Somerset, and also including Scotland. I carried out a major survey, initially by air and then for selected sites by road. Rosemary drove the car and I spent much time standing with my head through the sunshine roof viewing the land around.

We submitted detailed proposals for 16 sites, with full information including ordnance maps, names of owners, and reports on negotiations with the owners for the acquisition of their land – farming was in a depressed state and many farmers were willing to sell. The Air Ministry selected four and Wing Commander John Whitford from RAF Training Headquarters and I flew in the Puss Moth to view them. We landed at one of the sites near Southport in the early evening for an overnight stop. It was on a minor road with little traffic, but eventually an Austin Seven came along and we asked the driver if he would be good enough to give us a lift into Southport. He said he would, provided he could call and pay his water rate. We scrambled into the car and found that the point of payment was the local pub, where he paid his water rate and we had a drink before proceeding to Southport.

In December 1936 the Air Ministry telephoned to say that some of our sites might be of use to the Air Force but they were not near enough to centres of population for Volunteer Reserve (VR) training schools. (Some were developed as aerodromes during the war, including Arbroath in Scotland near Montrose.) The Air Ministry representative said that they appreciated the work we had undertaken and had good reports on our flying training. They were anxious that we should have one of the new flying schools and had nominated us to establish a school at Tollerton, the Nottingham municipal aerodrome. Our appointment was announced in *The Times* on Tuesday 12 January 1937. But by now we were preparing our new aerodrome at Cambridge which could be ready for RAFVR training by January 1938. We told the Air Ministry that we were proceeding with everything necessary for a VR centre. We asked to be excused from further Nottingham involvement and to be allowed to establish a centre at Cambridge. We knew that, if we were to make a quick impact with our flying training efficiency, it was vital to have our first VR school on our own aerodrome with our proven, enthusiastic Cambridge team. The Air Ministry had been concerned that the sparsely populated Cambridge area would not be a good recruiting centre, but they finally agreed to our proposal and a contract was signed for No. 22 E & RFTS to begin operations on 1 February 1938.

We would not have received this contract if our new aerodrome had not been available by then, and the latter without RAF flying training would have been, to say the least, a financial headache. The timings of the essential planning approval and the Air Ministry contract were interdependent to provide a successful conclusion – a close run thing.

The contract made the company responsible for the efficient running of the school to the satisfaction of RAF Training Headquarters at Hendon, which in turn had to approve the Chief Flying Instructor. In our case we were providing the aerodrome and buildings, whereas most other VR training centres operated from Ministry aerodromes with the Ministry responsible for the accommodation. Young men with acceptable standards of education and physical fitness were accepted for flying training as and when they were available from their normal work, including weekends, with a commitment of two weeks' continuous training a year. Initial training was on Tiger Moths, graduating to advanced Service training on Hawker Harts, Hinds, and later Fairey Battles.

This was a big step forward, but with our substantial financial commitment we were concerned as to how long such RAF flying schools might be required under pre-war, war or post-war conditions. One thing we were sure was that it was essential from the outset to do everything possible to give a good account of ourselves in order that, if there was a cut-back or any re-shuffling of the schools, we would be one of the survivors, regardless of whether we were east or west of the Newcastle to Somerset line.

Our garage made good progress during this period with the continuing expansion of the Austin range. The Austin Light Twelve/Four had been introduced in 1931. The Austin Ten was introduced in 1932 – a very important addition and a tremendous success. This was followed by the Eighteen and Light Fourteen/Six in 1934 and the Big Seven in 1937. A range of nine models, each with its own selection of bodies including some sports models. Austin sales, with their now established reputation for reliability and low depreciation and with a comprehensive range, were taking off. Austins were also doing very well in exports to all parts of the world, and in countries such as Portugal and Egypt, Austins were predominant.

Austin cars were very popular and the Austin franchise was the most sought after. The Cambridge motor trade was very envious of our distributorship and other garages tried to get a foot in the door. The most persistent, with an assurance that they would sell many large Austin Twenties, succeeded in pressurising Austin, who in turn pressurised us, to give them a retail agency under our distribution. They sold no Austin Twenties and the sub-agency lapsed at the end of the year.

With the increased competition which was developing in the garage world, in 1932 we engaged our first full-time car salesman, Len North, who had been in the motor business in Cambridge since he left school. When Len joined us he was in his early 30s. It was a very happy choice and he was with us, including the war years at the aerodrome, until his death in 1966. A very good personality, exceptionally popular with customers, and with the best handwriting I have ever seen, a skill which was inherited by his son. In recent years I received a letter and, seeing the handwriting on the envelope, I said, 'Good Lord; there's a letter from Len North who is dead' – it was from his son Richard. Len as Head Salesman built up a sales team of five during the thirties – Tony Reynolds, Jack Nichols, Ted Skinner, Percy Holman and North himself. When war broke out they all transferred to the aerodrome with the exception of Nichols, who was called up for military service.

I held 8.45 a.m. meetings daily, including Saturdays, with Len North and his team at Jesus Lane to go through who was doing what and actions to be taken to bring potential enquiries to fruition. On one occasion Reynolds had been trying to sell a new car to two elderly sisters living in the Huntingdon area who were waiting until their pigs, about six or seven of them, had reached a better market price. This had been going on for several weeks, when I suggested to Reynolds, 'Find out what price they are expecting and give it to them and take the pigs to the cattle market on Monday.' This he did. On another occasion Nichols had a potential customer who had a pony and trap which he was waiting to sell before he would commit himself for a new car. Again, after several weeks, we finally decided to take the pony and trap in part exchange for a new car. Nichols delivered the new car, drove the pony and trap back to my father's house and put the pony in the paddock. Shortly afterwards I had my father ringing me asking what a pony, which he understood belonged to the garage, was doing in his field? We sent the pony and trap to the cattle market on the following Monday.

1935 was the Silver Jubilee of King George V and Queen Mary. To mark the occasion the Austin Motor Company delivered by rail a set of three Austin Sevens, painted one red, one white and one blue, as a centrepiece for Jubilee showroom displays. The red and blue ones soon sold but Gilly Fromant had to spray the white one black to sell it. How things have changed. White vehicles are now popular.

Being able to land my aeroplane in the Longbridge Works brought Austins within an hour of Cambridge, which was a tremendous help. As for example in the case of Mrs Hopkinson (the widow of Professor Bertrand Hopkinson, the most brilliant mathematical engineering scientist of the early part of the century, who had been killed in 1918 in a flying accident) who was a wealthy and important customer. With her increasing age and her back problem she wanted a large chauffeur-driven car with easy access to the rear seat. She wanted a flap fitted in the roof which could be opened up when the rear door was open to provide access without stooping. We were anxious to sell her an Austin Twenty and were in competition with other makes. Negotiations with the Austin Sales Department were somewhat protracted and we were worried that we might lose the order. I phoned direct to Mr Challenor, the boss of the Austin body shop, and explained the position and said I could be with him in an hour-and-a-half and, if he could meet me on their landing ground, I was sure we could sort this out in a few minutes. He agreed and I returned to Cambridge and obtained the order that afternoon.

In spite of the University restrictions on the use of undergraduates' cars the garage business increased nearly five-fold between 1926 and 1936. Austin's pressure for increasing car sales became very intense during this period. Sir Herbert always met the distributors for the signing of their annual contracts. I used to go with my father and we were ushered into his office by the Sales Manager, Chris Buckley. On one occasion we had achieved above national average penetration of Austin sales and felt the increase in our contract obligation should be less than the general percentage being imposed throughout the country. I remember Lord Austin saying that, whilst pleased with whatever we had done in the past, his only concern at the moment was what we were going to achieve in the future.

In 1937 the garage workshops converted an Austin Twenty as a fire engine for our new aerodrome. It was designed to meet the Air Ministry specification of the day, with many additions as a result of our own aerodrome operating experience. It generated much police and fire brigade interest. The Austin Twenty chassis was chosen because of its great strength, reliability and long lasting qualities. A special feature was the fitting of an aircraft impulse magneto which, together with a dash carburettor flooder and an emergency gravity feed petrol tank, ensured instant and easy starting. It had accommodation for a crew of seven.

After dinner one Saturday early in 1936 we took Mrs Dimsdale back to Huntingdon Road where she was staying with friends and we had another piece of luck in noticing a house a few doors away – 'Broxton' – up for sale. The house belonged to Charles Ellis, who was deputy to Lord Rutherford, the atom scientist, and was now taking up a senior appointment in London. Rosemary and I knew Charles and Polly Ellis well. Broxton was just what we wanted, with its garden looking across the University Farm to Madingley Hill. We immediately entered into negotiations and purchased the house on the following Wednesday.

During these years there was much family activity. In August 1933 my eldest sister Margery married Monty Fry, a Trinity Hall graduate, then House Tutor at Crediton Grammar School. Monty was later a Housemaster and for many years Deputy Headmaster at Berkhamsted School, where he was held in universal affection by masters and boys alike resulting from his genuine interest in all their activities. Margery and Monty were married at St Andrew's Church, Old Chesterton, with the reception at Whitehill.

Mary, my fourth sister, took over from Margery as my secretary. She learnt to fly in 1935 and it is only recently I learnt that, in spite of all the regulations we rigidly enforced regarding aerobatics, she persuaded one of our instructors to teach her to loop, and that she succeeded in achieving a loop into her own slip-stream. If I had heard of this at the time there would have been some fun and games with her instructor. I also learnt for the first time that my father told Margery and Violet that he thought Mary was not as confident as she should be as a pilot and it would be a good idea if she gave them a flight to help build up her confidence, and off they went. At about the same time my father had a young married couple to lunch and, when talking about flying, he suggested that Mary would be pleased to give them a flight. The wife said 'No thank you,' but the husband had his flight. All this with less than 20 hours total flying.

In 1935 Brenda joined Molly at Slepe Hall, St Ives, and in 1937 went to St George's School, Ascot, when Molly went to finish her education in Paris.

My second sister Dorothy became a physical training teacher at St Clare School, Tunbridge Wells, and was a county hockey player. In 1935 Dorothy married Rupert Wagner, a brewery area manager. Dorothy and Rupert's wedding was at St Andrew's Church, Old Chesterton, with the reception at Whitehill. They then flew in the Monospar to Hatfield to pick up their car for their honeymoon in Scotland.

The family all went to Villars in Switzerland for Christmas in 1936. They had a large table near the centre of the dining room. The Christmas Pudding was brought to the centre of the room to be lit and hoisted towards the ceiling so that all could see. The chef shook some spirit, which proved to be pure alcohol instead of brandy, onto the pudding, which flared up immediately and flamed back into the bottle which burst all over Dorothy. Rupert threw Dorothy to the ground, took off his coat and wrapped it round her to put out the flames, but she was very seriously burned about the face, back and chest and was in Switzerland for some time. Violet stayed with her for the first four weeks.

Violet continued to run Whitehill and was garage reserve secretary for Margery and later Mary. Violet was a good all-round games player and a county tennis player for Cambridgeshire and Buckinghamshire. She captained the Buckinghamshire squash team and got through to the last eight in the Open Squash Championships in 1934. In 1936 she became engaged to Teddy Barbezat and they were married in July 1937 at St Andrew's Church, Old Chesterton, with the reception at Whitehill. Violet and Teddy first lived in Harley Street but soon moved to Effingham, having found London very expensive with many friends calling in for a drink.

In the meantime Mary and the Honourable Charles Cavendish had become engaged and planned to get married in June 1937. But my father would have none of it and said the girls must get married in the right batting order and that it would be quite wrong for Mary (daughter No. 4) to get married before Violet (daughter No. 3) so Mary and Charles put off their wedding till September, when they were married at St Mark's Church, North Audley Street, London with the reception at Claridge's and with Michael as one of the page-boys.

It was during this period that my father extended his great interest in horseracing to ownership, which occasioned much family excitement with my two youngest sisters, Molly and Brenda, being taken all the way to Ayr to witness his first win. Brenda recalls, 'Daddy used to take me out of school to go to Ascot, Fontwell and Goodwood and to Newmarket in the holidays. Miss Loveday, the Headmistress, did not think young ladies should be taught this sort of thing. I went with the family to Royal Ascot once and wore the bridesmaid's dress I had for Mary's wedding the previous September – it was blue. Daddy had a box at Ascot. I only remember three of Daddy's horses – David Mike, Jonquil and Brenda Mar.' His trainers were initially Gerald Laurence of Balsham, followed by Walter Earl who, on his appointment as private trainer to Lord Derby in 1938, handed over my father's horses to Henry Jellis.

One of my concerns now that we had a number of flying instructors was that my father might at any moment make up his mind to learn to fly and all hell would be let loose – he was a most ferocious and fast driver of motor cars, although I do not think he was ever had up for speeding, which was quite remarkable. My sisters recall that when they were driving he was very impatient and would encourage them by saying, 'Go on, go on – there's plenty of room to get through.' He had two car accidents in his life – both with the Cottin Desgouttes touring car. In 1913, when reversing to turn the car round on the beach road south of Yarmouth, the car hood blew up and the car went over the top – about a 12 foot drop to the sand – finishing with the car at 45 degrees with the tail on the sand and the front wheels on the wall. The only damage was to the tail lamp, but there was the problem of first getting the vehicle down on to the sand with some horses and then towing it up from the beach to the road. The second incident was soon after the 1914–18 war, travelling back from London and just leaving Epping on the way to Cambridge, with my mother, myself and other members of the family on board. We collided with the side of a lorry coming in the opposite direction, which ripped off part of the side of the touring car and bruised my mother's arm, but not seriously. She was sitting in the back right-hand seat. I would only add that my father had no mechanical sense whatsoever, and if he had been let loose in the air it would have been full throttle all the way regardless of weather.

We had been lucky to find our initial landing ground on our back doorstep in 1929. Now in 1936, acquiring the Teversham site suitable to develop into a large aerodrome next door to the family home and, in those days, within five minutes drive of our garage was another stroke of luck, and another piece of the jig-saw puzzle fell into place. With the Volunteer Reserve contract we now recognised that the experience we would gain in the maintenance of larger and more advanced aircraft could provide a springboard for the Company to undertake maintenance and repair work on large RAF aircraft.

The transfer was finally made from the old aerodrome to the new on 21 October 1937, with the aircraft flown over the hedge. The boundaries were only separated by a matter of one or two hundred yards, so when we came to move the aircraft it was fortunate that the wind was in an easterly direction. We just pointed the aircraft straight at the new Aerodrome, opened the throttle, climbed a few feet, closed the throttle and landed.

Chapter 13

Last Days of Peace

October 1937–3 September 1939

WITH ALL THE aircraft safely ferried from Cambridge (Fen Ditton) to Cambridge (Teversham), the honeymoon was over. Prospects looked good but we knew we would have to work hard and watch our step if we were going to have a chance of long-term survival. We were conscious of the fact that what we were experiencing was an artificial mushroom growth of the aviation industry in the atmosphere generated by the risks of war. But what was going to happen long-term? At the end of the 1914 war Government contracts were cancelled overnight, and many big companies such as the Sopwith Aircraft Company closed down. We remembered the near collapse of the Austin Motor Company left with a very big workforce, greatly increased factory capacity and no orders.

Most of our competitor flying training companies were lodgers on Government or third party owned aerodromes and buildings. They had no major fixed capital responsibilities and when the emergency was over could put on their hats and go home. We on the other hand had financed the rapid building of our new aerodrome to meet the potential war situation. With our own aerodrome and engineering facility, we had a better chance of controlling our destiny, but would have the challenge of finding a large volume of work to occupy the buildings and workforce when the emergency was over. This provided an explosive incentive to work hard to establish a widely recognised reputation as quickly as possible in the hope that this would stand us in good stead when life returned to normal.

Our initial task was to prepare for the opening of the RAF No. 22 E&RFTS during January 1938. This involved engaging additional aircraft maintenance engineers, a qualified and experienced parachute packer and flying instructors. An ex-RAF parachute packer Gerry Ball joined us in January 1938 and was to be with us until his retirement in September 1984. With the opening of our school, the AID (Aeronautical Inspection Directorate) required the nomination for their approval of a Chief Inspector. We had nobody at the time who was qualified, and the AID accepted me, with my experience of maintaining my own aircraft and responsibility for our Flying Training School for over eight years, backed by my university Engineering degree. I held the Company's No. 1 Inspection Stamp, which is still in the archives of Quality Control. We already had two very good ex-RAF Halton apprentices. At this time Halton was at the peak of its reputation for training first-class all-round tradesmen – they were quite excellent and I often refer to them as the salt of the earth. We were successful in engaging two more and recruited mechanics with little or no aircraft experience and additional apprentices. As Chief Inspector, I was responsible for approving the ex-RAF Halton engineers for signing for their own work and for the work of those working under them.

Peter May was appointed as our Chief RAFVR Flying Instructor. Leslie Worsdell, the first of our *ab initio* trained instructors, became Chief Flying Instructor of our civilian school and aero clubs at the age of 21, within two years of joining the Company. Peter May, aided and abetted by Leslie Worsdell, further developed our flying training efficiency. It was important to retain the tempo and operating efficiency we had achieved as a comparatively small unit and that the enthusiasm and excitement generated during those early days should overflow and become established in our new and much larger enterprise.

Our initial RAF establishment of six Tigers and six Hart aircraft was doubled within a few months. The big problem was the shortage of good flying instructors. Remembering our previous recruiting difficulties we decided to help ourselves by going ahead as a matter of urgency with what became known as Marshall's Ab Initio Flying Instructors Scheme training flying instructors from scratch. The milestones for completing the course, often improved upon, were: Elementary Flying Training, 50 hours (4 weeks); Additional Elementary and Advanced Flying Training, 100 hours (6–8 weeks); and Flying Instructor's Course 25 hours (1–2 weeks) – a total of 11–14 weeks.

We had a very good response to our advertisement for suitable applicants between the ages of 18 and 22 to be engaged on a probationary basis. We only accepted those who it was thought had good flying instructor potential and were employed in jobs which had little prospect of early promotion. This scheme was very attractive to young men, who were inclined to disregard all their former career prospects and the fact that the current urgent requirement for flying instructors might be short-lived. Fully qualified flying instructors were attracting salaries between £600 and £900 a year, which was a lot of money in those days. Under our scheme a successful *ab initio* instructor in his early twenties could earn this money within the first year or so, as compared with previous earnings of perhaps £4 or £5 a week.

During the training period the Company paid the apprentice instructors a few pounds a week, sufficient for them to live on. The scheme was a tremendous success. When these apprentices were passed out within a very few months by the RAF Central Flying School, Upavon, as advanced flying instructors they remembered all their own learning problems and rapidly learnt how to get the best out of their own pupils. These *ab initio* trained instructors were keen young enthusiasts, full of the joys of life, and they did sterling service during the drive to produce pilots quickly when pilots were so urgently required. Instructors trained in this way became some of our best instructors. Their enthusiasm for putting in as many flying instruction hours as possible quickly spread throughout the school and re-energised the older instructors.

The RAF could not understand our success in training very young men to become flying instructors in such a short space of time and without the benefit of years of squadron experience. The idea was considered quite revolutionary. We knew that our instructors' flying hours, aircraft hours and elapsed time for training pupils and instructors were well in advance of anything being achieved by any other civil or RAF operated Flying Training Schools. Marshall's flying training operated seven days a week for all hours of daylight, making flying instruction available to individual VR members whenever free of their normal employment.

The Air Ministry and the RAF initially thought Marshall was achieving these high flying times for financial gain. Such considerations were secondary to the importance to the Company of establishing an unrivalled reputation for all-round efficiency and, at this time of national crisis, doing everything possible to get more than a pint out of a pint pot. In any case, bearing in mind the urgent need to train pilots as quickly and as efficiently as possible at minimum cost, the more we could get out of aircraft and instructors the more economic it was for the nation. As far as profits were concerned our flying activities had cost us a lot of money in the first nine years of operation – all the work of my father and myself and the use of the land was free. Until after my father's death in 1942 the Directors did not receive any fees or salaries and no dividends were paid until after the war. From 1938 any profit in excess of that made prior to 1938 was subject to the Excess Profits Tax – the balance plus the established pre-1938 profit was then the basis for a company's normal taxable profit. For example, if a company had made £1,000 profit before 1938, and after 1938 made a profit of £10,000, there would be 80% excess profits tax on £9,000 of £7,200 leaving a balance of £1,800 to be added to the established pre-1938 profit of £1,000, making £2,800 on which normal tax was levied.

The real problem was that our flying instructor training scheme cut right across the RAF's long established practice of training instructors from carefully selected experienced RAF pilots. Not only were we not popular with Flying Training Headquarters, we were also becoming unpopular with competitor flying training companies because the RAF, despite what they were saying to us, were concurrently visiting them and asking why they were not achieving all that was being accomplished at Cambridge. Our competitors did everything possible to undermine us. We had one incident of a spy in the camp who fed anonymous reports to the RAF, including criticisms of standards of maintenance of aircraft. There was a general enquiry which clearly established that it was a put-up job and the source of the reports was identified. I was invited to attend a meeting where an apology was made and all relevant papers burnt in my presence.

In March 1938, the Ministry decided to establish four more Volunteer Reserve Flying Training Schools, and tenders were invited to which we responded. One centre was to be at Kidlington aerodrome, which was in the course of construction by Oxford City Council, with the Air Ministry erecting two prefabricated hangars and hutments to serve as a VR centre. A few days after submitting our tenders, I telephoned L. M. Jones at the Air Ministry Contracts Department and said, 'I am sure you know we have submitted our tenders and I hope we will be successful. If we are, Oxford goes very well with Cambridge.' L.M., as we came to know him, replied, 'We have already thought of that and, if you get a school, it would be Oxford.'

We opened No. 26 E&RFTS at Oxford on 24 June 1938. Bill Goode joined us direct from the RAF as our Chief Engineer. Peter May's deputy at Cambridge, Eric Grace, an ex-RAF instructor, was appointed our Chief Flying Instructor. At this time the Air Ministry decided that members of the Oxford and Cambridge University Air Squadrons who had attained a specified standard of flying and joined the RAFVR should attend Marshall's VR schools for advanced training on Hinds, Harts and Battles.

We immediately extended our *ab initio* Flying Instructor Training Scheme to provide instructors for the Oxford school. At the outbreak of war we were employing 35 flying instructors, over half of them Company-trained apprentices.

In August the Air Ministry, who had now gained confidence in our capability, decided on a major expansion at Cambridge for the elementary training of direct entry pilots to the RAF. We were to erect a very large hangar and administration block incorporating lecture rooms, a parachute room and a general assembly hall, and to be ready to receive pupils in the shortest possible time. This building was completed in six months and is now our No. 2 Hangar and Main Administration Block. A hutted camp with sleeping accommodation for direct entry RAF pupils was also built on the aerodrome. The hangar was constructed by Boulton & Paul of Norwich with building work by Coulson of Cambridge and electrical and heating installation by other contractors. Marshall undertook the direct supply of a number of materials and equipment including blockwood flooring, oak doors and surrounds, lavatory fittings and old Cambridge bricks. We co-ordinated the project ourselves, which resulted in a very high grade building at minimum cost. In 1939 the official report on the accommodation by Headquarters Flying Training Command stated: 'Cambridge has the best civil operated flying training centre accommodation in the country.' It was built at Government expense, as were the 'shadow factories' for aircraft and motor manufacturers, with the right to purchase when the national emergency was over.

The new building included a large Link Trainer room. The Link Trainer was one of the earliest forms of simulated flying training. An

American, Ed Link, whose father was a church organ builder, made a simulated flying machine operating on the principles of church organs. These became very popular at fairgrounds, and from this developed the simulated flying trainer which was used extensively by the RAF throughout the war and for many years thereafter. During the war each year we invited the Mayor and Mayoress to visit the aerodrome to see what was going on. We soon learned that we had to avoid getting the Mayor too interested in the Link Trainer. If the instructor got carried away and asked the Mayor, 'Would you like to try it, sir?' we knew we were stuck for at least half an hour.

For the official opening of our new aerodrome on 8 October 1938 by the Air Minister, Sir Kingsley Wood, we invited personally a few private owners who we were anxious should be there, and put a notice in the aviation press that all private owners were welcome. Aircraft were requested to arrive no later than 1.30 p.m. For those requiring lunch in Cambridge, a bus would leave at twelve o'clock, returning in time for the opening ceremony at two o'clock. We had a public enclosure for several thousand and a separate enclosure for invited guests, including 350 invited for the official luncheon. Rosemary and I received the guests as they passed through the Control Building.

Thanks to the good co-operation of Messrs Heffers printing works, a seating plan up-dated to nine o'clock that morning was handed to each lunch guest on arrival. The luncheon marquee was carpeted and draped in Cambridge blue and white. The catering was undertaken by Lyons of London, who were at that time considered the best catering company in the country. They put on the lunch as though it was being served in a London banqueting hall, with their 'nippies', as their waitresses were called, marching out in line to serve each course.

The Lord Lieutenant was going to propose the toast to the Secretary of State for Air but unfortunately he was indisposed and unable to attend on doctor's orders. He was represented by Field Marshal the Right Honourable Lord Birdwood who proposed the toast to Sir Kingsley Wood and said that the recent events in Europe indicated our vulnerability (this was at the time of Munich), that there was need for further effort and that the flying schools were doing great work. Norman de Bruyne, proposing the toast of the Cambridge Aerodrome, said:

> The partnership between father and son which we know as 'Marshall's' is something unique and this airport is a monument to two men who, working together in a perfect understanding founded on mutual respect, have always refused to do the easy thing if it meant turning back. They never lost sight of their goal so that now their vision is a reality for us all to see.
>
> It must be over ten years ago that Arthur Marshall first landed in the field behind his father's house and in so doing began the flying school and the aerodrome. I remember their ambition to build up the best flying school in the country and that recollection need cause them no embarrassment because they

have achieved their ambition and they have got the finest flying school in the country and I am very proud to have been the first of many hundreds of their pupils.

Now, 10 years is a fair slice of time out of a life and during that time these two young men (I hope Mr Marshall will forgive my presumption but he is as young in outlook as his son) – these two young men have never wavered in their enthusiasm and courage. And it was not easy to be enthusiastic or courageous because there were reverses which would have 'flattened' lesser men, if not embittered them. Everything had to be started from the beginning and everything had to be built up without the help of large amounts of capital.

To such difficulties were added what may be described as political troubles of no mean order. At one time it looked as though the Cambridge Town Council were determined to have a municipal aerodrome and would tolerate no other. How thankful we all are that the Council eventually came to a decision as wise as it was creditable to their reputation for fairness.

So as ratepayers we should be grateful for this airport, just as much as inhabitants we should be proud of it. I think that there is probably no airport in Europe, with the possible exception of Berlin, which is so conveniently placed in relation to the town.

Also as members of the University we should be grateful that the Flying School has always been run in full sympathy and understanding with the requirements of University discipline. An example which occurs to me is that at most aerodromes the club bar is the most profitable department of all. There has never been one here, and I know that has been Mr Marshall's special wish in view of the fact that we are a university town.

My father responded by thanking the previous speakers for their kind words and his guests for their presence. He said that since we began flying training in 1929 we had trained 500 pilots. He congratulated Sir Kingsley on his ministerial record, expressed confidence in his future and asked him to declare the aerodrome open.

Sir Kingsley Wood then declared the aerodrome open, and simultaneously three Harts took off, flown by members of the Cambridge Volunteer Reserve School. A flying programme followed, which included a formation of nine Avro Tutors by the Cambridge University Air Squadron, some aerobatic flying in a Hind by Leslie Worsdell, and a number of other events. The highlight of the afternoon was the first public showing of three Spitfires of No. 19 Squadron Duxford, with fixed pitch, two-bladed wooden propellers. The formation leader's orders to his flight were relayed to the crowd on the flying field.

The opening was nationally and locally very popular, reflecting the overwhelming national euphoria at the time of Munich. With all that has since been written and said criticising Chamberlain's Munich negotiations, it is useful to be reminded of the national anxiety and the relief and flag-waving when the Prime Minister came back brandishing his piece of paper and saying, 'Peace for our time'. There is no doubt that the year gained was of tremendous advantage to the Allies and that, in our state of preparation at

Munich time in October 1938, any effort to support the Czechs would have been disastrous.

Marshall's reputation for general efficiency and the rapid through-put of trained pilots had been established in a very short time between February and September. On 25 October 1938 Air Commodore Chamier, who at the time was advising a consortium on the possible establishment of a flying training centre near Bristol, wrote:

> I have been to the Air Ministry and have found out that you are 'a very blue-eyed boy' there. Apparently you succeed in getting more hours out of your machines, both elementary and advanced, than anyone else does. In fact you are a model school. I would like to congratulate you on having arrived so quickly at the stage of being a model for other schools. That is something to be proud of.

The Air Ministry appealed at Munich time for VR pilots who had reached an advanced standard of training to join an RAF squadron for a few months Service experience. Our VR schools at Oxford and Cambridge had trained more pilots to this standard in the short period of a few months than any of the other schools which had been established for a number of years.

In July 1938 Sir Kingsley Wood announced the Civil Air Guard Scheme to start on 1 October. In the CAG any man or woman, age unlimited, could learn to fly at a cost to the individual of five shillings an hour. Within not many days 30,000 applied. It was an interesting scheme, part of the national air-mindedness campaign, which trained many who were to play an active part in the war machine. Marshall's civil training aircraft fleet expanded from five to 10 Gipsy Moths and two Moth Minors by the time war was declared, with a substantial increase in flying instructors under the leadership of Leslie Worsdell.

Up to Christmas 1938 we had flown every day of the year, which gives an indication of Cambridge's good weather record for flying training. So as not to break the record for the full year, we flew on Christmas Day and Boxing Day.

In March 1939, with all buildings complete, our direct entry RAF flying school at Cambridge started operation with 50 resident pupils, all trained on Tiger Moths at the rate of approximately 40 pupils every eight weeks.

Night flying, as part of the VR training, was announced by the Air Ministry on 24 May 1939. Marshall's introduced night flying at both Cambridge and Oxford within two days (other schools followed somewhat later). That night I flew in our Leopard Moth to Oxford to see how they were getting on, and then returned to Cambridge; I had done no night flying since my Commercial Pilots 'B' Licence test of a flight from Croydon to Penshurst in 1930. Night flying was still looked upon as something a bit different for the first year or so of the war – but more of this later.

During 1939 Fairey Battle aircraft were issued to some VR schools. Equipment for the maintenance of these aircraft was very scarce. Most of the schools flew their machines until they became grounded because of the shortage of spares and equipment, and the aircraft were then put on one side until their problems were solved. We were determined to make full use of these Battle aircraft in the national interest, and improvised means of keeping them in the air. The Cambridge VR centre completed 832 hours flying on Battle aircraft during the few months prior to the outbreak of war. No other school achieved more than 12 hours Battle flying.

We were all delighted when Peter May in 1939 received the AFC for his services to RAF flying training.

During 1938 and 1939 Air Commodore Adrian Chamier established the Air Defence Cadet Corps (ADCC) on behalf of the Air League of the British Empire. He came to see me and I said we would give our fullest support, but I was anxious not to be personally involved. He had meetings with the Mayor and with Alderman Peck, an ex-Mayor, and Wing Commander Lockyer, CO of the University Air Squadron. The Mayor called a meeting at the University Lecture Rooms, Mill Lane, which was well attended, and it was resolved that a Cambridge Squadron should be formed. A Committee was elected and Alderman Peck, Wing Commander Lockyer and my father ganged up and told me I had got to be Chairman. Roger Parker (a Local Director of Barclays Bank) was elected Honorary Treasurer and offered Barclays Bank as a venue for our initial meetings.

The motto of the ADCC was devised by Air Commodore Chamier as a result of Major General Sir Thomas Marden, when addressing a meeting of ADCC Cadets, stating that 'They would find in the Corps something not to be found on sea or land unless specially sought out – adventure'. The Air Commodore cottoned on to the word 'adventure' and there and then invented the motto 'Venture, Adventure'. This inspiring motto has been a guiding principle of the Corps.

Tremendous initial support was given by Wing Commander Lockyer of the University Air Squadron, who provided two ex-RAF ground instructors and also introduced Arthur Chapman of the University Engineering Department, who became the Cambridge Squadron's wartime CO. The Squadron initially had its headquarters in a small building on the aerodrome along the Teversham Road, and had the use of the University Air Squadron Lecture Rooms at Scroope House.

Since the founding of our garage in 1909 big strides had been made by the motor trade nationally. Roads had become busy, and country villages (where a stranger was a rarity in the early part of the century) had now become towns, and much money continued to be spent on the building of new roads. As a result of the motor car, people could live further from their place of work and, most important of all, since the First World War motor cars and their maintenance had become progressively cheaper.

In 1937 Austin introduced an 18 hp saloon fitted with a Hayes automatic, infinitely variable gearbox. It was only a partial success because of its slightly reduced all-round performance and increased maintenance costs as a result of the short life of its roller components. In the summer of 1938, General Poole, who had an Austin 18 with the Hayes automatic transmission and lived at Newmarket, telephoned me at the garage at four o'clock one afternoon and asked if my father had taken his car by mistake from the Newmarket July Racecourse since he knew my father had a similar blue Austin 18 Saloon. General Poole had waited until all the cars had gone and there was one Austin 18 left which was not his. I asked my father if he had brought back General Poole's car by mistake. He said, 'I don't think so but I will have a look!' He came back and said, 'No, this is not my car, but it's a good job I brought it back because there is something wrong with the gears.' He had never driven a Hayes automatic gearbox before and just thought something had gone wrong with his own gears. As I have said, my father was not mechanically minded and all he was interested in was the throttle.

Our garage continued to make good progress until, as war clouds darkened, trade deteriorated rapidly during 1939. The motor trade had a large accumulation of second-hand cars, and car sales were at a standstill. Many distributors would have had financial problems but for the eventual recovery of the second-hand car market as the war progressed and most new cars were allocated to the war effort in various military, industrial and civil guises.

In 1939 Austin re-entered the commercial vehicle market with a 2–3 ton chassis in competition with Bedfords, and with plans for a full range of commercial vehicles. We were in the process of building a commercial vehicle depot opposite the aerodrome when war broke out. We completed it except for the showroom and offices and used it for the repair of aircraft throughout the war, when it was known as our No. 3 Hangar. It has now reverted to its original intended use as the Company's Commercial Vehicle Depot, known as Airport Garage.

Just before war broke out we completed plans with a Cambridge architect for a multi-storey rebuilding of the Jesus Lane garage at a cost of between £35,000 and £40,000. The plans were agreed with Jesus College, after careful consideration to avoid any shadow on the College hockey pitch, which was all important under frost conditions. With the advent of war the rebuilding was abandoned.

In March 1939 my six sisters and two or three of their husbands went with my father to Egypt, where they took part in a number of Arab horse races, some of which my father won. He was particularly taken by two Arab stallions which, with a stallion donkey, he had shipped to England. He retired during the year and moved to Hove where he did much riding on the Sussex Downs on his Arab horses. He kept a watchful eye on what was happening at Cambridge and returned to Whitehill for a few days each week.

Judith Rosemary Perdita, to our everlasting delight, was born on 10 April 1939 at Broxton. She was christened at Christmas while we were staying with Rosemary's Uncle Dick and Aunt Ethel at Llanstephan.

Rosemary had always been interested in farming, and in 1939 we decided to try to find a small farm and country house within a few miles of Cambridge. We looked at one or two but had got no further than buying a tractor and a few farm implements when war broke out and the idea was not resurrected until after the war.

My fifth sister Molly completed her education in France in 1938 and between terms had learnt to fly. After much discussion, to her amazement and delight, my father suggested she should do an engineering course at the aerodrome. She became our first woman engineering trainee in 1938. Rosemary and I were detailed from time to time to chaperone her at the Saturday evening dinner dances at the University Arms Hotel.

Molly later became a pilot in the ATA (Air Transport Auxiliary) ferrying aircraft during the war, and in recent years recorded a tape of her experiences for the Imperial War Museum. When asked about being the first woman aircraft engineer trainee at Cambridge and the only woman there, she said:

> It didn't really worry me in the very least. The fact was that obviously I was wearing dungarees like everyone else and, because I was a member of the family, I knew I had got to work harder than anybody else because, you know, if you are assumed to be in any sort of privileged position you have got to prove that you are not. I learnt that I didn't take days off and that I reported for work absolutely on the dot and the Chief Engineer there was extremely good about it – he made no exceptions either.

Asked about her specific duties, she went on:

> One used to strip engines down. One did all sorts of maintenance on them, but one also stripped them down and replaced component parts. I also did my stint on duty with the night flying that was going on, when they had to have an engineer on duty in case there was a heavy landing or something and, if there was, then one inspected the airframe and made sure it was safe to go on flying. There was one quite amusing incident when one chap found me bent double into a cockpit and gave me a quick flip on the rear. I am sure it caused a good deal of amusement to whoever was standing around at the time. I paid no attention and just got on with my work and the incident passed. I think this was a great relief to the Chief Engineer that I was not standing on dignity or being prim or difficult.

Molly has recorded on many occasions the great help and sympathetic support that she had from Peter Else – fresh from his engineering apprenticeship – during her initial training.

During this period my father decided to up-date his Will, and he arranged a meeting with Joe Taylor, our solicitor, at his office in Newmarket to tell us what he wanted. Our respective shareholdings in the companies were two-thirds my father and one-third myself. My father's instructions were to increase my number of shares sufficiently to provide me with a total holding of 50 per cent with the remaining 50 per cent and the residue of the estate to my six sisters. Joe Taylor was surprised and said that he would have thought, with my involvement and responsibilities, I should have been left with something more than 50 per cent. He finally said to my father, 'Surely you are going to leave the boy with something more than 50 per cent.' I did not enter into any argument, except to say that I thought I should be left with sufficient shares to maintain voting control, to which my father replied, 'If you can't maintain voting control with a 50 per cent holding plus the Chairman's casting vote, I don't think you will be a very good Chairman.' I knew my father had been somewhat shaken as a result of a friend of his, who had a son and four daughters, dying recently and leaving the whole of his substantial business and most of the residue of his estate to his son, leaving the four girls in a comparatively poor financial position.

Looking back, I do not think I was particularly hurt. I was a little disappointed and certainly surprised. It has in fact worked well. I think I can say without fear of contradiction that I have never worked for myself alone, and whatever I have gained personally has been a by-product of my life's work. I had a deep feeling of responsibility for my own family and for employment in the region. Fortunately I found that by nature the additional responsibility of a number of shareholders was good for me, and what could be better than that these shareholders should be the family. With give and take on all sides it has worked out very well for everybody. The Company required all the capital available for its day-to-day operation and development and, with the co-operation of all shareholders, we established a prudent dividend policy. Yes, I am very pleased with what has happened over the years and feel that for the family as a whole nothing could have worked better.

On 25 June 1939, we took delivery of an American Stinson aircraft – a very comfortable five-seater, high wing monoplane (rather like a big American car) fitted with a 290 hp radial Lycoming engine. This was our first experience of an aircraft with a self-starter. We used the Stinson for Army co-operation flying, and I used it in the few months left before the war, mainly for routine visits to Oxford.

On Sunday 30 July 1939 Rosemary, Michael, David, Norman de Bruyne and I flew in the Stinson to Hatfield and had tea on the clubhouse veranda – a beautiful day. Five year old David became very interested in the fountain and, much to the amusement of everybody, managed to fall in. In conversation during tea I said, 'I would like to know a bit more about what is happening at this place Danzig, which seems to be the big bone of contention with Germany. How about going next weekend and seeing what it is all about?' Rosemary immediately said, 'I'm not coming. I have Judy to look after' – but Norman said, 'I'll come.' And so, on Friday 4 August, Norman and I set out in the Stinson, landing to refuel at Amsterdam and then on to Templehof Aerodrome which is virtually in Berlin, where we stayed the night. Food was in short supply. It was a beautiful, hot weekend and, when we talked to any Germans about the possibility of war, they said, 'No war – lovely weather – we are all going on holiday.'

On Saturday 5 August we flew to Warsaw for lunch. Everything was gloom and doom, with the Poles hopelessly believing that somehow England and France would come to their rescue. There was general dilapidation all round, with long grass growing between the railway lines of the main Warsaw station. They were advertising 'Air trips to France avoiding Germany'. We visited the ghetto where the Jews lived, and what a dreadful sight that was. I asked a taxi driver in Warsaw, 'Is there going to be war?' and received the short answer, 'Of course.'

After lunch we continued to Danzig (now Gdansk), where everything looked prosperous and tidy. In the evening we motored to the seaside casino at Sopot, a few miles away. We had dinner on the casino terrace, sharing a table with a German architect and his wife. We talked about the situation generally – Norman spoke fluent German. We remarked that everything was very prosperous with plenty of food available in Danzig compared with little food in Germany. Their attitude was, 'We are Germans – we must go back to the Reich.' I understand that when Germany took over Danzig they were given special extra rations for six months to get them used to it.

On the return journey we had intended to stay the Sunday night in Warsaw and then proceed to Berlin on the Monday, returning to England on Tuesday. However, on hearing on our one-way wireless, during the flight from Danzig, the general broadcast from Warsaw expressing doom and war, war, war, we decided that the sooner we got home the better and that after lunch we would fly on to Berlin. We had lunch in the main hotel in Warsaw and, in spite of the general gloom outside, the dining room was full of people enjoying a leisurely meal which would finish very late in the afternoon.

We took off for Berlin, but as we got towards the German border the weather deteriorated, with low cloud and bad visibility. Time was also running out. We decided to turn back, and we scrambled into the Polish Air Force Station at Posen at dusk. There we were met by a number of young Polish Air Force officers who came out saying, 'War, War, War' and held up imaginary rifles to their shoulders saying, 'We will shoot them down – bang, bang, bang.' We stayed the night at Posen and set off first thing on Monday 7 August for a flight direct to Amsterdam for refuelling. We wanted to avoid a landing in Germany as we were worried that in poor visibility on the previous evening we might have flown over a German prohibited area on the Polish/German border. We got back to Cambridge on Monday evening. With all that has been written about what was happening in Germany and on the Polish border in the few weeks before the invasion of Poland, I think we were very lucky to have got back without trouble.

Fringe firms, other than the main aircraft manufacturers, were already undertaking the refurbishing and up-dating of RAF fighter aircraft, but not large bombers for which they had no large hangar capacity. Our new, very large, No. 2 Hangar gave us capacity for bomber aircraft, and we made this known to the Ministry early in 1939. In August we were made responsible for the refurbishing, modification and up-dating of Armstrong-Whitworth Whitley twin-engined bomber aircraft and eventually became solely responsible for their complete rebuilding throughout the war. Because all civil aircraft had been grounded since 27 August, Rosemary and Peter May's wife, Doreen, drove Peter and myself to RAF Shawbury to collect our first Whitley aircraft on Saturday afternoon, 2 September.

Companies operating RAF Volunteer Reserve Schools had become increasingly concerned about their future in the event of hostilities. All sorts of rumours were flying around, such as that all the schools would be closed down, or that some would be sandwiched together or requisitioned. I was therefore very relieved when, two or three days before war was declared, I received a phone call telling me confidentially that if war came Oxford was to close and the Oxford personnel and aircraft were to be transferred to Cambridge without delay. Detailed instructions were contained in a sealed envelope, delivered the next day by despatch rider, which was not to be opened unless war was declared. Nearly two-thirds of the schools were closed.

With all civil aircraft grounded, the Air Ministry had given me permission to use an RAF Tiger Moth when available for my personal transport. I flew to Kidlington with the sealed envelope on the morning of Sunday 3 September and was in the air at 11 o'clock when the Prime Minister made the announcement that we were at war with Germany. On arrival at Kidlington I opened the envelope and agreed arrangements with Eric Grace, our Chief Instructor and Manager, and Bill Goode, the Chief Engineer, for the transfer to Cambridge.

Chapter 14

Impact of War
3 September 1939–1940

AS A RESULT of the rapid build-up of German armaments throughout the thirties, the re-occupation of the Rhineland, the occupation of Austria and, after the Munich Agreement, the invasion of Czechoslovakia and finally Poland, people had become acclimatised to the inevitability of war. When war came they were more prepared for it and accepted it much more calmly than in 1914 when for a few weeks, as I well remember, there had been mild panic. The Government benefited from the experiences of the First World War and knew many of the actions to be taken and the national, regional and local committees to be formed.

At Cambridge some of the colleges were worried that famous and irreplaceable buildings might be bombed. I was involved in discussing the suggestion that King's College Chapel should be camouflaged. We advised that this was not practical and, in the event, it is fortunate that it was not attempted. On the other hand the Company received a directive to camouflage our aerodrome buildings without delay. This we did using any camouflage-coloured paint we could lay our hands on. Unfortunately this paint has proved very durable and we have tried without success to remove it, including with steam. We still hope that as time goes by the remaining camouflage will disappear. The brickwork most affected is that consisting of 'Old Cambridge' bricks used in the construction of our prestigious Administration Block.

During the summer of 1939 my sister Molly became engaged to Bernard Rose, an Oxford don. They planned to get married in 1940 but it was obvious that Bernard, at 23, was going to be called up. So, preferring to have the responsibilities of marriage, they were married from my father's flat at Hove at All Saints Parish Church on 23 December, with a reception at the Royal Pavilion. They had a normal life at Oxford until Bernard was called up early in 1940, when Molly returned to Cambridge as a ground engineer. My fourth brother-in-law, Mary's husband Charlie Cavendish, had joined the Buckinghamshire Yeomanry as a Territorial before the war and was called up when war broke out. Violet's husband, Teddy Barbezat, joined the RAF in 1940.

At the outbreak of war I moved my office from our Jesus Lane garage to the Flying Club Members' Room on the first floor of the aerodrome control building. My father, only just retired, returned to Cambridge and relieved me of all responsibility regarding the garage and the new aerodrome canteen. The garage undertook the manufacture of shell parts, as they had done in the First World War, and the servicing of military vehicles. The vehicle overhaul work continued throughout the war and was then transferred to the aerodrome works where it blossomed into a very substantial contract which continued until 1987.

There was much activity in making our preparations for war, including air raid precautions, fire fighting and the building of a decontamination centre against the possibility of mustard gas bombing. Temporary air raid shelters were erected, to be followed by more permanent structures. There was, of course, a complete black-out of all windows, including the hangar rooflights.

Norwich was one of the first cities to suffer serious air raid damage, including at Boulton & Paul, whom we knew well. Our Works Maintenance Manager, Percy Gipson, and I went to Norwich to see if there was anything to be learnt from their experience. Mr Taylor, Boulton & Paul's Managing Director, showed us what had happened and gave us a very good dinner at the Royal Hotel, Norwich – the last real steak of the war.

It was getting dusk as we started the return journey to Cambridge. The car headlights were blacked out except for two narrow slits. Shortly after we had left Norwich two young men waved us down and asked for a lift to Wymondham. We talked generally about the recent air raids and bombing, and dropped them at Wymondham. After a few miles we were stopped by the police, who said that we had been reported at Wymondham Police Station for our interest in air raids in the area. Having cleared this, we resumed our journey. We had not gone many miles, and I was about to pass a lorry, when a convoy rushed past on the off-side knocking a few bits and pieces off our car, including the door handles. We had a very narrow escape. The next morning a Major called to apologise, and he told us that somebody thought it a good idea to try out a convoy on a main road at night without any lights at all, which resulted in several accidents within the first hour. He was now going round to make his peace with all who had been involved.

During the first few months of the war our garage converted two Austin Twelve cars into armoured cars, using boiler-plate from a local stockist. Weight was a problem, so we restricted the spring movement. These vehicles were useful for patrolling the aerodrome at night. Somebody suggested we should see what happened if a rifle was fired at them. A rifle bullet fired at close range went straight through, which was not very encouraging.

Because of the risk of bombing, the Company was instructed to picket out all the Tiger Moth training aircraft and to operate from dispersed flights around the aerodrome perimeter. Each flight had its own garden shed type office, and all flying training and day-to-day servicing of aircraft had to be carried out in the open at the individual flight locations. Refreshments were sent out by the canteen to these flights and to the hangars and workshops. The 1939/40 winter was very severe. Many of the Tiger Moths were seriously damaged in a blizzard; one broke away from its picketing and finished wrapped round a telegraph pole on the opposite side of Newmarket Road. There was not so much anti-freeze about in those days and car cooling systems could freeze within a few miles. Flying instructor Herbert Tappin recalls that my father organised parties to play ice hockey on the frozen sewage works at Milton.

We were instructed to fit bomb racks to eight Tiger Moths to carry eight 20lb anti-personnel bombs under each wing for use against any invasion forces. This modification was known as the Banquet Light Scheme. The plan was to fly just above ground level until the enemy was identified and then to climb to 800 feet and dive-bomb down to 500 feet to release the bombs before, hopefully, returning home. With no dummy bombs available, practice descent approaches were carried out with the aircraft flown from the front cockpit and bricks thrown over the side from the rear cockpit but it was discovered that the bricks fell faster than a diving Tiger Moth, risking catastrophic damage to the propeller. An instruction was therefore given to eject the bricks very forcibly away from the aircraft.

It became a matter of urgency that I should find somebody to work alongside me and accept full responsibility for much of the Company's general administration, including ARP (air-raid precautions) and fire fighting. I spoke to Ronnie Bowles, the Personnel Manager, and he immediately responded with, 'We've got the very man on the aerodrome – Dick Lane.' A real stroke of luck – I saw him within the hour and he worked with me throughout the war. Dick, a partner in the well-known Newmarket solicitors Rustons & Lloyd, was over military age but anxious to play an active part in the war effort. He had applied to the London Fire Brigade but was turned down because of vertigo. He then enquired if Marshall's had anything suitable and as a result became a Link Trainer Instructor. After the war Dick returned to his practice in Newmarket and continued as a Director of our Company for many years.

Dick Lane assumed immediate responsibility for the ARP and Fire Fighting Services which became very efficient units and played an important part in the Company's operation throughout the war. S. J. Driver and E. D. Ankin, members of our Auxiliary Fire Service, were awarded the BEM for the risks they took and the success of their actions when a Whitley bomber caught fire one night in 1942 in our main hangar. They climbed on the aircraft and successfully played hoses on one of the mainplanes whilst the source of the trouble was dealt with. The Marshall team won the eastern region competition at the University rugger ground for 'Rescue' drill for teams of seven men, and went on to win the national final at Victoria Tower, London in 1944.

Following the blitzkrieg invasion of Belgium and France in May 1940, the Home Guard was formed to prepare for an invasion of England, and quickly grew to a force of one million. In the summer of 1940, the Marshall Company formed its own unit which had drill, operational exercises and rifle range practice, and provided a small nightly patrol of the aerodrome perimeter.

There was an acute shortage of skilled labour and we opened a training centre to provide the specific basic skills we needed. This included training a number of young women in a general way for aircraft repair in which there was very little repetitive work. We were particularly successful in training female labour to become good carpenters.

In May 1940, during the fall of France, Lysanders of 16 Squadron arrived back from that country in a battered state and were dispersed along the Newmarket Road and the eastern boundary of the aerodrome. For security, the Newmarket Road was closed and the traffic diverted through Fen Ditton until the middle of 1941. Marshall's had no responsibility for the decision to close the road, but we nevertheless became most unpopular as it was locally assumed that we must have been involved. Many applications were made to the appropriate authority for special passes, most of which were turned down. The Germans tried to bomb the Lysanders, and in December 1940 a Dornier 215 flying at low level machine-gunned the airfield and slightly damaged a few Tiger Moths, an Oxford, a Magister and a Lysander. A rumour quickly spread that the pilot of the Dornier had been an undergraduate at Cambridge and knew his way around. During the time they were at Cambridge, Lysanders went out on regular coastal patrols for any sight of invaders.

Peter May was always full of fun and bright ideas. During the Battle of Britain, when the Company was repairing Gladiator aircraft, he managed to scrounge some ammunition and thought it would be a good idea to have two Gladiators available for flight test during air-raid warnings so that he and I could take to the air to protect the aerodrome as an encouragement to those working to continue with their work during the air-raid warning period. This plan went into practice on three occasions in August 1940. The problem was to know when the 'all clear' had been sounded because there was no radio in the aircraft. However, during air raid warning periods it was the practice for buses to remain stationary. We would watch the buses and, as soon as they started to move, we landed. Fortunately, at least for me, no enemy aircraft appeared.

By 1940 the Cambridge Squadron of the Air Defence Cadet Corps had become firmly established. In October the Squadron's first Annual General Meeting was held at the Guildhall, attended by the Lord Lieutenant, as Patron, the Mayor, the Chairman of the County Council, and the Vice

Chancellor. The Secretary reported that officers and ground instructors had been appointed. The Squadron was attracting an excellent type of boy, and applications for membership had been in excess of the numbers that could be initially accepted.

Our Oxford flying training team was absorbed into our Cambridge RAF training centre, now known as No. 22 EFTS. Bill Goode from Oxford was appointed Chief Engineer. The Cambridge University Air Squadron, closed down on the outbreak of war, re-opened in October 1940 with some of its members gaining flying experience with No. 22 EFTS.

Wilkie Wilkinson, our pre-war Cambridge Chief Engineer, transferred to what became known as Marshall's Aircraft Repair Organisation, initially on Whitleys, Gladiators, Harts and Oxfords. There was a colossal shortage of intermediate twin-engine training aircraft during the first two years of the war, which made the repair of the Oxfords very important.

The Ministry of Aircraft Production (MAP) was established in May 1940 to be responsible for aircraft manufacture and repair. The MAP set up the Civil Repair Organisation (CRO) at Merton College, Oxford, who were responsible to the MAP for the provision of adequate aircraft repair, rebuild and conversion facilities and for allocating aircraft to individual contractors. The Director of the CRO, Jimmy Woodcock OBE, and his staff were seconded from Morris Motors by Lord Nuffield.

The instruction we had received that all trainer aircraft were to be dispersed and serviced in the open at the flight locations had made it possible for all the hangar maintenance of the EFTS aircraft to be undertaken in our original No. 1 Hangar and two blister hangars, one on the north perimeter and a second in the south-east corner of the aerodrome. This left our large No. 2 Hangar, which could accommodate a number of any type of aircraft operated by the RAF in World War II, available to the Company's developing Aircraft Repair Division.

With the rapid build-up of aircraft repair work, my father became extremely worried about our overall financial position and talked about this with Lord Chesham, Charlie Cavendish's father, who suggested that he should speak to Harold Smart, who advised Lord Chesham on all his financial affairs. Having studied the accounts, he said we were obviously seriously undercapitalised resulting from undertaking major Government contracts at overnight notice. He volunteered that this should not be too much of a worry whilst we were operating for one customer, the Government, provided we worked within the terms and conditions of individual Government contracts and were assured of regular payments, well backed with adequate and reliable banking facilities. He went on to say that the position would be quite different if we were carrying out the same volume of work with orders from many customers, with the commercial risks associated with the ups and downs of industry.

Lord Beaverbrook was the first Minister of Aircraft Production with direct responsibility to Winston Churchill to increase the output and availability of aircraft. Lord Beaverbrook's office established a practice of ringing every Friday evening at five o'clock to ask our Works Manager how many aircraft had been repaired and delivered that week. One Friday evening later in the war Lord Beaverbrook telephoned in person to ask the score and Freddy Hornsby, the Works Manager, thinking he would get a pat on the back said, 'I am pleased to tell you, sir, we have had a record week of 28 aircraft.' Lord Beaverbrook's only reply was, 'Make it 30,' and he put down the receiver. Our best weekly production was 33 aircraft made up of 11 rebuilds at Cambridge and 22 on site. Marshall's Aircraft Repair Organisation was to develop into the largest and most versatile of the CRO's aircraft repair contractors in the UK with a peak employment of just over 3,200. Over 5,000 aircraft were repaired or converted during the war.

On the outbreak of war Marshall's civilian aircraft, including my original Gipsy Moth G-AAEH, were requisitioned to be used by the RAF for general communications; G-AAEH never returned and was eventually allotted to the Air Training Corps as an instructional airframe.

Leslie Worsdell and all his instructors who were training civilians were members of the RAFVR and were mobilised. Leslie was instructed to report immediately to the RAF's Cambridge centre at Douglas House, Trumpington Road, where he was issued with a uniform and a truncheon and ordered to guard Marshall's aerodrome. The next morning he reported to the aerodrome where a few days before he had been the Chief Flying Instructor, and was now a Sergeant Pilot guarding with a truncheon from home-made sandbag pillboxes. After two or three weeks he was sent on indefinite leave and then, after a few weeks, instructed to report to the Initial Training Wing at Cambridge University, where he was billeted in undergraduate accommodation. Most of their time was spent learning how to drill, with lectures on airmanship and having inoculations or recovering from inoculations. Leslie in recent years recorded a tape for the Imperial War Museum, and of this period he said: 'We were quite a sight marching through the streets of Cambridge in groups of 100 or so, and rapidly became very smart, marching at a high rate, buttons well polished, gas masks slung and arms swinging so that they were almost higher than our heads – a typically exaggerated young man's marching as taught at that time.'

The majority of the RAFVR training schools had been closed when war was declared and the surviving schools, including Cambridge, were reduced to elementary flying training with the loss of their advanced training aircraft – the Harts, Hinds and Battles. The Company's flying instructors instructing RAF pupils were also members of the Volunteer Reserve but remained on the Company's payroll and continued to give their instruction in mufti. There was an immediate drop in the numbers of pupils. Many hundreds of pre-war VR pilots were left partially trained waiting to be called up as the war rolled on. If these schools had been allowed to continue with their Harts, Hinds and Battles, they could in a short space of time have completed the training of these Volunteer Reservists to an advanced standard ready for conversion to operational aircraft. The instructors were there eager and waiting with thousands of hours of unused instructional capacity. Our instructor Herbert Tappin's log book shows that his monthly flying instruction hours at this time dropped from an average of over 95 hours a month for the six-month period prior to the war to about 20 hours per month for the first six months of the war. The winter of 1939/40 was very hard from the weather point of view but would not account for these very low hours.

The civil operated EFTSs were virtually marking time. It was for us at Cambridge a very demoralising experience. Coupled with this, the Marshall practice of taking suitable pilots from within the VR and training them as instructors came to an end at the outbreak of war when we were restricted to elementary training of direct entry pupils for the RAF.

Above left Sir Kingsley Wood, the then Air Minister, and my father at the official opening of the new aerodrome on 8 October 1938.

Above right My father in 1938. (*Cambridge Daily News*)

Below Spitfires from No. 19 Squadron, RAF Duxford, at the opening of the new aerodrome in October 1938.

Above Our American Stinson G-AFRS at Hatfield on Sunday 30 July 1939 when we planned to fly to Berlin and Danzig on 4 August. Left to right: Rosemary, Michael, myself and David. (*Norman de Bruyne*)

Below EFTS aircraft under daily routine maintenance in blister hangar along Newmarket Road during World War II. (*Bedford Lemere & Co*)

Bottom Marshall's World War II Miles Falcon communications aircraft G-ADLI.

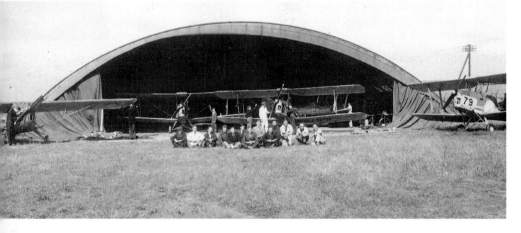

Mosquito NFXII (HK 117) in March 1943, one of many Mosquitoes we converted to night fighters. (*Air Ministry*)

Hawker Typhoons from the Second Front in 1944 under damage repair in No. 6 Hangar. (*Bedford Lemere & Co*)

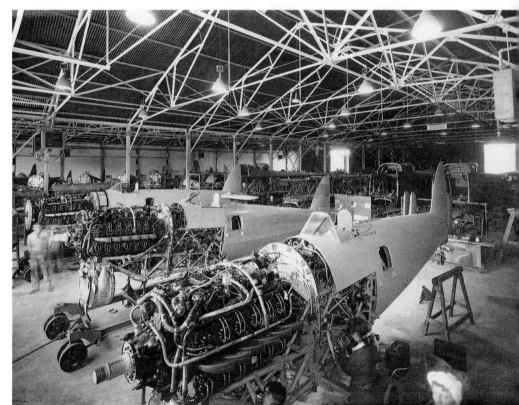

Above Mosquitoes in No. 2 Hangar during World War II. (*Bedford Lemere & Co*)

Below The first post-war civil UK pilot instruction flight on 1 January 1946. Tiger Moth G-ACDG on left and Miles Falcon G-ADLI on right in front of the camouflaged Control Building. Left to right: myself, Lady Bragg, Norman de Bruyne, Leslie Worsdell, and Douglas Winton-Smith. (*Cambridge Daily News*)

Bottom An aerial view of Horseheath Lodge. (*Cambridge Daily News*)

Whitbread's brewer's dray 1948.

Whitbread's low-loader, curtain-sided, brewer's dray 1987.

One of the first of 390 Marshall Leyland buses for Argentina, being loaded at London docks.

Vampire Cat IV rebuild at Waterbeach in the early fifties. (*Bruce*)

Above New Venom assembly 1955. (*Bruce*)

Below Vampire T11 WZ590 converted by Marshall to ejector seat standard in 1954 and now preserved at the Imperial War Museum, Duxford, Cambridgeshire.

Bottom Group Captain Johnnie Johnson, the inspecting officer of the Cambridge ATC Squadron in 1956. Left to right: Lord Lieutenant Captain Briscoe, Johnnie Johnson, Flight Lieutenant Snazle (Squadron CO) and myself.

Above Vickers Valiants in work in No. 12 Hangar in 1958.

Below New BOAC long-range Series 312 Britannia G-AOVK ready for delivery at Cambridge, 1958.

Bottom Iraqi Airways Viscount YI-ACL at Cambridge 1960.

Above left 'Cambridge boy Michael Marshall a gallant but losing stroke.' University Boat Race 1954. (*Cambridge Daily News*)

Above right Viscounts, DC7, Varsity, Gulfstream in work in No. 10 Hangar in the fifties.

Below The last of our air charter Rapides G-AGZO sold to France in 1962. Bill Goode is on the left.

Visit of HRH Prince Philip, Duke of Edinburgh, in July 1964. Left to right: myself, Roy Gates, Prince Philip, Lord Lieutenant Roger Parker and Norman Harry. (*Fox Photos*)

Arrival of the first Hercules C-130K (XV177) from America on 19 December 1966.

Concorde nose and visor on final check-out No. 2 Hangar.

Take-off of prototype Concorde – the first with Marshall nose and retractable visor – with a Canberra observer in December 1971. (*Flight magazine*)

'Snoopy' Hercules meteorological research aircraft XV208 at Cambridge in 1973.

Hercules C-130 XV204 at Cambridge in 1980 after completing centre wing change trials at Boscombe Down.

Completion of first Marshall stretch Hercules XV197 in 1979.

Hercules C-130 outer wing rebuild programme in No. 11 Hangar in 1979.

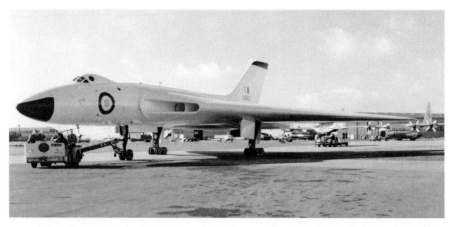

Above Vulcan XA903, used as a flight test bed for MRCA (Tornado) RB.199 turbo-fan engine, ready for flight in 1972.

Below Buccaneer MRCA avionic hack aircraft XT272 with Tornado radome fitted to a faired nose on trials at Bedford in 1974.

Bottom One of the 11 B(I)68 Canberras (PAF-247) supplied to the Peruvian Air Force in 1975.

Citations in work at Cambridge.

Gulfstreams in work in No. 16 Hangar in September 1979.

Chapter 15

Elementary Flying Training
1939–1942

AT THE OUTBREAK of war the German Air Force outnumbered the RAF by about three to one. It was estimated that it would take three years to achieve parity, and plans seemed to have been made to meet this hypothesis without considering what might happen and how we would survive in the meantime.

Whatever was achieved by VR schools before the war was with Volunteer Reservists only available to fly in their spare time at weekends and in the evenings; now in the RAF pupils were available to fly all day and every day. Knowing the shortage of flying instructors and fully trained pilots, we had assumed that with the outbreak of war flying training would be accelerated and schools worked to maximum capacity. But the reverse was the case. Flying schools experienced a serious loss of momentum and functioned at a fraction of their capacity. It has been recognised in many quarters that there was a serious failure to train pilots during the first year of the war and many reasons have been put forward. The simple fact is that there was no efficient national plan to train as many pilots and instructors as possible. The Air Ministry recognised what had already been achieved by Marshall's Volunteer Reserve schools at Oxford and Cambridge, but the RAF ignored how it was done and did not act on it.

Before the war our two Volunteer Reserve schools had operated two or three times more efficiently than any other flying school measured by the number of elementary and advanced pilots trained per instructor and per aircraft. We now felt the country was letting the grass grow under its feet, and we were convinced that there would soon have to be a change of direction towards maximum training of pilots and instructors. It would then be imperative to 'squeeze the pips' to produce as many first-class pilots as possible in the shortest possible time. Now, with much larger schools than before the war, the only way we could see to match or improve on our pre-war performance was to tighten discipline, start the day's flying punctually, eliminate waiting time between flights and decrease instructors' paperwork, all to achieve maximum flying hours per instructor and per aircraft, at the same time reducing instructors' attendance to eight hours a day, six days a week with no standing around.

We accordingly prepared a plan for flying training to be in full operation seven days a week. The pupils would be divided into Flights, each Flight having a rotational one day off per week provided the flying programme was up to schedule. In addition to daily ground instruction there would be training classes on three evenings a week. Our idea was to introduce a daily flying programme for each pupil for varying weather conditions and, making full use of all hours of daylight in the winter, to provide a continuous flow of flying instruction throughout the day and as much night flying as possible. We produced a 'Flying Programme Procedure' leaflet to make available to all new pupils and planned to give them time in class to read it and ask questions. The leaflet contained all relevant information including ground handling of aircraft, lectures, time off, air-raid and emergency alarms and general discipline. It emphasised:

> In the winter it will be necessary to fly every hour of daylight, and every available machine should be in the air for as many hours as possible with the aim of a minimum target of seven hours a day.
>
> All pupils must make themselves fully acquainted with the Flying Programme Procedure which will list daily: pupils' flight times; exercises to be carried out depending on weather conditions; refuelling times; machine numbers; and flying instructor's name.
>
> The alternative weather programmes will provide for: average weather conditions; very good weather conditions; below average weather conditions; bad weather which may be suitable for some pupils; very bad weather with all flying cancelled.
>
> Pupils must:
> i. Note on a piece of paper full details of their flying programme for the day, including refuelling and flight times (refuelling times were also indicated on a slip pasted inside the right-hand door of both front and rear cockpits).
> ii. Be equipped, ready and waiting before their flights are scheduled to start.
>
> Pupils will be detailed to assist with the general handling, refuelling and starting of aircraft engines between flights. The list of approved pupils will be posted, noting that these duties greatly facilitate the flying programme running to schedule and are of important educational value to the pupil.

We prepared all this in detail and put it on ice to await a change of climate.

Discussions had been going on since before the war between the Air Ministry and the RAF on whether civil Elementary Flying Training Schools should be taken over by the RAF under war conditions. The next step on 1 January 1940 was the mobilisation of all EFTS flying instructors with the exception of Chief Flying Instructors. The instructors who had been flying in mufti until now were mobilised as Sergeant Pilots and loaned back to the civil companies. This meant a reduction in their pay from £700–£900 a year to something in the order of £300. Our Chief Instructor Peter

May became the Commanding Officer with the rank of Wing Commander and continued as the Company manager, remaining on the Company's payroll. He was the link between the RAF and the Company, responsible to the RAF for the training and discipline of pilots and to the Company for the overall operation of the school. Peter had a Squadron Leader as his Chief Instructor.

The argument between the RAF and the Air Ministry smouldered on. As an experiment it was decided that, on moving de Havilland's No. 13 EFTS from White Waltham to Peterborough, it should be taken over by the RAF. RAF personnel had many extraneous duties and this resulted in a great many more Service personnel being used than the civilians employed by de Havilland's. In addition the RAF was restricted to personnel of military age, whereas a civilian contractor was able to employ male and female labour with no age restriction. The flying training hours also went down. The Air Ministry had made their point and the EFTSs continued to be civilian operated.

The practice of EFTS Commanding Officers being seconded to a company, and being on the company's payroll as manager, operated successfully throughout the war. There was no question of requisitioning our aerodrome, which might have happened if the Elementary Flying Training School had been taken over by the RAF; the aerodrome and works remained under Marshall's control throughout the war.

Things started to liven up in August 1940 with the allocation of more pupils and, although there was still no great pressure to increase our output, we introduced our Flying Programme Procedure. We appointed as the Flight Programmes Manager Gerald Laurence, my father's original race-horse trainer from Balsham, who had ceased training at the outbreak of war. This was a great success. Before going off duty the instructors gave him a brief indication of where each pupil had got to and his next possible exercises. The Manager and his assistant would prepare alternative exercises depending on weather conditions for the next day, with aircraft number, time of flight and name of instructor. These alternative flying programmes were posted on a prominent notice board. Early each morning the duty officer would select the programme best suited to the weather conditions and raise a flag of the appropriate colour to signify which programme had been chosen so that flying could start without delay.

As a result of this scheme our instructors had plenty of time off – those who started flying at 8 a.m. were away at 5 p.m. playing squash, having on fine days given five or six hours flying instruction. They were knocking up about 1,000 hours flying instruction a year compared with the few hundred hours being achieved by all other flying training centres operating without a similar flying programme procedure, whose instructors were on duty for longer hours. Night flying, always something of a bogy, was not tackled at other schools with the same degree of urgency as day flying, whereas we were getting in as much night flying as possible, and to us it was all part of the day's work.

We had only been operating in this way for a few months and were getting back to our pre-war tempo of pilot throughput when 50 Group (the RAF Group responsible for our flying training) started worrying about the high flying hours being put in by our instructors. Instead of giving them a pat on the back and telling them to keep up the good work, they sent a medical team in December 1940 to check their general health with the approach, 'You are putting in a lot of flying hours – are you feeling well? – are you tired?' Our instructors were found to be very fit, hale and hearty. 50 Group still could not appreciate that, as a result of our Flying Programme Procedure, the instructors had a comparatively short working day and were getting plenty of time for recreation and sport.

For the nine month period November 1940 to July 1941 our Cambridge flying hours, compared with other Elementary Flying Training Schools of 50 Group, were 64,696, with the next best (de Havilland at Hatfield) 33,066, the third 31,516, and then dropping to 25,624 and below. In the latter half of 1940 the Company broke all records by completing in three-and-a-half weeks the Elementary Flying Course scheduled for eight weeks. As a result, the original schedule was decreased to six weeks and any pupil who succeeded in completing the course, including ground subjects, in a lesser time was immediately posted to an Intermediate Training School. Many of our pupils also completed two or three hours night flying within the course.

Competitor civil operated training schools were being encouraged by the RAF to achieve all that was being accomplished at Cambridge but, in spite of this and in spite of the satisfactory result of the special medical check of the Company's flying instructors in 1940, Nos. 23 and 51 Groups of Flying Training Headquarters could still not understand how we were achieving such a high and rapid output of trained pilots, and the high annual flying hours of our flying instructors and aircraft. The Groups therefore decided that a thorough investigation of the operation of No. 22 EFTS should be carried out in May 1941 by a team headed by Group Captain H. Gordon-Dean AFC. The terms of reference were 'to examine the organisation of No. 22 EFTS as this unit has a reputation for high output, large number of flying hours and heavy loading on the instructional staff.' There were no adverse criticisms in the Group Captain's report which read:

> The EFTS at present carries a pupil population of 150, divided into 2 courses of 75 who arrive every 3 weeks on a 6-week course. The School is divided into 5 Flights of 30 pupils each. Every pupil is on a flying parade every day in the morning and in the afternoon alternately. Each pupil completes about 50 hours flying during the course, of which 25 is dual and 25 is solo. The instructors' times average between 80 and 100 hours a month and in some instances even higher figures than this are obtained. Full advantage is taken of solo flying during the lunch interval.
>
> The flying programmes are extremely well organised with a view to ensuring that aircraft are never idle whilst on flying parades. The actual

programmes are compiled centrally and issued to Flights. Flight commanders may vary these programmes as they consider desirable, but the staff who compile them are now so expert that I was told the Flight commanders seldom have to make any changes and they are thereby relieved of a good deal of office work. I collected a copy of the notes on this programme planning, together with specimen programmes, and was informed that copies had long ago been sent to the Air Ministry and HQFTC.

I visited Flights operating from dispersal points and saw the scheme at work and was impressed by the smoothness with which the organisation ran. There is a timekeeper at each point busily engaged with booking aircraft in and out. I collected a specimen copy of the booking sheets used. I spoke to as many Flight commanders and instructors as possible and enquired particularly into allegations of overloading. I was impressed with the alertness and keenness of everybody to whom I spoke. No one complained of overloading. Instructors admitted that they were kept busy, but they all seemed to be very fit and keen.

I had a long discussion with Mr Marshall, the Commanding Officer (Wing Commander May) and the Chief Flying Instructor (Squadron Leader Craig). All were convinced that, by utilising daylight hours to the full in the summer months, it would easily be possible to increase the national output substantially. Mr Marshall pointed out, however, that this school is already doing considerably more than any other EFTS and that the general attitude towards the school by higher authority appears to have been that they are already doing too much and would be more popular if they would reduce their efforts.

Conclusion

There seems no doubt that this school, in all its activities, is highly organised and efficient. I have, of course, no information regarding the quality of their pilots but I was told that, despite all criticisms, these are up to at least average standard. In a final discussion with Mr Marshall before leaving, I was told that every instructor in every EFTS could easily average 100 hours dual per month, and that without extending hours at all. If this standard were accepted throughout every EFTS and if the work of the instructors were properly organised, a very substantial increase in the output of pupils would at once be achieved.

Mr Marshall deplored the fact that all daylight hours were not being utilised at present but he thought that the stages by which increased output could be achieved were:

(a) Acceptance of a minimum of 100 hours per month flying instruction per instructor.
(b) The rapid production of more elementary flying instructors.
(c) The utilisation of these additional instructors by taking advantage of all daylight hours during the summer.

I left with the feeling that there is a great deal of force in the above views, and that in these highly critical days it was a great pity that such a school should have the impression that their efforts to set high standards have not been fully appreciated by higher authority.

Overlapping with all this criticism and investigation, L. M. Jones of the Air Ministry telephoned in June 1941 to say that they wanted us to be responsible for the new No. 29 EFTS to be established at Clyffe Pypard, near Swindon. This was planned to be second only in size to Cambridge and he assumed that we would obtain as good results at Clyffe Pypard as we were achieving at Cambridge. I said that we had our hands full and would like to be excused. The Air Ministry were very surprised and asked what was worrying us. I said this was going to be a station of over 700 Servicemen and civilians in a new hutted camp 10 miles from Swindon with little local labour available, and I anticipated catering was going to be a big headache. The Air Ministry brushed this on one side with 'Oh, no problem! There are many companies who would be pleased to undertake the catering on your behalf', and recommended one in particular.

We finally undertook the contract and appointed the recommended caterers. On the day of opening the catering company turned up with a staff of 12 when it should have been at least 40 and, as fast as they engaged new staff, some of the original staff left. It was chaos. In the circumstances Marshall's had to take over the catering overnight, with the responsibility to appoint a Catering Manager and staff. The appointment of Mr Bertola, with some recommendation from the Ministry, was no more successful. Whilst we partially recovered the position, after not too many weeks the CO telephoned me at home one evening to say we would have to get Mr Bertola off the camp as he was strutting about like a turkey cock in highly polished riding boots, adopting a very arrogant attitude towards the flying instructors and visiting the dispersed Flights in his car, for which he had obtained a petrol ration, whereas the flying instructors had to walk. At 24 hours notice Rosemary took a party of volunteers from Cambridge to Clyffe Pypard to hold the fort. Eventually we found a very good Catering Manageress who was with us until the station closed.

We began training at Clyffe Pypard in September 1941. Squadron Leader Donald Bennett (by then Chief Instructor of the newly established No. 4 Supplementary Flying Instructor School at Cambridge) was promoted to Wing Commander and became CO of the station and Marshall's manager, with Squadron Leader Tribe as his Chief Instructor. The school opened with 106 aircraft with six Flights, and was upgraded with additional Flights in 1942, when relief landing grounds were made available at Alton Barnes and at Manningford, which permitted more extensive flying. John Stearn, an *ab initio* instructor pupil at Cambridge in 1938, and one or two other flying instructors from Cambridge were transferred to Clyffe Pypard to help generate the same enthusiasm as prevailed at Cambridge. Several letters were received from 50 Group commending the results of the first few courses, including ground instruction results of 81 per cent, 87 per cent and 81 per cent, and expressing the hope that we would be able to maintain the high standards we had set ourselves. The school was a success and continued until October 1947.

From the summer of 1942 Clyffe Pypard also undertook the training of Army glider pilots. They were given 80 hours elementary flying instruction and were then passed on to a gliding school. Marshalls gave a challenge cup and medal to the best non-commissioned pupil of each course, which the Army recognised by automatically promoting the winner to the rank of sergeant.

At Cambridge our initial wartime training commitment was for 96 pupils living in the aerodrome hostel. This progressively rose to a maximum of 240 in 1942, with the excess billeted out, including four or five at my home at Broxton. Those billeted out had all meals at the aerodrome and were collected in the morning and transported back to the area of their digs in the evening. We reached a total of just under 180 aircraft, mostly Tigers. With the considerable training activity at the aerodrome at the peak of the war effort, dozens of Tiger Moths could be seen in the air at any one time, and they were often referred to locally as 'Marshall's Messerschmitts'. Two relief landing grounds were established – the first at Caxton, 10 miles west of Cambridge, and the second at Bottisham, three miles east of Cambridge. Each had two dispersed Flights. Caxton undertook most of the night flying training and was bombed on a number of occasions, unfortunately with the loss of one of our ground engineers. During night flying the training aircraft were sometimes fired on by German aircraft, and often the crew did not know they had been shot at until they landed and bullet holes were found. Marshalls at Cambridge became the largest of the Elementary Flying Training Schools.

Chapter 16

RAF Adoption of Marshall Flying Instructor Training Scheme

1939–1941

AT THE BEGINNING of the war we made immediate contacts with the Air Ministry and RAF to ask them as a matter of urgency to consider the immediate adoption at all flying training schools of our lively training policy and the training of young *ab initio* pupils to become flying instructors in a very short time. There were many phone calls and voluminous correspondence. We were forthright without being aggressive but little or no interest was shown.

After a short time I had a friendly phone call from L. M. Jones advising me that in our own interest we should not pursue this as it could damage our working relationship with the RAF. He said our suggestion of training young instructors was quite contrary to the long-established RAF tradition of selecting officers with some years of squadron experience to train as flying instructors. Our scheme would undermine the prestige of RAF flying instructors. There was no realisation of what could be achieved by all schools if Marshall's proposals were accepted. In short, without any discussion there was a complete rebuttal of our suggestions.

At that time we refrained from pressing this to the limit. But, with the fall of France in May 1940, we became so alarmed at the increasing shortage of pilots and instructors, and the fact that the instructors available were only being worked at 20–30 per cent of their capacity that we felt that, in the national interest and regardless of possible repercussions, we must do everything possible to get our proven pilot and instructor training procedures put into practice without delay.

I attempted unsuccessfully to make personal contact with the Air Minister, Sir Archibald Sinclair, and then persuaded Lord Milford, who knew the Minister, to intervene on my behalf. The Minister said he wanted time to consider all I had written to Lord Milford before seeing me. Two weeks later I received a message that the Minister would not be seeing me himself but was appointing for the first time an Air Member for Training (AMT) to the Air Council (now the Air Board) and requesting the new AMT to see me as a matter of urgency. Air Vice-Marshal Guy Garrod was duly appointed on 8

July and we met on 22 July. We discussed in detail all that had been achieved at Oxford and Cambridge before the war and particularly Marshall's Instructor Scheme under which, of our own volition, we had trained a number of *ab initio* pupils as advanced flying instructors, who in turn had trained several hundred Volunteer Reserve pilots, many to Advanced Standard. He said there had been a suggestion that I be put in charge. I said it was not a question of anybody being put in charge but rather that he and the Air Council should recognise what was done at Cambridge and Oxford and put it into operation at all RAF and civil operated training schools. The Air Marshal sent for the Director of Training, Air Commodore W. A. McClaughry, and others. The Director, who at previous meetings with me had not agreed with any of my proposals, was still not in sympathy and resigned within a few days. He was quickly replaced by Air Commodore the Hon. R. A. Cochrane.

I was expecting that our scheme would now have full official blessing. Instead, during August it was decided that there must be a trial course and we were offered 10 extra pupils over air-crew age to train from scratch to flying instructors on condition that we absorbed this extra commitment without detriment to our scheduled elementary training courses and without any additional instructors or aircraft. The trial started in September 1940 and was successfully completed before Christmas. On completion of the course all 10 were posted to flying schools as instructors, including two to Cambridge. There were still those in official circles who found it difficult to accept the scheme but, whilst the success of the trial was being finally considered, we were authorised to retain 10 selected pupils per elementary course to train as instructors.

Early in 1941 our scheme was at last adopted, and five Supplementary Flying Instructor Schools were opened in May 1941, No. 4 at Cambridge being attached to our Elementary Flying School with Squadron Leader Bennett as Chief Flying Instructor. No. 4 SFIS operated mostly with Tigers, a few Magisters and four Masters for the pilots to gain experience on advanced training aircraft.

The desperate shortage of pilots in 1940 is well described by Air Vice-Marshal Sir Keith Park, Officer Commanding No. 11 Group Fighter Command, in a letter to the author Richard Collier for the book *The Few, Summer 1940 – The Battle of Britain* by Philip Kaplan and Richard Collier (Blandford 1989):

> Thanks to Beaverbrook, who telephoned nightly, I was never dangerously short of Hurricanes or Spitfires. The pity was that he was not also given the supply of trained fighter pilots instead of Air Staff or Air Ministry; not till the Battle was nearly over in September 1940 did DCAS Air Minister Sholto Douglas appear to realise the critical shortage of trained pilots in my squadrons in the front line, also in groups in rear areas of Fighter Command. For many weeks I had been desperately short of pilots and kept reporting this daily to Lord Dowding who daily reported to Air Staff, Air Ministry.
>
> When I was posted in December 1940 for a 'rest' in Flying Training Command they were amazed to hear for the first time of a shortage of pilots in

> Fighter Command in 1940. The C-in-C Pattinson swore he had never been told by Air Ministry. Moreover, when I took command of 23 Training Group I found the advanced flying schools were working only two-third capacity on a peace-time routine complete with long weekends, Friday to Monday. Air Ministry records will show 23 Group's increase in pilot output in 1941 long after the Battle of Britain.

Sir Keith states that advanced flying schools were working only two-thirds of peacetime capacity, but this peacetime capacity was with instructors flying only a few hundred hours a year as compared with Marshall's instructors pre-war flying of a thousand hours or so.

Air Chief Marshal Sir Hugh Dowding, C-in-C Fighter Command, has stated that his biggest concern during the Battle of Britain was the shortage of pilots. It is generally accepted that Dowding began the Battle of Britain with about 1,200 pilots and during the Battle had a further input of about 1,000, a total of about 2,200, and at the end of the Battle he had few more than he had started with, having lost 1,000.

Had Marshall's procedure for the rapid training of pilots and young flying instructors been adopted at the beginning of the war there would have been no shortage of pilots and the pilots available would have had more air experience. Moreover, there would not have been the need for so many pilots to be trained in Canada, Africa and Australia under the Empire Training Scheme, and also in the USA. This would have saved much money and the lost training time and transport risks involved in this Scheme. Pupils earmarked for the Empire Training Scheme first underwent a 15-hour grading course at a UK EFTS to check their suitability for pilot training. The number of these grading courses could have been substantially reduced and more UK EFTS capacity would have been available for training direct entry pilots to the RAF.

When adopted, our Ab Initio Flying Instructor Scheme reduced the number of very experienced operational pilots, who were in short supply, being withdrawn from front line operations to train as instructors. Many of the young flying instructors trained under the *ab initio* scheme, after instructing for 12 months or so, were posted to operational flying with a total of 800 to 1000 hours or more flying experience – a much better insurance risk than going on to operations with less than 200 hours total air experience, which was the norm.

Over the years my Company has been privileged to have been in a position to play a key role in a number of national emergencies. In my view our revolutionary scheme for the training of young flying instructors in World War II has been our most important contribution to the nation. This scheme, as operated by Marshall before the war, trained many hundreds of pilots for the Battle of Britain who would not otherwise have been available. After official adoption by the Air Ministry in 1941 it snowballed the production of flying instructors and pilots. It was not only what was achieved by our own flying schools but the speeding up of training at all schools. This made possible the opening of new training centres sooner than otherwise would have been possible. All this must have contributed greatly to the progress and final outcome of the war.

By the end of the war Marshall's flying schools had trained 20,000 pilots, flying instructors, glider pilots and observers, and set new national standards for the rapid training of pilots and instructors.

There is good evidence of the quality of the young *ab initio* flying instructors the Company trained before the war and the success of the scheme.

'Tap' Tappin, one of our *ab initio* instructors trained in 1938, had many pupils who served with distinction in the war. At Oxford in 1939 he gave advanced flying instruction to Leonard Cheshire and Christopher Foxley-Norris. At Cambridge in 1940 one of Tappin's *ab initio* elementary pupils was Johnnie Johnson, one of the most decorated officers in the RAF who had the highest score of 38 German aircraft shot down. Johnnie Johnson in his book *Wing Leader* (Chatto & Windus, 1956) wrote:

> Personally I was lucky at Marshall's since four of us were assigned to Sergeant Tappin and 'Tap', although to his face we addressed him with a respectful 'Sir', was the very best type of instructor. A gentle, unassuming man, he flew beautifully and went to great lengths to foster a good spirit with his pupils. Tap could always find time to explain a tricky point of airmanship, and when we walked across the tarmac at the end of a period of dual instruction he would retrace the pattern of the flight and make certain that the various lessons were driven home.

In a recent Sunday morning three-cornered telephone conversation between 'Tap', Johnnie and myself I posed the question to Johnnie, 'Without being modest, to what do you owe your great success?' Johnnie's immediate response was, 'survival,' and he added the following interesting observations:

> Marshall's gave us a good start – no doubt about that – a first class start. We had some splendid times as well. The only regret I had was the time wasted playing football at St John's and Jesus. I was called up with the Volunteer Reserve on 3 September 1939 and spent nearly four months at Cambridge before my first flight at Marshall's on 20 December 1939. I succeeded in achieving 84 hours 45 minutes Tiger Moth experience at Cambridge. Maximum flying hours experience on any type of aircraft is important.
>
> It is also very important to have substantial experience of the aircraft one is going into battle with. I was lucky and got in more flying experience on Spitfires before going into battle because I was always hanging about to take the opportunity of a flight if they wanted an air test or anything like that, and managed to get in 23 hours 50 minutes Spitfire experience against the average 12 to 15 hours. I would say that the ideal was a minimum of 50 hours Spitfire experience before meeting the enemy, if that was possible. You were not really at home in a Spitfire until you had done about 50 hours or so. Having said that, survival was the all-important thing and with it the big build-up of experience and confidence as the Spitfire hours accumulated.

I first flew in the Battle of Britain on 6 September, the biggest day of the battle being 15 September. I survived the first few encounters at the end of the Battle of Britain. After the dreaded days of 1940 were over there was more time for me to get some considerable number of hours of Spitfire experience. With this experience you could stand it on its tail and do anything with it, whereas the previous year you were a dead duck.

Leslie Worsdell was our first *ab initio* trained flying instructor in 1936 and at the beginning of the war was Chief Flying Instructor of our Civil Flying School. We last left Leslie in 1939 at the Initial Training Wing at Cambridge University. After three weeks he was posted to the Central Flying School at Upavon to train as an instructor. His Imperial War Museum tape continues:

> It was quite an honour to be selected because the other students on the course were mainly very experienced RAF officers. In fact there were three young pilots from Marshall's – myself, Olley and Hubbard. Both Olley and myself had been trained as *ab initio* flying training instructors at Marshall's . . .

I am happy to say that Leslie was one of the two above-average assessments in the course of 30. After a short period as an instructor at Grantham he was posted to the Central Flying School on the Staff as a Pilot Officer, where he remained for two years. His frequent applications for posting to operations were turned down because the demand for instructors was insatiable to keep up with the demand for newly trained pilots. Eventually Leslie's wishes prevailed. He was awarded the DFC for his operational service in Malta and became a Squadron Leader at the young age of 23.

Leslie, in his Imperial War Museum tape, summed up the introduction of our Ab Initio Flying Instructor Scheme as follows: 'There was a lot of opposition by the RAF on this basic flying instructor scheme, but Mr Arthur Marshall persisted until finally a proper organisation was set up and a very large number of pilots with no experience other than their initial training were trained direct to become flying instructors.'

Chapter 17

My Father's Death
1941–July 1942

IN DECEMBER 1941 Peter May, with his gliding experience in China, was posted to RAF Brize Norton to play a responsible part in the rapid training of glider pilots who would be required as the war developed in Africa, Sicily, Italy and eventually for the Second Front. Wing Commander Bennett, the CO at Clyffe Pypard, was transferred back to Cambridge, and Wing Commander Goldsmith was appointed CO at Clyffe Pypard. Peter May made a great success of glider pilot training, and got them on to night flying very quickly. He later became CO of 296 Squadron and made the first operational sortie by an Albemarle over occupied Europe in February 1943. His Squadron was transferred to Tunisia, where Peter led the glider element of the invasion of Sicily on 9 July 1943. On 13 July Peter, flying Albemarle P1446, flew with a second Albemarle P1526, piloted by Flight Lieutenant Philip Smulian one of the first Marshall *ab initio* trained flying instructors, to drop 20 Special Air Service saboteurs behind enemy lines in 'Operation Chestnut I' to blow up the Catania Bridge in Sicily. Peter was shot down before reaching the target zone and all on board were killed. Philip returned safely having dropped his 10 saboteurs. Peter was awarded the American Distinguished Flying Cross for outstanding leadership.

In December 1941 Air Marshal Sir William Welsh, C-in-C Flying Training Command, told me he wished they could, in the early training stages, get away from looking at night flying as a bit of a bogy and get it firmly established as a routine part of flying. The Air Force had done comparatively little night flying between the wars, and whilst there was now plenty of operational night flying there was an indefinable feeling in the elementary flying training world that this was another barrier to go through. He thought I might take this as personal criticism and added that he knew we had done much more night flying training than anybody.

I suggested a way of breaking the barrier and disposing of the night flying myth for all time might be to teach pupils to fly by night before they were taught to fly by day. To my surprise the C-in-C cottoned on to this with enthusiasm, and within a few days it was agreed that we would be allocated six pupils for this exercise, who arrived at Cambridge on 3 January 1942; so not much time was lost. The training procedure and syllabus were left for us to devise.

For this exercise the six cadets were divided into two classes – three to be trained to fly by visual indications and 'feel', with instruments as a secondary back-up, and the other three to be trained to fly by instruments, with visual indications secondary. The instrument cadets were given five hours simulated Link trainer instruction to enable them to read instruments before beginning flying instruction. There were no real problems and all went solo after an average of 16 hours dual instruction. After 40 hours total dual and solo night flying we were instructed to train them to fly by day. I was disappointed about this. I had a pious hope that they would leave us without any day flying, proceed to an intermediate training school and then, after some 50 hours or so night flying, go to an Operational Training Unit still on night flying and on to night operations with the feeling 'I must get back before it's light.' The only two minor problems by day were 'three point' landings as compared with 'wheel' landings by night, and the considerable number of aircraft in the air during the day as compared with virtually having the sky to themselves at night.

It was concluded that the ability to fly by instruments was all that was needed for night flying. Both instructors and cadets independently recognised that those trained on visual indications and 'feel' benefited from clear moonlit nights and those trained mainly on instruments performed better when it was really dark. It is interesting to note that at that time when little was known about the nosewheel tricycle undercarriage the official report recorded that a tricycle undercarriage was the real answer to night landings to save training time and reduce accidents. The success of this exercise for us cleared away any remaining cobwebs of the night flying myth for both instructors and pupils.

After the six left Cambridge they went to a Service Flying Training School where the night flying exercise was repeated on intermediate training aircraft by flying first by night and later by day. I heard no more of our night flying guinea-pigs until a chap came to see me in the mid-sixties looking for employment for six months before emigrating to Australia. Having got this fixed up he said, 'You know, I was one of those six night fliers. We all got through the war and had good service records. Two of us finished up as prisoners-of-war in Germany. We have all kept in touch with one another.'

Marshall's Aircraft Repair Organisation (ARO) had now become completely responsible for the Whitley bombers, for which large component manufacturing jigs were installed. SS Cars (now Jaguar) and the Wolverton Railway Works near Newport Pagnell also repaired major Whitley components which Marshall assembled at Cambridge. I flew the first two Whitleys assembled from components repaired by these companies at low level over their factories at pre-arranged times to enable the workers to see the final results of their work.

Our ARO was developing into a very big undertaking. The volume of work made it necessary to do as much work as possible in the open. Until the fifties no hangars were heated and the health record of those working in an even temperature, whether in a hangar or outside, was good. Ted Skinner, one of our pre-war garage salesmen who every winter was frequently absent with various 'cold/flu' ailments, became a very good aircraft engine fitter during the war and never had a day's illness.

The aircraft rebuilt and modified at Cambridge during the war years included Harts, Hinds Gladiators, Ansons, Whitleys, Oxfords, Albemarles, Flying Fortresses, Mosquitoes, Typhoons, Dakotas and Hamilcar gliders. On site our working parties undertook work on all these and, in addition, on Spitfires, Hurricanes and Hampdens. Further buildings were erected at Cambridge on the north side of Newmarket Road to provide additional capacity for aircraft repair and assembly, a woodmill, a big store to accommodate large aircraft components and the extension of our Metal Detail and Machine Shops. Whitleys, Oxfords and Albemarles were completely assembled in the North Works and towed across the Newmarket Road for flight test and delivery.

All the aircraft repaired at Cambridge had to be flight tested, and during the first 18 months of the war Peter May and I undertook all the test flying. As the throughput of pilots for training increased Peter was less available, and at the same time our output of repaired aircraft was building up. We now required a full-time test pilot. Knowing of this, our Chief Ground Instructor encouraged his Armament Instructor Leslie Scatchard, a qualified pilot, to apply. Leslie had been a member of the VR and had been called up on the outbreak of war. Having accumulated 800 hours flying, much of which was on Hawker Harts, he suffered from neurasthenia and had been discharged from the Air Force in 1940. I interviewed Leslie and, after a test flight and an Air Ministry medical, he was engaged as a full-time test pilot in June 1941, with me helping out as and when required and always on Sundays. It was a very successful appointment and he remained with us until the end of the war. He recently wrote:

> My foremost duties were to test the aircraft to their specification as laid down. If I required a second opinion or became too busy, I would call Mr Marshall – or if (as often happened) there were several (4–5) aircraft awaiting testing about an hour-and-a-half before darkness. I often landed after dark.
>
> We ferried many aircraft to different parts of the country; on one occasion two Whitleys to Landau, Wales. We caught the train from Bridgend to London where Mr Marshall had a meeting at MAP and I returned to the aerodrome to find three Mosquitoes and one Oxford waiting to be tested. I finished at 8.30 p.m., but a 12-hour day was the norm.

We refurbished 20 Magister trainers towards the end of the war for the Brazilian Air Force, which we delivered to Reading. Peter Else, the ex-apprentice engineer and Battle of Britain pilot, flew one of the Maggies and was following me through some low cloud, when he lost me. He arrived at Reading an hour later having lost himself and landed at an American base, where they showed amazement at seeing a one-armed 'civvy' flying!

The only time I flew with Mr Arthur Marshall and Mr Michael Marshall was when I flew a Mosquito to Hatfield and Mr Marshall and his son picked me up in our Oxford ferry aircraft. Michael would then have been about 12 years old and his father was teaching him to fly on the way back while I read Michael's book, *The Wind in the Willows*.

Leslie and I had some good fun together. This flying was for me a tonic and relaxation away from the office and its telephone.

Up to 1941 I was allowed the use of one of the Cambridge EFTS Tiger Moths for personal transport, but now managed to find a good Miles Falcon aircraft G-ADLI which had not been requisitioned at the outbreak of war. I was given permission by the Air Ministry to use this low wing, four-seater aircraft with a Gipsy Major engine and a cruising speed of 120 mph. From August 1941 right through to the end of the war I flew to Clyffe Pypard every other Sunday and was very lucky with the weather – I never had a delayed or aborted flight. The Falcon was camouflaged and nobody showed any interest in it but, after the war, when we painted it white as soon as civil flying recommenced, it was most extraordinary how it immediately attracted attention, with small parties collecting round it wherever it went, including at Clyffe Pypard.

The Air Defence Cadet Corps had made such good progress nationally by 1941 that the Air Ministry, realising the importance of its work, decided to take it over lock, stock and barrel as a going concern on Saturday 10 February 1941 renaming it the Air Training Corps with a planned expansion to 200,000 cadets. I well remember visiting the Cambridge Squadron the next day during their Sunday morning parade at the Hills Road Cattle Market to explain what was happening. The Corps continued to run on the lines established by Air Commodore Chamier on behalf of the Air League of the British Empire, including administration through civilian committees. The formation of the Air Defence Cadet Corps was one of the Air League's greatest achievements. As the Air Training Corps the movement was of profound importance to the war effort and has continued to provide invaluable youth training to this day.

The major contribution of the Corps to the war effort is well illustrated by Commander Dick Reynolds, DSC, AFC, MRAeS, RN (Retd), Cadet No. 17 in the Cambridge Squadron, who writes:

If we as individuals had drifted into the war by awaiting call-up we would have finished up in the Infantry. Instead, those of us who realised and took advantage of the excellent training being given in 104 Squadron were commissioned into the Service of our choice – RN, RM and RAF. Because of minor medical defects – usually colour blindness, which was a particularly stiff test – not all became aviators. Bob Hales, for example, became navigator of MTBs which gave sterling service in and around the Norwegian fiords, and Jack Hiscock commanded a tank landing craft on D-Day.

Many of the cadets scrounged flights from the RAF and from various activities at Marshalls, particularly with the Tiger Moths located at the south-east corner of the airfield where the Squadron often paraded in the evenings. 'Cadging' a flight became a technique and Long and I became particularly good at it, and a friendly rivalry developed on who was achieving the most flying hours experience.

Alas, this friendly rivalry ended when Long, anxious to take a lead in hours hitched a lift to Newmarket and 'cadged' a trip in a Wellington training flight in May 1942. During the flight a wing failed and all on board were killed.

Arthur Chapman, the CO, was dedicated to the Squadron and loved by all. My training in the ADCC/ATC was so comprehensive in all subjects aeronautical that the only subject I didn't know about was deck landing – that was to follow.

There is no doubt that for most of the cadets their ATC days were happy, exciting and rewarding.

During the first few months of 1942, completely out of the blue three serious but unconnected financial problems arose.

With our bank overdraft building up, we had been pressing the Ministry of Aircraft Production to speed up payments for our aircraft repair work. We got to a position where we were claiming that £120,000 was overdue and the Ministry was claiming an overpayment to us of a similar amount, a differential of about a quarter of a million pounds which was a lot of money, and the equivalent now of £8 or £10 million. The Ministry decided to put in an audit team, and guaranteed our Barclays Bank overdraft in order that the business could be kept running whilst the audit check was in progress. The time had come when our Company needed an auditor with industrial experience. Barclays Bank recommended Layton-Bennett of London. This audit involved a lot of work and a great deal of worry over a 12-month period, but in the end our original claims were justified.

Whilst the investigation of these Ministry payments was in progress my father had a telephone call from the Local Inspector of Taxes to say that he and a colleague wanted to interview my father and myself at Jesus Lane as soon as possible regarding the Companies' and our own personal tax returns. The tone of this interview indicated that they considered it to be a very serious matter and we were advised to notify our auditor and solicitor without delay. This created a lot of work and worry and took over 15 months to finalise. Layton-Bennett were again involved. The outcome was that my father had underpaid by something under £5, I had a credit of a few pounds and the aerodrome and garage companies were OK. I never did learn what triggered off this enquiry.

The first I knew of the third problem was when I was at our fabric shop in the old Cambridge Knitting Company's premises in Abbey Walk and had an urgent message to return to my office where I found three plain-clothes police officers waiting to see me. They said it had been reported that we had claimed a major overpayment for the building of our No. 2 Hangar complex built, as were the aircraft 'shadow factories', with Government money with the option to buy when the war was over, which we did. The most extraordinary thing was that we had had no enquiry of any kind from the Ministry. The police officers warned me that anything I said would be taken down as evidence. I immediately telephoned Joe Taylor, the Company's solicitor, who said, 'Refer them to me and say no more!' I was pressed for time and arranged for Rosemary to go to see Joe Taylor the next day. She came back very depressed because he could not believe the position could be as simple as I stated or that the Ministry could have acted in this way without first making enquiries of the Company.

The Ministry auditor investigating the amount owing by the Ministry for our aircraft repair work had by chance come across Boulton & Paul's account for their steelwork for No. 2 Hangar of approximately £22,000 and had assumed that this was for supplying the complete building complex, for which we had a fixed price contract from the Ministry of approximately £33,000. Without making any comment he reported this, which sparked off the police enquiry. In completing the Ministry claim form for payment of the contract, to the question 'Name of Builder' we had simply inserted 'Boulton & Paul' and the total amount. As a matter of habit we have always named the steel constructors as the builders of our hangars. (If asked today who built our No. 17 TriStar Hangar in 1983, we would automatically say 'Boulton & Paul' although in money terms their involvement in the whole complex was a small portion of the total cost.)

What we had called our No. 2 Hangar was in fact a major building embracing one of the largest hangars in the country at the time of 60,000 sq. ft. clear floor space with a number of ancillary workshops and stores opening off and an administration block including an assembly hall, lecture rooms, parachute and Link trainer rooms, and offices for the RAF Elementary Flying Training Centre. In addition to Boulton & Paul, we had placed direct orders with a number of building contractors and numerous suppliers of materials and equipment such as oak doors and surrounds, door furniture, blockwood flooring, 'Old Cambridge' bricks and sanitary fittings. The result was a prestigious building at low cost. We have always been our own architect and managed such projects ourselves, unlike the standard practice of a company appointing an architect and then placing an order for the total work on one contractor who would place sub-contracts on trade specialists and suppliers and be responsible for the management, progress and completion of the whole project. The Ministry appointed another auditor, Price Waterhouse, to investigate the cost of the hangar building contract and to satisfy themselves that we had not received any commissions. Price Waterhouse went through all our books and records and those of Boulton & Paul and all the other contractors and suppliers. It involved a tremendous amount of work.

With my father's workload and his worries regarding the money owed by the MAP for aircraft repair work, followed within a matter of weeks with the tax enquiry, I did not initially tell him abut the hangar problem as I felt that, whilst it would incur a lot of work and we would have to go through all the motions, it must come out right in the end. I was, however, concerned that the police had been involved, and I was advised to see Charles Crocker (later Sir Charles Crocker, President of the Law Society 1953–54) who had a good reputation for dealing with police enquiries.

He also found it difficult to believe that the matter could be as simple as in fact it was. In view of the police involvement he was emphatic that, if the case was cleared up satisfactorily, he must on our behalf get a complete clearance from the Director of Public Prosecutions. The final outcome was that we had been underpaid by just under £33, which Charles Crocker insisted must be paid by the Air Ministry. I had a phone call from L. M. Jones to say how pleased and happy they all were that this matter had been cleared up satisfactorily, but did we really want payment of this £33? I said that after all the troubles and worry we had been through we certainly did. I really ought to have kept the cheque and had it framed.

My father died suddenly on 9 July 1942 whilst riding one of his Arab horses on Coldhams Lane near the aerodrome. He was found in the evening on the side of the road with his horse standing by. The first I knew of this was when Rosemary and I returned home from a cycle ride and walk on Stourbridge Common and Ditton Meadows and found an urgent message to ring the police. The Coroner's verdict was that he had had a sudden and severe stroke which caused him to lose consciousness and to lose control of his horse.

I had become anxious that my father should not hear about the hangar enquiry from a third party so I had told him all about this a few days before he died. With the three problems of the MAP payments, the tax enquiry and the cost of the hangar, I was at the sharp working end and in touch on a day-to-day basis, whereas my father, apart from his own tax worry, only knew what I told him from time to time. To him it was a much deeper black hole than it was to me. I had a meeting with him the evening before he died and, serious as things were, particularly the financial argument with the Ministry regarding outstanding payments, he was getting things very much out of proportion. He certainly kept his worries from my sisters, some of whom were living with him at the time and knew nothing of what was going on. I think the seizure may have been brought on not only by his workload but by the worry of these three problems. I have always regretted that he died before they were cleared up, which was not for another eight months.

Many obituaries made reference to my father having founded the garage company in 1909 and the flying school and aerodrome in 1929, the part he played in the formation of the Cambridge Squadron of the Air Training Corps and his work in World War I, but what I feel he would have appreciated most was a passage from the obituary in the Bloodstock Breeders' Review which read:

> A keen and all-round sportsman his activities were manifold. Until shortly before his accidental death he still played ice hockey. He loved racing, and at Newmarket rode out to training exercise. He intended to extend his stable. Last year he won races at Newbury and Newmarket (Exning Handicap) with Leading Topic and Brendy, also racing under National Hunt Rules with Jonquil and Noble King. Others of his winners in recent years were David Mike and Future Record – both exported. In the Furness Sale, October 1941, Mr Marshall paid 1,500 guineas for a filly-foal by Nearco out of Flinders. Named Brenda Mar, this filly was sold as a yearling at Newmarket on October 19th last for 3,700 guineas.

Titch Porter, Technical Director, on the occasion of the 50th anniversary of his service with the Company, remembered his first meeting with my father as follows:

> I had only been here a few days when our Crossley hire car was put in the workshops. It had just been painted and varnished and had a good coat of dust over it. I sketched out a cat on it – this looked good to me. Mr D. G. Marshall walked into the workshop just as I had finished my drawing and said in an angry voice, 'Who did this?' I, school cap in hand (overalls covering my bare knees and short trousers), said, 'I did'. Mr Marshall after that tore me off a terrific strip and then said, 'I am proud of you for owning up.'
>
> Ever after, if Mr Marshall was going to a race meeting, he would dig me out from the shop and tell me to go home and put on my best suit and tell my mother I would be out with him all day. I went with Mr D. G. to Newmarket, Yarmouth, Leicester and several other racecourses. When Mr D.G.M. was driving he would push out the clutch and say 'Change gear lad' (first automatic gearbox). When Mr D.G.M. was driving he would ask me to read out the horse jockeys and trainers. When at racecourses, I had to sit in the car (I was the first anti-theft device).

At the time of my father's death he had a number of racehorses in training, plus the two Arab horses and the stallion donkey which he had brought back from Egypt. The racehorses and Arab horses were sold without difficulty. My sisters were all keen to keep the donkey. After about six months I asked my sister Margery what to do about the donkey; we decided to sell it and I sent it to the Cattle Market. At eight o'clock that evening Margery phoned and said, 'You haven't sold the donkey, have you? The girls are furious.' She asked if I could get it back. It had been sold for £7 and had changed hands twice by eleven o'clock that night, when I bought it back for £12. It was finally sold two months later and did good service for many years after the war at gymkhanas ridden by a boy sitting backwards collecting money for charity.

My father had been the greatest influence on my early life and for me this was the end of an adventurous partnership.

Chapter 18

Second Front and Termination of Hostilities
August 1942–1945

AS A RESULT of my father's death we had to make quick decisions regarding the management of the canteen and the garage.

My four eldest sisters agreed between them to accept full responsibility for the canteen, which they did with great success. Violet progressively took the lead and continued as Manager until she handed over to Charles Baddeley in 1947. They set a very high standard of catering which has stood the Company in good stead over the years.

Eddie Parr, supported by Cyril Porter, accepted responsibility for the day-to-day running of the garage. I held a small management team meeting on the last Friday of each month starting at five o'clock and finishing when all business had been dealt with. These monthly meetings continued for many years until well after Michael took over responsibility for the garages.

In 1942 the Ministry of Aircraft Production asked a number of companies to look into the possibility of introducing bonus schemes with a view to decreasing the man hours for aircraft rebuilding and associated work. All the companies, including Marshall, turned down this suggestion as it was thought impractical to operate a bonus scheme effectively with the multiplicity of different types of repair and with very few operations exactly alike. The Ministry then virtually instructed Marshall to have a go, arguing that if anybody could make a success of this we could.

We took six months to prepare and plan the details and train ratefixers covering all trades. We used the 'Premium Bonus Scheme' for the wide variety of work associated with aircraft damaged in so many different ways and the 'Sterling Bonus Scheme' for straightforward repetitive work. The main difference between the two schemes is that if, for example, a job is assessed at 10 hours for a good average tradesman putting in a good day's work, the 'Premium Scheme' is more flexible and provides that some bonus can be earned if the 10 hours is exceeded by a limited amount, but under the 'Sterling Scheme', bonus is only earned if the job is completed within the estimated 10 hours. We progressively introduced the scheme from

September 1942, starting with Dickersons, our Whitley component shop on Newmarket Road, where it was an immediate success. In a matter of a few weeks the times taken for many operations were dramatically reduced.

Many companies came to see our scheme in operation but I do not think any finally attempted to introduce this or any other incentive scheme. It involved much training and required strict management control. If there was any loose ratefixing and prices got out of hand, a company would be in serious trouble and find it very difficult to retrieve the position. For us it has been a tremendous success to this day.

One company particularly interested was Sebro in Madingley Road, Cambridge, responsible for the rebuilding of Stirling four-engined bombers and a subsidiary of Short Brothers the manufacturers. Sebro employees were asking for Marshall's bonus scheme. We could not believe that they wanted the Marshall scheme instead of and not in addition to their present in-lieu bonus payments based on the average earnings of the production workers at Shorts' aircraft manufacturing works at Rochester. We explained to Shorts' directors that under our scheme some would earn more, some would earn less and some would earn no bonus at all – bonus earnings would be dependent on the individual's effort and capability. The Shorts' directors replied that they would not pay two bonuses and they wanted the Marshall scheme. Sebro spent many months training a team of ratefixers, much of this time observing our scheme in operation. In due course the General Manager, Hugh Gordon, told Sebro's Joint Production Committee that Marshall's bonus scheme which they had asked for would be introduced the following week. The Shops' Convenor replied, 'It is of course in addition to our existing in-lieu scheme?' – our scheme was never introduced at Sebro.

One very good thing which resulted from this was the meeting with Hugh Gordon, a delightful and entertaining personality who became a life-long friend of all members of my family. During the remaining years of the war Hugh, Rosemary and I had dinner from time to time at the University Arms on a Saturday evening. In the summer we could see through the dining room windows small crowds on Parker's Piece being addressed by all and sundry laying down the law for the future of the country when the war was over.

Of necessity, because of the speed of events and the immediate response required, most of the repair and rebuilding of aircraft was priced by the MAP on actual cost plus a percentage profit. Late in 1942 the MAP introduced the ingenious 'Balfour' incentive scheme for contractors, named after the company chairman who thought it up. This simply applied a fixed profit to a catalogued list of aircraft and components regardless of the actual cost of the individual repair. I seem to remember that the profit for the rebuild of a Spitfire was £8 regardless of whether the actual cost was £1,000 or £2,000 or more. Labour was in short supply and it was up to a contractor to get as much production as possible from his existing labour force.

At this time the Ministry, supported by Layton-Bennett, our auditors, thought our aircraft production was becoming too much centred on me. I felt we were a team who had grown up together and understood one another's language and that it was all running very efficiently and with good results. At the same time I appreciated that if anything happened to me there was no nominated vice-captain of the team to co-ordinate the departments, and I agreed to consider this.

In 1942 I appointed Fred Hornsby, who had been with the Company since the beginning of the war, as Works Manager of our Aircraft Repair Organisation, which worked extremely well. Fred built up a good personal working relationship with the CRO. He was particularly good at organising all our on-site working parties.

Towards the end of 1942 the Company was instructed to be ready to undertake any work that developed with the introduction into operational service of the exciting new de Havilland Mosquito. The Mosquito, a two-crew bomber with two Rolls-Royce engines, made a most important contribution to the progress of the war. A very versatile aircraft with a very long range, it carried a substantial load at high speed and at high altitude. It was made of wood with the use of Norman de Bruyne's synthetic glues and introduced woodworking companies and furniture manufacturers into the building of wartime aircraft in a big way.

The first Mosquitoes to arrive at Cambridge were the Mk. IIs, 98 of which we converted to Mk. XII night fighters with the fitting of a radome and British radar. The last Mk. XII delivered in July 1943 overlapped with the input on 6 June of the first of a programme for 100 Mk. II aircraft to be converted to the Mk. XVII fitted with American radar. The Mosquito became the principal home defence night fighter in 1943 and played a big part in Pathfinder operations. Vickers and Marshall between them converted 20 B.IV Mosquitoes to carry the 4,000 lb bomb and a number of B.IVs were converted for deck landing, of which Marshall completed the first 14. A multiplicity of Mosquitoes also came in for repair and modification.

Later we, with Vickers and Airspeed, converted 29 B.IVs to 'Highball' standard. 'Highball' was a spherical mine designed by Barnes Wallis to operate on the same spinning system as his larger bouncing bomb used on the Lancasters of 617 Squadron which was specially formed under the leadership of Guy Gibson, VC, for the Dam Buster raid which successfully breached the Mohne and Eder dams.

During 1943 Sir Stafford and Lady Cripps visited our Company. Sir Stafford was now Minister of Aircraft Production. Sundays during the war were normal working days for our flying training and aircraft work, and knowing this he chose a Sunday for their visit. Sir Stafford had long been a strong advocate of Joint Production Committees for companies concerned with war production, with equal numbers of management and workers. We were one of the first companies to establish a JPC. It was for us a happy and useful visit except for a hiccup at the end, which he took in his stride. We arranged for Sir Stafford to meet the JPC after lunch. The meeting went well. Before he left Sir Stafford addressed the assembled workforce. He delivered his address with gusto, commencing 'Comrades' – there were a few raised eyebrows but his speech was well received. The Shops' Convenor, Bill Everett, a good speaker and a good lay preacher but with a pronounced stammer, then proposed the vote of thanks. Bill started, 'I thank S-S-Sir Stifford and Lady Crapps . . . , and continued in this vein – not a titter from the workforce. When Bill was told what he had done he was almost in tears with his apologies to Sir Stafford, who patted him on the back and said, 'Not to worry, it certainly isn't the first time it has happened.' Bill Everett was for a great many years the Shops' Convenor and was awarded the BEM in 1980.

In March 1943 we had our first Mk. 1 Flying Fortress AM531 in for minor repairs and maintenance. I had arranged with Leslie Scatchard that he should test fly this aircraft if the test came up during the week, and I would test fly it if it came up on a Sunday. Sure enough, at eleven o'clock on a Sunday morning the phone rang to say that the first Fortress was ready and waiting for test flight. Never having sat in the cockpit of a Flying Fortress, I asked if Fred Burnett, our Chief Engine Mechanic, was available as he was very good at knowing the layout of cockpits and controls. Burnett and I then proceeded to give the aircraft its first test flight. It was a very wet period and the south-west corner of the aerodrome was very soft, with the wind coming from the north-east. The Fortress turned out to be easy to fly. Once Burnett and I had completed the first test flight and it was ready for a further and final flight in the afternoon, there were many requests for a ride. I took Burnett, Rosemary, Lodge our Chief Electrician, and the Chief of AID with me.

In 1940 I was averaging 12 test flights a month, which peaked to 45 by February 1945. I have made much of the spate of forced landings I experienced in the late twenties and early thirties but, apart from the Monospar fuel tap incident in the late thirties, I had no further forced landings until two in the war years, and have had none since. The first wartime problem was with a Whitley taking off to the north – the port engine failed just after take-off with much smoke coming from it. Fortunately Waterbeach Aerodrome was directly ahead. There was very little wind, and Waterbeach were operating from the opposite wind direction to Cambridge. I just scrambled in at the south end of their main runway and swung off the runway to the right to allow an aircraft approaching from the north to land. Clouds of hot oil smoke rose from the failed engine but there was no fire or physical damage to the aircraft. I had with me Charlie Charles, a good pre-war motor mechanic and by now a very good aircraft inspector, and this was his first flight. At the right moment, on instruction from me, Charles lowered the flaps and undercarriage and all was well. The second incident was an Oxford taking off to the west. Just after take-off the tip of the port propeller flew off and penetrated the fuselage just by my left foot and rudder. With the resultant vibration, the engine had to be shut down immediately. I just managed to scramble round the circuit and land with the undercarriage only partially down, but little damage was done.

Fred Hornsby, the Works Manager, was very good at organising concerts. He did a wonderful job for the Air Training Corps by arranging two concerts at the Guildhall to get the Cambridge Squadron's Welfare Fund on a sound footing. The main attraction was the appearance of members of the famous wartime wireless comedy series 'ITMA' ('It's That Man Again!') including Tommy Handley (That Man), Señor So-So, Colonel Chinstrap ('I don't mind if I do!') and Mrs Mopp ('Can I do you now, sir?').

In December 1943 the Company played an energetic part in the National Industry Salvage Campaign sponsored by the Ministry of Supply to urge companies and their workers to do everything possible to ensure that nothing was wasted in view of the increasing shortage of many basic materials. This was at a time when Japan held 90 per cent of the world's available rubber supplies. The campaign showed not only the type of industrial salvage required from paper to metal waste, but illustrated the practical examples of uses to which salvage could be put – rubber dinghies, tyres, ammunition cases and many other items of war equipment. Marshall's opened a Salvage Section which organised salvage of bolts, nuts, washers and many other items removed from aircraft and components undergoing repair. Jack Harvey, who was put in charge, accepted the challenge and did a tremendous job, to the extent that we had visits from many Ministry officials and other companies to pick up details of all that was being achieved.

Throughout the war the Company held children's Christmas parties which were always attended by the Mayor and Mayoress and reached a peak in 1944, when 525 children were entertained. The general pattern of these parties as recorded at the time was: 'Tea was provided for the children, after which they enjoyed a concert for which the Parsley brothers were responsible and in which many of the employees took part. The hilarity of the children was a sufficient token of its success. When the laughter died down each child was handed a present by Father Christmas.'

At four o'clock one afternoon the Director of the CRO rang me to say the MAP felt that some recognition should be given to an on-site foreman for all the good work which was being done throughout the country by contractors' on-site working parties in the repair and servicing of aircraft. As their biggest contractor, he asked us for a nomination, and this resulted in R. Wykes being awarded the BEM in 1943.

Towards the end of the war when Oxfords were being scrapped we obtained permission to use one for communications and the collection of air crews after delivery of aircraft, for which we had an increasing number of requests particularly during the days of the Normandy landings. We modified this aircraft by fitting passenger seats and the incorporation of self-starter batteries to avoid the need for ground starter trolleys.

It had been planned by the CRO that, as our Armstrong Whitley bomber work phased out, the Armstrong Albemarle would phase in and Marshall would have the same complete responsibility for the Albemarle as we had had for the Whitley. The Albemarle was a twin-engined bomber with tricycle undercarriage and two Bristol Hercules engines used in the African, Sicilian and Italian campaigns as a glider tug. By early 1944 we had reached a production of one Albemarle rebuilt per week with a floor holding of 24 aircraft. We were then advised that the Albemarle was to play an important part in the Second Front as a glider tug and to drop parachutists, and that we should now plan for a holding of up to 64 aircraft and increase production to three or four a week as quickly as possible.

The war was now coming to an exciting climax and the tempo increased. Early in 1944 the CRO advised us that we were to be responsible for Hawker Typhoon fighter aircraft rebuilds and fly-in quick-turn-round repairs. The Typhoons were fitted with the 2,200 hp Halford Napier Sabre 24-cylinder engine and were to be used in the Second Front as low level fighter bombers. They were therefore expected to suffer much battle damage from ground fire, and a big build-up of work was anticipated. The Typhoon really came into its own and was the backbone of the Tactical Air Force's Fighter Bomber Wing in the advance through France and Holland in 1944. It demolished ground targets by the score with its battery of rocket projectiles. Using both rockets and bombs, it devastated the enemy Panzer Divisions.

Up to now we had been responsible for nominating our own test pilots (Scatchard and myself) to fly the various types of aircraft. Early in 1944 a new procedure was introduced which required a technical exam and flight test for approval to test fly any additional types of aircraft. I went to the Gloster factory at Hucclecote, near Gloucester, for my Typhoon exam and flight test. (I remember at Hucclecote we heard weird noises and there were rumours of a new, mysterious engine. Gloster was responsible for the first British jet, the Gloster-Whittle E28/39, to be followed by the Meteor production line – the RAF's first jet aircraft.) The Gloster Company had been taken over by Hawker Siddeley in the thirties and Hucclecote, with a Typhoon production line, was the test centre for this aircraft. The Typhoon was a single-seater aircraft and, having cleared my oral technical exam, a Typhoon was made available for me to fly around for general familiarisation, followed by two or three observed circuits and landings. My first flight testing of a Typhoon was in May 1944. They were good, robust aircraft, with a near top speed of 400 mph and a big surge of response from the powerful engine; and they were good fun to fly.

In the middle of May 1944 Marshall was made responsible for the fly-in repair and rapid turn-round of the RAF's American Dakota aircraft which were to be used extensively in the Second Front as glider tugs and for dropping parachutists. It was anticipated there would be much damage to the aircraft from ground fire. We had no experience of Dakota aircraft and no special-to-type ground equipment was available, and only a few publications. It was said these things would be looked into as quickly as possible. In the meantime we collected all the information we could and ascertained what items of ground equipment, tools and possibly spares we might scrounge from United States Air Force stations on an 'old boy' basis – everybody was willing to help.

The Second Front began on D-Day, Tuesday 6 June. On Wednesday 7 June we were notified late in the afternoon that a meeting would be called in London to discuss the Dakota repair position. On Thursday 8 June late in the afternoon we were notified that three shot-up Dakotas would arrive that evening and we were instructed to deal with them with the utmost urgency. Fred Hornsby phoned me at 5.30 p.m. to say that the three aircraft were expected soon after six o'clock, and I asked what he planned to do with them. He said he was parking them at the bottom of the aerodrome for the night. Having put down the receiver, I suddenly said to myself, 'By Jove, they want these aircraft back as quickly as possible.' I got into my car and found Fred on the tarmac and said, 'They want those aircraft back quickly. We ought to put them immediately outside the hangar ready for the morning.' Fred said, 'I have already thought of that and have arranged for it.' I got back in the car and had not gone many yards when I again thought, 'We must start on these aircraft tonight.' I got out of the car and walked back to Fred and said, 'We must get these in work tonight. You move aircraft as necessary and get these Dakotas into the hangar. I will go and find Bayley to survey the aircraft tonight.' Lofty Bayley, the Chief Inspector, lived just down Newmarket Road but had gone to the cinema. I collected him at ten o'clock and he said he had been to see the Normandy landings. I said, 'Now you had better come and see the Normandy shot-up Dakotas.'

We found the first aircraft had very little damage except for a badly shot up port mainplane requiring a substantial repair scheme and manufacture of parts. The second machine had a splattering of gunfire damage, but nothing too serious. The third aircraft was badly shot up in the tank bays, the fuselage, the tug release cable and starboard mainplane, but had a completely undamaged port mainplane. We immediately decided to fit the undamaged port mainplane of the third aircraft to the first to give quick delivery of one aircraft. The repair of the damage to the second aircraft was completed over the weekend and the third aircraft, having cleared its repair scheme, was fitted with the repaired mainplane from the first machine.

There was then the question of Scatchard and myself getting Dakota test flight approval under the new procedure, but there was no technical flight test centre in the UK for the Dakota. I rang Group Captain Eustace Miles, the director responsible for test flying approvals, and asked, 'What do we do now?' He said, 'You and Scatchard are now approved Dakota test pilots and I will confirm to AID immediately.'

I test flew the first aircraft on Saturday morning 10 June and it was cleared ready for delivery. The RAF was informed and said the aircraft was urgently required and they would collect it without delay. They phoned shortly afterwards to say they had no pilots available – could we help? I delivered the first aircraft to Blakehill Farm near Swindon at 2.45 that afternoon and Don Bennett collected me in our Oxford transporter aircraft. The second aircraft was completed and delivered by Scatchard on Monday, and the third on Tuesday 13 June.

Within days of the start of the Second Front, shot-up Typhoons were flying in for quick turn-round repairs, and within 11 days Queen Mary low-loaders started to arrive with badly damaged aircraft. I remember the excitement on Saturday afternoon 17 June when the first six aircraft arrived covered in Normandy dust on the RAF tenders on which they had been loaded in Normandy. They were off-loaded at Dickerson's garage on Newmarket Road which we had made our repair centre for Typhoon fuselages.

A week after D-Day Albemarles were in very short supply and urgently required; the production of new Albemarles was running behind schedule. We were urged to increase our production to keep pace with increased arisings. The next week we had a visit from Air Vice-Marshal Frazer, the Director-General of repair and maintenance, and Mr Woodcock, the Chief of CRO, to stress the importance of achieving maximum production at once. By now Albemarles were coming in thick and fast and I said we would again review the position and report back immediately. We revised all our plans and explained the position to the workforce, committing them to continuous day and night work seven days a week, with individual undertakings that they would work 80 to 90 hours a week until the emergency was over. I rang Air Vice-Marshal Frazer and told him I was confident we were going to achieve all he was now asking for. I then asked him if he would please come and explain the serious position to the workforce and endorse all I had told them. This exercise was the most concentrated and best effort the Company had made to date and was fully justified by the results achieved. In due course a letter was received from the Ministry stating that the whole Albemarle position had improved as a result of our actions.

Late in 1944 we were notified that we were to convert the large Hamilcar gliders to powered aircraft by fitting two Bristol Mercury engines. These were to be used for the war in the Far East. The engines would provide the gliders with the capability of taking off light to get back to base under their own power after landing with their load in forward positions.

1944 was an intensely busy period with many requests for special action and maximum production. High as the pressure had been for increased production throughout the war, the demand for even greater effort was readily met. Everybody, with few exceptions, was more responsive and self-energising than ever previously experienced. People acted on their own initiative and got on with the job. The war was a tremendous worry and anxiety for all but, with our wide variety of fast-moving work, our part in it was very exciting and gave us little time to dwell on the tragedies of war.

VE Day was on 8 May 1945. My main recollection of this day is taking the family in the evening to Midsummer Common, where a colossal bonfire had been built, mainly with timber from aircraft we were now scrapping. The laminated spars of the Oxford aircraft provided excellent bonfire material.

Bill Goode and Fred Hornsby were both awarded the MBE; Bill for the sterling work he had done in the maintenance of aircraft for the biggest of the RAF Elementary Flying Training Schools, and Fred for all his work as Works Manager responsible for our aircraft rebuilding and maintenance work both at Cambridge and on site.

VJ Day, 15 August 1945, was almost a repetition of VE Day and the balance of the timber from our aircraft scrappage was made available for that bonfire. Hugh Wortham, the head of the 'Peterborough Column' of *The Daily Telegraph*, had previously arranged to come and see me at eleven o'clock on that day, and he and I were about the only ones left in the Works. Hugh Wortham, then aged 61, an old King's man and rather like an elderly don, was delightful company. A recognised connoisseur of food and wine, he was certainly a good convivial companion for the occasion. I do not think I can leave VJ Day on a better note than to record that we had a half-bottle of Sercial Dry Madeira between us and had a good old natter about the past, present and future.

The Aircraft Repair Contractors gave a dinner at the Dorchester on 8 November 1945 to members of the Ministry of Aircraft Production, the Civil Repair Organisation and the Air Force with whom they had worked during the war. The CRO suggested to the dinner organisers that, as Marshall's had been their largest and most versatile contractor, I should take the chair. It was a very happy occasion and an opportunity for all to express their appreciation of the co-operation and help we had given one another throughout the war years. I had not realised until recent years what an important part the CRO played in the war effort. For example, 2,148 aircraft were lost in the Battle of Britain – destroyed or damaged. During the Battle the total input of new and repaired aircraft made available to Fighter Command was 2,756 of which 772 (28 per cent) were repaired aircraft. Fighter Command finished the Battle of Britain with just over 600 more aircraft than they started with.

Chapter 19

Family – the War and Aftermath
1939–1949

ROSEMARY, I AND the children with Nurse Bessie spent Christmas 1939 with Rosemary's Uncle Dick and Aunt Ethel at Llanstephan, where Judy was christened. Michael and David remained there for the first few months of 1940 and went to Llanstephan village school, returning to Cambridge in March, when Michael went to Abinger Hill School, Surrey.

The question of our three children going to Canada arose at the fall of France. It became a complicated issue. Left to our own devices, I do not think we would ever have thought of it, but in the circumstances it just happened. With hindsight, Rosemary and I wished it had not – but that was knowing the course the war had taken, and things could have been very different. One has to try to remember the atmosphere of the times, with extensive air raids and the possibility of invasion with all its potential consequences. I also remember that when the subject arose we had the feeling that, with the children all safe across the Atlantic with somebody reliable to take charge of them, we would be able to concentrate entirely on the war effort and, if invasion came, we would have done the best thing possible for the children.

Rosemary's brother Wilfrid and his wife Helen lived in London. When their son Nicholas's school decided to evacuate to Canada, my mother-in-law Mrs Dimsdale agreed to take Nicholas. Mrs Dimsdale was given an introduction to Senator Cairine Wilson, Canada's first woman Senator, who was a very powerful and well-known character. The Wilsons, a wealthy family, lived at Rockliffe Manor House, Ottawa with a summer retreat at St Andrews, Newfoundland. Senator Wilson offered to look after our children if we decided to send them to Canada. Concurrently with this Michael's school, Abinger Hill, decided to evacuate to Canada. At the same time my sister Mary decided to take her young daughter, Jan, to friends in America, have her second child in America and take with her my youngest sister Brenda aged 13.

And so it was arranged that Rosemary would take our children to Canada towards the end of June 1940, in the hope of returning to England if she got them settled and was confident and happy about the arrangements. All these considerations were in the context of the strict wartime international financial restrictions.

Mary and Rosemary had various adventures in crossing the North Atlantic. Mary records:

> We embarked at Liverpool with over 700 unescorted children on board. We had one other liner with us loaded with internees and we were escorted by a destroyer. The engine of the other liner broke down and our captain decided to make a run for it and left the destroyer to guard the other liner. Just as we were getting out of the U-boat area, we were missed by feet by a torpedo, all of which was well reported in the press. I had a miscarriage during the voyage.

Rosemary's crossing, although very crowded, was comparatively uneventful but it was an exceptionally rough crossing with everybody feeling unwell. Michael recalls that he had a fight with David for the top bunk and lost, and so David had the top bunk and was seasick! On arrival in Canada they went to the Wilsons' holiday home at St Andrews for the rest of the summer. Mrs Dimsdale, already in Canada, became involved on a British propaganda lecture tour based on 'The UK At War'. Soon after arrival Rosemary wrote:

> Judy is frightfully hungry here and I have never seen her look so well. She stands alone now and talks quite a lot, but would you please send me a photograph of you because, when I say Daddy, she says 'Wow-wow-wow.' She thinks you are a dog. It makes the boys laugh a lot. David asks why you can't get a job in Canada, and Michael is just Michael-ish – I think he would be happy anywhere.

With the summer holiday over, the Wilson family returned to Ottawa. Michael and David were sent to Ashbury College. Michael was encouraged to produce *Michael's News* with an introductory poem by Senator Wilson. They had tobogganing, elementary skiing and generally an enjoyable life. David writes: 'One of the things I remember about staying with the Wilsons was the splendid train journey with all their staff lasting a day and a night, so it seemed, from St Andrews.'

Having settled the children in, Rosemary succeeded in travelling back to the UK in September via Halifax Nova Scotia and Liverpool. She was delayed for several hours at Bletchley Station during a big air raid on Coventry. I knew Rosemary was on her way back but had no idea when to expect her. When she arrived home the house was locked – Dorothy Deer, the housekeeper, worked in the canteen during the day – but she managed to get in, I don't remember how, and phoned me. I went home immediately and, if anybody asked me what was the most wonderful moment of my life, I would say without hesitation it was Rosemary's phone call and seeing her standing at the top of the stairs at Broxton – how delighted I was to see her and how relieved she was to be back. I gave her a big kiss and a hug and returned to work, and Rosemary went to bed to get some sleep after her hectic journey.

It is only now on looking back that I fully realise how vulnerable Rosemary was in Canada. She fortunately established a close and happy relationship with the Wilsons, but if the Wilsons had not been the tremendous success they turned out to be, what would she have done with three children with nowhere to go and no money?

Back in Cambridge Rosemary joined the Transport Department at the aerodrome, which was not running very satisfactorily, and eventually took over full responsibility as Transport Manager. She had over 150 vehicles of all kinds and was responsible for all Works transport, the maintenance of vehicles, and delivery of materials and parts without delay to the Company's 25 or so aircraft on-site working parties spread over RAF stations from Cornwall to the north of Scotland. Her road and route geography became very good. Her work included providing transport for personnel, including inspectors visiting the on-site parties. Those wanting personal transport always jockeyed for the biggest and best car. The most co-operative inspector was Peter Young who, although over six feet tall, never complained if he was given an Austin Seven to go, say, to Cornwall. After the war Peter became the Company's Chief Inspector – always ready to help anybody – a most successful appointment.

As her right-hand man, as it were, Rosemary had Mrs Leader, the wife of Brian Leader, the racehorse trainer. They had a good team working with them, including Rosemary's cousin Lelgarde Philipps, a very good driver who would go anywhere and at any time and did not mind roughing it. One of Rosemary's three motor bike despatch riders was named Jarvis. He was a good and willing worker but his machine was always catching fire. He went into the office one Saturday morning and said he had not had any time off for some weeks and he thought he would like to be off for a few hours on Sunday. Mrs Leader said, 'And what are you going to do on Sunday, Jarvis?' He replied, 'I think I'll do a little love-making,' and she said, 'How do you do that?' – she thought he had said 'a little glove-making'! Much laughter – they had their lighter moments. It was a very happy section and Rosemary thoroughly enjoyed her work.

Rosemary's Chief Mechanic was Bill Bailey, who joined the Company as an apprentice in 1930. On his retirement after over 50 years service, he wrote:

> The Transport Section had to overcome many difficulties during the war years. Petrol was in short supply and made the routeing of vehicles very important. Rosemary Marshall became an expert on UK road routes and would frequently advise her drivers on the shortest routes between airfields, particularly when re-routeing because of additional instructions to a driver since he left Cambridge. With very restricted vehicle and street lighting and the lack of signposts round the country, her advice was crucial to the successful completion of numerous delivery runs, many of which included instantaneous diversions for the re-routeing of vehicles in transit to meet emergency arisings.

Rosemary Marshall was also responsible for the allocation of petrol coupons for both Company and employees' vehicles, which was subject to a quarterly audit by Ministry inspection. This was an exacting task which she handled with her usual tact and diplomacy. Those who worked with her would remember that she sought no special privileges and was a very popular member of the staff.

(Rosemary's most difficult problem was to control my father's use of petrol coupons; he found it very difficult to understand petrol rationing.)

By 1941 Rosemary and I were becoming increasingly worried that we might never see the children again, and that if the parting lasted much longer we would not know them and they would not know us. There was a growing waiting list of children anxious to come back to England. Oswald Chivers, who had served on the Cambridgeshire County Council with Mrs Dimsdale, visited America on behalf of the Ministry of Food early in 1942. On his return he confirmed the worry we had that friction was developing between Mrs Dimsdale and Senator Wilson. Mrs Dimsdale was always critical and outspoken about anything when she was not in full agreement. The main problem was the suggestion that the Wilsons instead of Mrs Dimsdale should be the guardians of the three children in Canada, and Mrs Dimsdale's talk of getting the children back to England was not encouraged by the Wilsons.

We were now convinced that we must somehow get the children back home and in such a way that we didn't offend the Wilsons after all they had done for us. Approaching this subject with the Wilsons was not easy. So on 11 May 1942, with bated breath, I wrote a long and hopefully tactful letter to Senator Wilson, making it clear that Mrs Dimsdale would continue to be the children's guardian and that she would progressively make arrangements for their return to the UK. Something which helped oil the wheels at this time was the week's stay with Rosemary and me at Broxton of the Wilson's youngest son Angus who was stationed with the Canadian Forces in the UK. Angus recalls visits to Uncle Dick's racing stables at Newmarket and my father allowing him to ride his Arab horses, but only after my father had ridden them to take the steam out of them. The Marshalls and the Wilsons have remained good friends.

Michael was the first to return to the UK in August 1942. He travelled back with Professor Sir George Thompson and his son in a banana boat in a 12-day convoy to Liverpool. Professor Thompson, the famous atomic scientist, was returning from one of his many liaison visits to America at that important time.

David, aged eight, travelled back in November 1942 via the United States with my youngest sister Brenda, then 15, in a Portuguese boat, the *Serpa Pinto*, to Lisbon and after four days in Lisbon by plane to Bristol. Brenda, who went to a day school called Shipley at Bryn Mawr during her first year in America, used to visit my sister Mary's daughter Jan at weekends and felt very grown up going by train from Philadelphia to Baltimore alone.

Judy was the last of our family to return from America early in 1943 with Mrs Dimsdale and Jan Cavendish in a Portuguese ship to Lisbon and then a flight back to England via Ireland.

All were now back home except my nephew Nicholas (son of Rosemary's brother Wilfrid and now Fellow in Economics and the Estates Bursar of the Queen's College, Oxford). At the age of seven, in May 1943 he travelled back alone. He writes:

In May I left Ottawa for Philadelphia and there embarked on the Portuguese cargo liner *Serpa Pinto* of 7,000 tons. As a neutral ship she was supposedly protected against U-boat attack. Her cargo was grain and the chief activity among the refugee children was throwing wet grain in the faces of members of an opposing gang. The ship called at several islands in the Azores and took 21 days to reach Lisbon. At one of the stops I bought a large pineapple for my grandmother.

Upon arrival in Lisbon I stayed with a kind English lady and was found to be covered from head to toe in flea bites. I remember leaving the city by electric train for a local resort, only to be summoned back at short notice. I was informed that I was to fly back a day earlier than the flight previously arranged. Early in the morning I boarded a camouflaged DC-3 and flew to Bristol. Then I took a train to Paddington. I was aged 7 at the time and was looked after by a boy of 15 called George, whom I met when I climbed into the plane at Lisbon. George and I parted company at Paddington. I can remember sitting alone on my luggage on the platform in the growing gloom until my parents came to collect me. I was still firmly clutching an overripe pineapple which eventually reached my grandmother.

The following day the news came through that the plane on which I had originally been due to fly had been intercepted and shot down by German fighters in the Bay of Biscay. I can remember our cook and maid mourning the loss of Leslie Howard who had flown in the ill-fated plane as a result of a sudden change of plan. They commented rather unfavourably on my good fortune, since I was a poor substitute for their idol.

It was good to have our children home. They all settled down well, but we were conscious of indefinable gaps which confirmed that it was good that we got them back when we did. It was particularly good for Michael when David returned. Whilst I wish it had all never happened, we were very lucky that it worked so well and had a happy ending.

In 1943 Michael went to St Faith's School, Cambridge, and in 1944 to Eton. David was at King's College Choir School. During the school holidays I gave Michael and David a two-day outing in London to see the sights. We went to one or two theatres and I took them as a treat to one or two good restaurants but, regardless of what was available, all they wanted was 'Spam'. Rosemary and I managed to get a weekend or so at the 'Le Strange Arms' at Old Hunstanton and played some golf, better described as a good way of going for a walk as we weren't much good at golf but very much enjoyed the game. Our greatest golfing achievement was Rosemary winning the Ladies' Windsor Cup at the Gog Magog golf course near Cambridge soon after the war. Rosemary was the only competitor who turned up in a snowstorm and was declared the winner!

Soon after my father died in July 1942 and concurrently with her husband going to the Middle East with his regiment, my sister Molly applied to join the Air Transport Auxiliary which ferried aircraft for the RAF. She was accepted and reported to Luton for flying training in September 1942. After her initial training, and having some experience of ferrying Tiger Moths, Molly was posted to the all-women's ATA pool at Hamble.

The following is from Molly's Imperial War Museum tape recording:

ATA was very interesting in that, particularly amongst the women, you got a very extraordinary set of women doing it who had come from quite a number of countries and from all sections of the community, and this I found great fun – I enjoyed it. Once you had done a certain amount of ferrying on the light aircraft, they took you back into school again and you were trained on Masters. This opened up all the single engine fighters and the first of these that they put you on to was a Hurricane, and I think the moment that one took a Hurricane off for the first time was pretty memorable because it was much more powerful than anything one had been flying before, and, having had the excitement of take-off, you had then got to bring it down again! But these were a lovely group of aircraft to be flying. The Hamble pool had more fighter aircraft than any other to ferry and that was very enjoyable . . .

The Master was the one you were trained on for this type of aircraft, and throughout ATA they always picked out a type which had got either the virtues or the vices, whichever way you care to put it, of that group of aircraft and then it opened up the whole of that class to you, and your ferrying duties were then divided amongst that class. If they had a new type for you, you would have warning of it and you would get the handling notes out of the library for it, and we had these loose-leaf books which had the salient features of that aircraft and the speed at which you had to make your approach and so on and anything that was different about it and you would have these alongside you, so you could look at that as you were doing your final circuit. Basically aircraft are just like cars – there is a terrific similarity – but each of them has got unusual features and once you twigged this you were all right . . .

(I had one accident) which I am not very proud of. I was taking a Swordfish down from Shifnal and was due to take it to the south, near Southampton I think, and the engine cut going over the Wrekin and I had to force land. The fields round there seemed to me extraordinarily small and, having chosen a field and doing as rough an approach as one obviously would if you hadn't got any engine but heading into wind and aiming at this one, I didn't know that the field was slightly downhill and, instead of pulling up, because there were no brakes on this aircraft one didn't stop and I went through a hedge and on the other side of the hedge there was a young lad ploughing. To avoid him I had to swerve hard to the left, whereupon the aircraft turned over and a very angry woman got out of that aircraft, and because it had got secret equipment on it I had to get the boy to mount guard on it while I went and telephoned. The RAF had to come from Cosford and mount guard on it for the night – this was a Saturday and I was extraordinarily unpopular in the Mess because they had a dance on and two chaps had to miss the dance. However, on investigation they found I wasn't responsible for this and so they were very good about not taking any disciplinary action or anything else on my behalf. Happily I found that my brother-in-law, Flight Lieutenant Monty Fry, was at Cosford and he brought two bicycles and we cycled out for dinner, which was a very good way of spending a rotten Saturday afternoon. But that was the only accident I ever had in ATA, I am thankful to say.

As my sisters' husbands joined the Services, my sisters and their families had progressively moved to Cambridge and supported my father in the running of the Canteen, living initially at Whitehill. In August 1943 a twin-engined Oxford swerved on take-off and finished up with its nose in the window of the back bedroom, which was occupied at the time by my eldest sister Margery, her baby daughter Susan and a nanny. The bedroom door jammed and had to be broken down to let them out. The tail of the aircraft landed within a few feet of Nicholas Cavendish (the present Lord Chesham), who was asleep in his pram under a small laburnum tree which was uprooted by one of the wings of the aircraft. The aircraft was being collected by a woman ATA pilot, who was killed, but all members of the family escaped injury – fortunately there was no fire. As a result of the accident my three eldest sisters moved to Huntingdon Road and Girton, continuing their work at the canteen. My fourth sister Mary returned to her old home, White End, Latimer and in 1944 joined the Egham and Chertsey Battalion of the Surrey Home Guard.

My eldest sisters Margery's and Dorothy's husbands, Monty Fry and Rupert Wagner, had joined the RAF in 1941. Monty finished his war service as a Squadron Leader in the RAF Intelligence Corps, Herefordshire. Rupert became a Squadron Leader and was Senior Operations Manager, Coastal Command at RAF Banff.

Early in the war Violet's husband, Teddy Barbezat, had volunteered for aircrew duties but was turned down because of his age at 31. Nat Somers, who was to become a good friend, had similarly applied and been turned down. When the trial Ab Initio Flying Instructor Training Course started at Cambridge in September 1940 with ten pupils over air crew age, Teddy and Nat re-applied and were two of the 10. They then became instructors with 22 EFTS and later trained others to become instructors at 4 SFIS when it opened at Cambridge in May 1941. In June they were both posted to instruct at the EFTS at Sywell, Northampton and about a year later were posted together to the RAF Advanced Flying School at South Cerney, where they shared a room. They were converting Tiger Moth pilots to fly twin-engined Oxfords.

In August 1943 whilst at South Cerney they were offered operational experience, a bombing raid over Germany or sea surveillance in a

Sunderland flying boat over the Atlantic. Teddy suggested they toss for it, Nat tossed the coin and Teddy won the toss and chose the bombing raid. Nat flew in the Sunderland. Teddy was killed on the night of 17/18 August 1943 in the raid on Peenemunde where the Germans were developing their V1 flying bomb and V2 rocket. Although the RAF suffered colossal losses in this raid, its success resulted in a big delay in the start of the V1 and V2 attacks on Britain. Nat writes: I was lucky to have lost the toss and certainly lost a very good friend. I always remember Teddy as a perfect gentleman.' Nat had the unpleasant task of taking all Teddy's belongings back to Violet.

Nat Somers has been an adventurous, enterprising and very successful entrepreneur, with much of his business associated with the aircraft industry, including the purchase and development of Eastleigh Southampton Airport after the war. He has probably won more air races in Britain than anybody, which included the King's Cup, the British Air Racing Championship, and the Kemsley Trophy twice. He and his wife Phyllis continue to be close family friends.

My fourth brother-in-law, Mary's husband Charlie Cavendish, went to France with his unit in January 1940 and was one of the 338,000 British and allied troops miraculously evacuated from Dunkirk at the end of May 1940. The Army in due course asked for volunteers to become Air Observer Pilots. Charlie volunteered and, having qualified as a pilot, was with one of the first Air Observer Squadrons sent to North Africa to support the artillery. When Charlie returned from North Africa he became a flying instructor and later went to France during the Second Front.

Molly's husband, Bernard Rose, who had joined the Royal Armoured Corps as a trooper in September 1940, was commissioned into the 2nd Northamptonshire Yeomanry in March 1941. He was sent to North Africa in July 1942 and posted to the 4th County of London Yeomanry – part of the Royal Armoured Corps – known as the 'Sharp Shooters'. When sitting in a field near Tunis at the end of the North African Campaign, Bernard received a message that Captain Cavendish had landed his Auster in the allied lines and was looking for Captain Rose; even in wartime it seemed that family reunions were not uncommon.

Having returned from the African and Italian campaigns, Bernard took part in the Normandy landings. Molly was stationed at Hamble and saw the preparations for the D-Day Landings being made in that area, where they practised landings up and down the Hamble River. She records that 'The night it all started there seemed to be an added tension to the activities on the river and I remember taking a radio to bed to hear the next morning on the six o'clock news that the invasion had started and knowing that Bernard would be in it.'

Molly's Imperial War Museum tape continues:

Seven days later he was posted 'Missing, believed killed.' My first information of this was from a colleague of his, a fellow officer, who wrote to me, and his letter was the first thing I got saying he had seen my husband's tank burning and there was no way anyone could have got out of that tank – that he had seen it shot up and burst into flames. What he didn't know was that my husband was getting someone else out of a burning tank at that precise moment and so wasn't in the tank that was blown up. I did not know this for six weeks and during that time I had a communication from the War Office saying he was missing and then that he was missing, believed killed. My Commanding Officer and the ferry pool down at Hamble were extremely good to me. They had all known my husband and so were very sympathetic to me, and after three days I reported back for duty and it was accepted that I was capable of going on working and this was a great blessing.

At the end of six weeks I got a card from my husband's prisoner-of-war camp. Then of course one settled down for the duration and got on with dealing with things here and sending over relief parcels, which never arrived because by that time Germany was getting into a pretty good muddle.

During that time there was, of course, a great optimism going on because we were getting somewhere at last – the invasion was working – and we were obviously listening to the news avidly and very concerned about where they were getting to. In 1945 very soon after VE Day my husband came back from the prison camp and he was on, I think, two months leave then, and that morning I reported that he was back and ATA by then had got really more pilots than jobs and so released me promptly so I was able to concentrate on him.

Very soon after VJ Day my sisters held a family dinner party at Violet's house at Girton. I made myself unpopular after dinner when I remarked to Margery that if only we could now finish off the Russians we might have peace in our time. Margery was very upset and said how could I suggest turning on our Russian allies and at a time when my sisters, except for Violet, had only just got their husbands back from the war. I said we and the Russians had only used one another for our mutual convenience during the war with Hitler, but I fully recognised her point of view. As events turned out, life might have been much easier today if Communism had not been allowed to continue its hold on Russia and contaminate Eastern Europe and the Balkans, but it was a tactless remark for that family reunion occasion.

My sister Molly and her husband Bernard returned to Oxford and were living with friends until they found a house. Molly was expecting her first child in April 1946. One Saturday evening in the middle of January she rang to say that they had searched everywhere and had great difficulty in finding any house, but at last they thought they had found somewhere suitable. She described the house to me and I did not think it sounded very good. I had planned a routine fortnightly flying visit to Clyffe Pypard the next day but turned to Rosemary and said, 'I think we ought to look at this house. They are obviously worried.' So I rang Molly and got the address and said I would have a look at it on Sunday afternoon and report back.

We took the children with a picnic lunch. The house looked a bit of a shack, in a big garden with one or two Nissen huts – all very untidy. The front door looked as though it was made from orange boxes. I was standing at the garden gate looking at the house when a man came up and said, 'Do you want something a bit classier?' I asked why and he said, 'Well, there is a house at Bampton – a very nice house next to the church – which belonged to a Wing Commander who was killed in the war. If it is not occupied very quickly, I know it will be requisitioned.' He told us where it was and we motored another five miles or so to Bampton. It was a beautiful Cotswold stone house with a tennis court and a large garden – a very attractive property. By now it was about five o'clock and, just as we were leaving, an old boy came along to feed the few chickens he was allowed to keep in the garden. He repeated what we had already been told, that if the house was not occupied almost immediately it would be requisitioned by the local council.

The house agent was not available until late that night, when I spoke to him at his home and asked if he realised the house was about to be requisitioned? He said the price was £3,500 and I made him an offer of £3,250 subject to immediate vacant possession. He rang back shortly afterwards accepting the offer. I rang Molly first thing on Monday morning and told her, 'I have offered this on your behalf subject to vacant possession and I think you ought to be sleeping there tonight.' She could not believe it after all the search they had made of the area and, almost in tears, said they could not possibly do that. I left it, saying, 'Well, it is up to you.' Two hours later I got a message to say they were on their way. They were there by late afternoon and not long after their arrival a man walked up with a requisition notice, but all was well.

Brenda, on her return from America, returned to St George's School, Ascot until 1944, when she went to St James's Secretarial College which had been evacuated to Bridport, Dorset and during the holidays stayed with one or other of her sisters. In 1945 she was secretary for a time to her brother-in-law Charles Cavendish, and at the age of 21 became secretary to the editor of *The Evening Standard*.

Violet continued to run the aerodrome canteen after the war until she married John Hodgson, an estate agent, on 3 December 1947 and moved to Latimer, which was near Mary and Charles.

Rosemary had always been keen to have a small farm and we were looking for one when war broke out. Late in 1947 we resurrected our ambition and spoke to Francis Pemberton of Bidwells, the Cambridge Chartered Surveyors, who rang me in mid-February 1948 and suggested that I should go and have a look at Horseheath Lodge. It wanted a lot doing to it but it was otherwise just what we wanted and we bought it within a matter of days with vacant possession later in the year.

The area has an interesting and historic background going back to the Alington family, who had connections with Horseheath from the fourteenth century. There was a special relationship between Elizabeth I and the Alingtons in that one of the Alingtons married the step-daughter of Thomas More, who was beheaded by Henry VIII, and Elizabeth I's mother, Anne Boleyn, had suffered the same fate. The Alingtons were very good to

Thomas More's widow and Elizabeth I visited Horseheath Park. In the seventeenth century the Alingtons built Horseheath Hall, one of the most important houses in East Anglia at that time. As the years went by the Alington family's fortunes waned, the estate was sold and Horseheath Hall became derelict. What was left of the Hall was put up for auction, with staircases and marble fireplaces sold under the hammer. The superb wrought iron gates with gate posts carved in 1665 were re-erected at Trinity and St John's Colleges on 'The Backs' and at Cheveley Rectory, where they may be seen and admired to this day.

About 1800 the Batson's, a wealthy family from Jamaica, bought much of the estate and built Horseheath Lodge one-and-a-half miles from the original Hall, using the bricks from the old Hall for building the foundations and cellars. The Batsons were very keen on horseracing and bred and trained the 1834 Derby winner, 'Plenipotentiary', at Horseheath Lodge, and as a result extended the house and added a second floor. From the early part of this century there was a general run-down of the house and it had several owners. With farming becoming really bad in the twenties and early thirties, the house remained empty for many years, with a tree growing through the roof. My predecessor, Dick Parker, bought the house and its small farm in the late thirties and fortunately removed the second floor, which made it very practical to live in.

This is the house we moved into on 24 November 1948. It was a wonderful home for the family and played an important part in entertaining many of the Company's customers, particularly those from overseas. Horseheath is a beautiful part of the country which I always call 'The Cambridgeshire Alps' – it is approximately 300 feet above sea level as compared with Cambridge at 32 feet. Our life-long family friend and factotum Dorothy Deer moved with us to Horseheath in 1948 and was very much back on her home ground, being the daughter of a Balsham farmer.

The Aberystwyth Agricultural Centre carried out a survey of the farm during the first year. Their report was not very encouraging and started, 'This is a derelict farm.' I asked how long it would take to put right and they said 20 years. I said, 'Well it is hardly worth starting,' and they said, 'If you really get down to it you will achieve 50 per cent recovery within the first two or three years' – and this we did. It was ideal for Jersey cow dairy farming, and Rosemary turned out to have green fingers in building up a Jersey herd which within 20 years became one of the leading herds in the country.

Michael, prevented from qualifying for his Pilot's 'A' Licence on his 17th birthday on 27 January 1949 because of bad weather, achieved it the next day. He finished at Eton in the summer of 1950 as Captain of his House and was beginning to show promise as an oarsman.

The purchase of Horseheath Lodge began a close relationship with Francis Pemberton which, apart from our friendship, has been of considerable importance to the Marshall Companies and family ever since. From

1948 Francis has advised on all Cambridge property developments, antici-
pating what might be required for the future and dealing with intricate
planning applications associated with the owning and operation of an aerodrome. As a team, Dick Lane as a lawyer, Bob Thomson of Layton-Bennett
as an accountant (and later his successor Brian Herring) and Francis
Pemberton have over the years made valuable contributions to the development of the Marshall Companies. They individually and collectively
considered all matters appertaining to our Companies as if they had a
personal shareholding. As soon as I had a serious or unexpected problem, I
ran to one or other or all of them like a scalded cat (I still do!) – an
exceptionally happy personal and business relationship.

Chapter 20

Meeting the Challenges of Peace

1945–1949

NOW FOR THE future – VJ Day had come much sooner than anybody anticipated, which was wonderful but it certainly put us and other companies involved in war production on a spot – 'What are we going to do now, chaps?' With an employment of about 3,000 we faced our biggest challenge yet – to find viable work for this large workforce and to occupy six-and-a-half acres of extra factory floor space. During the war we had considered possible post-war plans, but there had never been time to get down to detailed planning and neither was it possible to predict the future of the aviation industry.

The garage's immediate task was to get back as quickly as possible to selling and servicing Austin cars and commercial vehicles and not miss any opportunity to expand. To clear the decks we transferred all the Ministry vehicle work to the airport works and carried out our pre-war plan to open the Airport Garage, used during the war for rebuilding Oxford aircraft, as our Austin commercial vehicle depot. The chauffeur-driven hire car service, on which the Company had been founded in 1909, was resurrected and is running to this day with Rover and Jaguar cars.

The Austin Ten, which had been used as an open military communications car throughout the war, was now available as a saloon car, followed by the Austin Light 16 hp (fitted with an overhead valve engine which had been developed for the Services) which was a good fast car. Post-war designed models started with the A40. During the immediate post-war years Austin made an important contribution to the balance of payments, and by 1951 their annual production had reached 162,079 vehicles, of which 114,609 were exported.

Before the war we had been anxious to extend our Austin distribution territory beyond Cambridgeshire and had discussed with Austin and Murkett Brothers the possibility of Murkett's dealership territory covering Peterborough and Huntingdonshire being incorporated in our Austin Distribution agreement. Murkett's main franchise and their main line of business was the distribution of General Motors Bedford trucks and Vauxhall cars. Bedford trucks had monopolised the commercial three-ton market throughout the thirties. Murkett Brothers had had a long personal relationship with Austin who agreed to our proposal subject to Murkett's accepting the position. I saw Harry Murkett at Huntingdon but could not persuade him, and the matter was dropped.

The position in 1945 was quite different. With Austin now making a range of commercial vehicles in direct competition with Bedford, Murkett had to decide whether their future lay with Bedford or Austin. Well established with their large Bedford commercial vehicle territory which extended beyond Peterborough and Huntingdon, they decided to remain with Bedford. Austin asked for proposals from three adjacent distributors, including Marshall, to establish an Austin distribution centre in the Peterborough/Huntingdon territory. We were the only distributor to submit a proposal which included opening our own Austin sales and service depot in Peterborough. Our Agreement was extended to incorporate Murkett's old territory in 1946 and we succeeded in renting Murkett's original garage in the centre of Peterborough. Dick Lane and I later negotiated the purchase of this property which stood us in good stead until the building of our new Peterborough garage on Oundle Road in 1963.

I thought I should take a wider interest in what was happening at all levels in the motor industry, and started attending the Distributors' Section meetings of the Society of Motor Manufacturers and Traders. We invited 12 French distributors to the Motor Show at Olympia in 1948 and to the SMMT banquet; they were with us for three days. On the last day we took them by train to the Austin Works at Longbridge and on the journey back to London we said, 'For the last three days you have told us you are losing money on new cars, second-hand cars, spare parts, motor repairs, hire of cars and forecourt sales. What are you living on?' They all went into a huddle and their spokesman laughingly said, 'Yes, it is quite right, we lose money on new cars, second-hand cars and all these things but if we do them all we make a profit.' In 1950 I succeeded Major Bradstock who had been Chairman of the Distributors' Section of the SMMT for many years.

Immediately after the war we obtained a contract to receive, store, service as necessary and generally sort out all the many thousands of Government-owned vehicles which had been loaned to companies and institutions throughout the war. We set up a reception and storage centre with a workshop at the wartime RAF aerodrome at Bourn and in the old Sebro Stirling bomber hangars alongside, using the aerodrome runways for the parking of vehicles. Bourn was used not only for vehicles but for a whole range of equipment, including cranes and electricity generating units. At peak periods we were holding over 5,000 vehicles in addition to other equipment with a considerable through-put. This contract provided important employment for a few years at a critical time. The Bourn centre was run by John Wellman who had been our Aircraft Stores and Buying Manager during the war.

February 1947 had some of the worst weather on record. Electricity cuts were severe and the power stations' stocks of coal were low. Even if coal could be got out of the mines, the railways were closed and fuel could not be got to the power stations. On the first Friday of the crisis it was very doubtful whether our works would be able to open after the weekend. The Bourn collection of equipment included eight big diesel generators which we transferred to Cambridge, and Tom Sayers, the Plant Maintenance Manager, got a team together to connect them to strategic parts of the works during the weekend. By Monday morning at eight o'clock when the day shift arrived, not knowing whether they were going to be able to work or not, it was possible for the whole works to be operating near normal. They gave Tom Sayers and his team a big cheer.

In October 1947, at an important time when the volume of aircraft work was still running down, another contract which provided useful employment was the rebuilding of a few hundred single and double-decker London buses which had had no major maintenance during the war. Immediately after the war no new buses were available. This work was undertaken in our No. 1 Hangar by aircraft tradesmen with an aircraft engineer in charge.

All new car and commercial vehicle production was required for export and the home market, with the emphasis on export. With the cessation of military vehicle manufacture the Services became dependent on refurbished vehicles for the foreseeable future. Transferred from our Jesus Lane garage to almost unlimited capacity at the airport works, our Ministry vehicle contract expanded enormously. When the Bourn contract was completed, John Wellman became Manager of this expanded Vehicle Overhaul Department. The main production line, the complete stripping and rebuilding of three-ton military cargo vehicles, built up to 48 a week for a year or so. It was a very versatile department successfully undertaking the servicing, overhaul and refurbishing of all types of military vehicles and equipment including mobile generators, bakeries, engines of all kinds, and tracked vehicles. This was very important work at the time supporting as it did the national export drive. This contract continued in various forms until 1988.

Before the war we had considered having a grass drying plant to make dry grass cattle fodder cubes from the cuttings from our aerodrome. Professor Sir Frank Engledow, Head of the University Agricultural Department, had advised us over the years on the growing and maintenance of the grass and had recommended that we should mow regularly and let the grass droppings remain as a fertiliser to avoid the use of artificial fertilisers. After the war, when cattle feed was in short supply, we went ahead with the installation of a drying plant, not only for grass from our aerodrome but grass and lucerne from farmers in the area. During the war aerodrome dry grass had got a bad name, as almost anything which was green had been cut and included in some mixtures. We therefore established a small company called Teversham Crop Dryers Limited, which operated successfully for a number of years without making any worthwhile profit. We collected grass and lucerne from farmers up to 10 miles away, including from my home at Horseheath. Unfortunately the work was seasonal and required the building up of a new team each year. We instilled into the team at the beginning of each season that once the season started it was a seven day week job. If grass was ready for cutting on a Friday and it was left uncut until Monday, the extra inch or so of growth would lose several per cent of protein. The selling price of dry grass was very much dependent on protein percentage, but just as one thought the price was rising and a worthwhile profit might be available the Government imported a quantity of decorticated cotton cake which deflated the price of dry grass overnight. We ceased production in the early fifties when world food supplies became more abundant.

Leslie Worsdell had rejoined Marshall's in 1945 to be responsible for the operation of the aerodrome and to re-establish and further develop the Company's pre-war reputation for all its flying activities. We set out to be the first to re-open civil flying on 1 January 1946 when the ban on civil aviation was lifted. The atmosphere of this period is well illustrated in the following extract from Leslie's Imperial War Museum tape:

On October 31st 1945 my log book shows that I made my last flight with the RAF and I was pleased to see that I got an exceptional assessment. I was demobilised on November 5th, and on November 7th I reported for work at Marshall's. My brief was to get the aerodrome licensed and get myself licensed.

Remembering that I had been away from Cambridge since 1939, I laid my hands on an Application for Renewal of Aerodrome Licence, although I couldn't find the old Aerodrome Licence. I discovered that the Ministry of Civil Aviation, or whatever it was at the time, was based in Bristol. So I flew myself down to Lulsgate, where the CO was an old friend I'd known in Malta. So that was a help, and he found some transport to get me to the Civil Aviation Department.

Well, I walked the corridors of power, which were between Nissen huts, for quite a long time before I found anyone who'd even give me the time of day. 'Renew an Aerodrome Licence? Nobody knows anything about aerodrome licences. We don't deal with that sort of thing.' But finally I did find someone who said he remembered something about it before the war and I said, 'Well here's the application form and I've filled it in.' He said, 'But you're not allowed to fill it in. It has to be done by an inspector.' I said, 'No it doesn't, it can be completed by any 'B' Licence pilot. Now I still have my pre-war 'B' Licence, and it's never been withdrawn. In fact I had a medical the other day.'

The ban on civil aviation was due to be lifted on January 1st 1946. Obviously we needed aircraft to fly, and Arthur Marshall had located a Tiger Moth which had been dismantled and stored in a barn and had not been requisitioned and therefore not militarised. He of course still employed licensed ground engineers with Tiger Moth aircraft on their licences so he managed to get this aircraft certificated and ready to fly on the day the ban was lifted, January 1st. So that was the day Cambridge Aero Club started flying activities. Our first student was Lady Bragg who was then Mayor of Cambridge and we had people queuing and knocking at the doors to join the waiting list to learn to fly. The price in those days was £5.10s. an hour. We were the first club to start operating, and in fact the next one was the Luton Aero Club which didn't start until Easter of that year.

Our civil flying certainly got off to a flying start, as was well reported by the press: 'The first civilian flying pupil for six years to leave the ground on a training flight in the UK took off in a Tiger Moth biplane G-ACDG (the only civil Tiger Moth in the country) at nine o'clock on Tuesday morning, January 1st, the first day of the lifting of the ban on civil aviation – the newly restored freedom of the air was nine hours old.' A number of other pupils were in the air during the first day of post-war civil flying, including Norman de Bruyne, having a refresher lesson.

The first British 'A' Licence after the war was obtained at Cambridge on 6 January. Remembering that Hugh Wortham, the Editor of *The Daily Telegraph* 'Peterborough Column', invited me on VJ Day to let his office know of anything we thought might be of interest, I phoned the 'Peterborough' number and said I thought they would be interested to know that Prince Birabongse of Siam (known as 'Prince Bira'), the well-known racing motorist of pre-war days, had that day qualified for the first Private Pilot's 'A' Licence to be issued since the war. The chap on the other end of the line said, 'Yes, yes, yes, yes,' and, just as I was about to put up the receiver, he said, 'Did you say he was a prince?' I said, 'Yes' and he said, 'Would you please say all that again?' They printed the story.

The Company progressively bought additional Tiger Moths, two new Percival Proctors and one new and three second-hand de Havilland Rapides for charter flights, particularly for the Newmarket owners, trainers and jockeys. For a number of years we operated a scheduled service to listed race meetings. Within a few months of the lifting of the ban, Marshall's charter flying was covering most European countries and as far afield as South Africa.

On 7 February 1947 the *Aeroplane* recorded:

So far as we know, Marshall's Flying School are comfortably in the lead with no less than 3,301 hrs. 30 mins. dual and solo flying by club members during 1946. Other impressive figures include 77 'A' Licence flying tests complete, 108 'A' Licence oral examinations. The Chief Flying Instructor, Sqdn. Ldr. L. V. Worsdell, had six Tiger Moths and two Proctors with six instructors for this achievement as well as over 1,100 hours charter flying, so no one is likely to object if we offer our congratulations on this very fine year's work.

Our EFTS at Clyffe Pypard continued until early 1947. Our Cambridge EFTS continued flying with Tiger Moths and an input of Oxfords and

Ansons to enable demobilised RAF pilots and Reservists to return for refresher flying. The School also undertook the training of Air Observation Post pilots for the Army, for which we had a number of Taylorcraft Auster high-wing trainer aircraft. In 1947 22 EFTS was re-designated 22 Reserve Flying School, continuing refresher training of RAF Volunteer Reserve pilots who had served during the war in addition to *ab initio* training of pilots to Wings standard. Leslie Worsdell was appointed Chief Flying Instructor of 22 RFS.

This was a period of twilight for the University Air Squadrons, during which their future was debated, but it was decided that 16 squadrons should continue. The Cambridge Squadron's flying was transferred from RAF Duxford to our Cambridge Aerodrome with Marshall's undertaking the maintenance of the aircraft. The Tiger Moth basic trainers were replaced by de Havilland Chipmunks in 1949. The Squadron had *ab initio* pupils, some of whom wished to enter the RAF or the Royal Naval Air Service, and also RAF pilots completing their interrupted education at the University, for which three Harvards were made available plus an Anson for navigation observer training. On 6 November 1949 a new town headquarters was opened in Chaucer Road by Marshal of the Royal Air Force Lord Tedder, whose son was one of the 128 CUAS members killed in the 1939–45 war.

At the end of the war there was overnight decimation of the aircraft industry, including the shutdown of the shadow factories. Whilst our garage had its problems, they were nothing compared with our aircraft engineering worries which were much more complicated. Most of our contracts were cancelled, reduced in quantity or had their delivery periods extended. Our contract for the conversion of large Hamilcar gliders for the Far East was cancelled following the sudden ending of the war by the Hiroshima and Nagasaki bombs. We had not reached the flying stage, but cancellation came at a time when the work was building up to a substantial contract which would have absorbed a big percentage of our workforce.

There was no earthly chance of getting sufficient aircraft work to fill all the floor space and employ all the workforce. With our own aerodrome and our big No. 2 Hangar we had our own home which was more than any of our competitors had. As far as our Aircraft Division was concerned we felt we could give the horse its head and take up the reins when there was a better indication of how quickly aviation was going to develop and what part we could play in it.

We knew from pre-war experience that aircraft manufacturers had substantial ups and downs of employment, but they were mainly located in or near large industrial areas where there was a pool of engineering labour. In the non-industrial area of Cambridge it was essential to have our own allied industry to occupy the extensive factory floor space no longer required for aircraft and to man peaks of aircraft work and absorb labour during troughs. Subject to giving a good account of ourselves on any aircraft work which was available, we decided we must concentrate our energy on establishing a new industry employing trades allied to the aircraft industry.

We considered possible alternatives and, encouraged by Austin having begun commercial vehicle manufacture, we concluded that commercial vehicle body building was the only answer. There was a big demand but we knew we would have to get firmly established very quickly if we were going to survive long-term after the immediate post-war demand had been satisfied. Hugh Gordon, the General Manager of the Sebro Stirling works at Cambridge, knew Sebro would be closed in the immediate future. We talked much about his and Marshall's future and Hugh joined us in February 1946 with the specific responsibility to train some of our aircraft labour to commercial vehicle body building practices and establish a Commercial Vehicle Body Building Department.

When he joined us – and I know Hugh will enjoy being reminded of this – I said, 'Hugh, before you get immersed in commercial vehicle body building, I would like you to attend the Fringe Firm Committee at the Society of British Aircraft Constructors on Wednesday. Here is the agenda – you know as much about this as I do.' On Thursday Hugh came back and said 'That meeting at the SBAC – you did say it was in the afternoon?' I said, 'No, Hugh, it was in the morning – anyway it was on the agenda.' Hugh said, 'Yes, I know, but somehow I thought it was in the afternoon and turned up at the SBAC Committee Room at two o'clock. It was not until four o'clock that I realised I must be at the wrong meeting, and said, "Mr. Chairman, I am sorry but I think I have come to the wrong meeting. I should be at the Fringe Firm Committee meeting. I'm frightfully sorry. I must go at once." But the chairman insisted, "No, do stay, you have made some most valuable contributions."'

Hugh worked like a Trojan, often into the small hours of the morning, to try to get our vehicle body building started with our existing labour and three or four aircraft draughtsmen. I had been foolish enough to believe there was not much in commercial vehicle body building – a box on wheels – but Hugh soon found that it was much more complex and said, 'You know, Arthur, unless we can get the real specialists in on this we are not going to get anywhere.' I took no notice at first because I thought this would be an impossible task and I was also worried that if we succeeded in getting in the specialists there would not be enough aircraft work for Hugh, and he would have talked himself out of a job. However, Hugh came back a few weeks later to insist that our only chance of success was to recruit men who had been in the industry all their lives to form a complete team of management and tradesmen covering all disciplines of commercial vehicle body building.

Hugh and I visited a number of vehicle body building works, not with a view to poaching any labour but to get some idea of what they looked like. At Spurlings of Edgeware Road, London, who were Bedford distributors who also built commercial vehicle bodies, we met St Clair Marshall, who had been in private car and commercial vehicle body building all his life. He had an encyclopaedic knowledge of all aspects of the industry and its personalities. He joined Marshall's as Manager of the Vehicle Body Building division in August 1946. He named a number of people in the industry who he thought would form a good nucleus of a commercial body building team. I remember visiting potential members of the team at their homes around London and walking up and down the street like 'Felix the cat'. One of the first and a very important member of the team was D. G. McMillan from Express Motor and Body Works Limited (now Pickfords) whom we appointed our Chief Designer. Mac and I well remember walking up and down Goswell Road, Islington in the rain whilst I successfully persuaded him that his destiny lay in Cambridge and that his destiny was important to Marshall's.

During this recruitment period Hugh Gordon's future became a worry. We had not sufficient aircraft work to absorb one with Hugh's all-round aircraft engineering capability and there were few aircraft jobs available. This concern for Hugh's future coincided with the demonstration tour of the new de Havilland twin-engined Dove, the replacement of the pre-war Rapide. The Dove, an aircraft for eight passengers and a crew of two, was initially priced at £18,250 which at that time seemed an astronomic figure. De Havilland arranged a demonstration at Cambridge on Sunday morning, 11 August 1946. The party included Whitney Straight, then a Director of British European Airways. I deliberately sat Hugh next to Whitney at lunch and after lunch explained the position and suggested that, if BEA wanted a first-class senior aircraft engineer, Hugh would fit the bill. Whitney phoned me the next day and asked if I really meant this? I said yes and reconfirmed that we had not sufficient aircraft work for Hugh at Cambridge. The following day Whitney sent for him and appointed him BEA Divisional Maintenance Engineer (Continental Division) forthwith, and a few years later he became BEA's Deputy Chief Engineer. Hugh and his wife, Irene, have remained very close friends of all members of my family over the years. Contact with them is a wonderful tonic at all times. Hugh finished his career as Westland's Sales Director and was awarded the OBE in 1973 for his services to export.

We owe everything to Hugh for so quickly recognising the essential need for specialists and identifying St Clair Marshall as the focal point for nominating potential members of our commercial vehicle body building team. He pressurised me into action regardless of his own position and, had we not heeded his advice at that time, our Commercial Vehicle Body Building Division would never have got off the ground.

Our intensive recruiting campaign was unbelievably successful. Within two months we had a complete team covering design, setting out, woodmill, metal detail, assembly, paint and illustrative signwriting. Housing was a big problem and we converted our wartime decontamination centre and an office block to provide temporary living accommodation within the works for a number of families.

Having collected the team together, all first-class tradesmen but all brought up at different factories with different long standing traditions, it took some time to establish Cambridge specifications for all types of commercial vehicle bodies. These were essential to avoid the detailed design of a vehicle body being progressively altered during design and manufacture by operatives working to their old firm's traditions. To overcome this I held a monthly meeting of the designers and operatives concerned to consider alternative methods of construction in specific areas of different types of body. On some occasions we put one or two alternative methods on trial for a period until we finally established the Marshall specification. Within two years we had an integrated team second to none.

Some of the early bodies built were for local customers, including Chivers, which resulted from my friendship with Oswald Chivers. Mr Wood, Chivers' Transport Manager, was a magnificent engineer and demanded on behalf of his company the very best. His advice and enthusiasm was a great help to us in the initial stages. Another all-important customer in the early days was Whitbread which arose from my father having known Colonel Whitbread since immediately after World War I when he was an undergraduate at Corpus Christi and garaged his large Sunbeam touring car with us at Jesus Lane; he played a big part in the University Steeplechases at Cottenham. We built a considerable number of vehicles for Whitbread during these post-war years. Mr Thompson, Whitbread's Transport Manager, was a stickler for detail and high quality. Marshall's high standards were beginning to develop.

We soon realised it was essential to market our commercial vehicle bodies in a professional and meaningful way. It was no good a company known as 'Marshall's Flying School' simply stating they were now making commercial vehicle bodies. Potential customers would say, 'What on earth does a flying school know about that?' Our customers were not private individuals but commercial operators who knew their vehicles and their particular requirements inside out. To overcome this we formed Marshall Motor Bodies Limited as the sales company in 1948.

By the end of 1948 we began to receive substantial orders for many types of bodies, including pantechnicons, brewers' drays, horse-boxes, cattle trucks, Post Office vans, military vehicles and multi-cell Black Marias for the Metropolitan Police. Because of the shortage of door furniture and similar equipment for the Black Marias, it was necessary for us to have at the works the vehicles which were being replaced, from which we stripped brass hinges, door locks, ventilation panels, etc. The vehicles had roof escape hatches controlled from a lever in the driver's compartment. The Police were particularly concerned about ventilation in each of the cells and also about the ability to thoroughly wash out the inside of the vehicle.

Whilst concentrating on the establishment of our Vehicle Body Division, we kept in close touch with de Havilland for whom we had continuing work on Mosquito and Hornet aircraft. Norman de Bruyne's synthetic glues had been used extensively in these aircraft, and the Naval adaptation of the Hornet just as the war ended, the Sea Hornet, was only made possible by the use of his Redux glue for the metal hinges of the upward folding wings to be glued to the wooden spars.

A temporary employment life-saver was the Berlin Air Lift which began on 26 June 1948. The Russians blocked ground communications to West Berlin, which became dependent on an American and British air lift for all supplies. Everything to make life possible had to be air-lifted, including oil, coal and salt. We were called to a meeting in London to discuss the major and rapid servicing of a number of different RAF aircraft. In view of our Dakota experience and quick turn-round during the Second Front we were instructed to undertake the maintenance, test flying and rapid turn-round of Dakotas. When an aircraft came in for service, the first job was to clear out all the coal-dust and flour which had collected in every nook and cranny.

The Berlin Air Lift continued to 30 September 1949, beyond the lifting of the actual siege on 12 May, to build up large stocks of food and general supplies. This was a tremendous exercise and resulted in 276,926 sorties covering 124 million miles. A large number of Dakota and other aircraft were used by the RAF and a number of British companies contributed to the airborne operations, some with improvised conversions of wartime bombers. Coal represented about three-fifths of all tonnage landed. The biggest lift in one day was 21,941 tons on 16 April 1949 in 1,398 sorties. To save weight the food flown in was dehydrated. Salt was flown in by RAF Sunderland flying boats which landed on Lake Havel in Berlin, these aircraft being suitable because they were internally and externally corrosion-proofed for operations on salt water.

During the war Fred Hornsby, our Aircraft Works Manager, had become friendly with Charles Sneesby, a senior designer at de Havilland Hatfield who had ambitions to be a chief designer. They both thought there was a future in continuing to undertake overflow work of servicing, repair, modification and conversion of role for the aircraft manufacturers as we had done, but they were confident that this could be extended to design and the manufacture of modification and repair kits. They were sure we would have a better chance of success if we could take over and be fully responsible for a complete package of design, manufacture and, with the backing of our very big hangar, work on the aircraft. This was a new line of thought as far as I was concerned. For our substantial and varied aircraft war work we had been in the main dependent on the supply of aircraft manufacturers' parts and modification kits, and on their drawing offices for final design and approval of repair schemes sketched by our handful of draughtsmen.

I know at the time I was not particularly enthusiastic but agreed that Charles Sneesby should join us in December 1946 and have a go. We put him with two or three draughtsmen in a rather dismal room with high windows at the back of the Aircraft Stores and left him, with Fred

Hornsby's co-operation, to get on with it. Initially progress was slow until such time as the aircraft manufacturers' design offices started to get busy with urgent work on the design of future military and civil jet and turbo-prop aircraft. We then began to receive orders for overflow design and manufacture of parts. By this time I had recognised the potential of this work in that it could result not only in expansion to a comprehensive design office but in addition a major expansion of our manufacturing capabilities. From this time on, Charles Sneesby and his Drawing Office had my most enthusiastic support to recruit a high grade team covering all disciplines. With this expansion Charles continued to work from his office at the back of the Aircraft Stores, with additional staff in vacant office accommodation throughout the works, until such time as we were able to provide a large, self-contained Aircraft Design Office.

Chapter 21

Aircraft Engineering – the Floodgates Open

1950–1958

SINCE THE WAR our Aircraft Division had done better than anticipated but the de Havilland Mosquito and Hornet work was coming to an end. As at January 1950 we did not know which way the wind was blowing or likely to blow. We hoped the new, small de Havilland Vampire and Venom jet fighters constructed of composite materials, with which the RAF was being rapidly equipped, would produce some work for us, but they were planned to have a short in-service life and to be replaced with larger, more sophisticated jet fighters which were in the course of development. Even if we got some Vampire and Venom work for a few years, with de Havilland concentrating on civil aircraft for the future the outlook for de Havilland work to follow looked extremely bleak.

Fortunately Vampire work started to become available during 1950. Damaged Vampire aircraft came to us for repair and rebuild, others came in for the incorporation of modifications, and new Vampires to be completed to overseas customers' specific requirements. We were lucky to be able to undertake most of this work at RAF Waterbeach which had a runway. Len Driver was in charge of our Waterbeach operation, which I visited daily and sometimes two or three times a day. I well remember working through many a night at Waterbeach to help ensure that we met some tight and important delivery dates, including – ironically now but with quite a different outlook in the early 1950s – the completion of a batch of new Vampire aircraft for Iraq. Mr J. A. MacKenzie, de Havilland's Works Manager, was thumping the table emphasizing that delivery of the Iraqi aircraft on time was of paramount importance and must be achieved at all cost for this very important customer.

Leslie Worsdell delivered the first Iraqi Vampire to Hatfield and recalls that Mr MacKenzie inspected it meticulously and in great detail. He suddenly got very excited and sent for his paintshop foreman and half the paintshop. Leslie thought we were in trouble, but when the paintshop foreman arrived Mr MacKenzie shouted, 'Look at this from Marshall's.

Why can't we paint aircraft like that? We have to get bloody Marshall's to
show us how to do it!' Our high gloss finish resulted from the Ministry's
Chief AID Inspector at Cambridge, who was a car enthusiast, insisting on
the same standard of finish on an aircraft as was achieved with cellulose
paint on a motor car. The AID Inspector's continued pressure to maintain
this standard on all aircraft enhanced our paint reputation but cost the
Company a lot of money.

Early in 1952 we had work on three pre-production Supermarine Swift
aircraft which we undertook at Waterbeach. The Swift was a contender for
the future RAF fighter. We carried out a number of urgent modifications
involving much design and manufacture of parts prior to the RAF final
trials. One of the problems was engine flame-out whenever the guns were
fired. We also had a Ministry contract to design the installation, equip and
flight test a Varsity aircraft ready for automatic landing development trials
at RAE Bedford and RAF Marham.

By early 1953 de Havilland's were becoming anxious to offload the
balance of their build of new aircraft for the RAF to enable them to concentrate all their efforts on their new Comet, the world's first jet airliner. They
asked if we considered we were capable of building the last 84 new
Venoms. We had no doubt about our capability and, with the Ministry's big
vehicle refurbishing contract now slowing down, we had our No. 4 Hangar
on the north side of Newmarket Road available. We could tow the
completed aircraft across the road for flight trials as we had done over the
years – but there was a problem. At the request of the Company's Works
Committee the 30 mph signs had been moved towards Newmarket to a
position where they obstructed crossing aircraft. I spoke first to Mr Arnold,
the Chief Constable of Cambridgeshire, who said he would do all he could
to help but this was primarily the responsibility of the Road Surveyor. He
was away, and so I spoke to the County Surveyor's Department who
assured us of their fullest co-operation and gave permission forthwith for us
to hinge the 30 mph signs on the clear understanding that we accepted full
responsibility for seeing the signs were only lowered for the few minutes
taken for the aircraft to pass – all was well.

Whilst we had flown an occasional Vampire or Venom from our
Cambridge grass aerodrome, we realised that for the new Venom contract a
runway was an absolute must and there was no time to lose. This decision
to build our own runway was a major one. At that time no concrete runways
had been built in this country without Government or municipal money. The
Government had subsidised the construction of runways for the main
aircraft manufacturers in the early post-war years, the amount of subsidy
depending on individual circumstances, including who would own the
runway when built. It was rumoured that de Havilland's, a conservative
company, adopted the attitude that, whoever paid for it, the runway must
belong to the company when built and it was said they received a 50 per
cent grant. A good old buccaneer such as Handley Page adopted the atti-

tude, 'Never mind who they say owns the runway, occupation is nine-tenths of the Law and we want as big a grant as possible'. It was rumoured that Handley Page received a 90 per cent grant.

With limited funds available we had to decide if we were going to lay as much concrete as possible with limited weight carrying capacity or build a short runway, half standard width but fully engineered, capable of carrying heavy aircraft and extendable. Whilst we were deliberating, the first Valiant flew into Wisley, near Vickers' works at Weybridge, onto the new Government-constructed runway built for flight testing the Valiant V-bombers. The Valiant was said to have chewed up areas of the runway like mud. The Wisley runway had been built with a new, cheaper process known as 'stabilised earth' which was not strong enough to carry a Valiant. We could not afford to have two bites at the cherry, and decided to construct the first section of our runway to a full engineering standard capable of carrying very heavy aircraft but only just over half standard width and of limited length. Since 1938 we had progressively bought packages of land on our southern boundary to make it possible at some future date to extend the aerodrome 500 yards to Coldhams Lane. The final plot of 43 acres was purchased on 14 August 1953, and the first stage of the runway was completed between 15 September and 18 December 1953, when Michael, then an undergraduate at Jesus College, dated it and signed his name in the wet concrete. The runway came into immediate use.

The Aircraft Division was now working to capacity and the remaining problem was shortage of aircraft labour. We took stock of the position and recognised that a production line of new aircraft assembled with proven interchangeable components was quite a different kettle of fish to the varying and individual work of rebuilding damaged aircraft. The time had come to take advantage of the buffer of labour we had built up in the Vehicle Body Building Division and of surplus labour from the military vehicle refurbishing contract. We decided that it would be possible during the building of our first two or three new Venoms to train non-aircraft operatives to perform repetitive operations, and that the whole programme could be undertaken with a team made up of a handful of proven skilled aircraft operatives and the balance non-aircraft personnel.

John Huntridge accepted responsibility for the new Venom programme and operated it as a separate unit within the Aircraft Division. Ben Breach, a foreman in the Vehicle Body Building Division, was appointed Production Manager for the new Venom build and was left to select his own personnel from the body building and vehicle refurbishing shops.

This is an opportune time to introduce John Huntridge. He had a successful Army career with the King's Own Yorkshire Light Infantry, seeing war service in Africa, Italy and France, and finished in Germany as Intelligence Officer of 15 Brigade with the rank of Captain. John joined Marshall's in 1947 at the age of 26 as my Personal Assistant, and I was disappointed when he left after 10 months to take up his early interest in farming and his love of horses. I had recognised his potential and we had established a close personal relationship. We kept in touch and met from time to time and, in due course, I suggested that he should return to Cambridge, which he did in November 1950 and never stopped working all hours and all days of the week. John rejoined the Company with the object of having a finger in every pie, including the garages and aircraft work but particularly the Commercial Vehicle Body Building Division. He was to play an all-important part in the development of our Companies.

John remembers that everybody was anxiously awaiting the first flight of the first Venom we built. Leslie Worsdell took off, climbed a few hundred feet, turned back and completed a low level roll over the aerodrome, which gave all concerned much confidence. The contract to build the new Venoms was a great success and was completed on time.

In 1954 we obtained a contract from de Havilland to equip 300 Vampire T11 trainers with ejector seats and ejector canopies. When we had originally decided to train some of our skilled body builders and motor mechanics for building new Venoms we never anticipated the possibility of a further contract similarly involving repetitive operations on a large number of aircraft becoming available to overlap and follow on – it just happened. The T11 ejector seat/canopy contract was a two-and-a-half year programme and, with in-service wastage, 284 aircraft were finally converted. Over the years ejector seats have saved a great many lives. When one of the remaining Vampire T11s unfortunately collided with a Meteor at a flying display at Mildenhall on Sunday 25 May 1986 it was good to know that the Vampire crew were able to eject safely. Tragically, the Meteor aircraft was not fitted with ejector seats.

Whilst we had worked for a number of other aircraft manufacturers, we had no personal commercial relationships such as we had had with de Havilland since the purchase of my first aircraft in 1928. Knowing Mr H. E. Hancocke, the Director of Aircraft Production, kept in close touch with the main manufacturers and felt some responsibility for the efficiency of the industry, I decided in 1953 to tell him of our worries and asked if any of the aircraft manufacturers might have an overload of work in the near future. He volunteered that one or two of them were becoming increasingly busy in their race to be first in the field with new jet and turbo-prop aircraft, and he gave me introductions to Tom Gammons, the Works Manager at Vickers, Weybridge; Don Crowe, the Chief Engineer (later Technical Director) at English Electric, Warton; and R. S. Brown, the Works Manager at Bristol. I met them all within a fortnight and it seemed that we had struck at the right time. They were all interested in varying degrees but all somewhat suspicious of the complete service we were offering. I progressively explained to all of them the work we had done to date and said we were ready and able to take over responsibility for any part of or complete projects including repairs, modifications, conversions, feasibility and definition studies, design, manufacture, aircraft trial installations, flight trials and certification, with all design completed to the individual aircraft manufacturer's in-house design standards and disciplines. I explained that we would plan to be as self-contained as possible with the object of establishing ourselves as their 'overflow works just down the road at Cambridge', leaving them to concentrate on their urgent development of new projects. There was no other company capable of taking on complete projects as I was suggesting. I also told them we had plans for a runway and large hangars to accept the largest aircraft envisaged at that time.

Tom Gammons of Vickers telephoned a few days later and said they would give us trial work on Viking, Valetta and Varsity aircraft. These were medium-sized twin-engine aircraft and could operate from our grass aerodrome; the Varsity was similar to the Viking but with a nose-wheel undercarriage. This proved to be a comprehensive package of work on 61 aircraft, including refurbishing one aircraft of the Queen's Flight.

English Electric were manufacturers of the famous Canberra aircraft, an aircraft they were rightly proud of, and they wanted to be very sure before entrusting any work to a third party. This was the first British jet aircraft to be built under licence in America in quantity for the United States Air Force where it was called the B57, which was later developed for long range strategic reconnaissance. Don Crowe was taken aback by our suggestion that we could undertake virtually anything that was offered to us as previously described to Vickers. Nevertheless, after a few trial orders we received our first Canberra at Cambridge at the beginning of 1954. Whenever an aircraft had to be on display at Cambridge in support of an MoD/RAF Canberra modification trial installation meeting, Don Crowe rightly insisted that the TI aircraft should be well segregated and everything about and around it scrupulously clean – a lesson well learnt.

R. S. Brown at Bristol said they had some Brigand Light Bomber work they might consider offloading, if they could satisfy themselves regarding our design capability. We received a two-year contract for a Brigand modification programme which included the incorporation of radar on 23 aircraft. This successful programme stood us in good stead with Bristol for the future.

In the midst of this avalanche of work, the de Havilland Comet suffered two serious accidents and all Comets were grounded in April 1954 – a terrible blow to de Havilland who with the Comet at that time had the world at their feet. This catastrophe provided de Havilland with an unexpected overload – not the sort of overload they wanted but it had to be dealt with. As a result of the reactions of some of the airline operators to these serious accidents, a number of Comets were accepted by the RAF including four to be converted into ECM (electronic counter measures) training aircraft over a three-year period which involved much design and manufacture, a complete strip-out of the aircraft and the installation of a vast amount of electronics and monitoring equipment. De Havilland could deal with the structural modification to overcome the pressurisation problem which had caused the accidents, but had no hangar space for the four RAF special project aircraft. De Havilland's Chairman W. E. Nixon visited Cambridge in mid-June 1954 with Mr MacKenzie and they were satisfied that we had the capability to undertake the work but, alas, our hangars were full. I said we would put up another hangar for the programme. Mac said, 'That's impossible – the first aircraft is due in during the first half of September.' I assured him we would meet the programme, proceed immediately with building our No. 8 Hangar, for which we had planning permission, and would have it ready for the first Comet. Mac said he did not believe it and would watch the position very carefully.

The new hangar was not a specially-designed building but the re-assembly of an RAF wartime prefabricated T2 hangar, 240 feet long and 130 feet wide. The Comet was one of the few jet nose-wheel aircraft which had a comparatively low tail and could be housed in a T2 hangar. On 7 September I phoned Mr MacKenzie to tell him that the first aircraft had arrived and was in the hangar. Mac replied, 'All I can say is that you are a bloody sight better at building hangars than you are aircraft!'

Mac was very friendly but spontaneously fierce if there was the slightest hitch in a programme. On one occasion I had to ring him to tell him that, because of the non-availability of a component, there would be a delayed delivery. I asked our telephone operator, as I thought, to get me Hatfield (this was in the days of manual plug-in exchanges) and asked for Mr MacKenzie. When I explained the position he said nothing – I expected an explosion at any moment. I repeated it all and still no reaction. I then said, 'You are Mr MacKenzie?' He replied, 'Yes.' I said, 'Mr MacKenzie of Hatfield?' He said, 'No, I am the boilerman at Vickers Weybridge!'

The new Vickers Viscount, the first turbo-prop airliner in the world, was progressively introduced into sustained service by BEA on selected routes during 1953. The Viscount provided increased cruising speed and less vibration and in-flight noise than piston engined aircraft. It was a revolutionary aircraft and a tremendous success, with over 550 sold worldwide. It was planned that BEA would take delivery of a substantial number before any were delivered to other operators. Apart from giving BEA the prestige of being the first and only operator of a turbo-prop airliner in the world, Vickers, Rolls-Royce and BEA would have the opportunity during the first 12 months of operation of this new generation aircraft to identify modifications which should be introduced before worldwide deliveries began. By mid-1954 a programme was planned to introduce modifications to the original BEA aircraft during the winter of 1954/55, the airline operators' slack period.

Vickers had no hangar capacity for this programme. We found that we could get five Viscounts in our pre-war No. 2 Hangar by the use of a nose-wheel jacking trolley to lower the tail to manoeuvre the aircraft through the entry door and to its work location in the hangar. The Vickers boss George Edwards decided to entrust this work to us. As was usual in those days, our pre-war No. 2 Hangar was not heated and it was a very severe winter. Some years later Sir George volunteered that our Viscount programme was one of the things that went really well that winter at a time when the pressure on Vickers was intense for the delivery of new Viscounts, completion of the V-1000 prototype and the start of design for the new, large Vanguard turbo-prop.

During the Viscount's initial period of operation Vickers, Rolls-Royce and BEA were keen to be identified as the only companies concerned with the manufacture and operation of this prestigious new aircraft. We recognised the importance of this and, as was our normal practice, kept a low profile and did not seek any publicity whatsoever. This policy paid off and further increased the confidence of Vickers and BEA in our working relationship. We became accepted as part of the team and, within 12 months, we were automatically expected to accept anything they threw at us, including collecting aircraft by air, dismantling damaged aircraft and collecting them by road and sea.

Viscount work further built up with emergency arisings. In December 1954 a Viscount crashed on take-off during a training flight at Blackbushe and, on 16 January 1955, another crashed when taking off on the wrong runway at London Airport in fog, and a third in Germany a few months later. In normal circumstances all three would have been written off, but the Viscount was in such great demand all over the world, including America, that we were instructed to collect them, improvise whatever jigs were necessary and somehow rebuild them. Everything possible had to be done to achieve a quick turn-round as the aircraft were desperately needed by the airlines for the expanding civil market. Our collection teams were made up of a handful of aircraft operatives covering all trades and the balance from our Vehicle Body Building Division. By increasing overtime at Cambridge it was possible to maintain our aircraft and vehicle production whilst these aircraft were being collected, so our buffer of labour provided by the Vehicle Body Division was working to good effect.

The Viscount winter programme of 1954/55 alerted us to the possibility of substantial future Viscount work and we realised that it would not be practical to rely on the improvised nose-wheel jacking trolley entry to our pre-war hangar. For aircraft coming to Cambridge for short periods of service work, quick and easy hangar access was essential. If we were to hold this work on new, large aircraft long-term we had to build hangars which would accept in numbers aircraft up to and beyond the size of any envisaged future jet airliner. Aircraft manufacturers' hangar accommodation for large aircraft in full flying trim was very limited. An aircraft manufacturer faced with an overload of work could find capacity for some design and manufacture but there was no company with a hangar big enough to carry out design, manufacture and incorporation of projects into large, high tail aircraft. The new generation of aircraft with nose-wheel undercarriages and resultant high tails required higher hangars than similar sized aircraft with tail wheels. We made a quick decision to build a big hangar to be known as No. 10 Hangar which was completed in 1955. During the building of this we applied for planning permission for a further hangar to be one-and-a-third times the floor area of No. 10 so that, if there was a requirement, we could build without incurring planning delays.

As at July 1956 we had planned our hangar accommodation for our winter commitments based on the completion of a Valetta programme by the autumn. Unfortunately an electrical component manufacturer ran into problems which meant that we would have to finish the Valettas during the winter months, for which we had no hangar capacity. We decided to go ahead with the erection of No. 11 Hangar, another T2, to be completed within six weeks with no floor – we would use the bare earth. I had previously visited a number of factories in Belgium in connection with our vehicle body building and found some had earth floors which provided warm working conditions and one was heated by improvised stoves using vehicle waste oil. We went ahead without planning permission and gave an undertaking to dismantle the building at some future date when there was no longer a shortage of hangar capacity. After a few years planning permission was obtained and the hangar up-dated as a permanent building with a concrete floor.

During 1955 Vickers entrusted us with much design work on their new Valiant jet V-bomber, and discussions developed regarding the possibility of Marshall becoming responsible for work on these aircraft after delivery to the RAF. The Valiant was an excellent aircraft which Sir George Edwards considers was his best; it was the first of the V-bombers and was planned to be in RAF service for several years before being followed by the Avro Vulcan and later the Handley Page Victor. These Vickers Valiant discussions again alerted us to the importance of having abundant aircraft hangar capacity in order that we could, without hesitation, accept any work which was offered to us. The first Valiant V-bomber arrived at Cambridge in January 1956 and went straight into our new, large No. 10 Hangar for incorporation of modifications and development work. In the atmosphere prevailing, we proceeded with the building of the second large hangar for which we now had planning permission, to be known as No. 12, which was completed in 1958. With the possible exception of one or two of the major airlines, we then had the biggest hangar capacity in Europe for servicing large aircraft.

Whilst we had been able to use our half-width and comparatively short runway for Venoms, Canberras and initial flying of Viscounts and Valiants, we realised that this would not be practical long-term for large aircraft and we took quick action in 1957 to widen the runway to the full standard width and lengthen it to the maximum dimensions available. We carried out this work without putting the runway out of action – quite an achievement. Leslie Worsdell writes:

> We started flying Valiants off the original narrow runway, much to the dismay of Jock Bryce, Vickers' Chief Test Pilot, who was insisting on a 6,000 ft. long, standard width runway at Wisley. Jock was getting embarrassed by his

board of directors who were asking how it was that they had to suffer the costs of operating the Valiants from very long and wide runways when Marshall's were landing on what pilots called 'The Cambridge Boot Lace'? Having decided to lengthen and widen the runway, the widening process was a little traumatic because we had at that time about ten Valiants in the hangar, and I went to the boss of the test flying units in the Ministry and said I wanted to dig a big hole on the side of the runway and fill it with rubble and then concrete, and would he mind if we went on flying his Valiants with only ten feet clearance between the Valiant wing-tip on take-off and the tall concrete mixer on the right-hand side and two foot clearance between my left wheel and the grass. He wasn't very pleased at this but I made it plain that we had to take action because of Jock Bryce's threat to withdraw approval to move a Valiant at all on our runway unless we took action. Finally he said that there really was no choice. He couldn't afford to have 10 aircraft locked up whilst we expanded the runway so we'd have to proceed. He added, 'But I'll tell you, Worsdell, if you prang that aeroplane in that hole I'll come and have your guts for garters.' I said, 'Sir, if I finish up in that hole they will be there for the taking. You will be welcome.' But it all went well.

Before work was started on the runway extension I carefully planned and practised initial take-offs and landings, and had established that if I kept my nose-wheel on the third bitumastic division between the runway 10-foot slabs – that is, 30 foot in from the concrete edge from the left-hand side – I had got two foot clearance from the grass verge and 10 foot clearance from the concrete mixer on the right-hand side and I was quite happy that I could operate the Valiant safely on the existing runway whilst the widening was still in progress. I said to Gordon Hubbard, my co-pilot, before the first take-off with the runway widening in progress, 'What you mustn't do is look out of the right-hand side when you go past the concrete mixer', but Gordon couldn't resist. We accelerated down the runway and as we came up abreast of the concrete mixer his eyes became fixed on it and he said, 'Oh my God! Oh my God! . . . Missed it!'

To complete the runway story, a further extension was made in 1972 which became possible with the building of the Teversham bypass, now known as Airport Way, for which the Company made a substantial financial contribution.

Marshall undertook many trial installations on Valiants, the biggest of which was Blue Steel, the stand-off hydrogen bomb. The Valiant was selected for all the development work for this advanced weapon which was planned to be fitted to the follow-on Vulcan and Victor V-bombers. We worked under strict security with a day and night guard on the aircraft. The work involved the complete strip-out of the Navigator's and the Flight Engineer's stations and precise installation of the then advanced Inertial Navigation System, which was the key to the success of the weapon, and its associated instrumentation. Inertial navigation equipment enables an aircraft to identify its exact in-flight position anywhere in the world without the aid of outside signals. This was the first British aircraft to be fitted with this equipment which is today standard fit in most modern long range civil airliners. The most demanding requirement of the Blue Steel conversion was to provide for the full-scale weapon in the bomb bay, together with the complex control and monitoring systems. The weapon was half buried in the bomb bay, and to interface this with the airframe and ensure structural and aerodynamic integrity was a substantial task. The extensive work we had undertaken on the Valiant on behalf of Vickers, with modifications involving changes in all systems on the aircraft and in particular the electrical and electronic systems, led to Marshall's appointment as Vickers' Delegated Design Authority for all future electrical and electronic development of the Valiant. We equipped a second Valiant with an Inertial Navigator System in support of the Blue Steel programme.

One Valiant TI which created much interest was the introduction of a Rapid Take-Off Procedure. Leslie Worsdell recalls:

This was at the time when the five-minute warning was being taken fairly seriously – one was expecting five minutes from the time the Russians launched the rocket until the time it hit its target. The fighter aircraft had all been organised so that they were on ready operational pans with the pilots sitting in the aircraft, and all they had to do was press the starter button, taxi a few yards and take off within five minutes.

The AOC of the Group which owned the Valiants didn't want his Valiants caught on the ground, so he asked Marshall's to find some means of getting the aircraft off the ground within the five minutes warning time. The Valiant pre-flight procedure normally took 20, 25 or 30 minutes by the time all the covers had been taken off and the crew had gone through all the pre-flight drills. Our engineers came up with quite ingenious devices. There were two pitot tubes on the aircraft for the pick-up of pressure for the airspeed indicators. These were about three/four feet long and fixed on each wing tip, projecting forwards, but of course quite out of reach of anyone on the ground, so to fit covers to keep out the weather and insects, and similarly to remove them and their attendant warning flags before flight, the ground crew had to get step-ladders.

There was also an air intake facing forward at the base of the fin on top of the fuselage to operate what was called the Q-Feel which was a device which made the controls go heavier as the aircraft flew faster to avoid over-stressing the aircraft. As the controls were pneumatically or hydraulically operated, normal 'feel' was absent. Starlings would nest in any opening if you let them! Normally the engines had to be started one by one as they put an initial very heavy discharge on the ground power units until they speeded up and their own generators came on line. All this took time, so Marshall's solution was to move the connection into which the ground power unit was plugged to underneath the fuselage, facing backwards, with heavy duty starter ground power units connected to that behind the aircraft. With a suitable system of elastics and levers as the aircraft moved forward the electrical and ground-to-aircraft intercom connections would disconnect by pull and the covering flap would spring closed and the electrical system was properly sealed off.

The solution for the pitot head covers and the Q-Feel air intake cover was to spring-load them and attach them by tapes to fittings on the ground so that, as the aircraft started to move, the triggers were pulled, the springs were released, the covers shot forward out of the way and the aircraft was 'clean'. To give more power for starting four engines at once the ground power units were doubled up or trebled in capacity. Well, we had several practices at this, myself and my co-pilot. We would sit in the aircraft, all strapped up and we had done 'vital actions' as far as we could. The only thing we had to do was to press four starter buttons together to start the engines, taxi on to the runway and open the throttles and take off.

One day the Officer Commanding said that he wanted to come and 'view the body'. He wanted to see what he was paying for. So he came to me for a briefing and I said, 'Well, sir, there is your slit-trench. You're going to be sitting there and you will receive the five minute warning. You will be plugged into my intercom and you are going to say, "Five minute warning – go" and we will carry on.' So he said, 'When do you want me to do that?' and I said, 'When you like. You know, this is a demonstration of its effectiveness. You can sit there for an hour if you want to, sir.' He said, 'Oh no, I'm with you.' So I said, 'I'll tell you when we are at readiness.' I told the AOC over the intercom we were now at readiness and almost immediately he said 'Five minute warning – go!' With that we opened the throttles, pressed the four starter buttons at the same time (opening the throttles during start-up to speed up the engines more quickly was quite against regulations). I throttled back, let the brakes off, started taxiing, turned on the 200 yard loop on to the runway which at that time was quite short and took off. At 500 feet we raised the undercarriage, turned down wind, lowered the undercarriage, put down some more flap, turned in and we had landed before the five minutes were up. So we had taken off and actually done a circuit and landing within the five minutes allowed for take off only.

We were terribly pleased. We thought we'd get medals for that so we taxied in grinning all over our faces, to be met by an irate Air Vice-Marshal who said, 'I've never seen anything so bloody dangerous in all my life. How did you know those covers were going to come off?' and I said, 'Well, somebody would have said stop if they hadn't.' 'You can't rely on that' and I said, 'Well we could see.' He said, 'You couldn't see the Q-Feel one because that's in the fin' and I said, 'No, you're quite right, sir.'

With this modification Marshall had in fact made a major contribution to the V-Bomber Force effectiveness. We were contracted to consider the feasibility of this procedure being extended to the Vulcan and Victor V-bombers, and the resultant modifications formed the basis of the 'Rapid Take-Off' facility for the entire Bomber Force.

During this time Vickers made us responsible for their Valiant CRSP (Contractors Repair and Supply Procedure) for the storage of major components such as wings, ailerons, flaps, spars and large billets of material required for major repairs or refurbishing, as compared with the day-to-day maintenance spares held by the RAF. Marshall purchased the old Sebro wartime Stirling bomber repair factory at Bourn for this contract.

Many years later, in December 1991, I was to receive a letter from my old friend Allen Greenwood which in a few words reflects the spirit and the working relationship which had developed at all levels between Marshall and the main aircraft manufacturers and our Royal Air Force at this time. Remembering these years he wrote: 'I will never forget my enormous good luck to have first met you there (at Cambridge). We walked down your runway together – Valiant was my problem – you said you would widen the runway – and built those huge hangars! What a friend – I will never have another like it.'

Within a year or so of receiving our first Canberra in 1954 English Electric entrusted us with all modification and development work for in-service Canberra aircraft, to enable them to concentrate on the later marks of Canberra still in production and on their new Lightning aircraft. We quickly became accepted as English Electric's overflow shop at Cambridge. We were of particular assistance by being able to accept special one-off projects which required much detailed attention, such as the equipping of a Canberra PR7, known as 'Aries V', for Arctic trials. Apart from other equipment, this aircraft had tanks fitted in every available space to provide for long range polar flights, and great care had to be taken in measuring the fuel flow from each of the tank positions.

Work on Canberra aircraft included the introduction of the American Low Altitude Bombing System (LABS) which provided a low-level bomb delivery procedure with the aircraft modified to carry the American 1,650 lb. nuclear weapon. This was the first RAF in-service aircraft with a nuclear capability. The delivery system was known as 'Loft or Toss Bombing', which entailed a low level approach to the target and a pull up at a pre-determined point with bomb release occurring automatically at between about 20 and 35 degrees depending on the throw required. Normally the aircraft would continue the looping manoeuvre and roll out in a dive back along the approach track. Apart from installation of the then very secret equipment, special instrumentation was fitted to safeguard the structural integrity of the airframe to meet the demanding low altitude manoeuvre. On behalf of English Electric, Marshall attended the LABS ground trials at RAF Laarbruch in Germany under the control of USAF. On the successful completion of the LABS trial installation and flight trials, we were awarded a contract to convert 73 further aircraft to the LABS role. It was by luck that this contract, made up of many repetitive operations, overlapped with the completion of the 284 Vampire T11 ejector seat/canopy conversions and was just what the doctor ordered for our North Works No. 4 Hangar team which we had trained from scratch to build the new Venoms some four years earlier. We got a record number of nine Canberras into our No. 4 T2 Hangar, with the aircraft running on rails providing two moving assembly lines.

The Canberra LABS programme was completed in time for John Huntridge and his Ben Breach team to undertake the modification and completion of 18 new long-range Bristol Britannia airliners for delivery to BOAC. This resulted from BOAC's change in flight deck operating proce-

Above HeavyLift Belfast G-BEPE taking off from Cambridge aerodrome.

Below left Marshall's Citation G-BCRM at Wichita 1976. Left to right: Bob Smythe, Rosemary and me. (*Cessna Aircraft Company*)

Below right Space sled for medical research undertaken in the Challenger space mission from Kennedy Space Centre on 30 October 1985.

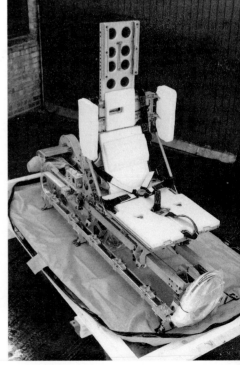

FH70 Howitzer crew compartment and gunnery equipment stowage.

The 15,000th 4-ton cargo body (1986). John Huntridge (left) and General John Willis, Director General Fighting Vehicle Executive.

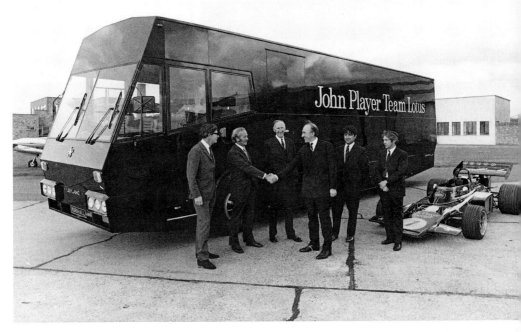

Handover of John Player Team Lotus car transporter in 1973 with Fittipaldi's car and (left to right) Jim Smith, Colin Chapman, St Clair Marshall, John Huntridge, John Arnold and Bill Lallyett. (*Phipps Photographic*)

Marshall Room, Jesus College. (*Reeve Photography*)

Family, Shareholders and Directors at the Annual General Meeting 1979 on and around Marshall's 1913 Austin Twenty (for key see Appendix 3).

Above left Percy Easter and myself in an 1897 Daimler at the Marshall 70th Anniversary Cavalcade in 1979. (*Michael Manni Photographic*)

Above right Hercules XV179 at Ascension Island with crew after 28 hours non-stop flight to the Falklands and back, refuelling in flight, 1982.

Below Leslie Worsdell presenting the Sir Arthur Marshall ATC Gliding Challenge Cup to Air Commodore K. J. Goodwin CBE, AFC, A-O-C Cadets RAF Newton 1982. (*RAF Newton*)

TriStars in work in No. 17 Hangar 1986.

Visit of Air Commander South Atlantic Operation Air Marshal Sir John Curtiss during Falklands conflict. Left to right: Flight Engineer David Ryding, Roy Gates, Sir John Curtiss and Maurice Kent.

TriStar ZD953 handover ceremony on 24 March 1986. Presentation of log book to the CA MoD Air Marshal Sir David Harcourt-Smith.

Above Gerald Coulson painting of a TriStar refuelling a Hercules over Cambridge Aerodrome, presented to 216 Squadron RAF on 24 March 1986.

Below Gulfstream III HZ-DAI of the Dallah Avco Company of Saudi Arabia 1985.

Bottom Spanish Navy Citation II with forward-looking infra-red camera pod installation, 1986.

John Huntridge explaining a point to the Prime Minister during her visit on 27 May 1988.

Apprentices presenting their chisel to the Prime Minister. (*East Anglian Daily Times*)

Above left Michael as High Sheriff lighting the Armada Beacon at Huntingdon in 1988.

Above right Michael High Sheriff and myself a Deputy Lieutenant, 1988. (*Michael Manni Photographic*)

Below DROPS (Demountable Rack Off-loading/Pick-up System), the MoD production contract which our Vehicle Division won in 1989.

Marshall/Bedford JJL Midibus. (*B. Nye*)

My 80th birthday in 1983. Left to right (back): Michael, Judy and David, (seated) Rosemary and me.

Norman de Bruyne and me at the opening of Ciba-Geigy's de Bruyne Room in 1987. (*Michael Manni Photographic*)

Cambridge airport 1938 – Aviation career of Sir Arthur Marshall. Gerald Coulson painting presented to me on my retirement (for key see Appendix 2).

HM King Hussein of Jordan presenting me with the Order of Istiqlal First Class in Amman 1990. (*Meledos*)

Gulfstream 'Appreciation Day' at Savannah, November 1991, when the management served employees in the canteen. Left to right: Bill Lowe (President), Allen Paulson (Chairman), Sibyl, Michael, and Goldie Glenn (Vice-Chairman).

Above left Villagers looking at Horseheath village sign.

Above right Rosemary Marshall Memorial Window, Horseheath Church.

Below Michael with General Sir Peter de la Billiere, Commander British Forces in the Gulf War, January 1992. (*Cambridge Newspapers Ltd*)

Toasting the future at my 90th birthday party at Jesus College on 4 December 1993 (*Michael Manni Photographic*)

Aerial view of the aerodrome and works from the north 1994. Our Boeing 747/TriStar hangar is in the distance.

dures which involved a complete rehash of the cockpit, including the provision of an engineer's station. It was a tightly scheduled programme to minimise delay in the aircraft entering operational service and was completed on time. John Huntridge and Ben Breach had by now formed a close working relationship and in 1959 were eagerly awaiting a new challenge.

In 1957 we undertook our largest and most complex task on behalf of English Electric – to convert Canberra B6 aircraft to the new B15 and B16 roles completely up-dating the aircraft's armaments and avionics. This involved a complete strip-out of the aircraft, including the cockpit, and installation of all the latest demands of the Air Staff, including extension of the LABS facility to take the now available 2,000 lb. British WE177 nuclear weapon. Prototypes were produced for re-certification by the Aircraft and Armament Experimental Establishment at Boscombe Down, to be followed, if successful, by a possible conversion requirement in 1959 for a total of 74 aircraft. The difference between the B15 and the B16 was that the B16 was fitted with 'Blue Shadow' sideways looking ground terrain following radar.

On 14 March 1957 Viscount G-ALWE crashed on the approach to Manchester Airport when a flap on one side of the aircraft inadvertently retracted losing lift on that side. The aircraft rolled over and dived into the ground with serious loss of life. Urgent modification action was necessary and we became the centre for the remedial work with an input of 19 aircraft from various airlines within a few days. The first few aircraft were collected by our own flight crews from Heathrow and other aerodromes and flown back to Cambridge, landing with flaps retracted. This was not an exercise which the average airline pilot had probably ever undertaken in his life (and neither had we!) but in fact we found there was no particular problem.

We were now undertaking Viscount work on behalf of a number of airlines throughout the world. The general atmosphere is well described by the following extracts from Leslie Worsdell's Imperial War Museum tape:

> We were helping Vickers deliver their Viscounts to Canada and America, and we were doing a lot of Valiant and Canberra flying. We had a great variety of aircraft then. We were still flying some of the older types, and one day I did fly six different types of aircraft, ranging from a Tiger Moth to a Valiant, and including a Viscount and a Venom. Of course, it was interesting that in those days one was allowed to do that. Now you can't get close to an aircraft – you can't sit in it until you have had a full brief on what to do when you sit in it.
>
> Whilst I was at Vickers learning to fly the Valiant, Trubshaw (Vickers' Chief Test Pilot) said he thought that I'd got the most interesting test flying job in the whole of the aircraft industry. They, as manufacturers' test pilots, were limited to about three aircraft, waiting for the Vanguard to start coming off the lines. De Havillands at that time probably only had three types on the go, and English Electric had only the Canberra and were waiting for the Lightning. So my log book full of different types put me in a very interesting and enviable position.

In the early fifties the University Aeronautical Engineering Department, led by Professor Mair, was experimenting with wing boundary layer control. The boundary layer is the slow moving layer of air adjacent to the wing which has the effect of increasing the frictional resistance of the wing and hence slowing down the aircraft. The theory is that, if this layer of air could be removed, the aircraft would behave as if the wing was much cleaner and the aircraft would fly faster. The Air Ministry was interested in this project and made a Vampire aircraft available for experimentation and flight trials. A replacement section of the port Vampire wing was installed with of the order of half a million very small holes drilled in it which were all channelled into a tube to a pump which sucked off boundary layer air. The 'suction-air on/off' was operated by a lever and, if the aircraft was flying straight and level and the suction-air then applied, the aircraft would make a smart roll to the right because the port wing was providing more lift than the starboard wing. The test flying was undertaken by our pilots. The experimental section of the Vampire wing is still held by the University Aeronautical Engineering Department.

In 1955, as a result of the success of the University Aeronautical Engineering Department to date, the Ministry awarded us a contract to work with them to design and produce a new version of an Auster aircraft, known as the M.A.4, as a research vehicle for a boundary-layer control project. The work consisted of producing a new wing, the installation of a Budworth gas turbine engine and extensive instrumentation to measure various parameters of interest to the research programme. Marshall's test pilots undertook most of the flying to explore the flight envelope in close co-operation with the University. Dr Head of the University Aeronautical Engineering Department, who was directly responsible to Professor Mair for the project, also undertook some of the test flying.

After 120 hours development test flying, the aircraft crashed when flying under low cloud conditions in March 1966, tragically killing both Brian Wass, one of our pilots, and the University observer, Krishnamurthy, a young Pakistani scientist. The cause of the accident was never satisfactorily resolved.

Brian Wass had flown with me on many of my overseas trips. We teamed up well together. I particularly remember one sticky winter journey when we were flying back from North Africa. Flying conditions were very bad all over Europe and the Mediterranean. It was a journey I think Brian would not have been eager to make but for the fact that his wife was expecting their second child within the next few days. Our machine iced up rapidly in an alarming way at a comparatively low altitude over the Mediterranean. We refuelled at Lyons and, in spite of adverse weather reports, continued to Cambridge where the conditions were minimal with plenty of ice, snow and misty visibility. I only remember one other occasion of bad icing and that was with the same aircraft with Gordon Hubbard on a flight from Vickers Weybridge to Vickers at Hurn. The machine iced up and became sluggish on the climb-out from Wisley. Both occasions shook me at the time.

In 1955 we received a contract from the Bristol Aeroplane Company for the design, development and manufacture of a recoverable supersonic ram-jet test vehicle called 'Bobbin' based on the Bloodhound missile, which we worked on with great urgency under great security behind barred windows; Eddie Fortin, our Machine Shops Manager who had joined the Company in 1941, had overall responsibility for the manufacture. Eddie established the high precision engineering standards in our Machine Shops and was an inspired improviser in times of emergency.

Marshall had a senior designer at the trials of 'Bobbin' at the Woomera rocket range in Australia. It was thought that if the initial trials were successful there could be a big follow-on order which might entail advanced electronic development, and Bristol hoped Marshall could become self-supporting in this respect. For this we required a boffin-type specialist with electronic research and development capability who would live with the progress of the missile and, if possible, one who had an idea for a marketable project and ambition to develop it. This project would be his day-to-day work and he would keep up to date with the missile and be available for any avionic problems or development work as and when required.

We engaged John Barron who had very definite ideas about the development and possible sales of pulse height analysers, known as Kicksorters, used for nuclear research to identify the strength of signals of radioactive materials. We had just got our Electronics Section going when the Bristol recoverable missile contract was cancelled in the 1957 Defence White Paper, which considerably reduced the size of the RAF and cut back many missile projects. We were then left with an Electronics Section to develop and market the Kicksorter. Although development took three years longer than originally forecast and cost three times as much, it was finally very successful and 69 Marshall Kicksorters were sold throughout the world, including 21 to the UK Atomic Energy Authority. We also developed three specialist items of equipment to assist us in the development of our Kicksorter and these, in turn, had good sales throughout the world. The project came to an untimely end when customers asked for transistorised equipment in place of valves, and suitable transistors for our Kicksorter were not readily available.

We had developed our Kicksorter under licence from the National Research Development Corporation based on the Hutchinson-Scarrott Analyser. Our many contacts with the NRDC and their first-hand experience of our capabilities stood us in good stead when the question of work on the Bacon Fuel Cell arose. A fuel cell is a piece of equipment which, fed with hydrogen and oxygen or some other gases or liquids, produces electricity.

Francis Thomas (Tom) Bacon lived near Cambridge and his life's work was the development of fuel cells. The NRDC decided to support further development of his work and a contract was established whereby Tom would provide the technical input and team up with Marshall with the object of developing a reliable, automatically controlled fuel cell to generate a substantially higher power than the lighting of a few bulbs which had previously been achieved under laboratory conditions. This was an exciting and challenging project. The Company appointed John Frost Project Manager responsible to John Huntridge. After two-and-a-half years' work, on Monday 25 August 1959 we demonstrated to those interested in fuel cells, including the Press, a fuel cell with an output of six kilowatts driving a forklift and a circular saw and providing power for arc welding. This unit was not commercially viable but it was one stage closer to a practical solution than anything that had been achieved before.

The principles of Tom Bacon's fuel cell as developed at Cambridge were further developed by Pratt & Whitney of America and used in the Apollo moon landing in 1969 for which the fuel cell provided electrical energy and, from the combination of hydrogen and oxygen, water for drinking and humidification. I posed the question to Keith Williams, who is writing on behalf of the Royal Society a biographical memoir on the late Tom Bacon's work, 'Would the Apollo moon mission have been possible but for Tom's life's work and his work with us at Cambridge?' Keith Williams replied that he could not do better than to record Tom quoting the occasion when President Nixon put his arm round his shoulder and said, 'Tom, without you we wouldn't have gotten to the moon.' Pratt & Whitney wrote to Tom soon after the successful Apollo flight congratulating him on the part his fuel cells had played in the mission and recording that the three fuel cells were one hundred per cent reliable. The electrical energy used during the mission was of the order of 400 kilowatt hours. The flight duration was 8 days 3 hrs 18 mins 35 secs (approximately 195 hours).

Tom Bacon was always modest and we found him easy to work with. Since Tom's work at Marshall's in 1961 hundreds of millions of pounds have been spent on the development of fuel cells in various parts of the world, particularly America, Germany and Japan. If, finally, it proves commercially and technically successful, fuel cell technology will have major applications in the production of electricity for domestic and commercial use, transport of all kinds, and silent power for submarines. It would decrease pollution, in motor transport for example, and it might be possible to provide the energy by making use of waste gases such as methane, which in itself is a major pollutant, and such gases would be rendered harmless. Bacon's pioneering work on fuel cell technology has made a significant British contribution to research and development worldwide. We are privileged and proud to have been associated with Tom's work during this important development of his life's work.

By December 1958 we had completed major work on, test flown and delivered from Cambridge 650 Vampires and Venoms, 95 Viscounts, 134

Canberras, 79 Valiants and 96 sundry aircraft made up of Brigands, Varsities, Valettas and Vikings and a substantial contract from BEA to modify 25 large twin-engined Airspeed Ambassador airliners.

In addition to all our engineering work with a physical aircraft involvement we had orders from various sources for tens of thousands of hours of basic design and manufacture for many types of aircraft not worked on at Cambridge, and we also helped out generally whenever required. Stan Cooper, a senior designer (later our Aircraft Engineering Design Office Manager), took a design team to bolster up Vickers with their work at Wisley for a short time, and similarly to de Havilland, Hatfield. This was not just supplying a few draughtsmen, but supplying people already familiar with the Vickers and de Havilland design office procedures as a result of work undertaken on aircraft at Cambridge. Having become recognised experts in aircraft armament installations, we were allocated the task of designing the complete electrical installation of weapons system circuitry of the English Electric Lightning Mk. 3.

The Company owes much to Charles Sneesby for the part he played in establishing our Aircraft Design Office. Charles had a good all-round background knowledge of aircraft design and of the industry and was uninhibited and full of confidence and bounce. The spirit in the Design Office is well described by Mrs Saunders (Miss Thora Tuck) who was my secretary during the war and returned to the Company in 1950 to work in the Design Office where she was responsible for the minutes of the MoD/RAF technical meetings, and herself made a big input to the enthusiasm of the Design Office team. She writes:

> Charles Sneesby made no secret of the fact that the formation of a Design Office – a design office team – was something he had dreamed about all his life and somehow we all got caught up in that dream. We were involved in the unknown, in the creation of a new venture. We had been given this once-in-a-lifetime opportunity and the road ahead lay bright and shining with promise right to the end of the rainbow. So we cared – about what we were doing and the team we were forming.
>
> Founder members of the Design Office were blessed with boundless energy and enthusiasm, and new members joining the team were soon swept along on that tide of enthusiasm – or else they did not stay – there were no half measures. The opportunities for those who cared to apply themselves were boundless.

Marshall's Design Office was rapidly developing into a pedigree team and the quality, versatility and quick response of their work and their enthusiasm were becoming recognised throughout the UK aircraft industry. There is no doubt that in his early days Charles Sneesby contributed in a big way to the general spirit of enterprise which prevailed, all supported with the first-class intake covering all disciplines during this period which included Roy Gates (from Vickers and Follands) and Norman Harry (from Shorts).

John Kellock, a young draughtsman at the time, wrote to me recently:

Charles was absolutely single-minded, thought only about work and it was an obsession with him. The sort of thing I can remember is he would call me into the office at perhaps half past five at night, 'There is an urgent thing up at Warton. Be there at eight o'clock in the morning.' No matter who he asked in the office, we would not think twice. We would just nip home, put some things in a bag and say to the wife, 'Sorry, I have got to go up to Warton tonight.' We knew we were on the threshold of something big. You never knew what new jobs would be coming up during the day's work. Charles's spirit was infectious, there is no doubt about it.

I had the offer of a job at Bristols and had quite a barney with Sneesby, and I thought it was going to be a punch-up. Do you remember that you, sir, got us together and metaphorically banged our heads together in your office and told us to go away and act like grown-ups? I decided to stay and am very grateful that I did because at Bristol I would have had work on one or two aeroplanes, compared with the very quick-moving work on many types of aircraft at Cambridge.

Norman Harry recalls that he wanted a challenge, and Marshall's big attraction was our wide range of work on many types of aircraft. Many of the first-class design engineers recruited during this period were attracted by this variety of work – all very fast moving and on occasions, by pre-planning, the manufacture of parts began before the drawings were complete.

We had reached the limit of spreading the Drawing Office personnel around the works wherever room was available, and in 1953 we up-dated a North Works building to accommodate the Aircraft Engineering Design Office under one roof. We had a small informal glass-of-sherry party, to which the wives were invited, to declare the new Design Office open. I well remember at the end of the party Charles coming up to me and taking my hand and, in that way of his of standing with his left shoulder lower than his right and his head cocked to the left and looking you straight in the eye, saying, 'I cannot thank you enough for all this, which makes it possible for me to achieve my life's ambition.'

By this time we had trained many of our non-aircraft engineers to be aircraft operatives, backed by a continuing input of apprentices and trainees. The introduction of a Company-assisted housing scheme played a big part in attracting many of our future key employees. We also provided hostel accommodation for up to 230 temporary employees to meet periodic peak requirements. With all this activity the time had come when Ronnie Bowles, the Personnel Manager, needed a deputy. Dick New, who had been with the Company throughout the war, was working in our Airport Garage and was serving with me on the Eastern Regional Board for Industry, made up of representatives of industry, trade unions and various Ministries. Dick was a union representative and I was an industrial representative. I thought Dick talked good common sense, and suggested to Ronnie that we should offer him the job. Dick was initially doubtful but finally decided to have a go and this he did with great success over the years. When Ronnie Bowles retired in 1956 Dick New was appointed Personnel Manager.

In January 1957 Group Captain Jock du Boulay CBE, one of the youngest Group Captains in the Air Force, joined Marshall as Manager of our newly established Aircraft Servicing Sales Office to initiate and maintain contact with overseas military and civilian customers. Jock in his unassuming way established a very friendly working relationship with many customers, particularly in the Middle East. His most important contribution was his advice that we should become Grumman's East of Atlantic Service Centre for their new Gulfstream de luxe executive twin turbo-prop aircraft fitted with two Rolls-Royce Dart engines which made it a very powerful, high performance aircraft. The Gulfstream at that time had a maximum seating capacity of 18 but was usually fitted out to accommodate 10 or 12 passengers in extreme comfort. Our first customer was Signor Agnelli, the head of Fiat, Italy in 1960. Jock when submitting his recommendation to the Company said he thought we would only have one or two aircraft a year to service for a year or two but he was confident that the aircraft had a great future. It developed into a total input of 1,555 aircraft over the next 30 years.

The fifties was an exciting, exhilarating period and full of the joys of life. Everything was fast moving and overlapping, and the provision of capacity and the development of capability had to be dealt with on a day-to-day basis. We did not realise it at the time but Sir George Edwards has since remarked on numerous occasions, 'There is no doubt you provided the right help at the right time.'

Chapter 22

Other Developments of this Explosive Period

1950–1958

IN THE EARLY fifties our Cambridge aerodrome was a hive of flying training activity. At the end of the forties tension was mounting in Korea. A number of RAF Reservists were called up and the flying training commitment of No. 22 Reserve Flying School and the Cambridge University Air Squadron was increased.

No. 22 RFS continued with the training of new pilots and annual refresher courses for ex-RAF pilot Reservists. Its fleet of 21 Tiger Moths was replaced in August 1950 with de Havilland Chipmunks. The School also had three Ansons for training navigators and wireless operators, and four Oxfords to provide radar interception to a unit of the CUAS known as 'Fighter Control'. No. 22 RFS was one of the last seven schools to be closed on 30 April 1954.

Bill Ison had joined the RAF Volunteer Reserve at No. 22 RFS after war service with the RAF. When the RFS was disbanded he and fellow enthusiasts formed the Cambridge Flying Group, which still operates from our Cambridge aerodrome and now claims to be the only flying school in the world offering basic tuition on the Tiger Moth, once the RAF's principal basic training aircraft.

The Cambridge University Air Squadron's general training responsibilities were increased to include other aircrew categories and fighter controllers. In addition to the Anson for navigation and observer training, a second Anson was attached to the Air Squadron for a period for the use of Professor St Joseph who established the Cambridge University Department of Aerial Photography. When this Anson was withdrawn Professor St Joseph continued his research using a Marshall Auster aircraft suitably modified with a hole in the floor for aerial photography, until in July 1965 the Aerial Photography Department obtained their own Cessna 337 in-line, twin-engined, push-pull 'Skymaster' G-ATCU, which they operate to this day.

During this period Air Training Corps Air Experience Flights were introduced at a number of centres throughout the country, including No. 5

AEF at Cambridge, to give cadets flying pupil experience in RAF Chipmunk training aircraft equipped with parachute seats. To supplement this further, Group Captain Eustace Miles, then Chairman of the Association of British Aero Clubs, thought up and successfully negotiated with the Air Ministry the Air Cadet Flying Scholarship Scheme. This gave a great boost to the Corps and the aero clubs. The Flying Scholarships provide 300 to 400 selected cadets with up to 30 hours dual and solo flying towards a private pilot's licence, which requires a minimum of 40 hours. Many of the cadets pay for the extra few hours training to obtain their licences.

The state of the order books of the individual aircraft manufacturers dictated the volume of test flying they required, and there were prolonged periods with little or no flying. Marshall had an increasing commitment for test flying many types of aircraft but could not afford the cost of slack periods. Remembering my experience before the war of flying instruction and air charter, and my test flying during the war, I decided that we should establish an élite team of pilots able to cover the whole spectrum of development and production test flying, air charter and flying instruction. This variety of work and flying many types of aircraft gave Marshall's pilots a busy and interesting time, but above all and most important it provided constant day-to-day experience of working in the element – the air – on which their professional livelihood depended.

Our post-war pilot team included 'Tap' Tappin who had had a distinguished Service career in many theatres of war, including leading the first sortie of the combined operations at Dieppe in August 1942. He served with Mediterranean Command in Greece and Southern Italy and was then posted to command 256 Squadron Mosquitoes with the Desert Air Force at Forli in Northern Italy. He destroyed a number of enemy aircraft, finishing his RAF career as Wing Commander, DFC and Bar.

We seconded 'Tap' to M.L. Aviation at White Waltham to carry out the initial test flying of two of their development projects. The first was a pneumatically operated auto-pilot for a pilotless aircraft which was fitted to a Provost aircraft for development purposes. The second was for the initial flights of the M.L. Utility (Mobile Army Spotter) at Defford, the centre of radar research and development. This aircraft had an inflatable rubber wing and a simple, single-seater fuselage into which the deflated wing was stowed. The machine was towed behind a road vehicle and when required the wing would be unpacked, installed and inflated and the aircraft was ready for flight. The wing in flight was kept inflated at .5 lbs. per square inch. An automatic safety valve maintained the pressure at altitude, and a pump operated by a generator which was powered by a wind-driven propeller was used to top up the pressure in flight. After extended Army trials at Middle Wallop this was not proceeded with and the aircraft is now a museum piece at the Museum of Army Flying.

One charter flight 'Tap' recalls was in one of the Company's Rapides during the very serious east coast floods of 1953. The Press reported:

BIRD'S-EYE VIEW OF DISASTER

Only one aircraft flew in the gale-torn skies above East Anglia the day after the disaster – a time when Britain's newspapers began to realise the extent of the disaster. It was a twin-engined de Havilland Rapide biplane, chartered specially by the Eastern Daily Press from a Cambridge firm – the only one that dared combat the hurricane force gusts.

In it were the E.D.P.'s late Steve Amyes and Don Rudd, the Eastern Counties Newspapers' Chief Photographer. Although Mr Amyes was severely sick and the photographic glass plates had to be watched so that they did not smash in the buffeting, they swooped down the whole stretch of Norfolk's devastated coastline bringing back a unique story and horrifying pictures which scooped the nation's Press. Mr Rudd, the photographer, an ex-wartime member of the RAF, said it was the worst trip he had had in his life. Ten miles from the coast before the aircraft turned for its long disaster run, spray from the sea was striking the plane at 1,000 feet. The 16-stone navigator had to lean his weight fully against the wind to remain upright when they landed at Langham to pick up Mr Rudd, and the pilot, Mr Tappin, refused to land anywhere after that except back at Cambridge.

As a result of all this flying activity, a series of biennial flying competitions was held at Cambridge in which 22 RFS, CUAS, the Cambridge Aero Club and the Varsity Flight (ex-CUAS members) competed for a challenge silver Rose Bowl donated by Marshall. The competitions included formation flying, spot landings calling for a three point landing as close to a defined mark on the aerodrome as possible, and a treasure hunt. These 'At Homes', as the competitions were called, were extremely popular with Reservists and their families and were unique at the time.

The Cambridge 104 City Squadron of the Air Training Corps had a proud war record with three DFCs, a DSC, a DFM and two AFCs. Flying Officer W. H. Franklin was killed early in the war having been decorated with the DFC. He had been an outstanding cadet from the Perse School and did much to engender the team spirit of the Squadron – fluent in German, he updated the cadets on Goebbel's version of the conflict. The Cambridge Squadron in its transfer from war to peace was fortunate to have Flight Lieutenant Arthur Chapman as Commanding Officer until he retired after wonderful service in 1947. I was personally very grateful for all that he achieved. During the post-war years the Squadron became fully established as a local institution. The importance of youth training by the Corps continued and in the Government 1957 White Paper introducing defence cuts and discontinuance of National Service it was stated that it would not affect the Air Training Corps which was of increasing importance: 'Because of its proved value of developing qualities of character, good citizenship and general interest in aviation among the youth of the country, everything possible will be done to maintain the present high standard of the Corps.'

I was awarded the OBE in 1948 for services to the Air Training Corps and was very pleased to become a member of the Air Cadet Council in 1951, and continued until 1959. I was re-elected in 1965 and carried on till

1976 – a matter of 19 years service. I think the only reason they put up with me for so long was that I have always believed in continuing to know from ground level upwards the details of operation of anything for which I have an active responsibility, and whilst a member of the Air Cadet Council I continued as Chairman of the City Squadron. Most chairmen of local Squadron Committees relinquished their Squadron responsibilities on becoming members of the Air Cadet Council.

In 1951 Marshall successfully tendered for the operation of the RAF Outstation at Swanton Morley, Norfolk. RAF Outstations are centres of activity which are not part of the normal day-to-day operation of the Royal Air Force, such things as the maintenance of University Air Squadron and ATC Air Experience Flight aircraft, flying target-towing aircraft and operating aerial bombing ranges. At Swanton Morley we maintained and flew Beaufighter, Oxford and Spitfire aircraft for target towing for anti-aircraft gunnery practice with live ammunition and simulated attacks on anti-aircraft batteries at RAF Little Snoring, Norfolk, for which our pilots had CAA certificates authorising low level flying. They also simulated enemy attacks for radar practice. A few years later this contract was transferred to RAF Langham, Norfolk, when the Beaufighters were replaced with Mosquitoes. As a result of winning this contract we decided to tender for similar contracts, and appointed as our Outstations Manager Jeff Barclay, who had considerable flying experience and held a Commercial Pilot's Licence; a very hard-working and buoyant character.

For the next 40 years Marshall's operated a number of Outstations, including one at West Freugh, Scotland for 20 years. West Freugh was an aircraft bombing range; the Company was responsible for the operation of the aerodrome, crash crew, maintenance of the aircraft and station equipment, and for flying two Dakotas for dropping sonobuoys which were used for the detection and tracking of submarines. The RAF flew all the other aircraft for bomb dropping practice in the sea. Marshall's marine craft operating from Portpatrick Harbour recovered the sonobuoys and also provided air-sea rescue cover when the RAF were operating over the sea ranges. Portpatrick, a very old harbour which in the days of sail was the main harbour for the northern crossing to Ireland, was owned by the local authority. Jeff Barclay heard that they had decided to sell the harbour and was worried that if it got into the wrong hands it might upset our marine craft activity. He arrived back at Cambridge one Saturday morning and without any pre-warning announced he had bought Portpatrick Harbour. Before asking the price, I automatically asked, 'As seaport owners, are we insured?' and he replied, 'Yes.'

For some years we had an Outstations contract to maintain the Sea Princes of No. 750 Naval Air Squadron at Lossiemouth in Scotland. These aircraft were used for training Observers at the Royal Naval Observer School. After four years the Lossiemouth activity was transferred to RNAS Culdrose and we moved lock, stock and barrel to Culdrose in Cornwall, about the greatest distance between Service aerodromes in the UK.

Our biggest and longest Outstations contract, for 30 years (1961–1991), was at RAF Shawbury, Shropshire. At Shawbury we were responsible for flying piston Provosts, Vampires and later Jet Provosts for the Central Air Traffic Control School, and for the maintenance of their aircraft and a number of Varsity and Valetta aircraft operated by various RAF units at Shawbury. In addition we maintained Air Traffic Control training simulators, airfield radio, radar and navigational aids, Gazelle and Wessex helicopters of No. 2 Flying Training School and Central Flying School (Helicopters) which were resident at Shawbury, and for many years undertook major servicing of Bulldogs and Chipmunks for the majority of the University Air Squadrons and Air Experience Flights in the UK. It was a very wide ranging contract, embracing the operation of the station work-shops and maintenance of all station motor transport.

In July 1954 Freda Short joined me as my secretary. This has proved a most successful partnership to this day – nearly 40 years and still running. Freda's office operated from 8.30 a.m. to 6 p.m. Monday to Friday and 8.30 a.m. to 12.30 p.m. on Saturday until recently, when Monday to Friday became 8.30 a.m. to 5.30 p.m. Miss Short and her two assistants had to contend with a tremendous volume of correspondence, internal notes and minutes of meetings covering a wide range of subjects, coupled with the operation of a very precise filing and 'follow-up' system on which my whole working life was dependent and which required a very strict disci-pline of operation. Freda has reminded me in recent years that when we first met I explained the importance of the filing and follow-up system and how dependent I was on it, and she said she had her own ideas of how to achieve this and would I like to know what she had in mind. I said, 'I don't want the details but leave it with you and will be quite happy as long as it works' – it did and does. Freda had a particular flair for training secretarial staff and for organising them into a loyal and cohesive team.

We were extremely fortunate to be working in a fast moving environ-ment with tremendous variety – there was never a dull moment. Our Vehicle Body Building Division had its own exhilarating excitements during this period. We were all delighted when St Clair Marshall was awarded the MBE in 1952, to be followed later by the award of the MBE in 1979 to 'Mac' McMillan, for their work as founder members of our Vehicle Body Building Division and for the part they played in establishing in the Cambridge area an industry compatible with the University environment.

Eddie Lush joined us in the early fifties, direct from the Ministry of Supply Vehicle Production Department, as a salesman for our commercial vehicle bodies in the London area. To date all our bodies had been of composite construction – that is timber with iron brackets and supports. Eddie was sure that in the very near future both commercial and military vehicle bodies would be of all-metal construction. This immediately roused our interest and we installed the necessary equipment as a matter of urgency. We began all-metal manufacture in 1953. In the post-war years vehicle body building had been very much a craftsman's job developed from the horse carriage coachbuilding industry, but with the introduction of all-metal construction using jigs and tools the assembler's part of the work became semi-skilled.

A number of annual vehicle body building apprentice awards were introduced. The highest award for the Best Apprentice of the Year was first won by Apprentice Keith Hall of Linton and presented at a Joint Production Committee meeting in January 1952. To ensure there was adequate training of vehicle body building apprentices, evening classes were started at our aerodrome in conjunction with the Cambridgeshire College of Arts & Technology.

In 1955 in support of our all-metal construction we installed a large phosphating plant specifically designed to our requirements to provide the most perfect anti-corrosive, anti-rust treatment available. Phosphating provides a blotting paper surface texture perfect for paint adhesion. This process had been used extensively for small articles but had never been used for large components. Our plant was unique and could handle the steel underframe of metal cargo bodies after the underframe had been completely assembled by welding and with all holes drilled. When the new Leyland bus factory was established in Cumbria in the late seventies, Leyland decided to install an anti-corrosive treatment plant identical to the one we had designed for our special requirements in 1955.

We executed many orders for television broadcasting vehicles for the BBC which had to be built to a very high standard and were considered to be a status symbol, with the inside and the outside of the vehicle reflecting the advanced state of the art at the time of the installed TV equipment. We also built television vans for Pye's and Marconi, many for export including to Russia, Venezuela and Canada. To keep the Company's name to the fore, we exhibited at a number of shows, including the Royal Show, the Cambridgeshire Agricultural Show, the SMMT-sponsored Commercial Vehicle Exhibition at Earls Court and biennially the MoD/SMMT-sponsored Fighting Vehicle Research and Development Establishment (FVRDE) Exhibition of Military Vehicles at Chertsey. During the Earl's Court Shows we gave a number of lunches and dinners in London for many of our customers.

In 1954 we received our first design and development contract from the FVRDE at Chobham, later known as the Military Vehicle Experimental Establishment (MVEE) and now the Royal Armament Research and Development Establishment (RARDE). This was an important step forward. The policy up to that time had been for the Research Establishment to produce prototype vehicles followed by full production drawings. The Ministry's plan to have the prototype design and manufacture and completion of production drawings undertaken by outside manufacturers was new, and Marshall was an early choice of contractor for this work. Over the years we became the principal extramural design establishment in the country for thin-skinned military vehicle bodies.

In 1955 the Ministry of Supply planned to place an order at the end of the year for 3,027 all-metal military three-ton cargo bodies, an urgent requirement to be completed within a 12 month period. To ensure delivery, the order was to be divided between three companies. We tendered not only for the one-third quantity requested in the Invitation to Tender but also for the total number of 3,027 which, if accepted, would require an immediate major increase in production to avoid affecting deliveries of our other orders. We had the impression that our tender for the total number was attractive provided we could achieve delivery. We also thought the Ministry were conscious of the fact that a contract placed at one centre would be easier and less costly to monitor. By this time we had gained the confidence of the Ministry not only for quality but for meeting delivery dates. John Huntridge and I went to see the Ministry Production Director and managed to satisfy him that we could undertake the total number. The order was placed in November 1955, was in full production by April, and completed with three months to spare. At one period we were producing 150 new vehicles a week, which included 120 three-ton cargo bodies.

The Bodies Division started in 1946 had taken root. By 1950 we were receiving orders at the rate of 450 a year, by 1951 1,000 a year, and in 1955 the floodgates really opened and we took total orders for 6,330 bodies. During the first seven years of the fifties we had received orders for 18,833 bodies – all very exciting and heart warming!

Our Cambridge and Peterborough garages held an Austin Festival Show Week to coincide with the opening of the Festival of Britain in 1951 to commemorate the Great Exhibition of 1851 and to demonstrate Britain's post-war development. Exhibitions in science, architecture, agriculture and the arts were organised throughout the country. The main exhibition site was in London on the south bank of the Thames, where the Royal Festival Hall was built by the London County Council specially for the occasion. Herbert Morrison, a member of the Government (later Lord Morrison of Lambeth), was a moving spirit behind the Festival and emphasised that this should be a joyous occasion, forgetting the difficulties of continuing post-war shortages, and in fact it gave people a tremendous lift. It was a wonderful improvement to the south bank area and King George VI, despite his ill health, took a personal interest in everything. When Herbert Morrison was showing the King plans for the Festival Hall, the King indicated that such a lovely building merited being titled 'Royal'. Morrison grasped the chance offered immediately and said, 'If you are giving permission to name it "The Royal Festival Hall", Sir, its success is assured.' The King smilingly agreed, and so it was.

Chris Buckley, Austin's Sales Manager, visited Cambridge during our Austin Festival Show Week and took the opportunity, at a luncheon in the Prioress's Room, Jesus College, to present Marshall's with a 30-Year plaque to commemorate our long Austin distributorship. Knowing how tough the business population of Birmingham could be, it was extraordinary how they all mellowed into almost a religious atmosphere within the College precincts. When thanking Mr Buckley, I said:

> My only regret is that my father is not here to share the honour of receiving this plaque commemorating our long association. I know he would have been delighted and very proud. I well remember the excitement of the first Austin Twelve we sold in 1914. My particular memories of it are the self-starter, which was operated by engaging the mesh of the starter with a small brass gear lever before pressing the button.

The garages continued to be run by Eddie Parr and his management team, which now included the Peterborough Manager. My monthly meetings at Jesus Lane continued and I paid regular visits to Peterborough and was responsible for most of the contractual dealings with Austin. As from 1956 there was a separate Distributor's Agreement for each county and the Peterborough depot was appointed as a direct Austin distributor. This change of Austin policy was not helpful, inasmuch as until then a company holding a distributorship covering a number of counties operated through one Distributor's Agreement, which gave large distributors a big advantage in bonus rebates which were based on the total new car sales turnover.

In the late fifties Austin established five Distributor Zones and the distributors in each zone met twice a year at a convenient central location within the zone. Austin's nominated me to be the first Chairman of our zone, and the first meeting was held at our aerodrome with a luncheon in the Prioress's Room at Jesus College. The meetings and luncheons for many years were held at our aerodrome.

The zone meetings at that time served a good purpose but never achieved all that could have been achieved had the distributors' warnings regarding design defects and quality been taken seriously. Had action been taken, it might have helped to minimise the progressive serious deterioration in quality over the years. Pre-war Austin's reputation had been high throughout the world, and it is a tragedy that the standards deteriorated as they did. A number of repetitive defects were reported at each zone meeting but nothing happened. In desperation our Zone Committee suggested that it might help if a senior Austin designer was present at our next meeting in order to hear our points first-hand. The distributors were very concerned and knew at showroom level the serious damage which was being done to Austin's reputation. Unfortunately George Harriman on hearing of this suggestion decided the distributors were exceeding their terms of reference and instructed his chief designer that under no circumstances was he to allow any design office representation at zone meetings as he was not going to have his designers dictated to by the distributors. It is good to know that there has been a major resurgence of quality under the Rover banner in recent years.

Our second driver of the 1909 days, 'Gilly' Fromant, retired at the end of 1953. In my letter to him I recalled:

> One of my earliest memories of you was a trip to Gorleston when we had a puncture at Attleborough. That must have been, I suppose, about 1909. Then there was the move to Jesus Lane and the temporary move to the stables, where Wesley House is now built, while the present garage was being built prior to the 1914 war. Then followed your period in the Army and in Salonika. I remember you came back with stories of the tremendous cabbages they grow out there. If my memory serves me right I had the impression that one cabbage was sufficient for a 'company's' lunch.

Alas for memory. He replied, 'The cabbage was a leek' and continued:

> I think we were some of the pioneers of the taxi and aeroplane business. Do you remember when I used to spray G-AAEH and G-ABIZ etc. at Jesus Lane and the stir they used to cause in the street when they were towed back, and when you turned on the oil drum tap in King Street – it went all down your Sunday suit and we had to clean you down with a can of petrol. I could think of dozens more memories.

During these years Rosemary began to get well established and accepted as a farmer and made rapid progress with her Jersey herd which became one of the best in the country. She had made a good start from what was described as a derelict farm in 1949 to be runner-up for the Pemberton Championship Cup for farms under 200 acres in 1951, and to win the Cup in 1952. In October 1952 in the Central Jersey Cattle Club Open Competition, which Club covers six counties, the cup was won by our Horseheath Jersey Herd, with Henry Webb's famous, long-established Snailwell Herd second and Harry Walston's Thriplow farm third.

It was a very happy time except for a set-back in 1955 when Rosemary woke up one morning and said, 'I think I have got a lump on my left breast.' It proved to be malignant and the left breast and arm-pit lymph nodes were removed. Not many weeks later another lump appeared on the right breast which again proved malignant and was removed, but on this occasion without the removal of the lymph nodes which was important because it meant that Rosemary was left with full strength in her right arm. She made a good recovery and was well for many years to come.

As learners, Rosemary and I attended many farmers' evening lectures. Rosemary was always worried about me bobbing up and asking what might have been silly questions. It was surprising how often a farmer came up after a lecture and thanked me for asking a question which he, as a life-long farmer, just dare not ask. We became quite an authority on silage and had many visits from neighbouring farmers. The poorer countries of the world had made full use of silage over the years, but it was only used extensively in this country during the two world wars. Silage making was hard work but, if you did not mind the hard work and were careful with temperature control and made good quality silage, it was a good and rewarding crop and particularly suited to a dairy herd. Our dry grass operation from the aerodrome, with collections of grass and lucerne from a number of farms in the area, helped Rosemary to get established with the farming fraternity.

On most Sundays Rosemary had lunch with me at the aerodrome and in the afternoon would work on her weekly milk sheets, planning the individual cows' rations for the following week based on current yields for her 70-strong milking herd. She really enjoyed this and found it very exciting and rewarding. Her enthusiasm in the progress of her herd is a very happy memory.

In 1950 Michael started his two years National Service in the RAF. His initial RAF flying training was on Harvards at Gimli in Manitoba, Canada, where he gained his Wings and commission. He finished his training on Vampires at Valley in Anglesey, where he had a forced landing on May Day 1952 and the aircraft was a write-off. For some undetermined reason his engine failed during aerobatics at altitude and the aircraft went into an inverted spin for which the Vampire had obtained some notoriety and from which he could not recover. He attempted to bail out but was unsuccessful because of the centrifugal forces of the spin and had a number of burns on his arms caused by the friction of his flying suit. At a lower altitude the aircraft came out of the spin and after pulling the stick back with his right foot to lower the speed he was able to climb back into the cockpit and managed to get it down in a small ploughed field near the village of Bryngwran. He was bleeding heavily from a cut in his forehead because he was not strapped in when he landed, following his efforts to leave the aircraft. It was perhaps very fortunate that he could not bail out; his Vampire had no ejector seat and, unless one left the aircraft in a very precise and practised way, there was every risk of colliding with the tailplane. He borrowed a bicycle from a farm and cycled to the nearest telephone to report the accident. He was flying again by 7 May but had received some damage to his back and spent a time at Headley Rehabilitation Centre. Michael was given a verbal commendation by the Wing Commander Flying, coupled with strong persuasion for him to remain in the Royal Air Force. He returned to Valley the following year for his annual two weeks Reserve flying commitment.

Michael then completed his education at Jesus College, Cambridge 1952–55. He was particularly successful with his rowing, stroking the Jesus boat to Head of the River in the Lents in 1953 and the Mays in 1955 and to win the Henley Ladies Plate in 1953. He stroked the Cambridge boat in the University Boat Race in 1954 and rowed for England in the European Championships Coxless Fours at Ghent, Belgium in 1955. Unfortunately Cambridge did not win the Boat Race in 1954 but the Cambridge newspaper caption under a photograph of a party leaving the works for the Boat Race said:

> In view of the intimate personal interest the Marshall organisation has in the Boat Race this year by the inclusion of Mr Michael Marshall as stroke of the Cambridge crew, the Sports and Social Club organised their works annual outing to coincide with the race. A record number of employees went on the outing. After the race most of them planned to visit theatres and other enter-

tainments. The organisation as a whole is looking forward to Mr Michael Marshall joining them after he has finished his university career.

In August 1955 Michael joined the Company at Jesus Lane. He served a training period in all departments, including the garage reception and fore-court, workshops and sales, and became a member of the management committee team. He took over full responsibility for the garages in 1958. Just as it was good for my father to have me to follow on in the twenties and thirties, so it was good for me to have Michael to follow on and take increasing responsibility over the years.

David finished at Eton in 1952, leaving with his Colours for the Eton Field (Soccer) Game and the Under-16 High-Jump record. David joined the Army for his two years National Service and was commissioned in the Oxfordshire and Buckinghamshire Light Infantry. After his initial training he was posted to Osnabrück in Germany and was the Standard Bearer to receive the presentation of new Regimental Colours on 7 May 1954 from General Sir Bernard Paget, who was nominated by Her Majesty the Queen to make the presentation. Whilst at Osnabrück David played an active part in regimental sports and on the hunting field. He in turn went to Jesus in 1955 to complete his education and obtained his degree in Estate Management. He went on to follow a career in estate management and joined Marsh & Parsons, established in 1856, the partnership of which he acquired in 1969.

My daughter Judy was at school at Downe House, Newbury and was in the school lacrosse and netball teams, and collected some A-Levels. She had a 'Coming Out' dance in April 1957 at the Hyde Park Hotel with her friend Jennifer Daw. They had Tommy Kinsman's Band and Winifred Atwell played her honky-tonk piano. In 1958 Judy went to Italy to look after two American children in Elba and then in Rome, and returned to London to do a secretarial course in Queensgate.

In 1951 my sister Dorothy moved to Sproutes, Coolham, near Horsham where she lived for the rest of her life. In 1954 her left eye started to cause problems and she was admitted to the Royal Free Hospital for tests and treatment. By 1958 the right eye was also affected and, after further treatment, she was left with no centre vision and only blurred peripheral sight called 'macula oedema'. This was thought to have been caused by a riding accident. She could not read and was no longer able to drive, but otherwise led a very active life. It was a very big handicap and worry to Dorothy, Rupert and the family, but Dorothy was very good about it and never complained.

In 1952 Lord Chesham died and Mary's husband, Charlie, inherited. He was a Delegate of the Council of Europe in Strasbourg from 1953–56 and Lord-in-Waiting to the Queen 1955–58. Charlie was Parliamentary Secretary to the Ministry of Transport 1959–64 and made a Privy Counsellor in 1964. As a result of his life-long interest in motor cars since his undergraduate days, he became known when he was a Minister as 'the motorist's friend'.

Molly's husband Bernard became a Doctor of Music in 1955. Over the years at Oxford Molly has played an energetic part in local affairs and charities and she became a Magistrate in 1957 and Chairman of the Bench 1977–87.

In 1952 my youngest sister Brenda joined Unilever's information service, LINTAS. She married Hoby Moore, Senior Partner of Moore & Stephens, the London accountants, on 23 December 1952. They lived initially at Grosvenor House until they moved to Thornhill, East Grinstead the following year. Thornhill was an ideal home for entertaining many overseas clients and friends of Moore & Stephens and for the holding of the firm's international partners' meetings. Having taken a farming course, Brenda entered into the farming world with her usual practical enthusiasm and established a very good, prize-winning Jersey herd, with one cow, 'Golden Delicious', holding the UK milk record for a four-year-old Jersey cow.

For the Marshall Company this was a period of much capital expenditure. The tenfold expansion of the vehicle body building production necessitated new buildings, one of which was for the new Phosphating Plant, and extensions to the Metal Detail, Wood Mill and Machine Shops. For our increased aircraft engineering activities we had built and then extended the runway, built large hangars and a new Air Traffic Control building consuming substantial capital, all within a four-year period. The Company had been continually short of capital, having started the war in 1939 with current assets over current liabilities of minus £9,000 and finished in 1945 with current assets over current liabilities of minus £12,000. As at 1953 our current assets over current liabilities had improved to plus £124,000. The bank rate at the time was fortunately of the order of 4–5 per cent. The capital commitment we made in the 1950s would not have been possible had the very high bank rates of the late eighties prevailed. Apart from the initial capital costs, we were now becoming conscious of the long-term liabilities of maintenance and rates if we did not achieve a sufficiently large continuing volume of work to make the project overall financially viable long-term. The Marshall Company during these years was carried on the crest of a wave. Things looked good for the future.

Chapter 23

The Tide Turns
1959–1966

1959 STARTED ON a high note. We were, without being over confident, sitting on top of the world. We had established a working relationship with Vickers, English Electric and Bristol, who came to treat us as an extension of their own works at Cambridge. We could, for the first time, feel that we were based on a solid foundation with prospects for the future looking good provided we worked hard to maintain our position.

Having successfully completed the flight trials of the Canberra B15 and B16 conversions, we received the order to manufacture the kits and convert a further 74 aircraft over the next year or so. The conversion enabled the B15 and B16 aircraft to be operated in the following roles:

(a) Normal bombing (including 28 lb. practice bombs).
(b) Integrated LABS for delivering the American or British nuclear weapon.
(c) Wing pylons to carry air-to-air Nord AS.30 missiles, or Matra rocket launchers housing 68mm SNEB rockets, or the 1,000 lb. retarded parachute bomb.
(d) Air sampling ducts for collecting dust after a nuclear explosion.

It was a big and urgent programme for which the RAF held six-weekly progress meetings in my office chaired by a Group Captain who had with him Squadron Leader Douglas Lowe. The Squadron Leader well remembered these meetings in years to come when, as Air Chief Marshal Sir Douglas Lowe, he became a famous RAF Controller Aircraft. At one meeting there was much amusement when we had nine working days production delay because of the late delivery of a component and we added nine days onto the date, which included a weekend. A junior member of the RAF team burst out laughing and said, 'But they just count Saturdays and Sundays as normal working days!' A five-and-a-half day week plus weekend overtime has always been for us a way of life. Had we not been working weekends the delay would have been 13 days embracing two weekends.

At another meeting the Group Captain warned us that only 19 of the new high output generators had been manufactured to date and some would be progressively required for other projects. He emphasised that ours was an urgent priority requirement which had first call on whatever was available and that we must make sure we got all we required to meet the programme. I rang Dennis Parrack, our Buyer, on the internal loudspeaker phone and explained the position. Dennis said he knew of this and I said, 'It's important we know where they are and that we get our fair share.' He said, 'Yes, I do know where they are.' I said, 'Well that's one thing, but how about getting our fair share?' and Dennis repeated, 'Yes, I know where they are.' He realised he was on the loudspeaker telephone and did not want to say more, but I pressed him and said the Group Captain wanted to know what was happening. Dennis hesitated and finally said, 'They are all in our stores.' Much laughter.

Marshall had been responsible to English Electric for the design of the weapon systems circuitry for the Lightning Mk. 3. With this background, in 1963, in preparation for an urgent wide-ranging modification programme for the Lightning fleet, we assisted with the manufacture of modification kits and planning instructions for incorporation in the aircraft. Then at 10 days' notice we provided a self-contained on-site team of 100 men made up of fitters, electricians, inspectors, supervisors, draughtsmen, storemen and cleaners to support English Electric's own teams in the field with the introduction of these modifications.

Apart from design contracts which incorporated manufacture and physical work on aircraft, we were fortunate to have had many contracts for design only on a wide range of advanced state-of-the-art aircraft. In the mid-1950s we had designed the wings of the Saunders Roe SR-177, a Mach 2.2 rocket-propelled aircraft, and the tailplane and rudder of the Bristol 188, a Mach 2.5 aircraft; we also had a big involvement in the design of the V-1000 planned to be the first UK jet airliner with a non-stop transatlantic capability. We had 400,000 hours of design on the English Electric TSR-2 advanced swing-wing aircraft planned to be the RAF's new Tactical Strike and Reconnaissance aircraft. Since by now we were recognised armament specialists, this TSR-2 work included the task of designing a major part of the aircraft's complex weapons system. All these projects were progressively cancelled but in-depth design involvement on such aircraft gave our designers unique experience and played a big part in the development of our Design Office and the recruiting and retention of designers of the highest calibre in all disciplines.

It is a tragedy that within a few years this all proved too much for Charles Sneesby. With the rapid build-up of design work, Charles became less inclined to delegate, and he worried that there were those who were lobbying for his position. Many of his colleagues were anxious to help him, but to no avail. I, in turn, during the last few years found it necessary to be with him at design meetings with important customers to maintain their confidence and to give reassurance that programmes would be met.

When Charles resigned in 1960, Roy Gates and Norman Harry, young as they were for this important responsibility, teamed up to take over where

Charles Sneesby had left off, Roy as Chief Designer and Norman as his Deputy. They continued to develop our Aircraft Design Office into one which won the respect of the aircraft industry worldwide and further extended our overall aircraft engineering design capability to undertake virtually any project offered, including eventually on the Concorde and the Space Shuttle Sled on behalf of the European Space Agency.

With a healthy workload, we had another stroke of luck. Having completed the BOAC Britannia aircraft delivery programme, John Huntridge and Ben Breach were ready for a new challenge. At the end of our regular Friday morning vehicle body building meeting on 17 July 1959 everybody was trooping out of my office when John turned back and said, 'Standards have just purchased Mulliners, the Birmingham bus builders. I expect they will require all Mulliners' capacity for cars. I wonder what Mulliners are going to do about their buses?' I immediately put in a phone call to the Chairman, Colonel White, who said they wanted to sell off their bus building interests. We met at Birmingham on the Monday and agreement was reached on Wednesday to take over Mulliner buses lock, stock and barrel, with Marshall accepting the responsibility to complete Mulliner's outstanding orders.

This was a heaven-sent opportunity – we had often considered single and double deck bus building but it was a highly specialised market, and to break into it from scratch would have been a long haul. We allocated to buses the hangar we had built for the Comet programme in 1953 and delivered 20 'Marshall Mulliner' buses by the end of the year. Mulliner, a long-established company, had specialised in a heavily built vehicle suitable for Third World countries' rough and rugged roads, for which it had a very good reputation. We immediately concentrated on overseas sales, and over the next 10 years succeeded in selling over 1,200 buses to more than 30 countries, such as Sudan, Argentina, Indonesia, Kuwait, Jamaica and Venezuela.

We realised from the outset that the heavy Mulliner bus was unsuitable for the home market and that the long-term viability of our Bus Division would depend on sales to UK bus operators and to the Ministry for our armed forces. For this home market a new bus would have to be designed. Our Vehicle Body Division had considerable vehicle engineering experience but lacked specialist knowledge of bus design. Fortunately we had recently recruited Ian Owen into the Vehicle Body Design Office. Owen had spent his life in bus design with Midland Red of Birmingham who were bus operators and bus body builders with a reputation for being in the forefront of bus building design. Owen was instructed to design a Marshall bus for the home market, and it was good that he realised that it was essential to get it right first time and that he needed all the up-to-date advice he could get from bus operators.

One day during lunch in our small Executive Dining Room I posed the question, 'How can we find a reliable Sales Manager with common sense, a comprehensive knowledge of the bus industry and well known to bus operators?' St Clair said, 'There's one man who meets that specification – Jack Davis.' Jack Davis for many years was responsible for bus sales for Metropolitan Cammell-Weymann, the major bus and railway coach builders at Birmingham. He was a likeable personality who had been nationally known as a tennis player, he knew the bus industry inside out and had a good relationship with bus operators. Jack had left Metropolitan Cammell-Weymann and St Clair thought he was now running a post office. I said, 'Can we find him?' St Clair said, 'Give me 48 hours.' Within a matter of days Jack Davis was working from Cambridge and proved to be a great success.

His first job was to assess the market, and he quickly decided that the British Electric Traction Company Bus Division must be the prime target as they operated the majority of the non-municipal buses in the UK and purchased 2,000 single and double deck buses a year. Jack was on very friendly terms with Peter Vince, the boss of BET, who was at that time keen to find a new source of supply. Mr Vince paid many visits to Cambridge and gave us considerable help in designing a bus to meet BET's requirements. Our first order from BET was for 270 buses in 1961. Everything proceeded from there to what became a very exciting and successful Division for which John Huntridge was entirely responsible, ably supported by Ben Breach who, back to his apprenticeship trade of bus building, was in his element.

And so, with full order books in all divisions and the birth of the new Bus Division, all in the garden looked rosy. But by the end of 1959 storm-clouds gathered with increasing Government pressure to rationalise the aircraft industry, with shot-gun marriages to include the formation of the British Aircraft Corporation (BAC) combining Vickers, English Electric and Bristol. We realised this must destroy the efficient and close working relationship we had established with these three companies over recent years. During the period of the amalgamation negotiations I spoke to my old friend 'Hank' Hancocke, still the Director of Aircraft Production, and asked, 'What do we do now?' He thought for a moment and then said, 'All I can say is try to be the last left in the field.'

The BAC shotgun marriage was finalised early in 1960. During the final stages of negotiation the planned new consortium was anxious to fill any vacant capacity within its own organisation immediately after agreement had been reached. As a result we received few new orders, anticipated orders did not materialise, and some existing orders were cancelled or reduced. Our English Electric order for the conversion of 74 B6 Canberras to the new B15 and B16 roles was halved, with the other half going to Bristol. There was at the same time some reluctance by the individual companies which were to comprise BAC to pass work to their new partners who would expect to have some input and work to their own design procedures. This was not the same as giving an order to Marshall, the specialist professional sub-contractor always anxious to please.

For 12 months the RAF had been discussing the possibility of an over-load of Valiant Major Inspections, and early in 1960 decided to offload nine to Cambridge. An RAF/BAC/Ministry meeting was held at St Giles Court to discuss the programme, with Group Captain Vic Otter representing the RAF. In the passage before going into the meeting, Allen Greenwood of BAC told me that BAC now had spare hangar capacity and was proposing that the Valiant Major Inspection programme be divided between us. BAC was an important customer and we had no alternative but to accept their proposal without argument. At a stroke the amalgamation of the main aircraft manufacturers had destroyed the basis of our working relationship with the individual companies.

However, the chairman of the meeting explained that the RAF had nominated Marshall for this work because they felt it would give them a better chance of containing the work within the strict limits of the Major Inspection schedule and of achieving the quick turn-round required. He then asked how many aircraft it was suggested should go to Marshall and said the RAF would do the rest. Allen immediately said, 'In that case they can all go to Marshall,' and a programme was agreed. A good indication of the close working relationship which had developed between the RAF and Marshall. The RAF established a representative at Cambridge to make quick decisions on any additional work that developed. They were anxious that the programme should be a success, with no delays in the supply of spares or bay serviced components for which the RAF were responsible. We completed and test flew the first aircraft for delivery within five weeks. Our average over the whole programme was six-and-a-half weeks per aircraft as compared with large aircraft Major Inspections previously taking several months.

Counting our blessings at this time we were lucky to receive a number of substantial but short-term orders which all helped to keep the wolf from the door, but we were living hand to mouth without a project which would provide a spine of continuous work. The variety and sophistication of these short-term orders continued the development of our all-round aeronautical engineering capabilities.

We received an order from RAE Farnborough to design and manufac-ture rocket-propelled sleds capable of accelerating to 500 mph to run on a rail system at Pendine Sands for testing ejector seats. The sleds were of timber construction, with the rockets fitted in the rear compartment; they were expendable and finished in the sea. An unsuccessful attempt was made to salvage them by fitting a 'retro-rocket' in the nose.

In 1961/2 we had a modification programme on BEA's large, four-engined turbo-prop Vickers Vanguard airliners after they had been in service for 12 months. The modifications included structural changes to the tail cone and the introduction of chain armour to protect the aircraft from any failure of the engine turbine blades. BEA entrusted the work to us because they felt that the quick turn-round required could best be achieved at Cambridge, and we had hangars which could accommodate these large aircraft in numbers.

In 1963, despite the amalgamations of the British aircraft manufacturing companies, a big order came from BAC Weybridge to re-work the first three VC-10 trials aircraft to bring them up to the final production standard. This work could be passed to Cambridge with minimum time and effort because of the old relationship and working procedures established between Marshall and Vickers. The question of hangar capacity was again a deciding factor – there was just nowhere else which could accept these very large aircraft. The turn-round time for 150,000 hours of work per aircraft was very demanding. I spent many nights with the night shift at critical times as we worked up to the pre-flight stages of the first aircraft.

A BEA contract was placed at three hours notice for an urgent programme of work to help BEA catch up on serious arrears of maintenance, with the first aircraft arriving on the same day as the phone call for help. Over a three month period we carried out maintenance schedules employing 200 operatives on a mixed bag of 17 aircraft made up of Argosys, Comets, Viscounts and Vanguards.

We received a contract from the Fighting Vehicles Research and Development Establishment, Chobham to design and manufacture for the Army the first air transportable container, to be known as the CB300, to be carried in RAF Argosy freighter aircraft. Marshall's Vehicle Body Division undertook this work and, taking advantage of aircraft design techniques, the container weight was reduced by 50 per cent compared with containers previously available. This led to our Aircraft Division being contracted to design and install a luggage roller system in the Argosy freighters to carry these containers. The original CB300 airborne containers were designed with a limited height so that they could be carried in the Argosy. When the Argosy was replaced by the Hercules, RAF containers were increased in height, but the Army still preferred the lower container because it was easier to camouflage in the battlefield. The containers had to be capable of being equipped for many different uses – sophisticated electronic installations, maintenance workshops, signal stations, bakeries, office and sleeping accommodation and for easy packaging of goods for transport and quick off-loading.

In August 1964 we suffered another serious setback when a Valiant experienced a wing spar failure in flight. It landed safely, but the entire fleet was inspected and some aircraft were scrapped immediately, the others being allowed only to continue flying under restricted conditions. With the Avro Vulcan and Handley-Page Victor V-bombers beginning to come into service, it was decided that the Valiants were beyond economic repair and all were scrapped in January 1965.

With the change of Government in the autumn of 1964, the TSR-2 was doomed for very early cancellation. As I have said, Marshall had major design responsibility for the TSR-2 armament systems. The cancellation of

TSR-2 in April 1965 also triggered the withdrawal of most of our Canberra work which BAC now needed themselves because of the major reduction in their own work resulting from the cancellation of the TSR-2 in the midst of its flight trials. For 10 years we had been responsible to English Electric for Canberra aircraft in service and had designed and installed 400 new modifications on Canberra aircraft, of which not less than 140 were directly connected to the weapon systems.

The TSR-2 and the 90-strong Valiant fleet were two projects in which Marshall was heavily involved. In spite of the shot-gun marriage, it had been expected that our work on these would continue for a long time because of our specialist knowledge of TSR-2's armament system design and our overall knowledge of the Valiant, our delegated design authority for its electrical system and our large hangars.

By 1965 things were becoming very difficult indeed. Spen Finch, the Company's Avionics Manager, returning from America after a two-month helicopter course, was horrified to find that our then largest hangar, No. 12, was completely empty of aircraft and partially occupied with vehicle body construction. We were fortunate to have a heavy load of vehicle body building at this time of recession in the aircraft industry. As originally planned, the Aircraft and Vehicle Body Building Divisions were complementary to one another, cushioning the ups and downs of their respective workloads. We always prayed that not everything would go up or come down on the same day.

Amidst all this gloom we were all highly delighted when Peter Young was awarded the OBE in 1966. He had been the Company's Chief Aircraft Inspector since the end of the war – a very popular colleague always ready to help everybody.

The Association of British Aero Clubs and Centres had long held the view that there was a need to provide civilian pilots with an authoritative guide to flying instruction. During the early sixties Leslie Worsdell, helped by his fellow instructors at Cambridge, played a big part in the discussions and wrote a new manual entitled *ABAC Manual of Flying and Ground Training*. This was first published in 1964, reprinted in 1967 and 1968 and revised in 1969. The foreword by Viscount Runciman of Doxford in the first edition read: 'Finally and particularly, our thanks are due to L. V. Worsdell, DFC who, as compiler and editor, has given form, substance and life to the whole, and without whose tireless efforts this publication could not have been achieved.'

In the meantime my old friend, a founder member and a former Master of the Guild of Air Pilots, Wing Commander Clem Pike, AFC, who had helped us with the opening of our aerodrome in 1929, had presented the Guild with 'The Pike Trophy' – a silver model of a Chipmunk aircraft – to be awarded for 'the most praiseworthy contribution to the maintenance of high standards of flying instruction and safety during the year, taking into account working conditions and opportunities.' We were delighted that the first presentation of the trophy was made by His Royal Highness the Duke of Edinburgh to Leslie Worsdell at the Guild of Air Pilots' Dinner in 1963 at the Guildhall, London.

In the sixties the Company's Civil Flying School, air charter and Rapide scheduled service to race meetings were doing well. One interesting contract we had was to fly a team of American technicians to carry out routine maintenance inspections of the 'Thor' ballistic missiles at a number of sites, including North Luffenham, Hemswell and Driffield. The 'Thor' was a safeguard weapon until such time as the V-Bomber Force was fully equipped to take over by the end of the sixties. The Americans were aghast when they realised they were to travel in the Rapide, a biplane aircraft which looked quite ancient to them. This initial reaction quickly turned to affection in the poor visibility conditions in which much of their flying was undertaken. They had not experienced the Decca navigation system which was fitted to our Rapides and were most surprised when the destination airfields came in sight out of the gloom.

Marshall's Cambridge Aero Club received a contract from the Civil Aviation Authority in 1966 to train student air traffic control officers to private pilot standard. The idea behind this was that air traffic control officers would better appreciate a pilot's problems if they themselves had experienced them, even in a minor way. This contract provided the stimulus for the Company to change from the famous old Tiger Moths to Cessna 150 heated cabin trainer aircraft with side-by-side seating and modern radio aids.

During this period there was a revolutionary development in the use of general purpose surface and seaborne transport containers. These had been progressively coming into use with containers of different sizes made to manufacturers' varying specifications. This new concept of moving freight around the world quickly and simplifying Customs procedure was developing into standard practice, and the International Standards of Operation (ISO) container was established and universally adopted with dimensions of 8 ft. high, 8 ft. wide and alternative lengths of 20, 30 and 40 ft. Concurrently Lloyds of London finalised a manufacturing specification incorporating strength and durability which was recognised worldwide. Marshall's Vehicle Body Division had developed a very good container, and, with the co-operation of the Welding Institute, had perfected a method of welding with galvanised material which was very successful and durable. We were the first company to meet Lloyds' specification and were No. 1 on Lloyds' list of approved companies for ISO container manufacture.

It was fortunate that we decided not to get too heavily involved in this revolution which we thought could be a nine-day wonder. We made containers to satisfy orders of a few hundred but did not go all out for the larger quantities of a few thousand. Quotations for these large orders became a rat race and a number of companies burnt their fingers badly, and some failed altogether. Had we taken orders for the larger quantities it would have absorbed too much of our capacity and when the tide went out, as it did within a year or so, we would have been left with empty workshops.

The Vehicle Bodies Division won an order for developing the manufacturing techniques for a number of Medium Girder Bridge components including the elaborate bottom panels; this was to be the Army's replacement for the famous Bailey Bridge. The manufacturing specification provided for machining before welding, but it was quite impossible to meet the tolerances with this procedure. We found ways and means of machining after welding with some brilliant improvisation on the part of our designers and machine shop engineers. We did all the pioneering work for this sophisticated construction on this section of the bridge, but we were fortunate not to get the production contract. Fairey, who won the contract, found the bridge absorbed much more of their capacity than they originally envisaged, which became a serious embarrassment. However, the bridge helped us to develop our machine shop techniques which proved to be of considerable benefit in the years ahead.

The Sixties was a very competitive period for the garage industry. There were many take-overs and there was much jockeying for franchises. We decided to remain 100 per cent loyal to Austin, having done business with them since 1914 and been their distributors since the immediate post World War I years. Franchise holders were either marking time with the risk of being taken over or on the up and up poised to absorb any distribution territories which became available. The competitive negotiations for possible territories took up much time and detailed attention to keep up to date with what was going on behind the scenes.

Our garage expansion out of Cambridge had started by taking over the Austin distribution for Peterborough and Huntingdon immediately after the war. During 1959 Michael negotiated the take-over of Austin's Bedford distribution. We built a completely new garage on the site of the old steam laundry on Goldington Road, Bedford. During the same period we purchased S. C. Sharp of Wisbech and Ireland Brothers in St Neots, followed soon afterwards by Maddox & Kirby, our Austin dealer at Huntingdon, and Varney's Garage, the Austin distributor in Jersey. In 1963 we built new garage premises at Peterborough on a larger site which Rosemary and I found by carrying out a general survey of the area one Sunday afternoon. As we took over more garages so the financial responsibilities increased; the garage industry is very speculative and much money can be lost in a very short space of time if very strict financial control is not maintained on a day-to-day basis. Michael progressively took control of the Garage Group and was appointed Managing Director in 1963. I was at the same time anxious to get him fully involved at the aerodrome as soon as possible but, with the expansion of the garage business and the increased amount of money involved, this did not materialise as quickly as we had hoped, and was not finally achieved until 1989.

During this period our children married. Michael married Bridget Pollock at Cliburn Church, Cumberland on 16 January 1960 and the whole Marshall family travelled to Penrith for the wedding. Judy started work with the Victoria League in 1959. She became engaged to Simon Boscawen, a stockbroker, in September 1960 and they were married at St Mark's, North Audley Street, on 21 April 1961, making their home in Sussex. David, now well established in his estate agency business, married Jennie Whitmore in Cambridge on 7 August 1965. Jennie, whose home was with her parents at Madingley, Cambridge, worked in London and David had met her on the train to London.

Rosemary and I made a number of overseas business flights, including one in 1964 to Ethiopia in the Company's Beech Queen Air. At the time we were undertaking at Cambridge the furnishing and equipping of King Constantine of Greece's new Gulfstream aircraft, so the first overnight stay was at Athens – then on to Beirut to meet our agent and the President of Middle East Airlines for whom we had work on their Viscount aircraft. Next, we flew to Cairo where we had a team working on Egyptian Airlines Viscounts. We then flew to Sudan to meet our agent, who was very successfully selling our buses in Khartoum. Having got so far, I thought I would explore the possibilities of any bus sales in Ethiopia, and flew on to Addis Ababa, where the Shell manager and his wife looked after us very well.

On the outward flight to Athens we had trouble with our oxygen system. My old friend Ivor Gregory, Chief Maintenance Engineer of British European Airways, knowing of our pending flight had asked his Athens office to look after us. BEA very kindly helped with some emergency oxygen equipment which we were very pleased to have on the flight from Khartoum to Addis Ababa aerodrome which is at an altitude of 8,000 feet. We had a point of no return on this flight and became worried because we could not get any wireless response from Addis Ababa and none of their direction finding equipment was working. Rosemary, our stewardess on these flights, was reading a book on the cannibals of Ethiopia. When we arrived at Addis Ababa the airport authority explained that they only switched on the navigation aids by special request made before the commencement of a flight.

On the return flight we landed at Luxor to meet up with my old school, college and family friend Henry Bateman and his wife Joan for dinner. Henry at that time was a ship's doctor on one of the Nile steamers. He and I sent Vera, our dear old Tonbridge Housemaster now retired, a greetings card from Luxor. The next day we refuelled at Cairo and left in a sandstorm which rose to over 12,000 feet, eventually landing at Benghazi in pouring rain at five o'clock – the airport all very dirty and 22 miles from Benghazi town. One of Marshall's ex-air traffic controllers, then an air traffic controller at Benghazi, recommended that we push on to Malta. It was a dark, dirty night with a strong head wind, and at the end of a long day I remember how cheered we were to know we were going in the right direction when our Distance Measuring Equipment started registering at 143 nautical miles from Malta. This was the early days of this new DME for small aircraft and our set had never previously registered at a greater distance than about 100 nautical miles. The next day I met representatives of Malta Airlines regarding possible aircraft work at Cambridge.

Most of my overseas visits were in the Company's aircraft, which saved much time and provided valuable flexibility with Customs clearance just outside my office window at Cambridge. I did the flying and the captain did all the hard and most important work of aircraft serviceability, flight planning, navigation and air traffic control communication and was ready for any emergency which might arise. For me flying has always been a form of therapy – complete relaxation from the outside world, free from office phone calls. These flights kept me up to date with flying, the efficiency of our aircraft maintenance, air traffic control and general aerodrome management. I took much trouble to learn all I could about aerodrome operation wherever I went, particularly from the private passenger's point of view, and also to learn all I could about the garage business. Jock du Boulay recently wrote of an occasion when we were delayed by fog and I got impatient: 'You didn't like wasting time, so you took me across the road to see a new garage and filling station and proceeded to take measurements of the courtyard, pumps, roof, etc., with a view to improving our own garages.'

During 1964 there were rumours of an RAF interest in Lockheed's Hercules C-130 transport aircraft. If this materialised into an order we thought the RAF would require a UK Hercules technical centre for which Marshall, with its large hangars and all-round engineering and design capability, was ideally qualified. Negotiations proceeded between the UK Government and Lockheed for the purchase of the aircraft, with consideration of possible UK manufacture of selected Hercules components as an offset against the dollar spend. In September 1965 a number of companies, including Marshall, were invited to attend a meeting at Lockheed, Marietta, Georgia to be briefed on Hercules components for which Lockheed considered British industry could tender. Rosemary and I went to America with some of our senior designers, including our Deputy Chief Designer, Norman Harry.

During this visit I managed to spend some time with Tom Morrow, the Vice-President responsible for the Hercules production line, discussing the possibility of Lockheed appointing Marshall as their Hercules East of the Atlantic Service Centre for the many aircraft operating in this part of the world, which could also provide the RAF with their UK technical centre. Lockheed were not keen on this and wanted the RAF to deal directly with them regarding all in-service requirements. A visit to America early in 1966 by Michael and John Huntridge followed. They had further discussions with Tom Morrow at Marietta regarding the suggestion of a Lockheed Hercules Service Centre in the UK, emphasising Marshall's all-round design and aircraft engineering experience and underlining the importance of our very large hangars which could hold many C-130 aircraft in work at any one time. We were in fact offering Lockheed the comprehensive, self-contained service we had successfully offered to Vickers, English Electric and Bristol in the early fifties.

We sent a number of engineers covering all trades to Lockheed to gain first-hand knowledge of the Hercules in anticipation of a possible invitation to tender for work associated with these aircraft. We also kept in close touch with our Ministry which eventually issued invitations to tender for a UK Technical and Engineering Support Centre to provide at minimum cost the same technical support as was available to the RAF for British built aircraft. This included the responsibility to receive the Hercules from America, introduce a number of RAF modifications, including the installation of the Smith's British auto-pilot, paint, test fly and make ready for delivery to the RAF. The increasing importance of our Aircraft Design Office as it became more sophisticated must not be forgotten. There is no doubt that our high reputation within the industry worldwide weighed heavily in our favour with the Ministry of Defence when considering appointing Marshall as the UK RAF Technical Centre for their Hercules fleet.

Our tender was accepted, and I well remember the first Hercules XV177 arriving at Cambridge on 19 December 1966 on a direct delivery flight from America and being received by Air Chief Marshal Sir Kenneth Cross. The Air Marshal, Lady Cross, Rosemary and I sat in the front window of my office overlooking the airfield having a cup of coffee awaiting the aircraft's arrival. We had been very eager to obtain this contract because we realised that the successful establishment of a UK Hercules Service Centre to support the large RAF fleet would be a good testimonial to attract work from overseas operators. Whilst this contract did not make up for all the aircraft work lost as a result of the shot-gun marriage, it was a major step in the right direction. As at December 1966, although there was still much to be done to re-establish our position, there was a sigh of relief all round.

Since 1959 our Aircraft Division had suffered a major change of fortune. Considerable capital expenditure had been incurred to contain the rapid influx of work in the mid-fifties, including the building of our second very big hangar in anticipation of Valiant aircraft work continuing for some years. When making this expenditure we realised there would be peaks and troughs of work, but never anticipated devastating overnight changes of national policy under peacetime conditions such as the shot-gun marriages in the aircraft industry and the cancellation of the TSR-2. The Division survived on what remained of old contracts and an unexpected input of some important but short-term work. The Valiant fleet had been scrapped, there was little prospect of work coming from the amalgamated aircraft manufacturers, the airlines were becoming more self-contained for their maintenance and new generations of aircraft were requiring less mainte-nance. The only bright spot was our appointment as the RAF UK Technical

Centre for their new fleet of Lockheed C-130 Hercules aircraft but, whilst we had high hopes of work developing on the RAF Hercules fleet in due course, we had no expectation of any major work in the near future. A period of great tension and worry. The future was by no means assured.

Writing this I feel very much like the captain of an airliner full of passengers flying in atrocious weather in South America announcing to his passengers, 'I have got some bad news and some good news. Our No. 1 engine has failed, our No. 3 engine is showing signs of trouble, oil pressure low and running rough, fuel is low and the compass is unserviceable. The good news is we are ahead of schedule.'

Nevertheless between 1959 and 1966 we had completed and delivered from Cambridge 857 aircraft made up of Viscounts, Vanguards, Canberras, Britannias, Gulfstreams, Valiants, VC-10s, BAC 1-11s and Constellations.

Chapter 24

The Hercules Story
1967–1981

WE BEGAN 1967 with the excitement of the Hercules delivery programme.
When going all out for the RAF Hercules Technical Centre contract we were
aware of the possible opportunity of establishing Cambridge as the Hercules
focal point east of the Atlantic. This could be the next best thing to an
aircraft of our own, with a large number of Hercules already in world service
and likely to be in operation for a great many years. Subject to satisfying all
RAF requirements as our first priority, we set out to gain Lockheed's confidence, build a good working relationship at all levels and become recognised
as Hercules specialists. With this objective we prepared a programme to
educate designers, aircraft engineers, inspectors and flight crew in all aspects
of Hercules maintenance and operation and I chaired weekly discussion
meetings to monitor progress. This provided the Company with the basic
knowledge which was the start of Marshall's continuous Hercules engineering learning curve for the in-service life of the RAF Hercules.

Leslie Worsdell's memories of this period are:

> I and co-pilot Doug Page and two flight engineers were sent to Stewart Air
> Force Base in America, which was the Air Force base for C-130 flight crew
> ground training. We had ground school backed with a lot of complicated
> working section models of various parts of the aircraft system. We then
> proceeded to the flight simulator, which was very exciting. We had a good
> hour's briefing by a USAF Major Instructor and a Sergeant Flight Engineer
> and they gave us a review of the systems and then practice at handling them.
> We did all sorts of emergencies and so on in the simulator, which was very
> good experience for anything, not just the C-130. We really loved it.
>
> We did not proceed to the flying course but went on to Marietta in
> Georgia, a big USAF station embracing Lockheed's C-130 manufacturing
> base, to get some first-hand aircraft experience – sitting in the aeroplane,
> starting the engines and switching off. We were there for two weeks having a
> marvellous time and then came back to England to await with breathless
> anticipation the arrival of the first aircraft.

After Marshall had completed the outstanding work for delivery to the RAF, it was test flown by one of the RAF crews we had met at Stewart. After the delivery of the first aircraft to the RAF, Doug Page and I went to RAF Boscombe Down and had half a dozen circuits and landings, including three-engine approaches and stalls, and that was our conversion. From then on we just carried on doing full test flights on each aircraft.

As a result of our early work together, Lockheed awarded us a contract to design and manufacture a full-scale engineering working mock-up of the mainplane of their new C-5A Galaxy giant freighter with a wing span of 247 ft. 10 ins. The mock-up was complete with leading edge, trailing edge and control surfaces, all of which were mechanically operated. This was to assist Lockheed's London design office with the design of the mainplane and control surfaces and to provide working information including tolerances to be allowed for moving parts.

After delivery of all the RAF's new Hercules, there was no prospect of any further RAF Hercules work for some time, but this was transformed at a stroke in November 1969 when a demanding challenge presented itself. An RAF Hercules was being prepared for flight at Cambridge when an inspector noticed moisture, a dew drop, under one of the mainplanes. He rubbed it off and it reappeared. The inspector then poked a piece of fine wire into what looked like a pin-hole and the wire went through into the wing tank. The fuel system was drained and the tanks opened up and ventilated for internal inspection. It was found that there was serious fungus formation and corrosion. Emergency action was essential.

We were instructed to inspect the whole fleet without delay and take samples of fuel for analysis from each of the 65 RAF aircraft. Many Hercules were abroad, including in the Far East, and inspection teams were despatched. The exercise was completed in a matter of weeks and confirmed that all aircraft were affected in varying degrees, and rectification categories were defined:

(i) Tanks to be scrubbed out and paint finish made good as necessary.
(ii) As (i) but with some grind-out within limits and the surface treated and re-sealed.
(iii) As (ii) but with local repairs where the grind-out was beyond limits.
(iv) Some of the 46 ft. long wing planks making up the inner surface of the wing tanks were corroded beyond limits and had to be replaced.

This was a major operation carried out on an emergency footing. The aircraft with minimum corrosion were dealt with as quickly as possible. Category (iv) necessitated the design and building of large wing turn-over jigs to hold the complete wing and maintain its profile during the replacement of wing planks. Special equipment had to be designed and manufactured to accelerate the curing time between the application of coats of protective paint. It was a very successful exercise, completed in a period of two years, and the value of Marshall's large hangars was again demonstrated. At one stage of the programme, with three from overseas operators, we had a total of 19 Hercules on our aerodrome. Our ability to cope with this emergency confirmed MoD and RAF confidence in their Cambridge Hercules Technical Centre for any problem that might develop during the in-service life of the RAF Hercules fleet.

There was an immediate investigation into the cause of the trouble. Fuel at all refuelling locations was analysed and found to be satisfactory. The problem was identified as bacterial fungus corrosion resulting from a bug which flourishes where condensation water collects at tank water drainage points. The trouble was attributed to an early Ministry decision for economic reasons to operate the RAF fleet without a fuel additive and without the installation of strontium chromate cartridges to eliminate the risk of fungus formation and corrosion. This Ministry decision was reversed overnight and no further trouble has been experienced.

At about this time we established a working party to support the RAF with their Hercules maintenance at RAF Colerne, which was transferred a few years later to RAF Lyneham and continues to this day.

In 1971 the Meteorological Research Unit required an aircraft to be converted for research of weather, atmosphere, and nuclear contamination. The Meteorological Research Flight operating from Farnborough is a department of the Meteorological Office and provides information to a team of scientists for the advancement of meteorological research and information to the Weather Bureau, all working in conjunction with several universities and scientific establishments throughout the world. The Hercules was chosen for this task and Marshall was contracted to convert and re-certify Hercules XV208 which was designated the W.Mk. 2. The conversion consisted of:

(a) Fitting a 20 ft. 6 ins. long probe on the nose of the aircraft to measure accurate air movements clear of aircraft induced turbulence.
(b) A drop sonde installation to deploy the sondes with the aircraft pressurised. (Sondes dropped by parachute are radio emitting devices fitted with sensing equipment which transmit temperatures, pressures, etc., back to the mother aircraft during descent.)
(c) The collection of air samples by side boom and under-wing pods.
(d) Installation of a sound-proofed and electrically shielded cabin in the fuselage for progressive in-flight analysis of the samples.
(e) Various electronic and cockpit changes.

We were very relieved to get the resonance test of the 20 ft. long nose probe behind us. There was a stringent requirement for this nose probe to be inherently stable because of the delicate measuring instruments installed in the nose. It was also critical to get the angle of ejection of the sondes controlled to eject them clear of the slipstream to avoid risk of damage or failure of deployment. When we removed the large radome from the nose and installed it on top of the aircraft to make way for the probe, we had to make sure that it did not have any impact on the fin and rudder.

Leslie Worsdell recalls some interesting test flying of the Met. Aircraft:

> We had been instructed that the performance of the aircraft must not be changed by more than a very small amount and so we were particularly careful to record the performance figures of the aircraft to be converted before commencing the conversion, particularly noting the stalling speed under various conditions, drag measurements and climbs with various engines throttled back, so that we had something we could go back to to enable us to compare the actual pre- and post-conversion performance. It turned out that there was very little difference, almost immeasurable – I mean the flickering of a needle or the thickness of a needle between one knot and two knots – difficult to tell.
>
> We had a requirement to carry out engine off approaches at maximum landing weight. Well, one didn't do many maximum weight landings anyway – you know, the requirement never arises. You take off with a full load – you land with less than a full load. We were taking off with more than the landing weight and coming back at the maximum landing weight, and then again one never made approaches with the engines throttled right back, but this requirement was put on our plate to do six of these landings. The runway at Bedford I think is more than 10,000 feet long and having given this some thought I decided we had to arrive over the end of the runway at 2,000 feet. We got overhead at 2,000 feet, closed the throttles, pointed the nose almost vertically down, dived at the runway and at exactly the right time pulled out of this dive into a three point landing and touched down. I was very surprised when the first one worked as well as it did, especially as the co-pilot, the flight engineer and the flight test observer were almost screaming with fear at this horrible sight of the aeroplane still pointing almost vertically at the ground to about 100 feet – it didn't seem that it could pull out. Anyway we managed to get six of these landings down without doing any damage.
>
> Another exciting test took place. The flight test schedule tasked us to determine the stalling speed at full power. I got to within about 20 knots of the stalling speed but, at full power and lightweight, the nose of the aircraft was so high I was really frightened that if the aircraft dropped a wing it was going to immediately spin. I chickened out and came back and said, 'That's not for me.' Some years later I met Sullivan, the Lockheed Chief Test Pilot, and we were talking about the aircraft and I said I was always very surprised that they had never got a British Certificate of Airworthiness because, you know, it was such a marvellous aircraft, it was so adaptable and I was sure there could have been a big civil market for it. He said, 'We didn't get it because your Air Registration Board insisted that we did stalls at full power and I tried it and frightened myself and I said if the British want the C. of A. they can do stalls at full power themselves. I'm not going to.'

The Hercules Met. Aircraft, affectionately known as 'Snoopy' because of its long red and white striped nose probe, still operates as a flying laboratory collecting atmospheric samples and tape recorded data to gain a better understanding of how the atmosphere works by observing and analysing its behaviour, which is crucial to improving forecasts of weather and predicting changes in climate. Dr B. J. Mason, CB, FRS, Director-General of the Meteorological Office at Bracknell, wrote in October 1974: 'Snoopy' made the most outstanding contribution of all the 12 aircraft taking part in the International Meteorological Atlantic Tropical Experiment centred on Dakar which has just finished. The aircraft flew 350 hours during the Experiment. We now have the best equipped meteorological research aircraft in the world.'

Following the Gulf War in 1991, 'Snoopy' was in action sampling the pollution and atmospheric effects of the oil well fires in Kuwait. I understand that a non-academic general summary of their findings was:

> Insignificant amounts of smoke present above 5,000 metres. The greater CO_2 emissions represent only 3 per cent of total annual fossil-fuel emissions and would still have a negligible effect on global climate through the greenhouse effect. Whilst the effects were significant on a regional scale, those on a global scale including the Asian summer monsoon, are likely to be insignificant.

The Lockheed Hercules was originally designed and developed at great speed in the early fifties as a stop-gap planned for a 10-year life with the US Air Force, but it has been so successful that it has continued in production to this day and over 2,000 aircraft have been delivered. The RAF knew of the short life expectancy of certain components of the aircraft at the time of placing their order and knew that Lockheed were working on the design and development of a strengthened centre wing to be introduced within a year or so. Early in the seventies the USAF detected cracks developing in some areas of their centre wings, which alerted the RAF to consider their centre wing policy. The Ministry of Defence first considered strengthening the original centre wings to provide an extended life. Marshall was instructed to build a centre wing test rig and to carry out a fatigue test programme representative of the RAF flight profiles with a view to identifying the problem areas to determine if these areas could be reinforced to provide a worthwhile longer life. The test proved that a general strengthening of the centre wing would not be economically viable, and a decision was made that the centre wings should be replaced over a period of years beginning in 1975. This required precise jigging of the aircraft to ensure that the fitting of the new wing tied up with the profiles of the individual aircraft, the location holes in the centre wings having been drilled during the original build to match the profiles of the fuselage which varied slightly from aircraft to aircraft.

In 1976, when the RAF was looking for economies in the operation of its Hercules fleet, the Major Inspections were transferred to Marshall. It was fortunate that we had the engineering capacity and virtually unlimited hangar accommodation readily available for this contract requiring working floor space for five Major Inspection aircraft at a time, in addition to the hangar space required for other Hercules arisings. It was very important to the Company to have the Major Inspections as a continuing spine of work.

In 1975 Hercules XV181 crashed during landing on an asymmetric training flight at Thorney Island. The undercarriage was pushed up through the cockpit floor doing extensive damage including the complete write-off of both wings, the electrical racking and the Engineer's Station. The right-hand landing gear was also badly smashed up, as was all the adjacent fuse-lage structure. The aircraft remained at Thorney Island for a year as a possible write-off but, with the rapidly increasing costs of new aircraft, it was transported to Cambridge in 1976 and in due course instructions were given to proceed with the rebuild. This was a most valuable exercise providing useful practical information to all departments, particularly the Drawing Office which designed many major repair schemes.

These substantial Hercules contracts, together with large orders for work on other aircraft, had all developed within a few years and the snow-ball was continuing to grow with new major projects still rolling in.

The Hercules had been in service for nearly 10 years and the MoD was now giving consideration to the life of the outer wings. Two alternatives were available – to buy new wings or completely refurbish and rebuild the existing wings and bring them up to the latest production standard. The question was which was most economic and efficient, coupled with the need for minimum dollar spend. We submitted comparative proposals for the two alternatives, and a decision was made to refurbish the wings at Cambridge. Our wing rebuilding experience during the tank contamination exercise in 1969, which entailed the building of large wing turn-over jigs able to accept the complete wing and contain its profile during plank changes, greatly assisted us in putting forward our submissions for this work.

It was essential for the RAF to know how long their refurbished wings were going to last – a minimum of 20,000 flying hours was required. Marshall was instructed to build a Hercules wing-tip to wing-tip test rig, which included the centre wing, to assess the anticipated fatigue life against RAF established missions. This rig, designed, built and commissioned in the early eighties, in due course confirmed that the original minimum target of 20,000 flight hours would be achieved.

The RAF found that operational demands on Hercules to carry large and low density cargo revealed a requirement for a larger cargo hold. Lockheed had produced an extended civil version, and the extension could be retro-installed increasing the aircraft length by 15 feet. Proposals put forward by Marshall and Lockheed for stretching some of the existing RAF aircraft were eventually accepted by the MoD. The task consisted of breaking the fuselage forward and aft of the wing centre sections, inserting two fuselage plugs, extending all the services and flying controls and rejoining the sections together. Considerable jigging was required and very careful planning of the sequence of work to ensure the overall aircraft integrity. This was the first time a retro fit had been attempted and 30 RAF aircraft were converted. The first was stretched by Lockheed at Marietta with Marshall representatives present and the remaining 29 by Marshall at Cambridge. The conversion increased the cubic capacity of the aircraft by 20 per cent.

The transfer of the Major Inspections to Cambridge located at one centre the important overlapping programmes of Major Inspections, Outer Wing Refurbishing, Centre Wing Change and Aircraft Stretch. To avoid down-time of individual aircraft we held two spare sets of wings, which meant that refurbished wings were ready for each aircraft coming in for a Major Inspection or for assembly on completion of a stretched aircraft. This involved much planning and an intricate forward planning diagram of where wings were coming from and to which aircraft they were going to be finally fitted. The central location of this work also saved transportation of the major components involved to and from other sites. When the programmes were all in full work, including Major Inspections, there was a requirement for 10 or more aircraft on the floor at any one time.

There was a happy luncheon at RAF Lyneham on 18 September 1978 to mark the first half million flying hours accumulated by the RAF Hercules fleet. There were presentations to the Station by David Crockett, Vice President of Lockheed-Georgia and by myself on behalf of Marshall.

At the time of purchase of the RAF aircraft Lockheed had not been enthusiastic about the RAF appointment of a UK Technical Centre, but with the build-up of our overseas Hercules work at Cambridge we were very pleased in 1974 when Lockheed invited us to become their first officially appointed Hercules Service Centre as a focal point east of the Atlantic for Hercules operators throughout the world. By 1981 we had carried out Hercules work for 31 military and civil overseas operators from 27 different countries with an input of 45 or so aircraft a year.

The Royal Air Force gains much from Marshall's experience of working on overseas Hercules which often have flown many more hours than any in the RAF in extremes of world climatic conditions operating to different flight profiles and maintained to varying standards of efficiency. And what better testimonial for us to attract overseas Hercules work than 'By appointment to the Royal Air Force's large Hercules fleet.' The increased total volume of work generated by having overseas aircraft in addition to the RAF fleet reduces Marshall's overheads and costs of work to the RAF. The total volume of work also makes it possible for us to compete and obtain overseas Hercules work, which in turn contributes to the UK balance of payments. Should we lose the RAF work at any time it would mean the loss of our overseas orders because of increased costs resulting from the lesser volume of work, with the RAF spending dollars for technical information currently available at Cambridge. Nearly 30 years build-up of knowledge and experience of the aircraft would be destroyed – experience cannot be bought – and another established hardcore of British industry would be broken up with no chance of recovery.

This mutual reciprocal benefit – this team effort to attract overseas work – is important because year by year we face increasing competition for Hercules work from overseas government-owned companies. Jealous of the success of our Cambridge international Hercules Service Centre backed with our Lockheed Service Centre and RAF Technical Centre appointments, overseas governments put extreme pressure on the US Government and Lockheed to appoint Hercules Service Centres in their individual countries. Ours was the first such appointment, but towards the end of the seventies this intense pressure from the governments of Belgium, France, Portugal and Greece resulted in Lockheed establishing Hercules Service Centres with government-owned companies in all these countries.

Chapter 25

Changing Fortunes
1967–1981

IN 1967, IN spite of the Hercules delivery programme, we were still short of large aircraft work, with one of our biggest hangars still empty of aircraft and being used for new vehicle body work – the refurbishing of BEA buses and the manufacture of their new luggage trailers. Once again the Aircraft and Vehicle Body Building Divisions, all under the same management and interrelated, were supporting each other. Len Driver, who had been in charge of the Vampire and Venom work at Waterbeach, was responsible for this BEA bus work and had with him many aircraft workers.

The American General Dynamics F111K was now being seriously considered by the British Government. In view of our armament systems expertise and leading involvement on behalf of BAC Warton in the TSR-2 armament installation, the MoD awarded Marshall the only contract issued concerning the possible purchase of the F111K. We were tasked to carry out a feasibility study for the installation and instrumented flight trials of UK armament equipment planned to be fitted to the aircraft. Instrumentation is commonly installed for flight trial programmes, with in-flight tape recordings of specified information such as temperatures, pressures and loads from a series of sensors for post-flight analysis. We sent a team to General Dynamics at Fort Worth to get first-hand knowledge of the aircraft and to assess the position. We submitted our findings which confirmed there was no problem, but the purchase of the F111K was not proceeded with.

Our Aircraft Design Office was still feeling the full effects of the aircraft industry shot-gun marriage and with it the loss of responsibility for all in-service Canberra design work. Then without warning a silver lining appeared – another piece of luck. I had an early morning phone call from George Gedge, the General Manager of the British Aircraft Corporation at Filton, Bristol. George said, 'We have a problem with the Concord droop nose and we've got to start all over again. Can you undertake the design and manufacture of the droop nose and its retracting visor?' I said, 'I'm sure we can. What do we do now?' He replied, 'Get down to Bristol as soon as possible.' Roy Gates and I were at Bristol by 11 o'clock and back at Cambridge during the afternoon with the go-ahead subject to agreement of contract conditions. We had committed ourselves to additional numerical control machine tools and other equipment required for the initial production aircraft noses and to install any further plant required for a full production programme. During the following year detailed plans were agreed with BAC for building up to 20 Concord noses a year.

The droop nose (known in France as the 'nez basculant') is a 23 ft. variable geometry nose fairing with a retractable glazed visor. The visor retracts into the nose fairing and the hinged nose fairing is lowered to provide cockpit visibility for take-off, approach and landing. The visor was designed to fit glove-tight to the aircraft in the raised position to meet aerodynamic requirements and reduce cockpit noise levels. Operating times were specified as six seconds for retracting the visor, 12 seconds for lowering the nose and 19 seconds for raising the nose and visor. The droop nose is a large moving component within the full air flow of the aircraft. This was an exciting challenge, and during the critical period of assembly I set up a second office in the main hangar alongside the assembly jigs for several months, and on a number of occasions worked through the night with the night shift. We delivered the nose with its systems fully tested ready to bolt on to the aircraft. Marshall was the only company in the UK outside the BAC Group with Concord airframe structure design delegation. We were also very pleased to have a team of 100 men, covering all trades and inspection, at Filton to help with the final assembly of the British prototype Concord.

I flew to Toulouse with the MoD/RAF party to witness the first flight of the French prototype on 2 March 1969. It was a very cold day with much champagne but little or no warming refreshment. Tony Benn was the Minister responsible for the Concord and I was a member of his Advisory Council on Technology. We talked about his overnight decision to give way to French pressure to adopt the French spelling of Concord with an 'e'. I was also at Filton for the first flight of the British prototype on 9 April 1969. The French prototype is now in the Musée de l'Air at Le Bourget and the British prototype is in the Fleet Air Arm Museum at Yeovilton. The Concorde at the Imperial War Museum, Duxford is the first British pre-production aircraft. The Concorde supersonic airliner is a great technical achievement but worries regarding sonic bangs over built-up areas delayed permission for the aircraft to fly to New York, and its introduction into airline service was not helped by major increases in the cost of fuel.

The Concorde droop nose, together with our other Concorde work on electrical installations, cockpit layout and instrument panels, was tremendously important to us and brought our Aircraft Engineering Design Office back to life, but it did nothing to provide large aircraft work for our big hangars. This balance of work between design and production is a continuing problem.

On 26 March 1972 the Freedom of the City of Cambridge was presented to RAF Oakington, with a march-past in front of the Guildhall 'with swords drawn, bayonets fixed, bands playing and colours flying', followed by a reception. The Mayor, Mrs Jean Barker (now Baroness Trumpington), introduced Rosemary to Air Chief Marshal Sir Lewis Hodges, Deputy Commander-in-Chief of Allied Forces, Central Europe. (Bob, as he was known, had been a very daring wartime pilot of Lysanders on Special Operations dropping and picking up agents in occupied territory.) Rosemary told him of our worries about the outlook for the future. He strongly recommended that I saw Air Chief Marshal Sir Neil Wheeler, known as Nebby, the AMSO, which resulted in a very useful visit to Cambridge. At the end of Nebby's visit we had not finished talking, and I went with him to the station and finally got on the train and travelled with him to Liverpool Street to complete the meeting. Up to then we had had no direct contact with the CA, AMSO or RAF Chief Engineer. We had always concentrated our contacts at the MoD with the Procurement departments at St Giles Court – as we still do – but since then we have kept the departments in the Main Defence Building up to date with what we are doing.

We received orders from the British Aircraft Corporation to furnish BAC 1-11 aircraft in the executive role for a number of important customers in Europe and America and install customer-selected navigation and avionic equipment. Two for the President of Brazil were described as 'the most luxurious and well equipped executive aircraft of the day' and included a double bed. The specification also required the design and fitting of an auxiliary long range fuel tank located within the pressurised area. This was possibly the first occasion that such a tank had been installed within the pressurised area of a large civil aircraft. To satisfy CAA requirements the installation had to be developed with complete double skinning of the auxiliary tank system. For the first time I realised what a large country Brazil is – about 2,000 miles long and 2,000 miles wide with few short range VHF radio stations. On long journeys over Brazil aircraft could only maintain radio contact with a long range HF keyboard Morse transmitter which is much more powerful and efficient than HF speech equipment. The installation of powerful keyboard equipment initially created electrical cable segregation problems, and the first testing of the HF system put all the lights out on the aircraft. De Havilland's ran into the same problem on an HS-125 which they were equipping for Brazil, and came to see how we had got over our segregation problem.

Geoffrey Knight, CBE, later Vice-Chairman of BAC, handed over the first BAC 1-11 to the Brazilians at a small luncheon party at Weybridge which I attended. I was fortunate to have got up to date with Brazilian aviation history having just read a most excellent book on Santos-Dumont by Air Marshal Sir Peter Wykeham, son-in-law of J. B. Priestley. Santos-Dumont was a very wealthy Brazilian who came to Europe at the beginning of the century and did much airship flying at Monte-Carlo and at rooftop level along the Champs-Elysées. He built his own aeroplane which he flew in France in 1906. The Wright Brothers' December 1903 flight was not well publicised, and Brazilians maintain to this day that Santos-Dumont's flight was the first flight ever. There was a revolution in Brazil at the time of his death and a truce was called for the day of his funeral. The new Brazilian aerodrome at Rio de Janeiro is named 'Santos-Dumont'.

Rolls-Royce commissioned us to design and manufacture a variable geometry ground test air intake and an aircraft air intake for flight testing the RB.199 engine designated for the new European Tornado MRCA (Multi-Role Combat Aircraft). We installed the aircraft air intake under the belly of a Vulcan V-bomber aircraft at Cambridge for engine flight trials.

The Tornado is a collaborative project of the UK, Germany and Italy with Panavia as the multi-national company based in Munich to co-ordinate it. During the initial stages of development it was realised that the programme would be unacceptably delayed if all the new avionic, navigation and weapons equipment and their systems were not fully developed and proven ready for installation in the first Tornado trials aircraft. It was decided that hack aircraft must be provided and equipped to undertake flight trials of the new equipment, and there was much competition between Germany and the UK for this work. The German proposals were based on the American F104 fighter but not all the equipment could be installed in one aircraft and they proposed splitting the development programme into different aircraft, using perhaps five or more aircraft for the full trials.

Allen Greenwood, the Panavia Chairman (the chairmanship rotates between the three countries every three years), nominated us to submit proposals based on the Buccaneer aircraft. Our first consideration was to provide a paper to satisfy all concerned that the Buccaneer Mk. 2 was the most suitable aircraft and that we could install all the equipment in one aircraft. We proposed that two Buccaneers should be fully equipped to represent Tornados. The Buccaneer was chosen and we received a contract from Panavia and became the design authority for these special Buccaneers. The conversion entailed the complete stripping out of the cockpit and replacement with a Tornado cockpit layout with head-up display, the fitting of a Tornado nose radome and the installation of an extensive instrumentation package in the bomb bay. The task was made more difficult as most of the equipment was in the course of development with multi-national participation. Roy Gates well remembers meetings with up to six contract officers representing interested parties from three nations and many equipment suppliers: 'Trying to obtain agreement from all was a daunting task, but in the end we managed it after countless meetings in the UK and Germany.' Panavia held regular Buccaneer progress meetings in my office and on one occasion Allen Greenwood brought the Managing Director of Panavia, Gero Madelung, a nephew of Professor Willy Messerschmitt. I was pleased to hear from Allen after the meeting that Gero had told him that it was the first time he had been to such a meeting with a managing director who knew all that was going on at production level.

On completion at Cambridge the Buccaneers were positioned for proving trials at BAC Warton, where the Tornado was being built. As Design Authority for these special Buccaneers, Marshall had two representatives at Warton for the two-year Buccaneer flight trials period. E.A.S.A.M.S. Ltd (BAC's Tornado programme co-ordinating contractor) held daily meetings attended by BAC and the various avionic and navigation equipment manufacturers. Our representatives attended these meetings to deal with any questions arising from the trials relative to the Buccaneer hack aircraft. The Tornado would have been delayed by two years but for the development work on the Buccaneers.

With the full-blooded support of BAC Warton, and particularly Glen Hobday, their Divisional Sales Director, we obtained an order to supply Peru with six B(I)8 Canberras – later increased to 11 – which when delivered to Peru became known as the B(I)68. Glen travelled with me to Lima to negotiate the order. Marshall purchased redundant aircraft from the RAF to refurbish and then flight test to meet the production standard of new aircraft. One problem was lack of lateral stability at varying speeds which, in the main, resulted from wings having been manufactured at different centres; this in some cases meant wing changes after having run out of all the adjustments available.

Doug Page was the test pilot for most of the test flights and also delivered the 11 aircraft to Peru between 1975 and 1978; Doug records:

When I was asked to deliver the Canberra B(I)68 aircraft ordered by the Peruvian Air Force I was rather surprised and delighted. It did not take long before I realised that one could not just fill up with fuel, head out south-west and wait until Peru came in sight. With the help of the Navigation Department at BAC Military Aircraft Division at Warton and the first class navigators who volunteered to come with me on a rota basis, the flights were soon organised and we looked forward to our first delivery flight.

The Canberra B(I)68 is a two crew aircraft with the navigator stationed low down in the nose with the pilot sitting just behind and above him, with his head in the perspex cockpit cover. This was like sitting in a greenhouse and made me very hot while the navigator down in the nose slowly became colder and colder at altitude as the heating system was not powerful enough to cope with the temperature.

The routes taken from Cambridge varied according to the seasons to avoid weather, particularly airframe icing. To this end we used the North Atlantic route during summer, i.e. Cambridge–Shannon–Gander–Baltimore–Jamaica–Lima. In winter we used the southern route, i.e. Cambridge–Morocco–Dakar (Senegal)–Recife (Brazil)–Caracas (Venezuela)–Lima.

The routes varied slightly according to air traffic and fuel or oxygen pick-up problems. Oxygen availability was a problem at times. We had to carry a selection of connectors to enable the main cylinders to be topped up from the supply truck and even then at times we had to make up a connector.

Oxygen was very important to us as with low cabin pressure in the Canberra we generally flew above 40,000 feet with the cabin altimeter showing 25,000 so we had to use oxygen all the time. If we tried to save oxygen by descending this would mean we would use more fuel which generally we could not afford to do.

As the two of us in the aircraft would have no ground-crew at the airfields en route, we had to carry out the inspections after landing and take-off. We only had ourselves to rely on and it was important the navigator helped, and this was where I was very lucky because one could not have asked for a better or harder working bunch.

One or two incidents regarding air traffic spring to mind. The first was when one particular unit asked us for our diplomatic clearance number. As we rarely knew this before starting off I just gave the first four numbers that came into my head and we were allowed to proceed normally!

Another incident happened when we were flying down the coast of South America at above 40,000 feet in order to reduce fuel consumption to reach Lima. On contacting the appropriate air traffic unit I was asked to reduce to 20,000. I knew we would have difficulty reaching Lima if I descended and, knowing we could not be reached by any aircraft sent to intercept us, I acknowledged the message, waited a few minutes and reported that I was at 20,000 feet, although remaining at cruising height.

Although the previous actions are not recommended, they just serve to show what one must do at times to achieve the desired result.

One or two sights I shall never forget and which stand out in my mind are Brazil with the Amazon and hundreds of miles of jungle and rain forest, small settlements here and there just visible by the river with the odd landing strip; the magnificent Andes, again with the villages up in the mountains and the highly coloured bright blue and green lakes in the mountains brought about by the high mineral content; the muddy Amazon river and the huge delta with the river water visible far out to sea.

The operation is one I would not have missed. There is something special about having to rely on oneself and one's crew. I also found a great deal of satisfaction in arriving at Lima on time and on the day forecast a week or so before.

Remembering my old friend Dermot Boyle's very successful pioneering sales mission to South America in the fifties with a formation of RAF Canberras, I sent him a copy of Doug Page's delivery flight impressions. Dermot replied: 'Doug Page's recording of his Lima flights certainly brought back nostalgic memories. What a lucky chap Doug Page was to have as his task delivering lovely aircraft like the Canberra to South America.'

With the introduction of the Hercules, the RAF had no further use for their large Belfast freighters. The sceptics were saying that there was no commercial use for the Belfast, but HeavyLift of Stansted, a subsidiary of Trafalgar House, saw the civil possibilities of the plane and, after discussions with us, decided to have a go. The conversion of a military aircraft to a civil role is a formidable task. We embarked on a programme of weight reduction and configuration changes and, in collaboration with the CAA, a complete recertification and flight test programme was prepared. I do not think I can do better than to quote Doug Page, who was our test pilot responsible for clearing all the CAA flight trials:

> The conversion included the problem of satisfying the CAA regarding the stall and the introduction of an automatic stick pusher. With a big four-engined machine it is dangerous to carry out a stall at full engine power but the problem was to establish by pressure on the stick the point at which the stick pusher was to take control and prevent the stall. To get the aircraft finally cleared, including the proving of the stick pusher action, involved 300 or 400 stalls to determine not only when the column had got to move forward to prevent the stall but also when it had to stop moving forward to prevent the aircraft diving. The number of stalls involved was to check for different weights, different centres of gravity and varying power settings and flap configurations.

Marshall became the design authority for the Belfast civil aircraft, a very successful freight carrier.

In 1974 we were pleased to be appointed Cessna's UK Service Centre for their Citation executive jet aircraft. This has resulted in the build-up of a warm working relationship between our two companies over the years, and to date we have had over 1,000 Citations into Cambridge for various degrees of maintenance, repair and modification for special projects. On the occasion of the Citation's 20th Anniversary in 1992 I sent Cessna a message of goodwill for their anniversary brochure: 'Citation – an inspired aircraft with an inspired name. I hadn't lived until we had our first Citation in 1974. I had nine trips to the USA including Alaska and to Peru – all on schedule.'

From 1974 onwards Rosemary and I made annual visits to America in September, travelling in the Company's Citation aircraft. It was all very interesting and saved much time. We could complete in seven days what otherwise would take a fortnight, and all the trips ran to schedule.

We would usually leave Cambridge at 11 a.m. on a Saturday, refuel at Keflavik in Iceland and fly on to Goose Bay in Canada arriving at about 4 p.m. local time. On the Sunday it was non-stop to Savannah, Georgia for a working breakfast with Gulfstream representatives, and I would spend the Monday at Gulfstream and late in the afternoon fly the 200 miles to Atlanta to spend the Tuesday with Lockheed, flying on to Wichita that evening. We spent Wednesday with Cessna and were home again by Friday evening.

Three times we extended the trip. Once to Alaska to meet Alaska International Air for whom we did much Hercules work, flying back via Edmonton, Thunder Bay and Goose. When we landed at Thunder Bay in one of the worst storms I can remember I was very pleased to hand over the approach and landing to Bob Smythe, our most excellent Captain on all these flights. On another occasion we flew on to Palm Springs for the announcement of Cessna's new Citation III. In 1976, when we were supplying Peru with Canberras, we flew from Atlanta to Lima crossing Cuba with night stops at Montego Bay, Jamaica and Guayaquil in Ecuador.

Having one's own aircraft made a tremendous difference – much more flexibility and relaxation by not being tied to catching scheduled flights, and much easier and quicker aerodrome access via executive aircraft Customs. On the westerly flight one is flying against the prevailing wind and with the clock and on the easterly flight one is flying with the prevailing wind and against the clock – very convenient for the westerly flight but not so convenient for the easterly return journey when you have to leave Goose during the early hours of the morning to make Cambridge at a reasonable time during the day.

To attract overseas aircraft for servicing it is essential that aircraft can fly direct into Cambridge from any part of the world without an intermediate landing in the UK for Customs clearance. Intermediate landings increase costs and create delays, including an overnight delay if a crew is running out of flying time and requires a rest period. With increasing overseas work resulting from our Gulfstream, Lockheed Hercules and Cessna Citation Service Centre appointments, the time had come to up-date our Customs accommodation, and we built a new Customs Building in 1974.

Grumman transferred their Gulfstream manufacture from Bethpage, near New York to Savannah, Georgia in 1967. In 1978 the Gulfstream Company was purchased by Allen Paulson and has prospered under his inspired leadership helped by senior colleagues who have been with the aircraft since its earliest days. The Gulfstream has always been in a class of its own and has maintained its position. We are very proud of the Gulfsteam/Marshall relationship of over 30 years which has resulted in an important input of work to Cambridge, and Gulfstream in turn have found that an advanced aeronautical engineering establishment east of the Atlantic is important to them. Our work has included the complete furnishing and avionic navigation equipping of new 'green' aircraft. Michael and his second wife Sibyl had a very happy visit to Savannah in November 1991 which happened to be on the Gulfsteam Staff Appreciation Day, when they joined the management in serving food to all employees in their restaurant.

In 1977, to modernise our facilities for executive Gulfstream and Citation work, we built our large No. 16 Hangar with a comfortable lounge, working desks and a shower bath for visiting air crews. With the avalanche of work then coming in, we found it necessary within 12 months to extend this new hangar to accommodate the Hercules Stretch Programme.

As was our usual practice, having built a large hangar we immediately considered where we could build another if a worthwhile long-term opportunity presented itself. Knowing from past experience that major projects usually arise without pre-warning and have to be actioned overnight, we carried out a new survey. To be operationally viable and efficient such a building must be as near as possible to our existing aircraft hangars, Design

Office and manufacturing shops without infringing on the aerodrome Flight Safeguarding Plan. The only site which met the specified requirements was on Barnwell Road on land owned by the City Council. We immediately started negotiations with the City Council for the purchase of the land and for planning permission.

In 1978 we won a contract from the European Space Agency to design and manufacture a space sled for medical research to endeavour to find ways of alleviating the problem of space motion sickness experienced by some astronauts, and to find possible training methods for conditioning the human balance system. The sled flew in the German D-1 space mission on 30 October 1985 for 7 days 44 minutes and 51 seconds in the 'Challenger' from Kennedy Space Centre and covered 121 orbits of the earth. The results of the work on the sled and the flight were described as being a first-class success, and the scientific returns were judged as substantial by the numerous experimenter teams involved. We produced two of these sleds – a flight model and a training model. Both models are in regular use at the Dutch flight research T & O and the French CNES.

We were now bursting with work, all of which had developed within a few years, and additional programmes continued to flood in which was splendid.

Our computerised Numerically Controlled Machine Shop had an over-full order book for many years ahead. It was one of the largest NC shops in the UK with machines capable of manufacturing components up to 35 feet long from solid alloy billets. Our team of experts could adapt and improvise to manufacture the most difficult components. The shop was working under intense pressure at peak production on a multiplicity of programmes. For over two years I held daily production meetings, including Saturdays and often on Sundays, in Eddie Fortin's Machine Shop Office. This work included such things as the manufacture of many hundred sets of Phantom leading edge slats, complex components which had to be manufactured to very fine tolerances over an eight foot length; moulded tools for Westlands to produce composite helicopter blades 30 ft. long containing variable profiles from root to tip to an accuracy of plus or minus .004 inches; many hundreds of major and intricate components over a period of seven years for SAAB of Sweden for their Viggen fighter aircraft; and many hundreds of main wing spars for various marks of European Airbus airliners and British Aerospace's 146 small airliner/executive aircraft including one for the Queen's Flight.

In 1971 I ceased attending the weekly Friday morning Vehicle Body and Bus Division meetings, which John Huntridge continued to hold right up to his retirement in 1991. In 1977 John became Joint Managing Director with me.

In the early seventies the bus export market was drying up because of lack of money in Third World countries. Our last big export order was 40 for Indonesia. Increased home market sales and orders for military buses initially compensated us for the loss of exports and cushioned us temporarily against the eventual run-down of the UK bus industry. The general decline in the use of buses over the years because of the increasing use of motor cars, motor bikes and scooters resulted, in the early seventies, in 50 per cent of the routes and 30 per cent of the mileage running at a loss. Bus operation is a labour intensive industry and substantial and continuous increases in wages accelerated the run-down.

This was a good period for our vehicle body and container building with average orders of over 2,000 a year, reaching peak production towards the end of the decade. An increasing percentage of our vehicle production capacity was being taken up with military projects. We were building over 80 per cent of the UK's military non-armoured vehicles, and 15 per cent of our military vehicle production was going to export.

Having built many thousand Army 3-ton cargo vehicles, we developed a replacement 4-ton military cargo body. When our new 4-tonner had cleared all its trials we obtained an initial Government order for 2,250 in 1977 and many more orders from Vauxhall, the Bedford chassis manufacturer, for export. In addition to volume orders for 4-, 8- and 16-ton cargo bodies, we had orders for design, development and manufacture of many complex military vehicles and containers such as for the FH-70 howitzer tractor and its limbers, which carry the ammunition, and a 'gunship' installation for fitting to the Land-Rover chassis to carry a 106mm recoil-less gun, the export customer providing the guns from we knew not where. We built ambulances in quantity, including many hundred for the Dutch Army on Land-Rover chassis.

In 1976 we had a contract to provide the Libyan Air Force with a full-scale timber replica of the C-130H as a simulator for paratroop ground training. We made this to aircraft drawings but built to commercial standards by our Vehicle Body Building Division; it was assembled in Libya by a Marshall working party.

During this period the demand for our high quality commercial vehicles was running down as cheaper, lower quality bodies came on the market. Our standards and consequently our prices were too high for many customers. We attempted to overcome this by building a lower quality body – the 'Granta' range – as opposed to the better version – the 'Cambridge'. We soon found that we could not build down to the lower standard and had to drop the 'Granta'. We just do not work that way – in fact our military vehicle standard was to build our bodies 'soldier-proof', intended to take the roughest usage and to last 15 years and then in some cases be transferred to new chassis. Our remaining commercial orders were for those who required prestigious and attractively styled vehicles such as Whitbread and John Lewis, car transporters for British Racing Motors and Lotus, and mobile schools for the British Motor Corporation.

When we introduced vehicle body building to Cambridge immediately after World War II it was very much a craftsman's job and we established for the body builders the same rates of pay as for our aircraft workers based on national aircraft industry conditions. This made it easy to transfer operatives from one division to the other depending on the individual workload of the two divisions. With the introduction of metal bodies with their jigs and tools for quantity production many of our skilled body builders, whilst still doing important work, were carrying out semi-skilled and unskilled operations. As a result our Vehicle Body and Bus Division costs and prices were severely affected by our aircraft wage rates. Our high rates of pay for the vehicle divisions became an increasing embarrassment.

Orders for containers were brisk, including equipping many to accept sophisticated equipment and black boxes. Most were for the British Aerospace Missiles Division for their Rapier ground to air missile, and for other avionic companies including Plessey and Marconi, mostly for export. A major achievement in 1969 was winning the container order for the multi-million pound Ptarmigan project – a highly sophisticated mobile field communications system and one of the most expensive projects of its time. We successfully converted our original container to satisfy the Plessey Ptarmigan requirements, which include electro-magnetic pulse protection. Apart from radio 'battle' facilities, Ptarmigan can be tapped into national telephone systems, including telex and fax, and has direct communication to Downing Street and the White House. We had to go to extreme lengths to convince those concerned that we had the capacity for the quantity required, which in effect only represented 15 per cent of our divisional manufacturing capacity. We completed the contract well ahead of schedule.

The 1960s was a period of re-organisation for the whole British motor industry. Leyland acquired Standard Triumph in 1961 and Rover in 1967. The British Motor Corporation (formed in 1952 with the merger of Austin and Morris) merged with Jaguar in 1966. The British Motor Corporation and Leyland then merged in 1968 forming the British Leyland Motor Corporation. Michael was Chairman of the British Leyland National Car Distributor Council in 1977 and 1983, and a member of the Council during the crucial years of 1975–1984. Our garage business was expanding and becoming established as a large, co-ordinated group of companies. The developments included the purchase of the Austin distributors Grimsby Motors, opening additional depots at St Neots, Huntingdon, Grimsby and Bedford, and in Cambridge taking over garages at Hills Road and Teversham Corner and the Car Centre on Newmarket Road, much of this to satisfy the respective vehicle manufacturers' requests for individual depots. We became the East Anglian distributors for Aston Martin/Lagonda cars. Another important development was our Thermo King distributor appointment for their American vehicle refrigeration equipment. We are now the largest Thermo King distributor in Europe with service engineers in the field based at eight service centres in England and Scotland.

The City Squadron of the Air Training Corps continued its good work. The Squadron had over the years been blessed with many distinguished

Annual Inspecting Officers. In 1980 Sir Douglas Bader was great fun. Douglas and his second wife Joan stayed with us at Horseheath and, before the evening ceremony, I took him round the works. While going through the Numerical Control Machine Shop I told him that the next man we were going to meet was ex-RAF, a good chap but very worried because of his wife's serious cancer illness. Douglas said, 'Oh, we'll soon cheer him up,' and called, 'Hello there – how are you getting on and what are you doing?' and then added, 'It looks as though you are doing bugger all' (the machine was tape controlled with the operative keeping an important watchful eye). We then talked for a few minutes and Douglas asked, 'And what did you do in the RAF?' The operative replied, 'The same – bugger all!' Much laughter. The next morning, when taking Douglas an early cup of tea, Julie, our general factotum, was quite alarmed to meet him in the long passage from the bedroom to the bathroom propelling himself with his hands along the floor backwards on his bottom without his artificial legs.

At one of the afternoon meetings of the Air Cadet Council in the Ministry of Defence building on the Embankment in 1972, I tried out the suggestion that the important and successful youth work of the Air Training Corps should be extended to help combat the increasing crime amongst teenagers by including some terrifying adventure exercises such as possibly the famous St Moritz Cresta Run. I argued that the spending of the odd million pounds in this way could save tens of millions of pounds on new borstals and prisons and save many wasted lives. I did not get any encouragement.

Afterwards I made myself known to Air Vice-Marshal Eric Cook, DFC, who had been listening in at the meeting before taking over the responsibilities of Director-General of Training in the Ministry of Defence, which included responsibility for the Air Training Corps. Eric was interested in my ideas about advanced adventure training and thought that in his new position he might be able to help. Within two weeks Eric came to Cambridge with his Group Captain responsible for RAF adventure training and within a matter of months positions were made available to Air Training Corps cadets for skiing in Scotland, sub-aqua diving, off-shore sailing and parachute jumping. Members of the Air Cadet Council were flown to Aviemore in Scotland to see the cadets' skiing in action. These adventure training exercises continue to this day with the exception of sub-aqua diving which ran out of steam because of the high cost of insurance. Courses in recent years have been extended to include girls. The off-shore sailing is good youth training experience for all and particularly for any Cadet who has had a difficult upbringing, now working as a responsible member of a small crew.

While writing this book I phoned Headquarters Air Cadets to confirm that all the activities, other than the sub-aqua diving, were still in full swing. Squadron Leader Bill Brankin confirmed that they were and, thinking he was speaking to Michael, added, 'But you know your father introduced

this.' I said, 'I am the father.' I was very pleased to know that my association with the introduction of these RAF adventure training courses was still
remembered.

Michael succeeded me as Chairman of the Cambridge Squadron in
1975, and continues to this day. He has also just been elected a member of
the Air Cadet Council. Between us we have had the privilege and honour of
serving the Squadron as Chairman for over 55 years. The Squadron very
kindly appointed me Honorary President when Michael took over.

1967/1981 was a vintage period for Company honours, awards,
commendations and prestige appointments, with a total of sixteen. In the
summer of 1974 came the excitement of my knighthood, a complete and
overwhelming surprise. I well remember the morning of 13 May. I had a
large meeting in my office when Freda Short, my secretary, came in with an
envelope labelled 'From the Prime Minister'. Freda thought I had better
have it at once. The meeting continued and I edged open the envelope to see
what it was all about. I contained myself until the meeting was over and
then immediately rang Rosemary.

We were all delighted when John Huntridge was awarded the CBE in
1976 in recognition of his contribution to the Company's work for the
Navy, Army and Air Force, including urgent support at times of national
emergency; an honour well and truly earned. A very popular award was
Leslie Worsdell's OBE in 1980 for his all-round services to military and
civil aviation over a great many years.

I was very honoured to be asked to present the prizes to the Royal
Aircraft Establishment apprentices at Farnborough in 1977. Farnborough
has been at the very centre of British aviation since the Royal Engineers
Balloon Factory, established in 1882, was moved there in 1905. Britain's
first authenticated powered aircraft flight was made at Farnborough by
'Colonel' S. F. Cody on 16 October 1908. There is still in existence the
Cody Tree to which he attached his aeroplane via a spring balance and
revved his engine to measure its horsepower. Farnborough was renamed by
Royal Warrant 'His Majesty's Aircraft Factory' in 1911. The first intake
of Farnborough apprentices, then known as 'trade lads', was in 1911.
The apprentice prize presentation became one of the highlights of the
Farnborough year with a large attendance of parents and friends. The
apprentices presented me with a beautifully made pair of book-ends
inscribed: 'Made by Craft Apprentices. Presented to Sir Arthur Marshall,
OBE, RAE Farnborough Prize Presentation 1977.' Thus I became a
member of their 'Book-End Club'. Rosemary and I stayed with the Director
RAE Mr. R. P. Probert CB and Mrs Probert – a very happy visit.

It was a great pleasure to be the guest of honour at the RAF Cranwell
Annual Dinner in 1979 and to become an Honorary Old Cranwellian. It was
good to be reminded of my first visit to Cranwell in 1922 as a member of
the Jesus College athletic team. In 1980 I had the honour of being elected a
Companion of the Royal Aeronautical Society.

In 1979, on the occasion of the garage company's 70th Anniversary and the aircraft company's Golden Jubilee, we made a donation to Jesus College to mark the long family relationship with the College going back to the garage's move to Jesus Lane in 1912, my own happy days at Jesus, followed by Michael and David and my nephew John Cavendish. The donation was to be used at the discretion of the College Council. We were delighted when the College allocated the money to the architectural refurbishment and furnishing of one of the oldest rooms, built about AD 1100, to become a new Junior Common Room, and called it 'The Marshall Room'. A mould of the family coat of arms was inserted over the fireplace. On 28 April there was a small opening ceremony attended by the Master, Sir Alan Cottrell, followed by a luncheon. Muriel Brittain, the Keeper of Records, remarked that the motto on the coat of arms, 'Felix Qui Laborat', was most appropriate for the Junior Common Room. The College has only three other named rooms – 'The Prioress's Room' which is a lovely old room used for special occasions and adjoins the Marshall Room, 'The Alcock Room' named after Bishop Alcock, Founder of the College, and 'The Cranmer Room' named after Archbishop Thomas Cranmer, a Fellow of the College.

To celebrate the Company's 70th Anniversary a vintage and veteran car cavalcade toured in and around the City, organised by Percy Easter. Percy, well known as an entertainer in local theatricals, had been responsible for planning all the Company's special occasions. He was Master of Ceremonies at our annual Long Service Award presentations. Percy had joined the Company at Jesus Lane in 1941 and created much goodwill by his friendly reception of customers. He married Rita Dean and was with us until he died in 1982 at the age of 82. Rita has been with us since 1937 and is still working.

I have indicated that I always like to be involved in detail and not superficially in whatever is going on. As the years went by I felt I must continue to be completely dedicated and active regardless of age. There must be no slacking off and increased reliance on colleagues and business associates or not pulling my weight. I have often said that one has got to be 'completely in' or 'completely out' and 'no half measures'. An amusing incident supporting this philosophy occurred in 1978 when the Company changed its communications aircraft from a Citation I to a heavier Citation II. The new aircraft weighing over 5,700 kg required a higher category pilot's licence and I had to undergo a further technical examination to upgrade my licence. The Air Registration Board air crew exams were held at Hatfield concurrently with ground engineers' exams. I went to the examination room and sat at a two-seater desk at the back of the room which I shared with a young man named Keith Holland. We got talking for a few minutes before the exam started. He was 18 and said he was enjoying his work and this was his first ground engineer's exam. I asked him where he was working and he said, 'I'm working for you, sir.'

Taking stock of our big build-up of work during the seventies, there was no other UK company apart from the two main aircraft manufacturing consortiums which could have tackled this conglomerate of work, and the main aircraft companies had no vacant hangarage available big enough for very large aircraft in numbers. From 1967 to 1981 we completed and delivered 2,719 aircraft from Cambridge, made up of Viscounts, Hercules, Gulfstreams, Canberras, Citations, Belfasts, Boeing 707s, Britannias, Buccaneers and BAC 1-11s. At one time in 1977 we had aircraft from nine different foreign countries in work – Norway, Sweden, the United States, Saudi Arabia, Kuwait, France, Austria, Oman and Peru.

As the Company's employment grew I became increasingly worried about the importance of Marshall's contribution to prosperity and employment in the Cambridge area which had one of the lowest unemployment records in the country. Our wage rates allied to the national rates of the aircraft industry were high and we employed a wide range of highly paid professionals. The Company's assisted housing scheme for the importation of specialist engineers played an important part in strengthening our engineering base on which to build for the future. I was concerned because I knew our industries were very speculative. We had been fortunate to date to have a number of contracts which provided a core of continuous work, for many years enabling short-term contracts to be absorbed without delay. I shuddered to think how a major overnight reduction of our work and employment would affect Cambridge.

I was relieved when the Cambridge Science Park was established by Trinity College, creating more employment in the region. This collection of high technology industrial companies and research institutes providing opportunities for interchange of ideas with a major scientific university is a tremendous national and international success. Many of the Science Park companies had small beginnings with six to 12 employees. Some expanded and required, for example, a highly skilled wood or metal worker, a specialist electrician or a draughtsman and we were a complete 'Aunt Sally' for such recruitments since we were employing skilled labour in many trades and professions. Although we did not like being an 'Aunt Sally', we were genuinely relieved to know that our major responsibility for employment in the area was diminishing.

In this time of deep worldwide recession, looking back I realise how fortunate we were to have lived through such a buoyant period with a large volume of exciting and challenging orders. It was a very happy and exhilarating time, but life was too intense for any let-up of effort. We had to work very hard and long and, no matter how busy we were, we were always hungry for future work. I often thought of one of the Rothschilds who, in 1882, said it was very hard work to build something up but it took ten times as much effort to try and maintain it.

Although the Aircraft Division was at peak production at the end of the seventies, clouds were once again gathering on the horizon. By 1980 things were beginning to go into reverse. Ministry of Defence money was in short supply and we had not received a substantial new Government aircraft engineering order for over four years. Orders were being cancelled and others decreased either in number or in the rate of production; the Hercules Outer Wing Refurbish production rate was reduced from three production lines to two and then later down to one, and the Hercules Stretch Programme was reduced from two production lines to one.

Then, in September 1980, came the Ministry of Defence moratorium on all defence contracts, which put a halt to the issue of any further aircraft or military vehicle orders until the Government had taken stock and re-assessed its overall financial position. Throughout 1981 we were once again on a slippery slope with no prospects of recovery.

Chapter 26

The Falklands and After
1982–1989

1981 FINISHED ON a dismal note. It seemed that nothing could prevent redundancies in the Aircraft Design Office within the first six months of the new year, including important members of the enthusiastic and versatile team which had been built up over the years with in-depth experience of work on many military and civil aircraft. Then, on 2 April 1982, Argentine forces invaded the Falklands. At five o'clock on Thursday 15 April Roy Gates received a phone call instructing us to proceed with all possible speed to provide the Hercules with an air-to-air refuelling capability. With the Argentinians in possession of the Falklands, the whole outcome of the war depended on providing the Hercules with air-to-air refuelling for the round trip from Ascension to the Falklands and back. The conversion had to be achieved in the shortest possible time and be one hundred per cent operationally reliable and efficient.

It was good to know that the MoD relied entirely on Marshall to achieve this. There had been no talk or rumour of such a proposal, and air-to-air refuelling technology was completely new to us. Having been in the doldrums for some time it was very exciting and good to feel that we were wanted again. We were pleased to know that there was still confidence in our reputation for spontaneous reaction and seeing any job entrusted to us through to a successful conclusion. The air-to-air refuelling capability of the Hercules was achieved from scratch; there had been no feasibility or definition studies and no committees – just an instruction to Marshall to get on with the job.

There was instantaneous rejuvenation of the Design Office and work began that night. By Saturday afternoon we were, in some cases without drawings, cutting metal. We were initially instructed to convert six aircraft, one as the leader with the follow-on aircraft as nearly as possible in parallel immediately behind the first. A long refuelling probe had to be designed, manufactured and mounted above the cockpit extending forward well clear of the nose, and the fuel system had to be revised to accept fuel from the probe.

Within 14 days the first aircraft completed flight trials at Cambridge and was delivered to Boscombe Down on 29 April for final flight trials including day and night transfer of fuel from a tanker aircraft. On 5 May the first aircraft was delivered to the RAF Operational Station at Lyneham, whose motto is 'Support, Save, Supply'. The modification was carried out in a fraction of the time it would have taken in peacetime with its formal committees and procedures. The aircraft entered service in the Falklands campaign within 21 days of the original request. Three further aircraft were delivered on 13, 25 and 31 May and the fifth and sixth on 3 and 6 June.

It was a tremendous relief to all concerned when the Hercules had this in-flight refuelling capability during the first week of May at a critical time of the Falklands operation. The *Cambridge Daily News* headlines on 30 April read 'Task Force Near Brink' and 'Air Lifeline Triumph For City Engineers'. This development had an overnight effect on the campaign. The Hercules played an immediate vital role carrying personnel and extremely urgent spares for the Harrier jump jets and Sea King helicopters, plus the all-important regular supply of mail to the Forces, all dropped by parachute. The aircraft were refuelled in flight from Victor tankers.

A good example of the importance of the Hercules air bridge was when Colonel 'H' Jones (posthumously awarded the Victoria Cross), Commander of the 2nd Battalion of the Parachute Regiment, was killed on Sunday 30 May 1982 during the successful assault on Goose Green. It looked as though the British thrust against occupying Argentinian forces in the Falklands might be impaired by this loss. Experienced leadership was essential for the impetus of the paratroopers' attack to be maintained. In the event Lieutenant Colonel David Chaundler was rushed out to assume command of the Battalion. Amazingly he was able to take over the leadership of his men in the field within five days of the death of 'H' Jones, having parachuted into the sea from a Hercules after a 14-hour flight from Ascension Island with two in-flight refuellings.

With in-flight refuelling, the flight time for the Hercules round trip from Ascension Island to the Falklands and back was 25 hours. Flight Lieutenant Terry Locke set up a world duration record for continuous flight of 28 hours 3 minutes during an Ascension Island/Falklands round trip. He said, 'It was just one of those flight quirks. We made the outward journey against a strong head wind and then ran into a head wind on the return journey.'

Air Marshal Sir John Curtiss, Air Commander South Atlantic Operations 1982, paid a personal visit to Cambridge on 10 June to thank all concerned. The Air Marshal said, 'The speed with which Marshall reacted to the initial request and the short time taken for the project to become a reality has earned the admiration of us all. It would not have been possible but for the highly professional, dedicated and skilled efforts of all the workforce. The conversion allowed the RAF to do a lot of important things they could not otherwise have achieved.'

In the meantime we had been given instructions to convert a further eight aircraft which were delivered to the RAF between 29 June and 23 July. Eventually the whole fleet was provided with this capability. Whilst it was Marshall's responsibility to get the job done, we had full support and encouragement from Ministry departments and RAF Boscombe Down at all levels, and the whole-hearted co-operation of Flight Refuelling Ltd.

The success of the RAF in providing support over such distances was one of the major technical achievements of the South Atlantic conflict. Providing the Falklands Task Force with an air bridge in this short space of time had a major influence on the final outcome of the war and the immediate aftermath. Although hostilities ceased on 14 June Stanley aerodrome was not operational for Hercules until towards the end of June, and round trips were the norm. The aerodrome was again closed for two weeks in August for lengthening, and again round trips had to be resorted to.

The initial refuelling trials had shown that the Hercules could not match the Victor tanker speed without using a toboganning procedure which entailed commencing the transfer of fuel at altitude and adopting a shallow descent. It was quickly realised that a Hercules converted to the tanker role would be ideal and would relieve the Victor tankers which were already overworked refuelling the all-important Nimrod maritime surveillance detection aircraft. On 30 April we were instructed to convert four Hercules to a tanker role, and the first trials aircraft XV296 arrived at Cambridge on 1 May.

On 3 May we had a meeting with Flight Refuelling Ltd, followed by an early meeting with MoD (PE), RAF Strike Command and 38 Group to discuss the fuel management and refuelling procedures. We installed a Flight Refuelling hose drum unit (HDU) on the ramp of the aircraft, which required much structural modification, a supply of high pressure air from the engines to drive the HDU air turbine and a supply of cold air to cool HDU components, plus extensive changes to the electrical control systems. All HDUs to date had been located in areas open to the atmosphere, such as a bomb bay, and ours was the first to be installed within the pressurised fuselage of an aircraft. With the HDU installed within the heated pressurised area, cooling had to be provided for three HDU components – the electric motor, the fluid coupling and the engine bleed air heat exchanger. The tanker conversion also included the installation of four ex-Hawker Siddeley Andover auxiliary fuel tanks, each with a capacity of 875 imperial gallons.

The lead aircraft cleared extensive ground functions, including dump tests, low and high pressure bowser tests, emergency disconnect of hose and the ground transfer of fuel into a receiver aircraft with surge pressure checks, and had its first flight on 8 June. The initial flight test was with the aircraft unpressurised, and the drogue was successfully deployed. On 10 June a pressurised test flight was carried out including a successful drogue deployment. Test flights proceeded at the Aircraft and Armament

Experimental Establishment at Boscombe Down and Cambridge, and some elevator buffet was detected. We tufted the aft fuselage and from the readings decided to fit strakes to the cargo door which overcame the problem.

In spite of adjustments and modifications to the cooling air flow, there was a persistent problem with the overheating of the HDU. On 15 June the aircraft returned from Boscombe Down at 8.30 p.m. and Roy Gates phoned me at 10 p.m. to say they were finding it difficult to make up their minds what to do next about this continuing problem. Knowing the great urgency, I said, 'Roy, let's all meet in half-an-hour. Who do we want from the Design Office and from Production?' We listed the people and Roy phoned half of them and I phoned the other half. We met on the basis that there was no time to be lost and that we had got to get over the problem without any ifs or buts, even if it seemed like taking a sledge-hammer to crack a nut. We concluded that the only certain answer was to provide for the three HDU components which required cooling to be fed from individual air intakes, and this meant fitting an additional air collector box and trunking. Instructions were given to the night shift and detailed instructions were prepared for the day shift.

Further test flights were completed on 21 June with the successful deployment of the drogue and a wet transfer of fuel to a Buccaneer. These tests confirmed that the HDU overheating problem had been cured. The aircraft was handed over to A&AEE at Boscombe Down on 22 June, and after extensive flight trials was delivered to the RAF Operational Station at Lyneham on 15 July, 76 calendar days from go ahead to delivery of the first Hercules tanker. Incredibly the three remaining tankers were delivered on 19, 21 and 26 July and are still in service today. The introduction of Hercules tankers simplified and increased the efficiency of Hercules air-to-air refuelling.

Emergency installations carried out at short notice are usually subject to re-work after the emergency is over if the conversion is required to be permanent. Both these Hercules conversions have continued to be successful in service to this day, the only up-dating being the replacement of two timber packers with metal distance pieces on the receiver probe installation.

Our Falklands work also included the installation of 'Omega' long range navigation equipment into the first of 14 Hercules within 13 calendar days and we also designed the installation of similar equipment for the RAF Chinook helicopters in record time, which was very generously acknowledged by Group Captain A. F. C. Hunter, the Station Commander at RAF Odiham.

Second only to our pilot and flying instructor training scheme in World War II, the provision of Hercules in-flight refuelling capability for the Falklands War has undoubtedly been Marshall's most important contribution to the national effort in times of emergency. The Company's efforts were recognised in the Falklands Honours List, with the award of the OBE to Roy Gates and later the OBE to Norman Harry for their leadership of our Aircraft Design team. Our Metal Detail Shop Foreman Gordon Mallion received the BEM for his outstanding work in the manufacture of parts with minimum drawings.

The Falklands over, our workshops and hangars were still busy with the completion of the RAF Hercules Stretch and Wing Refurbishing, Major Inspections and the balance of work left over from the Falklands conflict, plus a further two Hercules to be converted to the tanker role, and overseas Hercules, Gulfstreams and Citations.

But the Design Office position was quite different. Whilst we had the productionising of the air-to-air refuelling drawings for possible future requirements, we were rapidly running out of design work and getting back to the serious position that existed before the Falklands crisis. Had the war been one year later our Design Office would by then have been depleted by redundancies of key personnel and we could not have responded in the overnight 'instant coffee' fashion we did with the air-to-air refuelling conversions in 1982 – with what effect on the final outcome of the Falklands War if it had occurred in 1983?

The Aircraft Design Office was again facing big redundancies when towards the end of the summer it was rumoured that the RAF were becoming interested in wide bodied, long range tankers to provide air-to-air refuelling at a great distance from base, as in the Falklands. The rumours developed into meetings with the Ministry and meetings and discussions between the Ministry, the RAF and interested companies at the biennial Farnborough International Air Show in September 1982. Caledonian Airways DC-10s or British Airways long range L1011 TriStars were being considered for conversion to air tanker/receivers to carry 45 tons of extra fuel in the cargo bay with two hose drum units installed at the rear to provide for 'fail-safe' performance when operating at a long distance from base. The tankers were also to be capable of the alternative additional roles of a freighter to carry 44 tons of freight with a cargo handling system or a 204-seat troop carrier plus baggage accommodation.

With our long and close association with Lockheed our interest automatically centred on the TriStar, backed by Lockheed's assurance of their full co-operation and support if we submitted a tender for converting six British Airways long range TriStars to the multi-role requirement. As far as the DC-10 was concerned, there was a team-up of British Aerospace and Caledonian, backed by McDonnell Douglas. It was suggested that Marshall should tender for both the DC-10 and TriStar conversions but we felt we could not run with the hare and the hounds and in any case there was not enough time to prepare a meaningful tender for both aircraft.

The Ministry made it clear that they required a fixed price incentive contract which, in brief, means that the contractor estimates his anticipated costs to which is added an agreed percentage to cover contingencies and profit to establish the maximum price. If the final outcome is the original estimated cost, the contractor receives his normal risk percentage profit. If the actual cost is in excess of the estimated cost but does not exceed the maximum price, the contractor's profit is decreased progressively to zero if costs reach the maximum price. If the final costs exceed the maximum price, the total overspend is the contractor's liability.

Such contract conditions for this big and complex conversion seemed quite unreasonable. There had been no feasibility or definition studies and no prototype. This was the first time that a wide bodied civil aircraft was being converted to a military role. It was the biggest retrofit conversion undertaken on any aircraft to date. The work involved breaking much new ground, including provision for the extra 45 tons of fuel to be carried within the pressurised cargo bay. Such bulk tankage of fuel in the pressurised area of an aircraft had never previously been undertaken. Coupled with this there was to be a lead aircraft with three immediately behind, overlapping and being worked on at the same time. This meant that any re-work found necessary on the lead aircraft would result in re-working the same areas on the follow-on aircraft, and with the sure knowledge that there would be modifications resulting from the progressive ground testing of components and systems, including the complete fuel system. All this to be tendered for between the end of September and 22 December.

I rang Clive Redmayne, the Director General of Aircraft Production, and he confirmed they must have a fixed price. I said the Ministry must surely realise that what they were asking for was a colossal gamble which could easily bust a company. Clive replied 'No one wants you to go bust.' We talked further but he reconfirmed their insistence on a fixed price incentive contract. I said I thought my Company might be prepared to take a substantial risk of £5m if the maximum price was exceeded, with the Ministry responsible for anything in excess of the initial £5m loss. Nothing more was said and we finally tendered on this basis.

We recognised that a very large hangar would be required to house four or five TriStars and we knew that nobody in the UK including British Aerospace, had such hangar capacity available. In our tender we undertook to build a new hangar to accept five TriStar aircraft and made it clear that we were negotiating with building contractors to ensure that, if our tender was accepted by the end of January 1983 as indicated in the Invitation to Tender, we would have the new hangar complete and ready to receive aircraft within seven months. We pointed out that the RAF had no hangar of their own big enough to accept a TriStar and suggested that such a hangar at Cambridge could be a continuing asset to the RAF, particularly in times of international emergency.

It may be remembered that, when we increased the size of our No. 16 Hangar in 1978 to accommodate the Hercules Stretch Programme, we and Bidwells, our surveyors, entered into discussions with the City Council for planning permission for a very large hangar on land on Barnwell Road in order that we could proceed without delay if an urgent worthwhile project requiring additional large hangar accommodation presented itself. Detailed discussions had taken place over the years and so, when this opportunity occurred at the end of 1982, the Council was in a position to deal with the sale of the land and our planning application at short notice. This was at a time when national unemployment was on the increase and our hangar, called No. 17, automatically provided an uplift of employment not only in the aircraft industry but also in the building industry.

During the aircraft tendering period we completed the details of the hangar complex, including stores, offices, library, specialist workshops, water filtered air extraction for the paintshop, conference rooms and staff accommodation, and we obtained quotations for what was in effect a new, self-contained hangar factory to employ 500 men.

The precise positioning of No. 17 Hangar was by no means easy because of the lie of the land. In order to provide a taxi-way between the runway and the hangar apron within the gradients permitted for the towing and taxiing of large aircraft, the floor level had to be 20 feet below the floor level of the nearest adjacent hangar, some 100 feet away, and thousands of tons of earth would have to be removed before the foundations could be begun. This lowering of the floor level by 20 feet resulted in the hangar fitting in with the existing surroundings inasmuch as the skyline of the new big hangar is no higher than that of our other hangars. We also had to plan roadways round the hangar and a sloping approach road.

We did not have a prime contractor and, as was our usual practice, we managed all the work ourselves, negotiating with the contractors individually and then collectively as a team. Boulton & Paul, who had built our first hangar in 1929, was the steel contractor and R. G. Carter Holdings Ltd of Norwich was the main building contractor, with separate contractors for the electrical, heating, paintshop and other installations. There were no formal contracts, just an exchange of letters and a complete understanding. They were all contractors with whom we had worked over a great many years and we knew one another's language and could rely on and trust each other. The contractors gave an undertaking to complete within seven months, with the British Steel Corporation, who were supplying the large steel members to Boulton & Paul for fabrication, making a condition that they would require the order for the steel by 3 February, otherwise there would be two months delay for re-scheduling the manufacture of the large steel sections into their production programme.

As at the morning of 2 February we had no TriStar contract, we had not received final planning permission for the hangar and, if the steel was not ordered by 3 February, we would suffer a two month delay. At noon on 2 February the Council confirmed planning permission, and during the day there was much discussion with the Ministry, who knew the position regarding the supply of the steel. At 6.30 p.m. we had a conference telephone conversation with the Ministry's Director of Contracts to agree outstanding contractual points and we reached an understanding that the

TriStar contract would be placed with us and that it was up to us to get on with the job.

On 3 February at 8.00 a.m. we ordered the steel, at 10.30 a.m. the bull-dozers were on site to remove several thousand tons of earth before the foundations could be started. Weekly meetings were held in my office with all the contractors, with some intermediate emergency meetings. The main worry was that everybody wanted some critical area of the site at the same time, and keeping the peace between the respective contractors was like being King Solomon.

Nobody had believed it possible to erect such a hangar in seven months, but the first aircraft was in the hangar on 24 August. No. 17 Hangar is 480 feet long and 280 feet deep with a 70 foot door clearance and, at the back but as part of the hangar building, a two-storey building 480 feet long by 40 feet wide for stores and administration, boiler house and specialist workshops – the biggest hangar of its kind in the UK except for British Airways airliner hangars at Heathrow. Under normal circumstances such a building would have taken a minimum of two years to specify, design, obtain tenders and build, plus additional time to obtain planning permission if not previously negotiated.

In addition a fuel farm had to be built to provide for the storage and handling of the large quantity of fuel required for the fuel flow test of the aircraft fuel system and the extra 45 tons of fuel in the auxiliary fuel tanks. A fuel system test house also had to be built, and additional hostel accom-modation for 95 extra aircraft engineers required during peak periods of the contract.

Our Aircraft Design Office, so recently facing redundancies, was now faced with rapid expansion. The Design Office building was extended in a matter of months to provide accommodation for a further 100 designers of varying disciplines and to accommodate additional sophisticated equip-ment. We included a Computer Aided Design Centre and a full-scale Gerber Plotter, which accepts computer information and draws directly onto a film which prints manufacturing outline information onto metal sheets for use by the manufacturing shops as templates. A Plessey MODAS (flight test data analysis system) was installed which accepts 200 parameters which have been tape-recorded in flight from the aircraft instrumentation system at the rate of 5,924 samples per second. When the aircraft arrives back from flight test, the tape is installed in the MODAS and, on replay, provides an analysis of results showing such things as the rate, time taken and quantity of fuel transferred to a receiver aircraft, the altitude, air speed, temperatures, power settings, control column stick forces and position of control surfaces, etc.

The TriStar conversion was a demanding specification which had to be designed within tight weight limits. The first and most urgent consideration was to devise a method of manufacture of the double-skinned auxiliary fuel tanks within the weight limits. We considered various conventional methods, all of which were too heavy. We seriously considered an aluminium honeycomb structure assembled with synthetic glue which we researched in depth during the tendering period. My friend Norman de Bruyne had worked with and was very well known to Fokker, who had sufficiently large autoclaves for the curing of large tanks constructed with synthetic glue. Norman, Roy Gates and I paid a visit to Fokker, but the more we talked about this method of construction the more we felt it would be too experimental. In turn, the Ministry's flight test establishment at Boscombe Down indicated that they would require extensive trials over a two-year period before they would consider accepting the use of synthetic glue in this fuel environment.

This put us back to considering whether there was any means of decreasing the weight of a conventional method of construction. Much of the weight was in 3,970 feet per aircraft of 'top hat' extruded aluminium section which was assembled on the outside of the tank skins to provide stiffening and strength to the whole tank structure. A conventionally manufactured top hat section has top, sides and feet of the same thickness. Analysis showed that the best strength to weight solution would be achieved if the top of the stringer was thicker than the sides and feet. If we could find somebody able and willing to provide extruded section in variable gauges of thickness we could effect a saving of one-and-a-quarter tons per aircraft. Martin-Marietta of California said they could achieve this but later found that it was taking up too much machine capacity and wanted to withdraw.

We also required some lengths of titanium angled section to be fitted on the inside of the tanks at the top and bottom for the attachment of the tank skins. The titanium angle needed to be manufactured to close tolerances and with a very smooth surface to ensure that when the titanium angle and tank skins were riveted together they would provide a fuel leak-proof joint and be proof against air leaking in from the pressurised cargo bay. The only extruded section available in the UK at that time required machining. The machining of titanium is difficult and costly, and we had 640 feet of angle per aircraft to be machined to fine limits on four sides. Lockheed put us in touch with Teledyne Aero-Cal of America who offered to supply the angled section made from plate by a heat bending process which enabled them to bend within fine angle limits with no need for further machining. On the first production run Aero-Cal found the process was absorbing more capacity than they had anticipated and wanted to call it off.

The problems with these two suppliers arose within days of each other at a very critical stage of the tanker conversion design and coincided with the biennial Paris Air Show of 1983. The Deputy Managing Director of our Aircraft Division, Peter Hedderwick, and I met the Vice-Presidents of Martin-Marietta and Aero-Cal individually at the Paris Air Show and managed to persuade them to proceed with the manufacture of the top hat section and titanium angle.

The manufacture of the tank skins, the largest of which is 13½ feet by 6 feet, included the precision drilling of over 30,000 holes per aircraft –

which was very time-consuming. The holes had to be drilled to fine limits ready to accept rivets without further opening up, and to match exactly with holes similarly drilled in the titanium angle and top hat section for riveting together. For the drilling we adapted one of our large three-headed Max-E-Trace milling machines to allow 60 holes to be drilled simultaneously by removing the three routing heads and modifying the back plate to accept 12 multi-drilling units, each containing five spindles set at pitches specified by the Design Office.

The fuel system had to be designed to provide for transfer between the aircraft's main and auxiliary tanks and vice-versa, and with all fuel available to a receiver aircraft and to the tanker's own engines. To achieve this we had planned to use for the in-flight refuelling pumps a derivative of a J. C. Carter pump, proven in service with US Air Force tanker aircraft, which operated submerged in fuel. J. C. Carter had anticipated that this pump operated in-line as required by us, and not submerged, would give the same performance. However, extensive ground testing identified that the pump fell substantially below the required performance when operated in-line. After much research, modifications were carried out to improve the suction capability by tightening machine tolerances to reduce impeller clearances, by developing a venturi control system to adjust analogue pressure drop and eliminate unacceptable pressure fluctuation, and by introducing a flow limiter to eliminate speeding. The first proven production pumps were available by May 1985.

We had wonderful co-operation from all our suppliers, and very close personal contact had to be maintained with the American suppliers of specially designed or converted equipment. Our comparatively small orders of special equipment for half a dozen aircraft were almost of nuisance value to the individual manufacturers as compared with the volume orders they were accustomed to receive from American aircraft manufacturers and the United States Air Force. We had to make sure we were holding our position in the queue.

To ground test the fuel system we built a rig to represent the aircraft fuel system, and on test found some pipe and attachment failures which necessitated re-design. Dynamic testing of the fuel system revealed surge pressures in excess of the design limit of 120 psi to 185 psi. A pressure surge relief system was developed and proved on the rig. The complete fuel system was proved on the rig and demonstrated that the specification had been exceeded in all respects by a substantial margin.

We progressively got over all our problems, with the exception of getting the hose and drogue combination to react sufficiently steadily during contacts by receiver aircraft. After much trial and tribulation, it was found that the dimension of the baffle within the fluid drive was critical. The fluid drive is a key element in the hose drum unit power train and is responsible for maintaining the tension in the hose, thereby allowing smooth deployment both during extension and take-up of the hose following contact by the receiver aircraft. By trial and error it was found that a small increase in the size of the baffle, whilst having a minimal effect on the hose tension, produced a more stable response improving the pilot perception of the system from an acceptable minimum standard to an exceptionally good and steady characteristic, but it took a long time to resolve the problem.

The freighter conversion included the provision of a freight cargo door with an opening 11 ft. 8 ins. long by 8 ft. 4 ins. high and the installation of a palletised cargo handling system. The introduction of the large freight door giving external access to the passenger cabin necessitated a number of formidable structural ground tests on the completed aircraft to demonstrate compliance with the requirements of the relevant airworthiness authorities. These included:

(a) Cabin proof pressure test to 11.75 lb/in^2.
(b) Simulation of a 2.5 gravity manoeuvre case with cabin pressure.
(c) Simulation of a door hinge or latch failure during a 2.5G manoeuvre case with cabin pressure.

All aspects of this test programme were viewed with great concern by the management and all personnel actively engaged in the tests. The primary reason for this concern was the volume of the cabin (30,000 cubic feet) which was to be pressurised to 11.75 lb/in^2 – a quite frightening prospect. The site for the proof pressure test of the aircraft had to be carefully selected with the aircraft pointing in a direction which ensured that, if there was a problem with the large freight door, there was adequate clear space of Marshall land between the aircraft and the nearest public road. The pressure test was spoken of in awe as the 'Big Bang'. The other tests in this series, which involved applying very large loads to the fuselage structure, were known affectionately as the 'Big Bend' – the vertical deflection of the fuse-lage at the tailplane was in excess of 14 inches. The tests were without inci-dent and completely satisfactory, and all were able to sleep again at night!

The official handover of the first TriStar Mk. 1 tanker – Zulu Delta 953 – was held in No. 17 Hangar on 24 March 1986 and was for Marshall a very proud occasion.

In my speech I referred to the close Hercules working relationship established between Lockheed and Marshall which played a big part in the choice of the Lockheed TriStar and I emphasised the wonderful co-opera-tion we had received from Lockheed. Stressing the importance of the Hercules and the TriStar having an in-depth technical engineering focal centre in the UK, I said, 'With the inevitable changes of RAF and Ministry personnel over the years, this provides continuity – a data bank. Boscombe Down and the Royal Aircraft Establishment, Farnborough do not have detailed engineering knowledge of the aircraft from conception as they have of UK designed military aircraft.'

In accepting the aircraft, Air Chief Marshal Sir David Harcourt-Smith, the Ministry's Controller Aircraft, referred to it as the RAF's first genuine multi-role air-to-air refuelling/tanker transport and the first wide-bodied transport operated by the RAF or any air force outside the United States, and said that the TriStar tanker/passenger/freighter brought a new dimension to RAF operations. He then handed ZD953's log book to Air Marshal Sir Joseph Gilbert, the Deputy C-in-C Strike Command, who confirmed that the TriStar multi-role aircraft would enable the RAF to mount operations at short notice almost anywhere in the world. He said that, with the support of a VC-10 tanker, they could keep three Phantoms on station prepared to intercept Soviet aircraft 650 nautical miles north of Scotland for two hours but now, with a Tri-Star, they could keep 12 Phantoms similarly stationed; and when deploying aircraft to the Middle East and beyond, via Akrotiri in Cyprus, a Victor tanker could take two Phantoms to Akrotiri but the tanker itself would have to land in Italy, whereas a TriStar could now take four Phantoms to Cyprus plus 150 passengers and 5,000 lbs in freight with the TriStar itself landing at Akrotiri. (Given the Gulf conflict in 1990–91 this statement can only be regarded as prophetic.)

Michael presented to 216 Squadron RAF Gerald Coulson's painting of a Lockheed TriStar refuelling a Lockheed Hercules over our Cambridge Airport, which we had commissioned for the occasion. (Gerald Coulson, now a world famous artist, was at one time Marshall's Aircraft Design Illustrative Artist.) In presenting the painting Michael said, 'It is highly appropriate that 216 Squadron should be equipped with TriStar tankers and freighters in view of the Squadron's distinguished history since its formation in 1918 and its association with its first Lockheed aircraft, the Hudson, in 1942' The painting was received by Wing Commander K. D. Philbey, Commander of 216 Squadron, whose motto is 'Donna Ferens' (Bearing Gifts).

At the Fairford International Tattoo in October 1987 there was a flypast of 15 Lockheed Hercules C-130s to commemorate the 20th anniversary of Hercules entering service with the RAF. Marshall presented the RAF with another Gerald Coulson painting, in this case a Hercules being refuelled by a Hercules over our Cambridge aerodrome.

We were now again worried about hangar and engineering capacity becoming vacant with the progressive completion of the RAF TriStar programme, and we were pleased and relieved to win the British Airways 'Sunset III' contract for a complete new interior configuration including a new company livery for their TriStar-200 long bodied, short range aircraft. BA themselves were heavily involved with giving a parallel facelift to their 747 fleet and were working against time to meet marketing requirements.

'Sunset III' was a very large programme involving 10 TriStar aircraft to be completed between November 1986 and March 1988. The size of the task may be better judged when it is realised that we had to set aside an entire hangar to contain the kits supplied by BA and many other suppliers for installation, including 10,000 parts per aircraft from Lockheed alone. The refit included new toilet compartments (for the first time, two with facilities for the disabled), new galleys on the main deck to replace the original galleys positioned downstairs on the cargo deck, and the removal of the cargo deck stairs, all of which provided capacity for an additional eight freight containers. The interiors were re-vamped with new side walls, curtains and carpets in the new corporate colours, new overhead passenger baggage bins and the introduction of passenger entertainment. As part of the contract Marshall carried out a corrosion survey and undertook substantial rectification of the entire under-floor area of the freight bay. The first input was 'Bravo Romeo' which was delivered to Cambridge immediately after bringing the Queen back from her triumphant tour of China in October 1986.

Winning this BA contract against overseas competition helped the national balance of payments since we were the only British company able to undertake this work on these large aircraft other than British Airways themselves. But for Marshall, foreign currency would have had to be spent. As a result of the vast TriStar engineering experience gained from our RAF TriStar tanker conversion and the BA programme of work we were now also receiving TriStar work from a number of overseas operators.

On 27 May 1988 the Prime Minister paid us a visit. Mrs Thatcher was enquiring and interested in everything she saw. She had not been with us long before she posed the question – which she repeated later – 'How is it that your company has built up such a versatile and sophisticated design team?' This was a question I had never been asked before. I replied that we had been fortunate to have been involved in some form or other in every British military and civil aircraft designed since the war and that our large hangars had made it possible for us to work on even the largest aircraft.

Mrs Thatcher was particularly interested in our RAF TriStar tanker work which was then in progress. She related her own experience of flying to the Falklands in a Hercules which was refuelled in the air.

As an ex-curriculum project our first year apprentices had made a beacon to be permanently installed at Huntingdon which was to be lit by Michael as High Sheriff of Cambridgeshire on 19 July 1988 to mark the 400th anniversary of the victory over the Spanish Armada. For the Prime Minister's visit we had the beacon in the large TriStar hangar with the apprentices gathered around it. Mrs Thatcher was very interested and talked to the boys about their work and their manufacture of the beacon. She encouraged them to have ambitions to get on in life and to start an album in which they could record their happy days and their achievements and told them that, if we sent her photographs of them together around the beacon, she would sign them. This she did and the boys were delighted. The Armada beacon was later flown to Huntingdon and dropped into its foundations by an RAF helicopter.

The apprentices presented the Prime Minister with a hardened steel hexagonal cold chisel. The precision fabrication of a hexagonal chisel by hand is extremely difficult and has become a test piece for every first year apprentice; each year the maker of the best chisel is awarded the Huntridge Cup. John Huntridge explained that the chisel being presented was that made by the cup winner of the previous year, and added that the presentation of a chisel had no political implications, which amused her.

A photograph of the Prime Minister was taken on the steps of a BAe 146 which we were completing on behalf of British Aerospace for Air British Columbia. Mrs Thatcher was very careful to position herself in such a way that the Air British Columbia insignia was prominent, remarking, 'Never mind about me. You get the name of the airline in this photograph. That's what they want to see.' Air British Columbia were delighted to receive copies.

It was a very happy visit and there is no doubt that it was a tremendous success with everyone. When she wrote in appreciation of the visit, she finished her letter with, 'And of course your work for the Falklands campaign will never be forgotten.'

It was good to know of 11 further honours and awards received by members of the Company during this period for valuable work on behalf of the RAF.

In 1988 we were very pleased to undertake substantial design and manufacture for McDonnell Douglas to increase the load carrying capacity of their DC-10, followed by completing at Cambridge a number of their new MD-11s to satisfy operators' special requirements.

Between 1982 and 1989 we delivered 1,745 large aircraft from Cambridge, which included the design and installation of infra-red counter measures for the British Airways TriStar aircraft used by the Queen for her visit to Jordan in March 1984, and work on the Jordanian Royal Squadron TriStar JY-HKJ. During this time we were also working very closely with British Aerospace Hatfield as the completion centre for BAe 146 aircraft which were flown to Cambridge 'green' to be finished to individual customers' requirements, including one to complex and demanding standards for the Queen's Flight.

I have from time to time made reference to our hangar capacity for very large aircraft. Our accommodation since 1983 has been sufficient for 22 Hercules, or 13 Hercules plus either 5 TriStars or 2 Boeing 747s or 2 Lockheed Galaxys – all in full flying trim – and much additional hangar capacity for smaller aircraft such as Viscounts and Gulfstreams. Additionally we have established large external aircraft parking areas.

Having built No. 17 Hangar in 1983, as usual we immediately asked ourselves where we could build another large hangar if a worthwhile opportunity presented itself and what size of hangar should we be thinking about? Again it would have to be accessible to the Design Office and manufacturing shops, and free of any infringement of flight safeguarding regulations. We decided that any new hangar should be big enough to accept three Boeing 747 jumbo jets and that each aircraft should have direct access to its working position and be able to be moved in and out of the hangar without moving other aircraft. The only site we could identify was on the north side of Newmarket Road, towing the aircraft across the road for flight as we had done in years gone by. We designated the proposed new hangar No. 19.

We entered into discussions with the South Cambridgeshire Planning Authority and these discussions coincided with the public enquiry into the Cambridge Green Belt in 1985. We made outline planning application and South Cambs were minded to approve the hangar but felt that the issues – particularly affecting the Green Belt – were such that they should ask the Secretary of State if he wished to 'call in' the application. The Secretary of State so decided in September 1986. A public enquiry was held in September 1987 and, in March 1988, the Minister gave outline planning consent subject to agreeing conditions. Detailed planning consent was finally obtained in September 1990 after a number of difficult issues had been resolved and at a time when national unemployment was again on the increase.

Unfortunately during this five year delay a major opportunity occurred in 1986 when hangar accommodation for very large aircraft was in short supply worldwide. Trouble developed on the older Boeing 747 jumbo jets which resulted in substantial mandatory refurbishing of identified areas of the aircraft within a specified number of pressurisation cycles. Whilst our No. 17 TriStar Hangar could have accepted two Boeing 747 jumbo jets, its capacity was required for work on RAF and civil TriStars. For economic operation of the 747 refurbishing work we would have required unobstructed floor space for at least three 747s.

Had we been able to build No. 19 at the right time to undertake the Boeing work we could by now have become established as a world centre for Boeing 747 aircraft, and the employment position in the region today might have been substantially better, just as the building of our TriStar Hangar in 1983 at a time of increasing unemployment continues to have a substantial impact on employment now. It seems strange to remember that in the late sixties planning permissions were given on the understanding that no additional employment would result!

During the last few years of the eighties, hangar accommodation for very large aircraft was being built worldwide, including in Third World countries with their very competitive wage rates. The Boeing 747 opportunity was lost and we must now wait for the right industrial atmosphere to return, and endeavour to be in a position to take overnight action to build additional hangar space as and when required. The world recession of recent years and the Gulf War of 1991 seriously affected the world airlines, and the buoyancy of the industry in the mid-eighties has evaporated.

We are recognised worldwide as a TriStar centre. Whilst on a visit to Toronto in 1991 one of our staff spotted an item in the Air Transat house journal which read:

> During the second half of 1991 TriStar aircraft C-FTNA is spending a month at the overhaul facility of Marshall of Cambridge, England undergoing a 'C' Check which must be accomplished every 3500 flying hours. C-FTNA is

scheduled to return to Canada on 20 November, while C-FTNB will ferry to Cambridge on 17 November for the same check, returning to service in mid-December.

Marshall's proven track record with Royal Air Force tankers and transports has gained them the reputation as one of the world leaders in TriStar heavy maintenance.

In spite of the MoD moratorium of September 1980 our Vehicle Body Division began this period with a full order book and contracts running over a number of years. The Division gave extensive support to the Falklands campaign in 1982 with expedited deliveries of equipment and spares used in the conflict. But the last few years of the eighties were a traumatic time for the Vehicle Division. There was a decreasing demand for military equipment, and Ministry orders were fewer and for smaller quantities than in past years. The writing was on the wall for the future.

Until the 1980s, for military projects, quality had been an important consideration with tenders invited from 'approved' companies. In the early eighties the Government adopted a free-for-all tendering policy enabling small firms, some with lower quality standards and limited capacity, to tender for the smaller quantities now being ordered. In general terms the MoD's new policy encouraged the acceptance of the lowest tender, risking any possible consequences and without considering whether contractors had long-term given a good and efficient all-round service to date. Vehicle body building is a labour intensive industry but, in spite of labour rates far in excess of the rates of competitor vehicle body builders, for quantity production nobody could beat Marshall on price, quality or delivery. For the smaller numbers we could still compete quality for quality but we found it difficult to lower our standards.

In 1984 the Ministry introduced the prime contractor policy for projects involving more than one contractor. Cargo vehicles involve chassis manufacturers and body builders; in the past the Ministry invited tenders for the chassis and, having decided on the chassis, invited tenders for the bodies. They then placed separate orders for the chassis and bodies. Under the new procedure the chassis manufacturers were invited to tender for the complete vehicle. We realised that this procedure would adversely affect us when new, up-dated military equipment was introduced. This occurred with the up-dating of the 4-tonne cargo vehicle to improve its cross-country performance and provide additional comfort. Immediately we heard of the new specification we began redesigning our body to fit any make of chassis selected, with a view to reducing its cost without decreasing quality and durability. Under their new procedure the Ministry invited tenders from Bedford, Volvo and Leyland for a complete new generation of 4-tonne cargo vehicles, and vehicles were to be provided for Ministry trials.

We had to deal with invitations to tender from each of the three chassis manufacturers as compared with previously one invitation from the Ministry after the chassis had been selected. The cost of the trials vehicles was in the main industrially funded, supported by a token payment from the Ministry. The Marshall bodies passed all official track and cross-country tests at the Fighting Vehicles Research & Development Establishment and were selected for all three makes of chassis.

In 1989 the contract was awarded to Leyland and specified the Marshall bodies, with Leyland as the prime contractor. Having received the order Leyland asked the Ministry if they could, for commercial reasons, order the bodies from a company who Leyland considered could undertake the work only a few miles from Leyland's works in Lancashire. We had been pipped at the post and our production of Ministry cargo vehicles came to an end. At a stroke we lost this spine of continuous work which we had established in the early fifties and had continued to hold against successive tenders for nearly 40 years.

Our CB300 airborne container had been a tremendous success but, early in the eighties, John Huntridge decided the time had come when it should be up-dated to provide improved state-of-the-art protection from electro-magnetic pulse, i.e. high level atomic emissions, which was not a serious hazard to humans but did affect much of the sophisticated transistorised equipment in the containers. Our new container, which we called the 'Matrix', became an international leader. The first production version was equipped with Laser Equipment Repair Facilities and passed the very stringent EMP protection tests with flying colours.

Amidst all the general despondency there was a bright spot when in 1989 our Vehicle Division won the Ministry of Defence DROPS (Demountable Rack Off-loading/Pick up System) production contract. These are flatracks or platforms which can be pre-loaded to await a prime mover and carry a load of up to 15 tonnes. It is a one man operation for the driver of a prime mover to load the rack on to his vehicle, take it to its destination and off-load it. The system is used for carrying loads of ammunition to battle lines and can also carry vehicles and ISO containers. We submitted a proposal using the most sophisticated equipment and production methods, planned to minimise the man hour content, and we won an order for over 9,000 units with production to run over a four-year period. During the Gulf War in 1990–1991 the production rate of DROPS was increased and their performance in the war zone was a great success.

John Huntridge had anticipated the bus recession and developed a small chassis-less bus with a rear-mounted engine and a very low floor to provide ease of passenger entry and exit – a boon to old people and young children alike. It was a one-man operated bus with seating capacity for 24 and standing room for 10 with plenty of headroom made possible by the very low floor. The bus was designed for urban precincts or rural routes and future park-and-ride. It was a very manoeuvrable vehicle, 25 feet long with a turning circle of 43 feet between kerbs with a large glass area and slim pillars providing outstanding visibility. Our development vehicle received the British Design Council Award, with the Design Council judges commenting: 'A very attractive and well resolved design. It sets new standards of design in the main operating characteristics such as economy and reliability, coupled with the needs of passengers in terms of ease of access and comfort. Exceptional all round vision from extra deep windows.'

The Managing Director of Vauxhall (Bedford), owned by General Motors, saw the prototype and said, 'By Jove! I want that as a Bedford bus to include in the Bedford range.' Together we developed the vehicle to the production stage using, where possible, Vauxhall components. The bus, which was many years ahead of its time, attracted tremendous attention. It was thought to be scheduled for considerable success but unfortunately, as a result of the recession, it was guillotined by Bedford, together with a number of other General Motors projects. We called it the 'BB 82 – the Busman's Bus for the eighties'. Vauxhall designated it the 'J.J.L. Midi-Bus'. It was a unique vehicle which generated a happy, friendly atmosphere all its own and it is a great pity that it was not possible for it to go into production.

With national bus orders dwindling from 7,000 to a few hundred a year by the mid-eighties, we delivered our last bus early in 1985 having produced a total of 4,981 units, of which over 25 per cent were exported virtually all over the world. It had been a most interesting and exciting project and good fun while it lasted. It also provided employment at the right time, particularly in the difficult years of the early sixties when the volume of aircraft work was running down. With hindsight, with increasing road congestion, many of us have thought that we ought somehow or other to have tried to keep a trickle of buses in production in anticipation of a possible resurrection of public transport. But in the context of the time I do not think this would have been possible – much money has been lost in the industry and many bus and coach building companies have gone out of business. Our decision at that time was also influenced by our bus building capacity and labour force being required for our RAF TriStar tanker contract.

Michael's main concern in the early eighties was to establish a Garage Group Board headed by a managing director who would relieve him of responsibility in order that he could take over all my aircraft engineering responsibilities within the next few years.

With this objective Archie Clayton, who had reached retirement age and retired as Managing Director of Mann Egerton of Norwich, joined the Marshall Company in 1985. He was a warm personality, knew the motor industry inside out and was a great success. He started at the right time when the industry was beginning to find its way out of recession and into a few exceptionally good and profitable years – a golden period for the industry. Archie's main input was in the marketing of second-hand cars. We as a Company had always concentrated on selling new cars, and looked upon second-hand car sales as 'the poor relation'; most of the cars taken in part exchange for new cars we disposed of to second-hand car dealers. This stemmed from the early days when Austin's distributor agreements provided for a rebate related to the total sales value of new cars sold during the year. Archie's policy was to sell as many new cars as possible but at the same time to market and present second-hand cars to the best advantage – not only cars we had taken in exchange for new cars, but in addition to buy in good second-hand cars in order to offer a representative range of makes.

Under pressure from the manufacturers for separate facilities for each of our franchises, three new depots were opened during this period – two at Peterborough, where we established separate premises for Jaguar and Land-Rover, and a Leyland-DAF truck depot at Ipswich.

Michael was listed to be High Sheriff of Cambridgeshire in April 1988, which now included Huntingdon and Peterborough, and we agreed that I would continue as Chairman until the end of 1989 to give him the opportunity of carrying out all his Shrieval responsibilities to the full.

We have had over the years our ups and downs and worries, but also, much luck and by and large a very good run. But taking stock of the position at the end of 1989 was not a very cheerful exercise. The Aircraft Division, whilst busy with short-term work, had no potential new programmes of work ahead – the Bus Division had been closed since 1985 – and the Vehicle Body Division, which over 33 very successful years had built 125,000 vehicle bodies and containers, including 12,000 military vehicles for export, was reduced to completing the important DROPS ammunition loading flatracks contract over the next few years and the manufacture of small and spasmodic orders for Matrix containers. The garages were also now beginning to have a rough time. All this in the atmosphere of a national and worldwide industrial recession at the beginning of what has proved to be a very deep and long slump.

Chapter 27

Postscript – Family and Friends

1969–1989

I HAVE NOT spoken of the family for some time and now give a brief resumé of how some of us had been faring.

I was High Sheriff of Cambridgeshire and the Isle of Ely in 1969, a very happy and enjoyable year. It was the last full year of the Assizes being held at Cambridge with all the ancient ceremonial traditions, the Judge staying at Trinity College where he received the High Sheriff, the Vice-Chancellor and representatives of the University and the Mayor with members of the City Council to form a procession to Great St Mary's Church for a service at the opening of the Assizes. For each quarterly session as High Sheriff I gave a luncheon at the University Arms to a number of distinguished guests, and a dinner to the Judge at Horseheath, and in the summer a garden party.

Rosemary continued to make good progress with her farming and building up her Jersey herd. At the Royal Show in Cambridge in 1960 the Queen Mother presented William Atherton, who had worked at Horseheath Lodge Farm for 48 years, with a Long Service Medal. We were also very pleased in 1974 when Vic Mayes, who had been on the farm for 46 years, received his Long Service Medal at the East of England Show at the hands of the Lord Lieutenant, Colonel Hurrell, representing the Queen.

In 1971 Michael, at the age of 39, was the youngest man to be appointed a Director of the Eastern Electricity Board; it so happened that he succeeded his godfather, Dr Norman de Bruyne, who had been a Director of the Board for many years.

Violet Hodgson, my third sister, had a very serious skiing accident in Switzerland in 1972 during a holiday with her husband and Charlie Chesham. Violet managed to catch an ice peak after a heavy fall of snow and fractured her femur in more than one place. Charlie could speak German, which helped a lot, and Violet was taken to Interlaken Hospital where a nine-screw plate was fitted. After a week she was still in great pain and it was realised the knee was also broken. An orthopaedic surgeon friend who happened to be at the same hotel in Wengen arranged for her to be brought back to Westminster Hospital, London, where she was in traction for four months. She then had a further six months at Halton Hospital learning to walk again. Now, with not too much pain and one leg a good bit shorter than the other, she feels she is 'pretty lucky'.

All was going well with us at Horseheath until early morning on Thursday 28 November 1972 when Rosemary woke up and, feeling her head, said, 'I feel absolutely awful – I think I've got shingles in the head,' and she had. She was very ill indeed for a few days and then seemed to make a remarkable recovery and was more or less her normal self by Christmas. But after Christmas she fell seriously ill and was up and down and in the hands of doctors, nursing homes and hospitals until early 1974, when the doctors managed to get her medication balanced. Then, apart from not being quite as robust and energetic as before, she was otherwise back to normal and in good form.

With Rosemary's illness, 1973 was a write-off. I had not the time or aptitude to run the Jersey herd and decided to sell it whilst it was in top form. The dispersal sale was at Horseheath Lodge on Friday 1 June 1973; the herd sold well and the *Farmer's Weekly* reported:

> The highest average at a Jersey cattle sale for nearly 20 years was realised at the dispersal of the accredited Teversham Herd at Horseheath Lodge, Cambs. The sale included a 1,400 gallon cow and the Queen bought the bull 'Royal Silver Dreamer'. Mrs Marshall's work and constructive breeding were of the highest order and she has every reason to be very proud of her very fine herd.

Rosemary was very pleased to be invited by the Board of Governors of the Papworth Trust to become a Vice-President in September 1976, particularly bearing in mind the important part played by her mother in the foundation of the original internationally famous tuberculosis hospital. Later in 1987 Rosemary received the Red Cross Badge of Honour and life membership in recognition of devoted service.

In 1976 Michael's marriage was dissolved; Michael and Bridget had two sons and two daughters. Michael married Sibyl Walkinshaw at Henley in 1979.

My fifth brother-in-law, Bernard Rose, was the Fellow in Music at Magdalen College, Oxford, for 24 years, and for two years was Vice-President of the College. He was a well-known choral conductor and was for two years President of the Royal College of Organists; he was awarded the OBE in 1980 for his services to British music. His best known composition is his setting of the responses and Lord's Prayer called by the family 'Pa's Pop Piece'; these are sung in many English-speaking churches throughout the world.

On 19 April 1981 my sixth brother-in-law, Hoby Moore, died after a heart attack. Brenda and Hoby had had a very happy, full and exciting life together. With close ties with the shipping industry, their business travels had taken them to practically every part of the world, except the Iron Curtain countries, with some launching of ships which Brenda described as the most exciting occasions of her life. Hoby became Prime Warden of the Worshipful Company of Shipwrights in 1979, when Brenda became an Honorary Freeman. Hoby gave Brenda full encouragement in her considerable charity work, including as Chairman and finally President of the Friends of the Royal Marsden Hospital, Governor of the Royal Shakespeare Company and a member of the Royal Shakespearian Trust.

On 22 April 1981 Rosemary and I celebrated our 50th Wedding Anniversary with a small luncheon party at the Dorchester. Michael, David and Judy gave us for our Golden Wedding one of the three silver gilt cups which Sir Joseph Dimsdale, a distant cousin of Rosemary's, had had made when he was Lord Mayor of London in the Coronation year 1901–2. He had presented one of these cups to each of his Sheriffs, and one to Eton as he was very proud of the fact that he was the first Old Etonian to be made a Lord Mayor of London. Michael's old friend, Dr Gordon Simpson, recently a Master of the Grocers' Company, knew of the Dimsdale connection and let Michael know that one of the cups was on the market in 1980. Sir Joseph Dimsdale had himself been twice Master of the Grocers' Company.

Rosemary's brother Wilfrid died in 1983. With a First Class Degree from King's College, Cambridge, he had joined Ilford Ltd. and, although a nephew of the Chairman Sir Ivor Philipps, started as a chemist at £3 a week when chemists with First Class Degrees were normally paid £4. He developed the research engineering of the company, introduced the manufacture of film-base for the first time in the UK and eventually became Managing Director. He was held in great esteem and affection by his Ilford colleagues, who turned up in force at his funeral at West Mersea. Wilfrid had an encyclopaedic memory and one of his interests and hobbies in life was the history of the motor car, which he knew in great detail.

In March 1985 Norman de Bruyne wrote:

Dear Arthur,

The letter you sent me ('we struggle on') sounded a bit sad so here is an extract from a letter I received on my eightieth birthday anniversary:

'I have good news for you. The first eighty years are the hardest. The second eighty, so far as my experience goes, is a succession of birthday parties. Everybody wants to carry your baggage and help you up the stairs.

'If you forget your name or anybody's name, forget to fill an appointment, or promise to be in 2 or 3 places at the same time, spell words wrong, you need only explain that you are eighty.

'If you spill soup on your necktie, fail to shave one side of your face, or if your shoes don't match, or if you carry a letter around a week before mailing it – it's alright because you are eighty.

'At eighty you can relax with no misgivings. You have a perfect alibi for everything. Nobody expects much of you. If you act silly it's your second childhood. Everybody is looking for symptoms of softening of the brain. It's a great deal better than being sixty-five or seventy. At that time they expect you to retire to a little house in Florida and become a discontented, grumbling and limping hasbeen. But if you survive until you are eighty everybody is surprised that you are alive, surprised that you can walk and surprised that you can reveal lucid intervals.

'At seventy, people are mad with you for everything. At eighty they forgive you for anything. If you ask me life begins at eighty.'

Love to you both, Norman

Rosemary continued to play a full part in everything and had reasonable health until she started getting tired during the summer of 1986. After two visits to Addenbrooke's Hospital her trouble was finally diagnosed as cancer of the bone marrow. She was told that with treatment and blood transfusions she would have up to two years to live. Rosemary was very good, and between her transfusions led a normal life. We had our last five days' annual holiday at the Old Beach Hotel just outside Monte-Carlo in 1987 but, for the first time, Rosemary did not bathe.

Rosemary and I had a very happy few days with Judy and Simon at the end of May 1988 at their house right on the sea on Arran. We flew by helicopter from Glasgow and the pilot was very excited when he learned from Rosemary that she had flown in an autogyro, the forerunner of the helicopter in 1935. He was very helpful and lifted Rosemary in and out of the machine. Arran is a lovely spot – a different world where the clock stops. If you meet anybody on the road in a car or on a tractor and whether you know them or not, you just stop and pass the time of day – all very peaceful and relaxing. The house had a boat-house within a few yards, which provided a lovely peaceful sun-trap alcove sheltered from the wind where Rosemary spent a few hours every day. It was a very good and happy visit.

In mid-June Rosemary's health suddenly took a nose-dive. She had two nights in the Evelyn Hospital and came out on Monday 20 June. First thing Tuesday morning I was trying to hold her up and we fell together – she was not hurt but it was obvious that she was very unwell. Rosemary was carried downstairs and put in the car and I took her to the Evelyn, where she had another transfusion. All the family were with her at the Evelyn on the Wednesday evening and all very cheerful. But on Thursday Rosemary went into a coma and died early on the morning of Friday 24 June. Rosemary – a wonderful help-mate – a great loss, and I continue to miss her very much to this day and always will.

Rosemary's death happened to coincide with Horseheath Church restoration work, including the refitting of the windows, and we were able to take advantage of this to have a memorial window.

The funeral was at All Saints Church, Horseheath on Friday 3 July. The officiating clergyman was the Revd Laurence Marsh, Rector of Fen Ditton and Chaplain to the Cambridge ATC Squadron, assisted by the Revd William Girard, the Priest in Charge, and the Revd Canon V. C. Ryder. Some years earlier Rosemary had been to Robert Adeane's memorial service at Babraham when her old friend Harry Walston had made the address. Rosemary was enthusiastic about Harry's address and expressed the hope that if anything was said at her funeral it could be said by him. I told Harry of this and he readily agreed to make the address:

Rosemary Marshall was born nearly 80 years ago. Her father was a distinguished scholar, a Fellow of King's and a close friend and colleague of my father. Her mother was a Fellow of Newnham, a remarkable and, I must confess, a somewhat frightening lady. She had many things to her credit. She was one of the founders of Papworth. She also – and I hope I am not letting any skeletons out of the cupboard – stood as a Liberal candidate for the County of Cambridgeshire. She failed unfortunately – I have much sympathy with her, some of the best people have stood as Liberal candidates and have failed, but that is not a matter that I shall pursue now, but with that background Rosemary for some reason decided to go to Oxford where she took an Honours Degree and after that, as we know, she married Arthur. She became involved in a very direct way, especially during the war, with the work of that great company and she helped Arthur in the enormous up-surge that between them they were able to achieve, but I'm not here to give an account of the sort that one reads in the formal obituary notices.

I am here because I think I can claim to be probably the oldest of Rosemary's friends. We were children together. We went to children's parties together. I can't say I enjoyed them, I was a very shy little boy and any company of others was always frightening to me, but I do remember, even then, although Rosemary was a few years older than I was, I wasn't frightened of her. She was kind, helpful and she was fun, and on from there to other enjoyments we had together; weekends at the Mill in Norfolk. I recall her sister wore a monocle – enough to frighten shy young men – but I was not frightened with Rosemary, although I repeat I was always frightened in the presence of her mother, a fine but formidable woman. And then, after the carefree joys of youth, the wonderful – for some of us – years between the wars when shadows were not yet cast upon us.

After that she, of course, developed into that wonderful woman that all of us here knew and loved. I won't go into the work that she did with Arthur, but she did create a lovely home and a family, always warm, always welcoming anybody who came and always with great simplicity. She had many loves, as well as people, as well as her family and her grandchildren. Of course she had her dogs, the Great Danes, one of whom was still at home barking as we left. She had her Jersey cows and she was at heart a farmer, and I think some of you may be wondering and perhaps may be a little shocked why I am not wearing today the conventional black tie that is the correct wear for this sort of occasion, but instead I am wearing the tie of the Young Farmers' Club because I have always felt that Rosemary was at heart a farmer and she was always young, and so it seemed to me suitable to recognise that by departing perhaps a little bit from convention.

We had lovely days together – the Cambridgeshire Show, when it was a small show and we could stand at the side of the judging ring and see if her heifer or my heifer was going to be pulled in first or second or third – always cheerful, always excited and always very knowledgeable.

And, of course, her work didn't stop there. She did so many other things too – with Papworth following on her mother's tradition, with the Red Cross from whom she received some recognition of the work she had done and, again, I saw much of her with the Cambridgeshire Society for the Blind where she was always helpful, always present until the last year or so at our meetings, often offering us hospitality at the Lodge and always there to support the work that she was doing, and at the same time always working with Arthur, with the family. And I think it is in a way typical of Rosemary that, although ill and suffering, she insisted – such was her strength of mind over matter – she insisted on staying alive until after Michael's Sheriff's Party in which she took so much interest because of her pride in his achievements and in those of all her family.

All of us who have known her – and it is good to see so many people here and I believe outside too – all of us are indeed fortunate to have known her. Our lives have been the richer because of her and we shall not forget her no matter how long we may live, but it is good that there will be here in this church a lasting memorial of her for those who did not have the privilege of knowing her. There will be in one of these south facing windows stained glass with the coat of arms and the crest of the family, and that in itself is important, but through that stained glass the sun will shine and its reflection of blue and gold and bright colours will be on this floor and will in a way reflect the beauty, the brightness that Rosemary brought into the lives of so many of us, so it is good to know that her brightness and joy will continue long after we have gone.

Of course, now there inevitably must be deep sadness, especially for Arthur, the children and the grandchildren; deep sadness that she is no longer here, but she would be one of the first to echo the words of the first lesson that there is a time to plant and a time to pluck up what is planted, and she would never have wished it otherwise, but although that sadness inevitably is there and rightly is there, there is an even greater gratitude, a deeper gratitude, that we were privileged to know Rosemary, and so we must give thanks for that, and in time as the immediate sadness fades the gratitude will remain.

Bernard Rose played during the service and later lamented to Molly the state of the organ, which resulted in the family having it restored in Rosemary's memory by E. J. Johnson & Son, Pipe Organ Builders, Cambridge. It is a very old organ and had previously been restored by A. T. Miller & Sons, Cambridge about 1865.

My friend Jonathan Barker then suggested that Horseheath should have a village sign as a memorial to Rosemary. Jonathan made enquiries and found that the village would like this very much. I suggested the sign should be a painting of 'Plenipotentiary', the Derby Winner of 1834, which was bred and trained at our home, Horseheath Lodge. The village had forgotten all about 'Plenipotentiary' and welcomed the suggestion (See Appendix 1). The restored church windows, the organ and village sign were dedicated by the Rt Revd Peter Walker DD, Bishop of Ely, on Sunday 30 July 1989 and Bernard Rose played the restored organ at the service.

Michael, with the lively support of Sibyl, had a very busy year as High Sheriff in 1988. He held his High Sheriff's Party at Swaffham Prior House on Friday 17 June, fortunately a week before Rosemary's death. After a very successful year Michael was commissioned a Deputy Lieutenant of Cambridgeshire in 1989 and in 1992 Vice Lord-Lieutenant.

Henry Bateman, my life-long and family friend from Tonbridge and Jesus, was killed in a tragic road accident in June 1989 – a great loss. Henry, himself a doctor, had retired to Cambridge, where his son Anthony is a doctor. Our families had seen much of one another over the years, and Henry and I went to the Tonbridge and Jesus Old Boys' Reunions together, the last at Tonbridge in the summer of 1988. He was a delightful companion – Sunday afternoon walks both at School and College and staying with one another's families. It was always good to know that he was around and I miss him very much.

Julie Callary, who had worked at Handley-Page's aircraft works at Cricklewood during the war and was our very good cook for 35 years, died early in 1991. Julie's son Victor phoned to say that his mother had always considered the happiest days of her life were at Horseheath and she had asked if her ashes could be buried there. The family and I were delighted, and Julie's ashes were buried on a Friday afternoon between her flint cottage and the chicken run. The Revd Girard presided over the simple ceremony in the presence of her son and her colleagues.

For the family this was a difficult period with many deaths. Rupert Wagner, my second brother-in-law, died after a long illness in August 1987 having been a Church Warden at St Mary's, Shipley, West Sussex since his retirement. John Hodgson, my third brother-in-law, died after a very long illness in January 1988. Dorothy Wagner, my second sister died in October 1988. Monty Fry, my first brother-in-law, died in March 1989. Charlie Chesham, my fourth brother-in-law, died in December 1989. In May 1990 the family experienced the first loss of one of the new generation, then totalling 20, with the death of Violet's eldest daughter Jill Cornell at the age of 51 after a long illness.

There is no doubt that as a family we have been very fortunate with our brothers-in-law. The more I think about this the more I realise we have been exceptionally lucky. They all got on well with one another and became completely integrated as part of the family team. I have often said of my brothers-in-law, in the nicest possible way, that in marrying one sister they had married the lot. I am now reduced from six sisters to five and from six brothers-in-law to one.

A few years ago, at the end of a telephone conversation, George Edwards, my old friend of Vickers days, said, 'I met your sister at dinner last week – quite a girl!' I said, 'Which one? I've got six of them.' We identified Mary and I said, 'I often wonder what would have happened if they had all been boys.' George paused for a moment before saying, 'I think you've had more fun on your own.' Another pause and then, 'No, I think you would have formed a government.'

Chapter 28

Handing Over the Reins
December 1989

FOR MICHAEL, IF I had tried I could not have picked a worse time to 'pass the buck' and I still feel bad about this. The outlook was bleak. Financially the Company was in very good heart but the order book was low with nothing on the horizon, and the Company had grown to a size which created substantial future financial and employment responsibilities.

On 8 December 1989 for the last time I presented the Long Service Awards. We initiated these presentations in 1976 to recognise 30, 40 and 50 years service, and as at December 1989 the score was 366 for over 30 years service (the presentation of a silver Armada Dish), 85 for over 40 years, 10 over 50 years, and one over 60 years – a total of 462 awards. This is an indication of the Company's efforts to provide and maintain the continuity of employment which has made a major contribution to our successes since 1909.

I took this opportunity to recognise my eldest sister Margery Fry's service to the Company for 45 years as a Director. Margery was my secretary in the late twenties and early thirties and kept the Flying School books, and in World War II she helped run the canteen. She was succeeded as a Director by my third sister Violet Hodgson, who was very much on her home ground having been Canteen Manager during the war and until 1947.

I went on to say:

> The Company and the nation are facing a difficult period but don't forget that we have had many worries over the years, such as the overnight scrapping of the Valiant V-Bombers and the TSR-2, and then there was the Defence moratorium of 1980, but we are still here and much has happened since 1980. And so we keep our fingers crossed.
>
> We have been extremely fortunate with the teams we developed together and in the variety of work which we have had the privilege to undertake. There are no words which would adequately reflect my feelings but I will just say a very, very sincere and affectionate 'thank you' for all that you have done and – most important – all that you are going to continue to do in the future.

And so, with the hope of plenty of excitement ahead, I hand over to you, Michael, and wish you and all your colleagues the best of British luck and, what is more important, the best of Marshall luck, which has been a major contribution to the Company's successes to date.

With your success over the last 30 years in building up the garage business – few perhaps realise that the turnover of the Garage Group is over twice as much as the Aircraft Company – I look forward with the greatest confidence to you leading the Group into the next century.

As for myself, I am going to have the time of my life – I am available, if asked, to do anything that is wanted from sweeping up to standing in for anybody, and all without any responsibility, which is wonderful. I have at least two years work in tidying up records and archives and generally gadding about – I am going to the Falklands in January and to Jordan in March. Paul Wheeler has given me a 640 to collect so that we can obtain payment for goods delivered to the Falklands last February. I will be just up the road and so, as Mae West used to say, 'Come up and see me some time'.

Michael then, on behalf of the Company, presented me with a silver Armada Dish inscribed 'With gratitude from all for over 63 years inspired leadership of, and over 70 years active commitment to, the Marshall of Cambridge Group of Companies.'

Michael and his Directors gave me lunch and presented me with a most excellent painting by Gerald Coulson entitled 'Past and Present – a fly-past depicting the aviation career of Sir Arthur Marshall'. It was Michael's inspired idea that the picture should represent our Cambridge aerodrome as it was in 1938 with, on the ground, G-AAEH my first Gipsy Moth of 1929, our Puss Moth G-ABIZ of 1931 and an Austin Seven and, flying overhead, some of the hundred or more aircraft types for which we have had a major responsibility. I sent a copy of the picture to my old friend Dermot Boyle and he replied, 'I know it is sacrilege but the thing which interested me most was the Austin Seven – I had one.'

The Aircraft Design Office presented me with a brilliantly executed graphic portrayal of my career, from the airship of 1912, my time at Jesus, athletics, Austin Seven, aircraft and vehicle body building to the spacecraft sled – a very heart-warming finale.

At Christmas 1989 I finally handed over all my responsibilities as Company Chairman and Chief Executive to Michael, and the shareholders kindly elected me Life President of the Marshall Group.

*   *   *

Michael picked up the reins with much courage, determined to make the best of the deteriorating national and international economic situation.

There had been much discussion on where I should be relocated. I had been thinking of two or three offices at the aerodrome, but Michael and Francis Pemberton thought otherwise and were emphatic that this would be difficult for all concerned. Francis, always tremendously kind and considerate of what is best for his friends, vigorously insisted that the Company's Greenhouse Farm house, opposite the aerodrome, was the perfect place to put me out to grass. This has proved ideal, and I now realise that to have continued in 'an attic over the shop' would have been disastrous. Freda Short, my secretary, and I vacated our old offices and moved to Greenhouse Farm just before Christmas 1989. Michael made Greenhouse Farm as welcoming as possible by having my father's old Jesus Lane desk renovated and installed in my new office, together with a montage of photographs from the gallery of historical Company pictures which hang on the staircase leading to my old office.

Greenhouse Farm is a delightful location. The house, standing well back from the road, is approached by a long curving drive bordered by a deep plantation of flowering cherries which are a magnificent sight in the Spring. My office is on the first floor and, sitting at my father's old desk, I look through a very large bay window to a backdrop of trees which reflect the passing seasons – a wonderful inter-blending and overlapping galaxy of changing colours – a complete inter-mix of sycamore, weeping willow, purple beech, silver birch, chestnut, maple and evergreens intermingled with lilac, japonica, broom, syringa, honeysuckle and roses.

This complete change of life from full steam ahead with all guns firing to no executive responsibility was difficult to visualise. It has turned out to be a very full, enjoyable period with never a dull moment. There has been much to do, including sorting out the Company archives (the equivalent of 20 or so coffin-sized chests) which were transferred to Greenhouse Farm. The main consideration was the Company's request that I should write this book, and I soon realised that this formidable task would require a period of uninterrupted concentration.

With the full co-operation of the RAF, Michael planned what was for me – remembering the race against time to provide the Hercules with air-to-air refuelling capabilities – a nostalgic visit to the Falklands with my daughter Judy and her husband Simon. It was a very kind thought and the RAF prepared a very exciting programme. Michael felt this would help me make the break from my 60-year slog, and I think at the same time he thought it would be good for him and his colleagues to get me out of the way for a few weeks!

Before I left the Islands, and after my return, I was continually asked what was my main impression of the Falklands. My most memorable impression was sitting on the jump seat in the cockpit of the TriStar as we approached the Falklands at six o'clock in the evening with an overcast sky and imagining I was the Commander of the Task Force having my first sight of the Islands with instructions to take possession as quickly as possible and – regardless of any plans and guidelines received from the UK – with this mass of spreading and interlocked land and water where would I start – and having started how would I establish and maintain physical communications? There is no doubt that our Forces, with limited equipment and 8,000 miles from base, did a wonderful job, but one has got to see the Islands in person to have some idea what they were up against.

A few days after my return from the Falklands the Master of Jesus, Professor A. C. Renfrew phoned me to tell me that I had been elected an Honorary Fellow of the College – a wonderful surprise – I was quite over-whelmed.

The next excitement was a visit to Jordan in March. In September 1987 I had flown as a guest of King Hussein in his TriStar into the Fairford RAF Benevolent Fund International Air Tattoo of which the King was Patron. During the flight the King invited Rosemary and me to visit him in Jordan. Because of Rosemary's illness we had been unable to accept. On a similar flight to Fairford in September 1989 King Hussein said, 'You have not been to see me yet.' I explained the position and he kindly extended his invitation to include Judy and Simon. The highlight of a memorable and very enjoyable visit came out of the blue after lunch at the Basman Palace with King Hussein and Queen Noor and members of the Royal family when, to mark my long friendship with the Hashemite Kingdom of Jordan, His Majesty graciously conferred on me the Order of Istiqlal First Class, the highest order that can be awarded to a non-Jordanian other than a Head of State. I was deeply moved and expressed my sincere thanks.

The RAF invited me to be a member of the council of the RAF Benevolent Fund Appeal on the occasion of the 50th Anniversary of the Battle of Britain in 1990. I entered into this with gusto circulating many of our prewar and wartime flying pupils, and business contacts all over the world, and had a response so much beyond my initial imagination that it encouraged me to widen the range of my appeal. It was all very heart warming and I felt it was a fitting culmination of my association with the RAF for more than 60 years.

I enjoyed the informal launching at Heffer's bookshop in February 1991 of the publication of *A Last Eccentric*, a symposium edited by Canon Eric James depicting the life of the late Canon Simpson of Trinity, and I remembered again my 1929 meeting with 'Simbo' and all that stemmed from it.

In May 1991 I attended the ATC Bedfordshire and Cambridgeshire Wing Service of Thanksgiving at Ely Cathedral to commemorate the 50th Anniversary of the Corps. Michael, as Chairman of the Wing, read one of the lessons. It was good to meet many old friends there, including Commander Dick Reynolds, who in 1937 was Cadet No. 17 of the Cambridge Squadron.

To the delight of everybody, in 1991 Freda Short, then my secretary for 37 years not out, who has been a tremendous support over the turbulent but happy years, was awarded the British Empire Medal. The Lord Lieutenant of Cambridgeshire invested Miss Short at a ceremony at the aerodrome at which the whole Short family was present. A happy day made complete by the presence of Freda's mother at the lively age of 105, which was quite wonderful. I suggested to Mrs Short that her presence made it a unique occasion qualifying for consideration for inclusion in *The Guinness Book of Records*.

Whilst I am not making reference to the Company's day-to-day activities since 1989, I am pleased to record the very active part we played in supporting our Forces during the Gulf War 1990–1991, including work on Hercules and TriStar aircraft and accelerated deliveries of Army flatrack front line ammunition carriers.

1991 was the 25th anniversary of the very close association between Lockheed and Marshall, first on the Hercules and then the TriStar. Michael gave a Silver Jubilee dinner at Jesus – a very proud occasion for the Company. Jesus was an appropriate setting with the many connections between the College and the Marshall Company and family dating back to 1912, when David Gregory Marshall first leased from the College the stables which were to become his garage premises in Jesus Lane.

Michael, in proposing the toast to the past, present and future of the Lockheed/Marshall association, referred to it as a relationship 'based on technology, trust, enterprise, initiative, mutual respect and above all friendship' and said, 'With regard to the future, only one thing is certain, and that is that there will be unexpected demands from the most unlikely quarters and that we must be ready for them.' The AOC-in-C Strike Command, Air Chief Marshal Sir Michael Graydon, thanked Lockheed and Marshall for providing and sustaining the Hercules and TriStar, emphasised their importance to the RAF, and concluded, 'This partnership between industry and the Service has been a good one. It deserves to be sustained and fostered.'

One of the nicest things which has happened to me during my long career in aviation was on 12 June 1992 when I was created an Honorary Doctor of Science at Cranfield. I was proud to receive the Honorary Doctorate at the hands of the Chancellor, Lord Kings Norton, one of the great men of aviation who has done such wonderful work for all branches of British aviation over the last 75 years. Lord Kings Norton's life's work made flying safer and faster, and anyone who flies is to some extent in his debt. I was overwhelmed and highly delighted. The citation read 'In recognition of his great contribution to British aeronautical engineering.'

Michael, David and Judy gave a 90th birthday luncheon for me at Jesus College on Saturday 4 December 1993. Fifty members of my family were present and about 100 friends including many from the University, the Royal Air Force and the aerospace and automotive industries – several of them friends from the very earliest days. A contingent of the Cambridge Squadron of the Air Training Corps was in attendance. It was a very, very happy occasion and the 'Happy Birthday' descant sung by the Jesus choir brought tears from the heart. All eyes were on Michael proposing the toast, while I waited to blow out the candles, when the assembled company were astounded to hear me yell, 'Michael, we're on fire!' The cake had so many candles it was beginning to go up in smoke.

Looking back over my 90 years I realise that I have been a lucky fellow. Lucky to have been born in Cambridge – this story could not have taken place anywhere else. Fortunate to have had parents who saw that I had a good upbringing, laying the foundations for a large, loving family, good health and stamina. Lucky in the constant support of my sisters and their husbands and many lifelong friends. Lucky to have wonderful people to work with, a great many with 40, 50 or more years service, with much fun and games together – Felix Qui Laborat.

My greatest luck was my long and happy marriage to Rosemary, and our own family, Michael, David and Judy, Sibyl, Jennie and Simon. And now 11 grandchildren and two great-granddaughters all to keep me young. They are all quite wonderful.

A lucky fellow.

Appendix 1

Horseheath Village Sign

THE SIGN DEPICTS the 1834 Derby winner 'Plenipotentiary' which was bred and trained at Horseheath Lodge, later to become the home of Sir Arthur and Lady Marshall. The sign shows two different pictures of 'Plenipotentiary', one of which includes the Trainer, George Paine and the Jockey, P. Connolly. Both of these pictures, based on originals, were painted by Mr Donald Viveash, who sadly died a few weeks before the sign was unveiled. They are therefore his last major work and one of which he was very proud.

There are two different crowns on top of the village sign. The Tudor crown commemorates the visit of HM Queen Elizabeth I to Horseheath in 1578 when she visited Sir Giles Alington of Horseheath Park. The second crown represents the visit of HM King George V to Horseheath in 1912 when he reviewed his troops on the termination of the Army manoeuvres in the area; his visit is also commemorated by a plaque on the wall of the church.

On the plinth of the village sign there is the Marshall family crest with its motto 'Felix Qui Laborat' – 'Happy is he who works' – and Lady Marshall's Dimsdale family crest. The Marshall coat of arms was granted to Arthur Gregory George Marshall in 1976 and the arms and crest symbolise the life story of the work of Marshall of Cambridge. The Dimsdale coat of arms was granted posthumously in 1830 to Thomas Dimsdale, MD, who had been created a Baron of the Russian Empire in 1769 by Catherine II upon his travelling to Russia and successfully inoculating her and her son the Grand Duke Paul against smallpox. The Russian Eagle is the centrepiece of the crest.

A time capsule recording details of the inhabitants and life in the village of Horseheath in 1989 was sealed in the foundations of the Village sign. The location of the capsule has been marked with a brass plug so that it can be recovered and opened in its centenary year 2089.

The sign was accepted on behalf of the village by Mr R. W. Daynes, Chairman of Horseheath Parish Council, who said:

My Lord Bishop, Sir Arthur, Ladies, Gentlemen and Children.

It would be difficult for anyone assembled here today not to feel a sense of the enactment of real live history, for the unveiling of this village sign surely embodies just that.

It establishes for posterity this very occasion – the here and now – with us all.

It re-establishes a Derby legend in the paintings.

It evokes, too, a sense of momentous occasions when Sovereigns visited this small but historic village, and in the case of the Sovereign Lady Queen Elizabeth we are told she liked it well.

Moreover, and perhaps more importantly, it prepares for the future when – and who knows when – the capsule inside the monument will be discovered, and the discoverers will reveal life in this village towards the end of the twentieth century.

Above all, however, it will establish a monument to a Lady of this village. A Lady many knew well – with whom, like me, many more held a passing acquaintance – but who was to all who met her an indelible example of the graciousness of a passing era.

From such truths, I suggest, are folk-tales born as many a village sign bears witness to – thus I tell a tale:

Once upon a time in a land of rolling hills and wide, smooth valleys there was a village set high. Below that village in a grand house lived a Knight and his Lady. The Knight's Lady was gentle and gracious to all who spoke to her, speaking with humble wisdom. Alas upon an empty day the Lady died. The Knight and all who knew her greatly mourned her loss, but in happy memory the Knight built a monument, a sign, set upon the very heart of her much loved village. All the villagers marvelled at the sign with its fine and famous horse, its eagled crest and gilded crowns. Through the years many a traveller would stop to wonder. The bold amongst them would enquire of the people there asking, 'Wherefore so much splendour – what great occasion, deed or battle has been here?' and smiling the people would answer, 'No deed nor battle yet no great occasion only that once upon a time there was a real and lovely Lady now herself set high.'

Sir Arthur, it is with a sincere sense of personal honour, much civic pride and, I know, parish wide gratitude that I accept on behalf of the parishioners of Horseheath your magnificent gift of this village sign and in consequence I call upon all assembled here as witnesses to this historic event to show their great appreciation to you, your family and especially to the Lady who inspired it.

Appendix 2

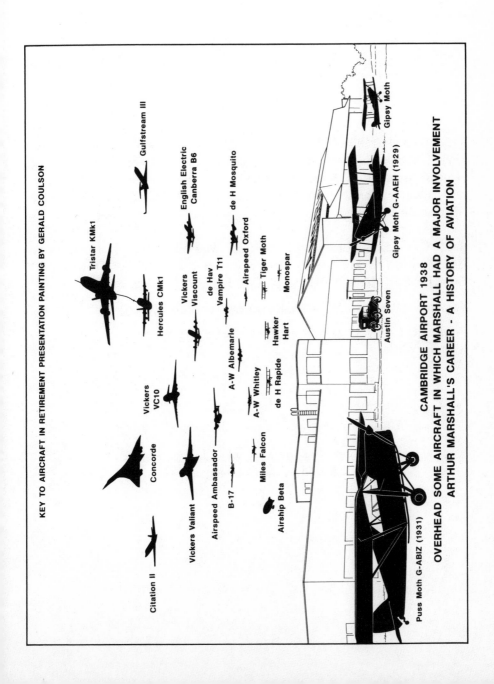

KEY TO AIRCRAFT IN RETIREMENT PRESENTATION PAINTING BY GERALD COULSON

Citation II
Vickers Valiant
Concorde
Vickers VC10
Tristar KMk1
Gulfstream III
Hercules CMk1
Airspeed Ambassador
B-17
Vickers Viscount
English Electric Canberra B6
de Hav Vampire T11
de H Mosquito
Miles Falcon
A-W Albemarle
Airspeed Oxford
Airship Beta
A-W Whitley
de H Rapide
Hawker Hart
Tiger Moth
Monospar
Austin Seven
Gipsy Moth G-AAEH (1929)
Gipsy Moth
Puss Moth G-ABIZ (1931)

CAMBRIDGE AIRPORT 1938
OVERHEAD SOME AIRCRAFT IN WHICH MARSHALL HAD A MAJOR INVOLVEMENT
ARTHUR MARSHALL'S CAREER - A HISTORY OF AVIATION

Appendix 3

KEY TO PHOTOGRAPH of Family, Shareholders and Directors on and around Marshall's 1913 Austin Twenty on the occasion of the Annual General Meeting on 3 October 1979 – the 70th and 50th anniversaries respectively of Marshall (Cambridge) Limited and Marshall of Cambridge (Engineering) Limited.

Back Row: Bob Horsbrough, Michael Marshall, Derrick Hirst, Peter Hedderwick, John Huntridge, Violet Hodgson, Brenda Moore, Owen Tebbs, Brian Herring, Hugh Day (hidden), Cliff Baigent, Jonathan Barker.

Seated in car: Arthur Marshall, Rosemary Marshall, Margery Fry.

Front row: Penny Wagner, Dorothy Wagner, Tikki Adorian, John Stancliffe

The car is a similar model to the first Austin car sold by the Company in 1914.

Appendix 4

Honours, Awards and Public Appointments (Company and Family)

1918	D. G. MARSHALL Founder of Company	Services at Woolwich Arsenal, World War I	MBE
1939	PETER MAY Chief Flying Instructor 22 E&RFTS	Services to RAF Flying Training at Cambridge	AFC
1942	S. J. DRIVER Company Auxiliary Fire Service	Extinguishing Whitley bomber fire in hangar regardless of personal safety	BEM
1942	E. D. ANKIN Company Auxiliary Fire Service	Extinguishing Whitley bomber fire in hangar regardless of personal safety	BEM
1942	H. E. TAPPIN On active service with the RAF	Leading his Flight in first and three other sorties in Dieppe raid	DFC
1942	L. V. WORSDELL On active service with the RAF	Leading attacks on shipping in defence of Malta	DFC
1943	PHILIP SMULIAN On active service with with RAF	Services to RAF flying training at Cambridge	AFC
1943	PETER MAY On active service with the RAF	Squadron Commander Airborne Operations, Sicilian campaign Killed in action	American DFC
1943	R. WYKES Foreman, RAF Aircraft Repair Outstations	Services to the RAF	BEM

1944	H. E. TAPPIN On active service with the RAF	Day and night fighter operations	Bar to DFC
1946	E. W. GOODE Chief Engineer 22 EFTS	Services to the RAF at Cambridge	MBE
1946	F. T. HORNSBY Works Manager, Aircraft Repair Division	Services to the RAF at Cambridge	MBE
1948	A. G. G. MARSHALL Chairman & Managing Director	Services to the Air Training Corps	OBE
1951	A. G. G. MARSHALL Chairman & Managing Director		JP Linton, Cambs.
1952	M. ST CLAIR MARSHALL Director, Vehicle Body Division	Introduction of new industry to Cambridge	MBE
1952	MOLLY ROSE Sister		JP Bampton East, Oxon
1953	A. G. G. MARSHALL Chairman & Managing Director	Services to the Air Training Corps	Coronation Medal
1953	L. V. WORSDELL Chief Flying Instructor, 22 RFS	Services to the RAF	Coronation Medal
1964	LORD CHESHAM Brother-in-Law	Parliamentary Secretary, Ministry of Transport	Privy Counsellor
1964	VIOLET HODGSON Sister		JP Chesham, Bucks.
1965	L. V. WORSDELL Chief Pilot and Airport Manager	Services in the Air	Queen's Commendation
1966	H. F. YOUNG Chief Aircraft Inspector	Services to the RAF	OBE
1968	A. G. G. MARSHALL Chairman & Managing Director		Commissioned a Deputy Lieutenant of Cambridgeshire

1969	A. G. G. MARSHALL Chairman & Managing Director		High Sheriff of Cambridgeshire & Isle of Ely
1974	SIR ARTHUR MARSHALL Chairman and Managing Director	Services to the RAF	Kt
1976	J. H. HUNTRIDGE Deputy Managing Director	Services to the Armed Forces and Exports	CBE
1977	P. ELSE Chief Engineer, Light Aircraft Division	Services to the Cambridge University Air Squadron and Air Training Corps Air Experience Flight	Queen's Silver Jubilee Medal
1977	I. G. F. BALL Chief Parachute Packer	Services to the RAF, Cambridge University Air Squadron and Air Training Corps Air Experience Flight	Queen's Silver Jubilee Medal
1977	H. B. BREACH Production Manager, Bus Division	Introduction of new industry to Cambridge	Queen's Silver Jubilee Medal
1977	J. CRITOPH Production Manager, Vehicle Body Division	Introduction of new industry to Cambridge	Queen's Silver Jubilee Medal
1977	L. V. WORSDELL Director of Flying	Services to military and civil test flying and training	Queen's Silver Jubilee Medal
1978	I. G. F. BALL Chief Safety Equipment Engineer	Services to the RAF, Cambridge University Air Squadron and Air Training Corps Air Experience Flight	AOC's Commendation, RAF Support Command
1979	SIR ARTHUR MARSHALL Chairman & Managing Director		Hon. Old Cranwellian
1979	D. G. McMILLAN Chief Designer & Quality Controller, Vehicle Body Division	Introduction of new industry to Cambridge	MBE
1980	W. H. EVERETT Chairman of Works Committee	Services to industrial relations	BEM

1980	DR BERNARD ROSE Brother-in-law	Services to British Music	OBE
1980	L. V. WORSDELL Director of Flying	Services to military and civil aviation	OBE
1980	SIR ARTHUR MARSHALL Chairman & Managing Director		Companion of Royal Aeronautical Society
1981	E. A. G. PAINE Foreman, Vehicle Body Division	Services to the Armed Forces	BEM
1981	G. G. BORLEY Chief Inspector, Hercules Aircraft	Services to the RAF	BEM
1981	N. WOOLLEY Foreman, Aircraft Maintenance	Services to Cambridge University Air Squadron and Air Training Corps Air Experience Flight	AOC's Commendation, RAF Support Command
1982	P. ELSE Chief Engineer, Light Aircraft Division	Services to Cambridge University Air Squadron and Air Training Corps Air Experience Flight	AOC's Commendation, RAF Support Command
1982	R. O. GATES Executive Director Chief Aircraft Designer	Services to the RAF – Falklands War	OBE
1983	I. G. F. BALL Chief Safety Equipment Engineer	Services to the RAF, Cambridge University Air Squadron and Air Training Corps Air Experience Flight	AOC's Commendation, RAF Support Command
1983	G. MALLION Manager, Metal Detail Workshop	Services to the RAF – Falklands War	BEM
1983	W. D. PITTHAM General Manager, Peterborough Garage	Services to the Air Training Corps	OBE
1983	MOLLY ROSE Sister		Commissioned a Deputy Lieutenant of Oxfordshire

1984	N. A. J. HARRY Executive Director and Deputy Chief Aircraft Designer	Services to the RAF – Falklands War	OBE
1988	M. J. MARSHALL Chairman Garage Group & Deputy Chairman Engineering Group		High Sheriff of Cambridgeshire
1988	R. J. NEW Personnel Director	Outstanding services to industrial relations, including at times of national emergency	OBE
1989	P. D. N. HEDDERWICK Managing Director, Aircraft Division	Services to the RAF	CBE
1989	M. J. MARSHALL Chairman Garage Group & Deputy Chairman Engineering Group		Commissioned a Deputy Lieutenant of Cambridgeshire
1989	S. G. WHEELER Manager, Hercules Engineering Design Office	Services to the RAF	MBE
1990	R. G. BIRT Chief Designer, Vehicle Body Division	Services to the Armed Forces	MBE
1990	MOLLY ROSE Sister	Services to Oxford	OBE
1990	SIR ARTHUR MARSHALL Life President		Hon. Fellow Jesus College, Cambridge
1990	SIR ARTHUR MARSHALL Life President	Marking the long friendship with the Hashemite Kingdom of Jordan	Order of Istiqlal 1st Class, Jordan
1990	GRAHAM TAYLOR Marshall's Chief Pilot, RAF Shawbury	Valuable services in the Air	Queen's Commendation
1991	FREDA SHORT Sir Arthur Marshall's Secretary	Exceptional contribution to the Company's work in support of the RAF	BEM

1992	SIR ARTHUR MARSHALL Life President	In recognition of his great contribution to British Aeronautical Engineering	Hon. Doctor of Science, Cranfield Institute of Technology
1992	M. J. MARSHALL Chairman & Chief Executive		Commissioned Vice Lord-Lieutenant of Cambridgeshire

There were of course many more deserving recognition
and those honoured were carrying the flag for all.

Index

Page numbers in *italics* denote illustrations

Aircraft Design Office portrayal of my life presented to me on my 90th birthday December 1993